FOOD PRODUCTION OPERATION AND MANAGEMENT

About the Book

This book has been designed keeping in mind that there is no such text book on food production available as of now. The key note of this book is comprehensive details of each subject. "Food production is neither dull nor difficult if you study it intelligently. Indeed it might be argued in the hotels industry food production ranks higher among the arts." Food production is specially designed to meet the requirement of student's undergraduate, post graduate course in food production operation and management. This book will also be perfectly suited to those who are already in the industry. The inspiration to write this book came from the Hospitality industry where I have worked for seven years in a diligent manner. This book has all the necessary chapters relating to all different aspects of kitchen training in world cuisine.

The book is divide into seven unit's. The first unit of this book contains eight chapters which serve an introduction to hospitality and professional catering. Also provide details about raw materials, methods of cooking and basic preparation.

The second unit of this book contains four chapters which mainly emphasis on Commodities and farinaceous. This unit provides you detail about egg, rice, wheat, corn and dairy product with their composition and there structure, with some standard recipes.

The third unit of this book contain six chapters which mainly emphasis on meat and seafood cookery. This unit provide you details about their standard cuts with their used. With some standard recipes.

The fourth unit of this book contain four chapters which mainly emphasis on garde manager section. This unit provides you in details about the Hors d'oeuvres, salads and sandwich. With their composition and types. With some standard recipes.

The fifth unit of this book contain includes nine chapters which mainly emphasis on International cuisine which includes Chinese, Japanese, Indonesian, Philippines, European, Arabic, Mediterrian, Mexican, Spanish and India. In this unit you recognized there culinary regions with their common Ingredients and there method of cooking with their glossary and with the end of unit you find some regional recipes.

The sixth unit of this book contain six chapters which mainly emphasis on bakery. In this unit you know about the bakery, with their Ingredients, method of mixing and its preparation. With some standard recipes.

The seventh unit of this book contains four chapter which mainly emphasis on kitchen management. In this unit you learn about how to design a kitchen, how to plan a menu, detail about material management, how to control food cost, different law food regarding food and certain management standards of hygiene.

FOOD PRODUCTION

OPERATION AND MANAGEMENT

Volume I

GULSHAN SONI

Ph.D. in Hotel Management
and Tourism Studies (U.S.A.)
M. Phil. Tourism Management,
M.Sc. H.M. and C.T.,
Executive MBA,
Diploma in Training and Development,
G.H.O.T.P. (Jaypee Hotels Limited)

AP

AMAN PUBLICATIONS

NEW DELHI

Published by
Rajiv Jain for Aman Publications
LG-4A, Ganpati Bhawan,
4675-B/21, Ansari Road,
Darya Ganj, Delhi - 110002
PH: 23255012, 23282127
E-mail: sshjbs@yahoo.com

First Published – 2010

ISBN-81-8204-056-4
ISBN-978-81-8204-056-4

SOLE DISTRIBUTOR
JINDAL BOOK SERVICES
LG-4A, Ganpati Bhawan,
4675-B/21, Ansari Road,
Darya Ganj, Delhi - 110002

Jacket Designed by :
S.M. Graphics

Printed by:
Abhinav Prints, Delhi - 110041

Preface

Food production operation and management has been developed with the vision of being one of the most sought after literature available. I have tried to capture all the details of cookery books which I think it has been developed in such a new pattern. The increasing competition and complexity of hospitality industry as well as high demand of travelers has meant an increase demands in terms of hospitality needs. Hospitality industry is the most diverse and specialized industry in the world. The emerging role of private sector in planning, organizing, managing and financing in the hospitality industry and the introduction of hotel management courses at senior secondary level by some of state boards shows the importance of hotel management in modern times.

This book was published to meet the need of the complete book on food production operation and management for the rapidly expanding educational institutes associated with Hotel management and Catering Technology, The Food Craft Institute and emerging requirements of the chef in the industry.

Food production is one of the major departments of the hotel. According to my experience, a student who enters in this field wants to be either a Chef or a Manager. Today the demand of chefs is on the rise around the world. All my efforts in this book are directed to arouse the interest of the student who will become future chefs of the industry.

The book is divide into seven unit's. The first unit of this book contains eight chapters which serve an introduction to hospitality and professional catering. Also provide details about raw materials, methods of cooking and basic preparation.

The second unit of this book contains four chapters which mainly emphasis on Commodities and farinaceous. This unit provides you detail about egg, rice, wheat, corn and dairy product with their composition and there structure, with some standard recipes.

The third unit of this book contain six chapters which mainly emphasis on meat and seafood cookery. This unit provide you details about their standard cuts with their used. With some standard recipes.

The fourth unit of this book contain four chapters which mainly emphasis on garde manager section. This unit provides you in details about the Hors d'oeuvres, salads and sandwich. With their composition and types. With some standard recipes.

The fifth unit of this book contain includes nine chapters which mainly emphasis on International cuisine which includes Chinese, Japanese, Indonesian, Philippines, European, Arabic, Mediterranean, Mexican, Spanish and India. In this unit you recognized there culinary regions with their common Ingredients and there method of cooking with their glossary and with the end of unit you find some regional recipes.

The sixth unit of this book contain six chapters which mainly emphasis on bakery. In this unit you know about the bakery, with their Ingredients, method of mixing and its preparation. With some standard recipes.

The seventh unit of this book contains four chapter which mainly emphasis on kitchen management. In this unit you learn about how to design a kitchen, how to plan a menu, detail about material management, how to control food cost, different law food regarding food and certain management standards of hygiene.

I am sure that this book will be a source of inspiration and each page will awaken a longing to pick up the phone and talk to me.

I express my gratitude to the management of Banarasi Das Chandiwala Institute of Hotel Management and Catering Technology, and Shri. Bhuwan Mohan ji, Secretary, Shri Banarsidas Chandiwala Sewa Smarak Trust Society for their motivation and encouragement to undertake this relatively less explored but highly poignant area of hospitality. I also extend my thanks to Principal Mr. R.K. Bhandri and Deputy Director (Administration) Mr. Pradeep Gupta, for their altruistic support.

I would like thanks to the Mr. Rajeev Jain and Mr. Pradeep Jain of Aman Publications, New Delhi for their persistence and support. Finally, I would like to thanks to all my friends and my well-wishers.

GULSHAN SONI

Authors Profile

Gulshan Soni is at present faculty in Banarasidas Chandiwala Institute of Hotel Management and Catering Technology, New Delhi. Earlier he had been associated with Hotel Jaypee Vasant Continental, New Delhi. After completing his graduation from Delhi University he joined Graduate Hotel Operation Traning Programme in Jaypee Group of Hotels (Hotel Jaypee Palace Agra). Simultaneously he completed his MSc in HM and CT and Executive MBA and has recently completed his M.Phil in Tourism Management .

He is presently working on his Fellowship Research in the area consumer protection

Contents

VOLUME I

UNIT 1: BASIC OF COOKERY

1. **Introduction to Hospitality and Professional Catering** **1**
   - Origin of Hospitality Industry
   - History of catering
   - History of food and beverage service industry
   - History of Indian catering
   - The evaluation of Indian catering
   - Scope of caterers in the industry
   - Relationship of catering industry to other industry
   - Role of catering industry in travel and tourism
2. **Introduction to Professional Cookery** **15**
   - Aims and objectives of cooking
   - Preparation of Ingredients - Mise-en-place and methods of mixing
   - Background skills of culinary professional
   - Hygiene and safety practices in handling food
   - General rules regarding sanitary and food handling.
   - HACCP objectives and principles
   - HACCP and ISO 9000
   - Hurdlel technology of food safety
3. **Kitchen commodities** **28**
   - Raw material - introduction
   - Characteristic and use according to their functions
   - Herbs and spices introduction
   - Herb and spices with their general description and ethnic uses
   - Vegetables types and description
   - Potatoes varieties and standard recipes of potatoes
   - Vegetable boiling techniques
   - Guidelines for proper doneness of vegetables
   - Tips to preserve the nutrients content of vegetables
   - How to choose vegetables
   - How to preserve vegetables
   - Principal of storage vegetables

- Flavourings and seasoning
- Texture of food
- Different cuts off vegetables

4. Methods of Cooking **112**
- Principles of cooking food
- Types of fuels
- Various methods of cooking
- Effect of food on heat
- Ways to leading the decomposition of food
- Solving difficulties
- Cooking effect on foods
- Food for health

5. Kitchen Organization and Management **152**
- Kitchen organization chart
- Duties and responsibilities of kitchen staff
- Kitchen equipments and tools
- Safety precautions of handling equipments and tools

6. Stock **172**
- Introduction
- Definition and meaning
- Elements of stock/fond
- Types of stocks
- Preparation of stocks
- Thickening of stocks
- Preparation of stocks components
- Standard recipes of stocks
- Methods of preparation of stocks
- Evaluating quality of stocks
- Flavouring of stocks
- Savoury aspic and jelly
- Courtbouillon
- Conveniences bases and glazes

7. Soups **190**
- Introduction
- Types and definition
- Classification of soups
- Clear soups and its types
- Consommé and its preparation
- Jellied soups
- Thick soups and its division
- Velouté soups
- Cream soups
- Vegetables soups
- Specialty soups - national and regional types
- Cold soups
- Quality of soups based on . . .
- Garnishes of soups
- Soups and its recipes

8. Sauces **228**
- Introduction
- Definition and meaning
- Essential of good sauces
- Characteristics of a good sauces
- Components of sauces
- Finalization or liaison finale
- Wines in sauces
- Milk and cream in sauces
- Reduction of sauces
- Making of mother sauces
- Five physical property of mother sauces
- Depouillage of sauces
- Classification of sauces
- Characteristics of a mother sauces
- The compound sauces
- Espangole sauce and its method of preparation

- Demi-glaces and its method of preparation
- Quick demi-glaces
- Velouté sauce and its method of preparation
- Béchamel sauce and its method of preparation
- Tomato sauce and its method of preparation
- Emulsified sauces
- Production of emulsified sauces
- Remontage of a broken sauces
- Hollandaise sauce and its method of preparation
- Béarnaise sauce and its method of preparation
- Béurre blañc sauce and its method of preparation
- Butter sauce
- Compound butter and its some types
- Miscellaneous sauces
- Derivates of mother sauces
- Cold sauces and its types
- Mayonnaise sauce and its method of preparation with their derivative
- Boiled dressing and its methods of preparation

UNIT 2: COMMODITIES AND FARINACEOUS

9. Eggs **261**

- Composition and its test of freshness eggs
- Grading, storage and handling of eggs
- Various ways of beating of eggs
- Mixing eggs with other ingredients
- Different ways of cooking eggs
- Standard recipes of eggs

10. Rice **275**

- Introduction and its composition
- Types of rice
- Different stages of rice processing
- Method of preparing rice
- Method of loosing nutritive value of rice

11. Wheat and Corn **280**

- Introduction and composition of wheat
- Varieties of wheat
- Introduction and composition of corn
- Principles of cooking cereals

12. Pasta, Noodles and Other **286**

- Introduction
- Factory produce pasta, its composition and structure
- Fresh pasta, its composition and structure
- Types of fresh and factory produce pasta
- Method of preparing fresh pasta
- Cooking pasta
- Noodles and its types
- Polenta
- Gnocchi
- Spatezle
- Different shapes of pasta
- Stuffed pasta

13. Dairy Products **296**

- Introduction
- Milk
- Pasteurization and homonization

- Varieties of milk
- Fermented milk products
- Process milk products
- Prevent curdling of curd
- Butter and its forms
- Cheese and its determined factors
- Cheese ripened process
- Types of cheese
- Process cheese and its types
- Storage and service of cheese
- Standard recipes of cheese

UNIT 3: MEATS AND SEAFOOD COOKERY

14. Meats 313
- Introduction
- Choosing your meat
- Boiling of meat
- Storing of meat
- Freezing of meat
- Cooking of frozen meat
- Thawing of frozen meat
- Storing of cured meats
- Storing of minced meat, sausages and variety of meat
- Standard cuts of meats and their uses
- The art of carving meat and seafood

15. Lamb and Mutton 324
- Introduction
- Boiling of meat
- Roasting of meat
- Stewing of meat
- Grilling or broiling of meat
- Frying of meat
- Braising of meat
- Frozen of meat
- Preparing of meat
- Marination for meat
- Gravy for roast meat
- Time table for cooking meat
- Standards cuts of lamb and mutton
- Grading quality of lamb and mutton
- Standard recipes of lamb and mutton

16. Poultry and Game 339
- Introduction
- Popular breed of poultry
- Choose quality of poultry
- Draw and truss of poultry
- Classification of chicken
- Selection of chicken
- Standard steps to cut chicken
- Cuts of chicken
- How to cut chicken
- Cooking of chicken
- Chicken nutritional facts
- Safe and storage of chicken
- Recipes of chicken
- Game introduction
- Cooking of games
- Varieties of games

17. Pork 357
- Introductions
- Standard cuts off pork and with their use
- Ham, Bacon and Gammon
- Standard recipes of pork

18. Beef and Veal 371
- Introduction
- Standard cuts off beef with their use
- Standard recipes of beef

- Veal introduction
- Standard cuts off veal
- Standard recipes of veal

19. Fish and Sea food **386**
- Introduction
- Fish structure
- How to check the freshness of fish
- Storage of sea food
- Universal freezing method
- Classification of fish
- Choosing fish
- Quantities of fish
- Preparing of fish
- Filleting and method of fillet a fish
- Method of cooking fish
- Courtbouillon
- Varieties of sea food with their used
- Standard recipes of seafood
- Point to remember to cook fish

VOLUME II

UNIT 4: GARDE MANGER

20. Cold Preparation **423**
- Introduction and meaning of garde manager
- Aspic and its preparation method
- Chemiser
- Chaud froid and steps to used chaud froid
- Charcuterie and its types
- Product created with force meat
- Salt cured and brined product
- Fermented sausages
- Terrine de viande
- Terrines and pate
- Mousse and Galentine
- Glazing cold meats
- Savoury cream and aspic garnish

21. Hors d' oeuvre and Appetizers **436**
- Introduction to hors d' oeuvre and appetizers
- Types and definition of hors d' oeuvre
- Hot hors d'oeuvre
- Use of hors d'oeuvre
- Composition of hors d'oeuvre and appetizers
- Types of canapés
- Barquettes and tartlets
- Some common hors d'oeuvre
- Standard recipes of hors d'oeuvre and appetizers

22. Salads **449**
- Introduction
- Salads and salad dressing
- Kinds of salads
- Classification of salads
- Certain rules for salads
- Parts of salads
- Types of salads
- Side vegetable salad
- Leafy green vegetable salad

- Side fruit salad
- Side rice salad
- Side meat salad
- Side chicken salad
- Side seafood salad
- Standard recipes of salads

23. Sandwich 462
- Introduction and meaning
- Classification of sandwich
- Type of sandwich
- Spread and dips
- Caviar and its types
- Some variation of cold closed sandwich
- Tools and equipment needed for sandwich products

UNIT 5: INTERNATIONAL CUISINE

24. Asian Cuisine 475
- Introduction of Asian cuisine
- Division Asian cuisine
- Common equipments used in Asian cuisine
- Basic Ingredients in Asian cuisine

25. Chinese Cuisine 482
- Introduction
- Regional cooking
- Chinese cooking schools introduction and with their speciality
- Chinese philosophy
- Chinese cooking methods
- Chinese glossary

26. Indonesian cuisine and Philippines Cuisine 515
- Indonesian cuisine introduction and their specialty
- Glossary of Indonesian cuisine
- Philippines cuisine introduction and their specialty
- Philippines cooking terms
- Philippines common vegetables

27. Japanese Cuisine 521
- Introduction of Japanese cuisine
- Glossary of Japanese food
- Method of cooking Japanese rice
- Culinary terms of Japanese cuisine
- Japanese menu guide and its ingredients

28. European Cuisine 536
- Introduction and division of European cuisine
- French cuisine introduction
- French culinary regions
- Italian regional food
- Italian meal course
- Italian basic ingredients
- German cuisine introduction
- German cuisine region and specialty of German cuisine

29. Arabic Cuisine 553
- Introduction and its features
- Common ingredients
- Culture influence on Arabic cuisine
- Common element of Arabic cookery
- Glossary of Arabic cuisine

30. Mediterranean Cuisine 562
- Introduction
- Lebanese cuisine introduction and their specialty
- Thailand cuisine introduction and their specialty
- Essential Thai Ingredients

31. **Mexican cuisine and Spanish cuisine** **569**
- Introduction
- Key element in Mexican diet
- Regional cuisine of Mexican
- Spanish cuisine introduction
- Ingredients and typical food
- Typical Spanish ingredients lists

32. **Indian cuisine** **576**
- Introduction
- Different aspects of Indian cuisine
- Northern Indian Regional cuisine
- Southern Indian regional cuisine
- Eastern Regional cuisine
- Western Regional cuisine
- Central Indian cuisine

Recipes on International Cuisine **599**

UNIT 6: BAKERY

33. **Introduction to Bakery** **665**
- History of bakery
- The art and science of baking
- Ingredients and their functions
- Temperature and baker

34. **Yeast, Bread and Dough** **672**
- Components and their contribution to whole
- Method of preparation
- Forming loaves
- Storage and handling of breads
- Types of mixture
- Types of quick breads
- Bread, Scones and Buns introduction
- Recipes of breads
- Scones introduction
- Scones recipes

35. **Pastry Dough** **685**
- Types of dough
- Preparation of dough
- Ingredients of dough
- Mixing procedure of various dough
- Cookie dough, ingredients and its types
- Choux pastry and recipes
- Flaky pastry and recipes
- Puff pastry and recipes
- Ingredients making puff pastry
- Pastries, savoury and sweet
- Savoury fillings for choux buns
- Vol-au-vent
- Éclairs
- Choux buns
- Pastry horns or cornets

36. **Cakes** **700**
- Introduction
- Method of mixing the ingredients
- Ingredients of cakes
- Chocolate and chocolate handling
- Types of cakes
- Preparation of cakes
- Mixing of different cakes
- High altitude baking
- Storage of cakes
- Different cake recipes

37. **Biscuits and Petit/fours** **714**
- Introduction
- Standards recipes of Biscuits
- Petit four introduction

- Shaping the mixture
- Short bread
- Shaping short bread
- Baking short bread

38. Cake icings and fillings 721

- Introduction
- Decorating
- To use the syringe
- Different icing recipes
- Chocolate dipping

UNIT 7: KITCHEN MANAGEMENT

39. Kitchen Designing 739

- Introduction and meaning
- Kitchen layout and its types
- Computer based kitchen layout design
- Steps in designing kitchen
- Kitchen layout and functions
- Equipment purchased guide lines
- Budget and time line
- Investment
- Space requirement
- Energy usage
- Shipping and delivery
- Additional expenses and consideration
- Equipment and energy
- Ways to save energy
- HVAC and there basic rule
- Managing energy consumption
- Heating system and air conditioning
- HVAC equipment maintenance
- Special requirements
- Kitchen layouts

40. Menu Planning and Material Management 764

- Introductions
- Types of menus
- Most important aspect of a planning a menu
- Food production control
- Material forecasting
- Culinary skills to minimized wastage
- Recycling used oil
- Material management
- Seven steps to food cost control
- Purchase procedure - perishable and non-perishable
- Receiving and storing of food
- Method of store accounts
- Computerization material management system

41. Laws Regarding Food 779

- Introduction
- Meaning and definition of food
- Unwholesome food
- Food adulteration
- Prevent of food adulteration act 1954
- Objective of PFA Act 1954
- Different PFA acts
- Prohibition and restriction on some food
- Purchaser food analysis
- Offence and penalties
- Central committee for food standard and central
- Food laboratory
- Central food laboratory
- Analysis of food
- Food inspectors and its procedure

- Food standards code in India
- Truth menu laws and labeling laws

42. **Management Standard of Hygiene and Storage** **798**
- Food hygiene and contamination
- Tips to reduce food poisoning
- Storage of food
- Personal hygiene for handling food
- Premise hygiene
- Guidelines for hygiene standards buffet and catered meals
- Preserving fruits and vegetables
- Bottling fruits and vegetables
- Garnish and saving

Culinary Teams **812**

Bibliography **832**

Index **835**

Weight, Volume and Liquid Measures

WEIGHT MEASURE

Oz	Gram	Oz	Gram
½ oz	14.17 grams	3 oz	85.05 gram
1 oz	28.35 grams	4 oz	113.4 grams
2 oz	56.7 grams	5 oz	141.75 gram

lb	oz	lb	oz
¼ lb	4 oz	1 lb	16 oz
½ lb	8 oz	1½ lb	24 oz
¾ lb	12 oz	2 lb	32 oz

lb	gram	lb	oz
¼ lb	114 gram	1 lb	454.45 gram
½ lb	228 gram	1½ lb	682.50 gram
¾ lb	340 gram	2 lb	908.80 gram

WEIGHT MEASURE

Gallon/British measurement	Litres	Gallon	Litres
1 gallon	4.5 litre	4 gallon	18.2 litre
2 gallon	9.1 litre	5 gallon	22.7 litre
3 gallon	13.6 litre	6 gallon	26.12 litre

VOLUME LIQUID

Cup	ml	Cup	ml
¼ cup	60 ml	1 cup	250 ml
½ cup	1255 ml	1½ cup	375 ml

DRY MEASURE EQUIPMNETS

3 teaspoon	1 tablespoon	½ Ounce	14.3 grams
2 tablespoon	$^{1}/_{8}$ cup	1 Ounce	28.3 grams
4 tablespoon	¼ cup	2 Ounce	56.7 grams
12 tablespoon	¾ cup	6 Ounce	375 pouns

OVEN TEMPERATURE GUIDE

Description of oven	Celsius (°)	Fahrenheit (°)
1 Cool	100	200
2 Very slow	120	250
3 Slow	150	300
4 Moderate	180	350
5 Hot	220	425
6 Very hot	230	450

Unit 1
BASIC OF COOKERY

Chapter 1

Introduction to Hospitality and Professional Catering

After studying this chapter, the student must know:

- Know the origin and evolution of hospitality industry
- Understand the scope of Caterers in the Catering industry
- Co-relate the hospitality sector with other industries
- Analyze the significance of hotel industry in terms of global perspective and to objectively know the development of catering industry with reference to the travel and tourism sector

INTRODUCTION

Hospitality is probably the most diverse but specialized industry in the world. It is certainly one of the largest, employing millions of people in a bewildering array of jobs around the globe. Sectors range from the glamorous five-star resort to the less fashionable, but arguably more specialized, institutional areas such as hospitals, industrial outfits, schools and colleges. Yet of these many different sectors, catering has to be the most challenging. Whatever the size of the catering operation, the variety of opportunities available is endless. "The sky is the limit with catering.

The hospitality industry includes all establishments of food and beverage services to the public. It is one of the fast growing industries in the world and it employs many more people than all the other service sectors combined. The hospitality industry is a virile force in the world society and for all who aspire to be a part of the industry it offers a wide range of jobs and careers which vary according to the style service in each establishment. The major advantage for a professional to be trained as the hospitality professional is that people with service attitude in the hospitality sector are easily absorbed in any service sector easily.

In India, the hospitality industry has grown over the past decades. Reasons behind this are - people generally have more money to spend outside the home for recreation or any other ways and eating patterns have changed, with an increase in the number of meals bought as take – away meals or eaten out.

Indian tourism and hospitality sector is growing at the rate of 10 to 15 % per year. Over a last few years tier II cities like Jaipur, Gurgaon, Pune, and Hyderabad are seeing growth both in occupancy and room rates. Indian hospitality corporations' mission is to acquire and successfully operate Indian business or assets in the hospitality, leisure, tourism, travel, and related industries.

The hospitality industry is 3.5 billion dollar industry with in the global economy.The success of hospitality industry worldwide has come to such an apex that the leading players in the process of expansion are not leaving any opportunity untouched. The industry depends mainly upon business, planning, market selection, strategy, human resource management, leadership qualities, communication skills, team roles and team building and behavior based evaluation.

1.2 Origin

"Hotels" or Inn are defined by British law as place where a bona fide traveller can received food and shelter, provided he is in a position to pay for it and is in a fit condition to received it. The hotel industry is perhaps the oldest commercial service industry in the world. The first inns go back to the sixth century B.C and were the products of the urge to travel, spurred by the invention of wheel. The earliest inns were invented by husband and wife teams who provided large halls

Fig 1.1 Inns in 19th century

for travellers to make their sleep on the floor with their bed and also provide some beverages to travellers include some alcoholic beverage. With the development of inns as competition, family members also provided some entertainment facilities to the travellers.

These things went on for several hundred years. The advent of industrial evolution brought more ideas and progress in the business of inn keeping. The development of different mode transportation this inn keeping business is more popular and changes according to present demands of travellers.

Earlier there used to be "Inns." Over the century they took bigger shape according to the demands of the market and took the shape of "Hotel Keeping". This concept was eagerly welcomed by the emerging nations of Europe, especially Switzerland. It was in Europe that we can see the birth of the "Hotel Industry" and the "Hotel industry as organized sector" in Europe took place in the name of small hoteis and chalets, which provided a variety of food and services provided to the travellers.

The opening of city hotel in New York, USA, in 1794 was the advent of the real growth of industry. With 73 rooms at that point in history, it was considered a very large property. This hotel building was the first edifice, specially made for hotel purpose. The first five star hotels (termed as U.S. modern hotels) were opened in the year 1829 by the name of Tremont hotel, in Boston, USA.

This is often referred to as the beginning of first class service. It had 170 rooms and featured such incredible innovations as private single and double rooms for those who have privacy. But the real boom in the industry came in the 20th century. This industry was booming in 20th century with beginning of chain operations under the guidance of E.M Stalter.

When the industry was booming, in 1930s, hotel industry had disastrous effect due to the great depression during that period. Everybody was convinced that the hospitality is doomed. But the outbreak of World War II brought tremendous change throughout the war years into the fifties. There were two new concepts coming 1) motelsand 2) International chains operation.

The concept of hospitality industry again launched itself with new vigor and enthusiasm

HISTORY OF CATERING

The history of catering late started in the 6th century B.C. when traveler's radius of movement widened. The modern catering industry dates back to the inns of the biblical period which served food to the travellers. The food service industry (catering industry in British English) encompasses those places, institutions and companies that provide meals eaten away from home. This industry includes restaurants, schools and hospital cafeterias, catering operations, and many other Formats, including 'on-premises' and 'off-premises' caterings. Catering is a multifaceted segment of the food service industry. There is a niche for all types of catering businesses within the segment of catering. The food service industry is divided into three general classifications: commercial segment, noncommercial segment, and military segment. Catering management may be defined as the task of planning, organizing, controlling and executing. Each activity influences the preparation and

Fig 1.2: First hotel in Switzerland

delivery of food, beverage, and related services at a competitive, yet profitable price. These activities work together to meet and exceed the customer's perception of value for his money.

HISTORY OF FOOD AND BEVERAGE INDUSTRY

Food and beverage service industry is enigma. The food and beverage service goes back to 6th century B.C where inns are started by husband and wife and they offered food and beverage to the travellers with the development of inns. As competition arose, people offered a variety of food and beverage to the travellers. This went on for hundreds of years.

After the invention of mode of transport travellers could visit all around the world. So with the increase in demand of food, lodging and beverage, competition soon made its way in to the industry. Those who provide these services tend to learn different regional foods so that travellers could feel "home away from home". As the industry boomed, Food and beverage industry also grew. When the first hotel industry originated in Europe especially in Switzerland, they called people from different parts of world for employment to serve different varieties of food to travellers according to their country.

The first five star hotels (termed as U.S. modern hotels) were opened in the year 1829 by the name of Tremont hotel, in Boston, USA. This was era often regarded as the beginning of first class service and E.M Stalter vision of the chain operations. In these chain operations, menus are common in all chains of particular groups to provide uniformity of products and services to the travellers. After the outbreak of world's war II tremendous change occurred in the industry, as people travelled around the world for different purposes and started demanding good services related to food and beverage industry. Now a day, it's a huge industry in the world with the numerous forms of food and beverage variations.

The eating patterns of worlds have changed as a result of economic, demographic and social changes. This has affected the hospitality industry, which has grown rapidly over a last few decades. Today trend has changed as more men and women both work outside the home and therefore there is even lesser time to cook food. Families with double incomes are often able to spend more on eating out; it is gradually becoming increasing popular. So, food and beverage industry will be growing until there is human life on planet earth.

HISTORY OF INDIAN CATERING

The history of Indian catering started late in the 6th century and with the help of various transportation method and improved technology. India is known for its varied cultural heritage, because India is vast country with diversity of culture from one to another and that is included in the variety of food and beverage.

India's hospitality is derived from the ancient text " Athithi Devo Bhava" when its translated means "the guest is god". In India it's mainly started with the pilgrims who went from one place to another for various religious purposes. From the ancient time, India is country of god and goddesses. People go from one place to another and homes are converted into place of stay to travellers. This was how; probably one can see the first start of catering industry in India. Later the Mughal and British rule in India gave rise to mosques and churches all over the country. In fact pilgrims are the major source of propagating the growth of catering industry in India.

The hotel industry has undergone a constant evaluation throughout its 2000 years history and has become one of the largest and most complex industries in the world. In India, the concept of shelter can be found in our historical records with the reference of Viharas, Dharamshalas, Sarais, Musaphir khanas etc. These shelters under various names have always been a part of India's rich cultural heritage. The ancient budhist monks were probably the first to institutionalize the concept of shelter by "chaitya"(sanctuary) for worships and prayers and a Viharas (monastery).These primitive forms of lodging establishments were mostly located on the ancient trade roots and important deities of the reason signifying there huge contribution in the development of tourism in that region. The traders travel with their merchandised and money went on these routes and the viharas were there hotels.

Over a last decade, the catering industry in India has grown gradually. We can see its impulse with establishment of hotel management and catering institutes, supply chains for food and beverage catering and hospitality recruitment agencies throughout the country. International as well as domestic tourism and business travel has increased manifold worldwide leading to a great demand for hotels, restaurants, resorts, etc., which in turn has created a demand for hotel management education across the world. India is the market place for leading hotel chains from overseas with the main thrust being provided by local hotel chains that are increasingly active in this versatile industry.

There are 30 Institutes of Hotel Management (IHMs) and 6 Food Craft Institutes spread all over the country that offers three-year degree programmes in hotel management and catering technology. Besides, a number of colleges / institutes are also offering 3/4 year programmed in hotel management / hotel management and catering technology.

The Indian Institutes of Travel and Tourism Management (IITM) offer short-term courses. Courses designed for travel and tourism are also provided by private institutions. The institutions run on the guidelines provided by the Indian Institute of Travel and Tourism Management, a reputed national body established by the Ministry of Tourism.

The degrees offered by the Indian institutions equip the students with all required skills and knowledge to effectively discharge supervisory and managerial responsibilities in star category hotels, airline catering, ship and cruise line catering, restaurants and bars, institutional catering, etc.

The degree programmed offered by the Institutes of Hotel Management (IHMs) are regulated through a statutory body, National Council for Hotel Management and Catering Technology (NCHMCT), which is responsible for establishment and prescription of standards/norms. All Institutes uniformly follow standardized course curricula prescribed by the Council. All India Council for Technical Education (AICTE), a statutory body of Government of India or the affiliated universities regulate the norms and standards in other institutions offering hotel management courses.

According to the recent estimated more than two million restaurants are dominating the present scenario of Indian catering industry.

EVOLUTION OF CATERING

The first evolution of catering industry started when the first city hotel opened in New York in 1794 and some of the finest hotels build in these decades, but real boom in the catering industry comes in 20th century.Because in this period the chain operation and the outbreak of the world war II brought a upsurge, and it never went through the down fall, especially, catering, because people are more fond of food and beverage Today more people eat outside the home than ever before. To meet this demand there is need to expansions of catering industry as well as increasing pressure for improved professional in catering industry. From the last decades there are three things which have not changed over a time;

- Food (people have to eat)
- Lodging (people want a safe place to sleep)
- Beverage (people like beverage)

The hospitality business has evolved over a definite period of time. Since we will always be travelling and requiring a place to stay and eat, the industry will continue to grow at a rapid pace.

Hotel and inn are defined by the British Law as a place where a bonafide travellers can received food and shelter provide, he is in a position to pay for it and is in a fit condition to be received. Hence a hotel must provide food and beverages and login to travellers on payment and has in term the right to refused if a travel is drunk disorderly or is not in position to pay for services.

Fig 1.3 The motel in U.S

The Hotel Industry is perhaps is one of the oldest commercial endeavors in the word the first inns go back to six century B.C where the product of the eager to travel spared by the invention of the wheel but it was not as easy today to eat while traveling around the country. Travel belongs to the certain section of the community. The move ability of pilgrims wondering minster religions order and military most of the other people do not move outside the confines of the village. The noble lord ladies travel their and horseback and where entertain by their own class. In the castles or manors of the great state. They were fed and log befitting their standard with exotic meals and wines.

The monastery provides shelter for religious order and pilgrims and soldier never had any trouble finding bed and board. It's fairly over's that same time an astitute villages, and farmers. Show the potential in providing at cost lodging to varied travels. The important in the road and the advent of the carriages may in-keeping more profitable and compative. The earliest inns where the ventures of husband and wife teams who provide large hall to travellers to make their on the floors. They also provide them modest whole some food thirst and quenchers like wine, port etc and stabling facilities. These condition privileges for several hundred years. The advent of industrial revolution in England bough ideas and progress in the business of in-keeping with the development of railways and steam ship mode traveling more prominent. The industrial revolution also changes travellers from social or governmental travel to business travel. There was a need for clean and quick service.

The need of hotel keeping by taking up the nation of Europe specially Switzerland. It was Europe that was the birth of an organized in the shape of chalets and small hotels which provide a variety of service and mainly patronized by the astrocase of the day.

Around 1760 a type of establishment a common in that type of Paris called "Hotel Garni" or large house in which apartment were let out by day weeks or month came into vogue in style. In appearance significance a departure from the customer method of accommodating guest in inns and hostelries into something more luxuries. Hotel mongers and receptionists and uniform staff arrived gradually only at the beginning of the 19th century. Scotland at that also started providing cheap and well furnished rooms to the travels. The ideas of resorts hotels are also developed in that time. In North America accommodation of travellers followed a similar pattern as in England by the burn of the 18th century services cities on the eastern seas coast has some purpose built hotel and in 1st half or the 19th century hotel building spread across America to the pacific coast. The evolution or the hotel industry therefore proceeded in parallel in the old and in the new world in the 20th century. The idea of hotel changed was developed by E M Statler. It involves big investment big profit and trained professionals to manage the business the dispersion In 1930 and the out breaks of the world ward started the development of two new concepts:

(1) The motels and international chain operation and
(2) Establishment of different, catering school to produce trained and skills professional to face the challenges of the rising industry of the day.

SCOPE OF CATERERS IN THE INDUSTRY

The scope of industry is range of vastly diverse hospitality business, all required staff capable of delivering forms of services which required variety of applied skills.

1. Catering jobs span a broad range of specializations from sales and marketing to food and preparation management and culinary arts.
2. The catering industry offers a wide range of jobs in food and beverage or accommodation so every catering job requires a certain skills.
3. Different levels of programme are also offered by luxury catering establishment which attract professionals.
4. The schools and college attract youngsters to the industry; this will help in bring new skills and enthusiasm to the industry.
5. This industry is closely related to tourism business; since people are become more travel conscious, so it becomes more vital industry.

So, in short, there is tremendous scope for caterers in the hospitality industry. The hospitality industry is growing at a faster than ever before. So high is the confidence that the only restriction is high ambition. In a fast changing world, the hospitality industry has become an ideal place for those having an in burnt talent to mingle with people, work with them and serve them.

RELATIONSHIP OF CATERING INDUSTRY TO OTHER INDUSTRY

Food is the sustainer of life regardless of whether they belong to animal kingdom or plant kingdom. All living beings consume food as they come in nature. Subsequently they may convert the raw natural food into usable form on their own. This transformation never involves the art and science of coking, which is a specialty of human beings alone. Importance of food for the human beings is amply, accurately and appropriately stated in the following age old sayings: "hungry man is an angry man" and "even the army marches on stomach" where stomach implies food Employment of largest number of people in the world in general terms (at home) and in commercial terms (catering) is in food preparation and servicing.

Roughly half the world population (women) is actively engaged in the art and science of food production and then alone comes reproduction. Food production, simply stated, is the transformation of raw food material into palatable, appetizing and easily palatable tasty food. Unlike all other living organisms, man has to "buy" food by paying money. Where does the money come from? It comes only from industries.

Any industry in the world has the primary objective of making money. Money so generated by the industrial activity is shared between the employer and the employee, however disproportionate it may be. Money so shared is used to take care of the three important objectives: food, clothing and residence. Whatever left after meeting these primary objectives may go towards acquiring wealth.

As clearly stated above, food is the very basis of existence or survival. To buy food, man needs money. The money comes or must come from industries, all of which have the primary objective of making money and share with those who help generate it. Since the raw food needs to be transformed into palatable food fit for consumption which is achieved, as already stated, through general cooking (household) or commercial cooking (catering). Therefore, there is no industry in the world which is not directly or indirectly, one way or the other, related to the food (catering) industry. Commercial food industry or the catering industry is the only industry that provides food, at a price, away from home. Various types of catering services available would include general or specialty services such as transport catering, welfare catering, industrial catering, etc.

ROLE OF CATERING ESTABLISHMENT IN TRAVEL AND TOURISM

Origin

Hotel facilities constitute a vital and fundamental part of tourist supplies. The need for traveller for food and temporary lodging has grown significantly in the past century and adequate supply of different segments of hotels tailor made to needs of the customer, is one of the basic components of any tourist market.The development and growth in terms of lodging establishment indicates a stimulating economic development at most tourist destination of the world.

Tourism, to a great extent, is depending on type and quantity of accommodation available in the area. It's rather the core of tourist industry. Many countries have recognized the vital importance of hotel industry in relation to tourism and there governments have coordinated their activities with industry by providing big incentives and concession to the hoteliers.

The hotel industry has undergone a constant evaluation throughout its 2000 years history and has become one of the largest and most complex industries in the world. In India the concept of shelter can be found in our historical records with the reference of Viharas, Dharamshalas, Sarais, Musaphir khanas etc. These shelters under various names have always been a part of India's rich cultural heritage. The ancient Buddhist monks were probably the first to conceptualized the concept of shelter by "chaitya"(sanctuary) for worships and prayers and a Viharas(monastery) money.These primitive forms of lodging establishments were mostly located on the ancient trade roots and important deities of the reason signifying there huge contribution in the development of tourism in that region. The traders travel with their merchandised and money on these routes and the viharas were there hotels.

With the passage of time the age old sarais or the inns adapted to the ever changing market and has evolved into the modern hotels. With the growth of travel in the mid18 century, London saw the prototype of the modern hotels with the opening by one David Low in 1774. In the USA hotels emerge from Taverns by the simple expedient of a change of name. By about 1800 the tarvens and hotels were used to describe a same thing.In the mid 18 century, Palatial establishment called grand hotels were constructed in New York, Chicago, Sanfrecco and other rapidly growing town in Sydney.these hotels were build exclusive for wealthy people.These hotels symbolized the emergence of United states as an important nations and tourist destination. By the year 1820 "hotels" become accepected term to describe a place where people stay for the night took their meals on payment. In the 1820 the first tourist hotel appeared in Switzerland.

Emergence of the hotels with reference to travel and tourism industry.

Although the earliest hotel dates to the 1800 century, there growth on the large scales occurred in the 19th century with the advent of railways as a major mode of transportation. This created sufficiently large markets to help make different types of hotels possible. The hotels were developed mainly along a major railway station and highways routes in major cities. These hotels catered to the increasing volume of the traffic thus boosting the economic development of major cities and towns in India and abroad.

Development of hotels (of all categories) at a tourist destination leads to many types of changes in social set up. It comprises of various factors namely –

Economic (in terms of more job creation, more business entrepreneurs, gradual increase in the cost of living index, more income generation leading to the multiplier effect in tourism, more foreign exchange earnings, etc.)

Socio-Cultural (leading to cultural amalgamation of two uniquely different cultures, Communicational exchanges leading to development of human knowledge, better awareness regarding the different cultures which improves their resilience towards new and practically unknown practices in different societies etc.)

In short, catering establishments play a very vital role in the emergence of travel and tourism industry. Developments of both the sectors.i.e. hotels and tourism industry are interlinked with each other. The growth and gradual advancement in one sector leads to the growth of the other sector.

LEARNING OUTCOME

This chapter is a student's guide into the world of hospitality. The unit as a whole gives you an insider's perspective when it comes to hotel industry. Hotels were developed based on the needs and requirements of all persons around the world for global appetite for lodging and food requirements. Starting from taverns and Inns in western world and Sarais and musafirkhanas and viharas in India, the hotels have come a long way in terms of scale, type of service, food offered and it continues to grow as we write this book. The best competitions, of hotels are surprisingly, not their contemporaries but the home of the traveller. To be a successful hotelier, hotels should go to as near as to the concept of "Home away from Home." There is no industry in the world which is not directly or indirectly, one way or the other, related to the catering industry. Commercial catering industry is the only industry that provides food, at a price, away from home.

LESSON END ACTIVITY

- Visit a restaurant and take a note on the food serving method.
- Visit a hotel that serve buffet lunch and note down the food items served.
- Attend a function and note down how the food is prepared and served to the visitors at the function.
- List down all the luxurious hotel properties in India with details about rooms outlets and facilities.
- Identify the current trends in hospitality industry in your town or city.

QUESTIONS FOR DISCUSSION

1. Give a brief note about catering establishments.
2. Explain in your own words about the evolution of hotel industry.
3. Give a brief note about the relationship between the catering industry and all other industries.
4. Briefly address the growth and development of hotel industry in India.
5. Increase in hotel professional institutes will help to provide trained man power to the hospitality sector. Discuss.

STATE TRUE AND FALSE

1. The hospitality industry is 1.5 billion dollar industry with in the global economy.
2. The first evolution of catering industry started when the first city hotel opened in New York in 1792.

3. The Oberoi Amarvilas, Agra and The Oberoi Rajvilas, Jaipur are the Leisure category hotels of the Oberoi group of hotels.
4. ITCH was originally incorporated as Rama Hotels Pvt Ltd in 1975.
5. The first five star hotels (termed as U.S. modern hotels) were opened in the year 1829 by the name of Tremont hotel, in Boston, U.S.A.

KEY TERMS

* Catering
* Hospitality
* Hotels
* Inns
* Motels
* Visitor

Chapter 2

Introduction to Professional Cookery

After studying this chapter, the student must know :

- Aims and objectives of cooking.
- Preparation of ingredients—Mise-en-place and method of mixing.
- Background skills of culinary professional.
- Hygiene and safe practices in handling food.
- General rule regarding sanitary and food handling.
- HACCP objectives and principles.
- HACCP and ISO 9000.
- Hurdlel technology of food safety.

AIMS AND OBJECTIVES OF COOKING

Cooking is an application of heat to food. The purpose of making it more digestible safer to eat more palatable and to change the appearance. To cook food serve flame of heat to be must be introduced to the food.

OBJECTIVES OF COOKING

Is make it pleasing to the eyes and in order to help stimulate the flow of digestive juice thereby creating an appetite. To render food more digestible by physical and chemical changes and by attention of texture thereby assisting masticating and to easiest way to remove the harmful bacteria and pesticides. The aim and intention of cooking to see the food that is cooked under blows a physical or chemical changes that is acceptable.

COOKING RENDER FOODS

1. Digestibility
2. Its sterilize the food,

3. Make more palatable,
4. Make more appetizing,
5. Brings in more variety,
6. Renders a balanced meal.

Digestibility

Complex food are broken down into similar substance which help to absorb and utilized the food more easily to facilitated the digestion and it's break-down cellulose and soften that connective tissues.

Sterilized

Partly sterilized food above 40° C or 15° F growth of bacteria cells rapidly and in general in seizes 40° C or 150° F above non spurring bacterial are killed at 60° C for varying period of time for example to make milk safe it's pasteurized at 63° C for 30 minutes or 72° C for 15 second. Spore bearing bacteria take about 4 to 5 hours building to be destroyed.

Palatability

Cooking food make it more tastier addition of flavouring and seasoning make it more palatable.

Appetizing

Using difference garnishing decorating it food become more pleasant and tempting, cooking food also take out the flavour make it more tempting to our senses.

Varieties

Different techniques of cooking can give difference varieties using the same component that used in different recipes of same ingredients gives a different varieties which are different in taste and look.

Cooking balance meal

It helps to provide a balance meal difference ingredients combined together in one dish make it easier to balance meal.

Preparation of Ingredients

Preparation of ingredients is popularly termed as Mise-en-place.

Mise-en-place (Pronounced Mizaplas) is literally meaning "Set in Place", it is a French phase defined by the "Culinary Institute of America" as "Everything in Place".

Preparation of Ingredients is done according to the requirement of various dishes. Recipes are reviewed by the Chef time to time. Preparing the ingredients a head of time allows the Chef to cook without having to stop and assemble items, which is desirable in recipes with time constraint. The following are the Points which are mandatory for the Preparation of Ingredients.

1. **Washing:** - Washing is a form of cleaning food before preparation. To remove dirty by wash in cold before any preparation. Meat, Fish, vegetable and fruits are washed in cold water before any preparation. The following parts are important while washing vegetables or fruits. Remove and discard outer leaves in case of cabbage, Reddish, fruit etc.
   - Rinse under clean, running water just before preparation in case of spinach rise two to four time to remove sand from it.
   - Rub briskly by scrolling with a clean vegetable brush or hands to remove dirt especially for root vegetable.
   - Use Chlorine tablet in water.
   - Don't use soap or detergent.
   - After washing dry with clean cloth and set in refrigerator. Cut away bruised and damage areas.
2. **Peeling and Scraping**: - Peeling is done to remove the outer most skin of vegetable and fruits. It's done through peeler etc. Scraping is done to removed unwanted particles, for example in potatoes sand like black in colour it is remove by scraping it.
3. **Paring:** - It's removing the surface layer in a circular motion by a pressure of knife to provide a good shape like potatoes etc.
4. **Grating:** - It is reducing a large piece of food to small particles or thin shreds by rubbing it against a coarse, serrated surface called grater usually a kitchen utensil.
5. **Slicing:** - Slicing is cutting into a thin piece but not as fine as shredding.
6. **Shredding**: - Shredding is cutting of vegetables into long narrow pieces by means of a shredder e.g. cabbage.
7. **Mincing:** It is method in which food ingredients are finely ground. In this method the effect is to create a closely bounded mixture of ingredients and a soft or fine chop texture flavouring ingredients with spice or condiments such as garlic, ginger and fresh herb may be minced to distribute flavour more evenly in a mixture.
8. **Slitting**: - Making a slit in the middle length-wise e.g. green chilies, long brinjal.
9. **Grinding:** To make a fine Powder. It is done reducing to small fragments or powder by crushing like grinding of India masala.
10. **Mashing**: - Its means breaking up of soft cooked food usually after boiling example boil potatoes mashed with fork, banana mashed with spoon.
11. **Pressing:** - It's the process separate the liquid from the solid content by using weight.
12. **Pureeing:** - It is grounding pressing and or straining vegetables or legumes to the consistency of a Paste or thick liquid.
13. **Sieving:** - Its means separate desired element from immaterial.

14. **Refining:-** From any of various processes for separating impurities from crude or semi finished materials
15. **Milling:** - Process by which removing of husk from grain.
16. **Skimming**: - Its means the act of removing floating material from the surface of a liquid.
17. **Rendering:** - Separate fat from connective tissue by heat.
18. **Filtration:** - The act or process of filtering the mechanical separation of a liquid from the undissolve particles floating on it.
19. **Flavouring**:- A bundle of herbs and vegetables to impact flavour of stock and sauces.
20. **Evaporation or reduction**: Removal of excess moisture by healing.
21. **Sprouting:** - It is the practice of soaking draining and then moistening seeds at regular intervals until they germinate.
22. **Emulsification**: - A suspension of small globules of one liquid in a second liquid with which the first will not mix for example emulsion of oil in vinegar.
23. **Homogenization**: - Subdivision of large drops into smaller one by force them through a small opening under great pressure for example fat and cream.
24. **Separating:** On the basis of difference in specific gravity as in the elimination of the over immature peas in a batch by used of brine of appropriate strength.

Combining and Mixing in the Preparation of Foods

Food preparation often involves the combining and mixing of different food or food material. Important effect of the method of combining food or ingredients is related to palatability.

1. **Beating:** - Beating is mixing material briskly, lifting and dropping them with an appropriate tool. It's done with electric mixer or by hand with fork. Spoon or hand whisker beating changes the consistency of the ingredients when we mixing egg white and sugar the changes into white opaque colour and look like a double white cream.
2. **Blending:** - It is a technique where two or more ingredients are combined so they are smooth and equally white cream.
3. **Cutting-in**: - It is a techniques used in a Pastry making. Mainly incorporated of fat in flour and other sifted ingredients with knife.
4. **Creaming:** - It is mixing or beating technique that combines ingredients to make a uniform mixture and also incorporates air into this mixture softening fat with hand or machine followed gradually by sugar.
5. **Kneading**: - It is a technique both used in bread making and pastries. It's pressured the mixture with knuckles and final what is out from the bowl is dough. These techniques can be done by hand or electric dough maker.
6. **Whipping**: - It is a mixture technique in this basically incorporate air into an ingredients or mixture.
7. **Marinating**: - It is process to steep meat or game in flavoured liquid for a certain length of time to tenderize and flavour the flesh.

8. **Folding:** - It's a simple to but crucial techniques used when combining light and airy mixture into a heavier ingredient or mixture in such a way as each ingredients maintain its original volume.

9. **Rubbing Inn:** - Rubbing fat into flour using the tip of finger until the mixture look like a bread crumb.

10. **Sealing:** - It is the sautéing or pre-cooking roast to develop colour and flavour.

BACKGROUND SKILLS

Knowledge of culinary: - Culinary preparation is both art and science in modern kitchen requires more than just a knowledge of food been prepared and method of preparation. Adherence to sanitary standards and the ability to communicate in the common language in the kitchen are a must. It is through knowledge of basic skills terminology and the rules of kitchen that achieved final goal preparation and services of quality food.

Sanitation: - Reports published by the world health organization in 1983 dealing with food handles are as follows. Food handling personnel play an important role in insuring food safety throughout the chain of production processing storage and preparation mishandling or disregards of hygienic measure on their parts may enable pathogenic to come into contact with food and in some case to survive and multiple in sufficient number to cause illness in the consumers. Occasionally food handling person may transfer pathogen that they carrying in on their bodies and such pathogens may service and multiple in the food may subsequently cause disease.

The sequence of events where by the food transfer may contaminated food in such a way as causes food borne disease is an follows:-

1. Pathogen are shed infuses, toilet, urine, discharge from the nose, ears or other areas of exposed skin in sufficient quantities.
2. Pathogens are transferred to the hands or exposed parts of the body which came into direct or indirect contact with the food.
3. The organism survives long enough to be transferred to the food.
4. Food that is contaminated is not treated in such a way as to destroyed the organism before they reach the consumers
5. Either the number of organism or the food constitutes and effected dose or the nature of the food and its condition of storage are such as to allow organizing to multiply and produce effective or to produce toxins in quantities sufficient to causes illness.

Pathogens or specific causative agent disease is most often transmitted or allowed to grow due to improve handling the kitchen worker.

The ability of food handler to entire the wholesomeness of the food prepared and served will depend upon the following few basic rules or personal hygiene and good food handling.

These rules can be divided into three groups.

1. General personal hygiene

(a) Should bath daily

(b) Should wear clean uniform, it also a sign of personal pride.

(c) Hair should restrained by either a bat or hair net to be wear to reduced the possibility of contamination of food.

(d) Finger nails should be short clean and free of nail polished.

(e) Open sores cut or burns should be carefully check for infection and covered with an antiseptic bandage and water proof protector food should never come in contact with open and infected source, cut or burns.

(f) Accomplished physical examination is recommended by all food handlers that they have no communicable diseases.

(g) Smoking or chewing tobacco products should never take place in food preparation or serving area.

2. Clean hands Healthy foods

The following action required immediate hand wash.

1. Contact with infected or offer wise unsanitary areas of bodies.
2. Use of handkerchief or tissue.
3. Hand contact with unclear equipment and work surfaces solid clothing or cleaning towels.
4. Handling raw food particularly meat, poultry fish items.
5. Clean away spoil dishes and equipment.

3. General rule sanitary for food handling

(a) Tasting or sampling of food should always be done by using two spoons.

(b) Never taste anything from stirring utensil.

(c) Perishables food should be kept out of the "temperature danger zone". This is the temperature range of 45° to 145° F in which bacteria multiplied most rapidly keep hot food hot above 145° F. Keep cold food cold under 45° F.

(d) Clean and disinfect surface and utensil after processing raw food, in order to prevent cross contamination.

(d) Thaw Food under refrigeration.

(e) Cook potential hazardous foods (meat, fish, poultry egg and dairy products) to the recommended internal temperature to prevent the growth of bacteria.

(f) FIFO food receives means first in used first out.

(g) Always used whole some food for approved sources.

(h) Discard questionable food. "When it doubt through it out"

HACCP

HACCP is an acronym or an abbreviation for hazardous analyses for critical control point. This is a complex name for whittle part of kitchen management. A critical control point is a point during processing of food item when a mistake in the storage preparation handling cooking for service of the item can result in the illness or even death of a customer. A food safety programme is a set procedure to produce safe and hygienic food every time. It involves a thorough examination of a process in order to identify and control the hazards that could make the food you produce harmful to eat. Simple stated in asks "What might go wrong, and how do I make sure it doesn't?" Food safety programme make sure that all the people working in your business are committed to producing safe and hygienic food by involving in the entire production, processing and distribution stage of the product. Food safety problems become easier to spot before they happen which leads to confidence in your product because you will have control ever the process.

General Objectives of Food safety Programme

- Identify the essential principles of food hygiene applicable throughout the food chain (starting from raw material reception to final product), to achieve the goal of ensuring that food is safe and suitable for human consumption.
- Recommend a HACCP based approach as a means to enhance food safety.
- Indicate how to implement those principles.
- Provide guidance for specific codes which may be needed for sectors of the food chain, processes or commodities to amplify the hygiene requirements specific to those area.

Food safety programme will need an expert technical advice to help in identifying the hazards and to take necessary controls. Internationally it is recognized that the ideal tool to give assurance of food safety is the Hazard Analysis Critical Control Point (HACCP), a Food Safety Quality Management system.

HACCP System

HACCP is an abbreviation for the Hazard Analysis Critical Control Point, which is synonymous with food safety management. It is a system which identifies, evaluates, and controls hazards which are significant for food safety. HACCP is a system that gives confidence that food safety is being managed effectively. HACCP was developed originally as a microbiological safety system in the early days (1960s) of the US manned space programme, as it was vital to ensure the safety of food for astronauts. The Pillsbury Company working alongside the national Aeronautics and Space Administration (NASA of the USA and the US Army Laboratories developed the original system.

A Hazard as used in the HACCP system is defined as "a biological, chemical or physical agent in or condition of food, with the potential to cause an adverse health effect".

Critical Control Point (CCP) is "a step at which control can be applied and is essential to prevent or eliminate a food safety hazard or reduce it to an acceptable level". HACCP is based on the principle that hazards affecting food safety can be either eliminated or minimized by prevention during production rather than by inspection of the finished product. Its goal is to prevent hazards at the earliest possible point in the food production or distribution chain. The HACCP approach can be applied right from harvest to the point of consumption. Adding HACCP to traditional inspection and quality control activities would lead to a preventive quality assurance system in a company. Companies using the HACCP system will be able to provide greater confidence about food safety to consumers as well as to food regulatory authorities.

The application of HACCP may require a fundamental change in the culture or attitudes of those involved in food processing. It also requires focused record keeping and documentation even though many of the procedures to be documented themselves may remain unchanged. It is very important that all the people working in the company understand the HACCP system and that they maintain it. The adoption of HACCP simply to satisfy a regulatory requirement has the potential to lead to failure in that company. The HACCP system and guidelines for its application were developed by the Codex Committee for Food Hygiene on the Codex Alimentarius Commission, a Joint food Standards Programme of the food and Agriculture Organization (FAO) of the United Nations and the World Health Organization (WHO).

HACCP Principles

Food is easily contaminated by bacteria's. The source of contamination affecting the food supply can be chemical, physical or biological. Biological contaminants accounts the majorly of illnesses or modern lifestyle which involves transport of food over long distance a movable population are frequently eat the food which tends to increase the risk of food infection and contamination

Hazard Analysis Critical Control Points (HACCP) is a tool that can be useful in the prevention of food safety Hazards. While extremely important, HACCP is only one part of multi-component food safety system.

The system of HACCP is based on science and systematic rules, identifies specific hazards and measures for their control to ensure the safety of food. HACCP is a tool to assess hazards and establish control system that focus on prevention rather than relying mainly on end product testing. It is important to identify the possible hazards that can occur at every stage of the food business from growth, processing, manufacturing, storage and distribution, until the point where it is sold to the customer. As far as possible manufacturer should consider how the customer might handle it too. The HACCP system consists of seven principles, which outline how to establish, implement and maintain a HACCP plan for the operation under study.

Principle 1: Identify hazards.

Identify potential hazards (microbiological, chemical and physical) associated with all stages of the production, using a flow diagram of the steps applied in the process. Assess the likelihood of occurrence of the hazards and identify preventive measures for their control.

I. Microbiological Hazards

Any bacterium, virus, or protozoan that is capable of causing illness and that grows or may be carried on food well-known example of bacteria are Campylobacter, Listeria and Salmonella. It is important to have some understanding of the risks associated with different types of microbiological hazards.

II. Chemical Hazards

Examples include excessive or toxic amounts of heavy metals, chemicals, pesticides, herbicides, insecticides, vitamins, minerals, preservatives, disinfectants, detergents and cleaning compounds. Some hazards may be naturally present such as in green potatoes or rhubarb leaves.

III. Physical Hazards

Objects that get into food are already present in food may cause illness, injury or distress to the person eating it. Some examples are glass, metal fragments etc. Other contaminants such as hair or insects may be offensive but not necessarily a danger to health.

Principle 2: Determine critical control points

Determine the points/ procedures/operational steps that can be controlled to eliminate the hazards, or minimize the likelihood of occurrence or reduce the hazards to an acceptable level. This means identifying whether it is the essential step to control an identified hazard. Also different types of hazard may have critical controls at different steps in the process.

i. Control points are the points in the food processing chain where it is possible to control or remove hazards.

ii. Critical control points are the control points in the processing chain where it is essential to a hazard, usually because there is no later step at which to establish control.

Principle 3: Establish critical limits

Establish critical limits (target levels and tolerances), which must be met to ensure the CCPs are under control. They must involve a measurable parameter and may also be known as the absolute tolerance or safety limit for the CCP. After each control point is identified, decide how to check whether it is under control during processing. This may be by observation or by measurement (such as temperature or time). Critical limits for critical control points are measurements such as temperature and time. Critical limits need to be validated after a certain time period regularly.

Principle 4: Establish a monitoring system

It must assured that the critical limits are always effective, it is important to set up a system to monitor and record control at the critical control point. Monitoring is the regular measurement or observation of a critical control point to ensure it is not beyond its critical limits. The monitoring system must ensure that any loss of control at the critical control point can be determined in certain time period to take corrective action before the product is rejected.

Information obtained from monitoring must be assessed by someone who has the knowledge and authority to carry out corrective actions when needed quick on-line chemical and physical measurements and observations are better than microbiological tests that take time to analyze. In practice a system is required to record observations. All records and documents must be signed by the person doing the monitoring and by a responsible reviewing official of the food production system.

Principle 5: Establish corrective action.

Corrective action to be taken when monitoring indicates that a particular CCP is moving out of control Decide exactly what corrective action to be taken to control a particular critical control point which is out of control. We need to think about reprocessing or dumping the affected product. Take corrective action to bring the process back under control before the problem (deviation) leads to a safety hazard. Consider proper management (disposition) of any adversely affected product. Document each and every corrective action taken in the HACCP records.

Principle 6: Establish verification procedures:

Once the HACCP system is established set up procedures to verify (check) that the system works. Verification procedures are tests and programmes that make sure the HACCP system working properly. Examples of verification include reviewing and HACCP system and its records to ensure that controls are effective. Reviewing corrective action reports to ensure that the corrective actions were undertaken to demonstrate that control has been maintained.

Principle 7: Establish record keeping and documentation requirements:

The level of documentation required will depend upon the needs and the complexity of the food business. In a small business, a simple log book or diary may be all that is needed. If your business is bigger or more complex, more detailed or formal documentation will necessary. Record keeping and documentation systems must meet the needs of the business and be adequate to show that the food safety programme is working without any deviation.

HACCP AND ISO 9000

The food industry is highly regulated by local, national and international laws relating to food safety. More importantly consumers are very careful in their buying decisions relating to raw or processed foods. Consumers usually feel more confident when they have evidence of quality management during the manufacturing of food and beverages, in addition to supervision by food regulators.

The ISO 9000 family of standards is generic in nature and has been developed to assist organization of all types and sizes that wish to implement and operate a Quality Management System (QMS).

There are no restrictions on its implementation by any sector of industry, including the food and beverage industry. Large and small companies that process and /or package food products worldwide have implemented ISO 9000 and obtained third party certification. These companies may also use HACCP or similar systems as part of their quality assurance system. Many companies today are using both ISO 9000 and HACCP as an integrated food safety and quality management system. Applying HACCP within an ISO 9000. QMS can result in a food safety system that is more effective than applying 9001 or HACCP separately. The emphasis of both systems is prevention rather than correction of problems or deficiencies after they occur. A company implementing a HACCP system does not have to comply with ISO 9001 but it is desirable. HACCP forms tool in controlling hazards that may be harmful to humans and provides a hurdle to microbes to multiply further. Hence a safe food is guaranteed by increasing the number of hurdles which can tackle growth of microbes effectively. These hurdles may include Good Manufacturing Procedures (GMP), ISO etc. together with HACCP system. An example of Hurdle Technology is clearly depicted in the figure represented below.

HURDLE TECHNOLOGY SAFE FOOD, GMP, HACCP, ISO MICROBE.

Hurdle Technology provides good number of hurdles for spoilage microorganisms either in the form of Food Quality Management System (GMP, HACCP, ISO etc.) or in the form of processing parameters (Acidity, Temperature, Pressure etc.) before they can reach the food item. The whole process takes enough time in the form of hurdle for any microbe to spoil the food product thus increasing the shelf life, quality, sensory attributes of the food item. Practicing different Food Quality systems together in the whole system will be of great advantage for achieving better quality product and consumer satisfaction.

Food Safety, HACCP and other Quality management System looks for hazards or anything that could go wrong regarding product safety and implements controls subsequently to ensure that the product will not cause harm to the consumer. Food Safety system mainly focuses on identifying and preventing hazards that may lead product to deteriorate. Food Safety system permits more efficient and effective government oversight and places responsibility for ensuring safe food to consumers from the food manufacturer. It helps food companies compete more effectively in the world market by reducing barriers to international trade.

HACCP helps in reducing the risk of manufacturing and selling of unsafe products and thus providing better confidence to consumers. Food regulatory authorities in many countries are adopting or like to adopt HACCP and other Food Quality Management systems as a part of their Food Safety system in order to ensure safe food reaching the consumers.

LEARNING OUTCOME

This chapter is a student's guide into the world of Professional cookery. The unit as a whole gives you an insider's perspective when it comes to commercial kitchen. Commercial kitchen were developed based on the needs and requirements of all persons around the world for global appetite for food requirements. Starting from the aim and objective of cooking. Cooking is the application of heat to food. The purpose of making it more digestible safer to eat more palatable and to change appearance. To cook food serve flame of heat to be must be introduced to the food. To render food more digestible by physical and chemical charges and by attention of texture thereby assisting masticating and to easiest the introduction of harmful bacteria and pesticide the aim and intention of cooking to see the food that is cooked under blows physical or chemical changes that are acceptable. Preparation of Ingredients and the method of mixing are done according to the requirement of various dishes. How important the hygiene and safety practice to be handle by food professional and the most important aspect of food safety such as know about the Hazard Analysis Critical control Points (HACCP) is a tool that can be useful in the prevention of food safety Hazards. While extremely important, HACCP is only one part of multi component food safety system.

LESSON END ACTIVITY

- Visit hotels in your place which are HACCP certified.
- Lists down various mixing method which are used in your home as compared to commercial kitchen mixing method.
- Make a questioner related to hygiene and sanitation and fill these forms from hospitality professional, either they used these practice in there working place (special reference to Chef).
- Make a chart presentation why used HACCP and when it was started.
- Cooked the following food item and observe the cooking effect and make a short note :

  i) Milk

  ii) Pulse

  iii) Apple

  iv) Raw banana

  v) Any pulses

  vi) Mutton

  vii) Fish.

QUESTIONS FOR DISCUSSION

1. Explain the aims and the objective of cooking.
2. What are different methods used in mixing the ingredients?

3. Explain the different techniques of preparation of ingredients.
4. Why we used hygiene and safety practices for handling food?
5. Explain the background skills of culinary professional.
6. What is HACCP?
7. Explain the different principles of HACCP.
8. Explain the food safety programme and its system.
9. What are HACCP and ISO 9000?
10. Explain the hurdle technology of food safety.

STATE TRUE AND FALSE

- HACCP and ISO-9000 only deals with foods.
- HACCP come in quality management system of any organization.
- Cooking made food less digestible.
- Cooking render the food easily.
- Cooking give varieties to the ingredients.
- Cooking reduce the bacteria contamination of the food.
- ISO-9000 is implemented for package food industry.
- Tasting or sampling of food should always be done without using spoon.
- Culinary preparation is both art and science in modern kitchen.

KEY TERMS

* Bacteria.	* Contamination
* Cooking	* Digestible
* HACCP	* Hazards
* Hygiene	* Ingredients
* ISO	* Renders
* Sanitation	* Culinary

Chapter 3

Kitchen Commodities

After studying this chapter, the student must know

- Raw material charactertics and their functions
- Different Herbs and Spices with their description and ethnic use
- Vegetables types and description with their boiling techniques
- Flavouring and Seasoning
- Tips to preserve the nutrients content of vegetables
- How to choose vegetables and how to preserve it
- Principal of storage vegetables
- Texture of food
- Different cut off vegetable.

Different raw materials are used in cooking to produce a complete dish. Each ingredient in a dish has a special part to play and knowledge of what each food does is necessary to understand cooking thoroughly. The materials are classified according to the part they play in making a dish. An ingredient is any substance used in the manufacture or preparation of a foodstuff and still present in the finished product, even if in an altered form. Contaminants and adulterants are not considered to be ingredients.

The foundation ingredient can be a liquid or a solid, for example: flour in bread, meat in roast, milk or stock in soups. Every dish has a foundation ingredient on which the other ingredients are based. It is necessary to know the proportions of various ingredients and also the composition of the different ingredients and the action of heat on these. Heat may not affect the whole material but only certain constituents.

CHARACTERISTIC OF RAW MATERIAL

To prepare good tasty colourful food its essential to have basic knowledge of raw material and their characteristic and the part they play this knowledge help to substitute material when necessary rectified the texture and taste if something's goes wrong it also help to improve the quality of the end product. The raw material are classified according to part of the play making a dish.

1. Salt
2. Liquids
3. Sweetening
4. Thickening
5. Fats and Oils
6. Raising agents
7. Flavourings and seasonings
8. Eggs
9. Clarified agents
10. Binding agents.

Salt

Through used in small quantity its special agent for both sweet and savoury dishes its help to bring out the flavour of other ingredient. If two much is added becomes in addable two light makes its supid. The right amount is added to know by experience. The common salt we used sodium chloride. It is ready available all part of the world in solid rock salt form or solution of sea salt form.

Uses

Salt has physical effect on gluten of flour in reasonable quantity. It is strength the gluten and increase its resistance to the softening effect of fermentation. Too much salt on the other hand will remove the power of gluten to hold gas. It act has disinfection for example Cauliflower or other leafs vegetable put in salted water make insects come out. It has controlling effect on the yeast activities in bakery product to control fermentation hence has mark effect on the crumbs, crust and colour of baked products. Salt added to water in cookery green vegetable help in colour retention and hence it effects the taste.

Salting

This operation preserves the meat. Fish ham, bacon other substance with salt or insuling than in bring for preservative. Its speed up coagulation of egg. Lower the freezing point of ice. Salt is an essential nutrients.

TYPES OF SALT

Grain or rock salt: - It's less pure but the impurities consists valuable nutrients.

Iodized salt: - By adding phosphate of lime has the advantage the salt keeps the powder form for a longer time where as pure salt tends to return to crystiling form under action of humidity.

Salt Petre and Potassium nitrate: - It's a fresh tasting piquant are little bitter. There is tang to it gives an admirable red colour to the meat but has to be used in very small quantity or else its toughing the meat.

Liquid

It is necessary to bind to dilute food to act as a cooking medium and to thin down gravies or a sauce, milk, water, stock and fruits juices and are commonly used liquids when two little liquid is added to the food it does not get cooked as in the case of cake retards the actions raising agents. Resulting in hard heavy food. Gravies, soups containing insufficient liquid are soggy. Too much liquid make food also soggy as in case of cakes or pudding hence liquids helps in maintaining the consistency of food, water and milk are used for making cooking liquors.

Butter milk is used for Indian curries and Kadi.

Stock: - stock is the liquid containing nutrients and flavours they are used in the foundation of soups gravies, sauces curries etc.

Sweetening:

When they are used to other food it hence a combined sensation or odour and flavour of the dish produce it also add to its own sweetness, its use in the kitchen in its varied substitution of one sugar (castor and icing) to another in a baking formula give allowance it difference in sweetening effect sugar available in following various form.

1. Granulated
2. Fine ground or castor
3. Powdered
4. Icing
5. Brown sugar.

Type of sweetening used is:

Sugar treacle, jaggery or molasses like corn syrups, maple syrups, golden syrups, corn syrups, and honey and fruit juices. If too much sweetening is used food becomes sticky to little is added sweet dishes become tasteless or bad cook generally add to much of sugar to cover of other faults.

Used :- Low concentration of sugar speed the effectiveness of baked yeast by providing a fast source of nourishment for its growth, does hastening the leveling process and the ability of sugar leveling crystallized gives delightful variety in cooking sugar gives pudding breads buns and bread rolls. A good light and even texture fermentation it's added by sugar in brewing wine making in the distillation of spirits. Sugar is also used as a preservative and can dissolved in water in very high concentration it's an energy food which can be stored a long home without getting spoil.

The uses of artificial or non nutritive sweetening like sugar-free requires special develops recipe while these products sweetness to food they do not have same effects of tremendous crust colour and velocity of the bad food.

Types of Sugar

Granulated sugar: White grain and refined

Cube sugar: It's actually granulated sugar which has been moisture with water moulds into cubes and then dries in that shape.

Frosting Sugar: It is manufacture of easily dissolve bubbles used in uncooked icing unlike icing sugar, frosting sugar does not have cornstarch added to it.

Icing Sugar or Confectionery Sugar: They are used for uncooked icing for sweetening fruits etc. It's made by pulprising granulated sugar assign cornstarch at the level or 3 % than corn starch is added to absorbed moisture than prevents cooking of the powder sugar

Brown sugar: Has a pleasing and distinctive flavour. The colour and flavour of brown sugar are due to its state of refinement. A dark strong brown colour sugar as under gone less purification.

Disadvantage

Those sugar promotes a smooth texture a vary sweet mixture will requested a lager time to freeze. It will also melt at lower temperature marking very sweet product is more difficult to serve without being too soft because sugar help growth of ice crystal

Thickening or Liaisons

They give gaudy consistency and palatability when used they also improved the nutritive value flavour liquids are converted into soups sauces, curries, gravies, bavarios(type of desserts), mousse, pudding etc. the thickening agents are : starch and starchy food agar-agar, egg, gelatin and for Indian gravies and curries thickening agent are coconut, tamarind, curd, poppy seeds, onion paste etc.

Starch is abundant in common food such as corn, rice, wheat, and potatoes arrowroot, tapioca they are classified into cereal starches, root starches and instant starches.

Cereal starches found in rice, wheat and maize when cooked they gelatins at about 71° C but requires about 85° C to 96° C. For maximum thickening cereals starch when cooked and cooled tends to jell.

Blood: - It's used in thickening

Binding Agent: - Are used to form a mixture of ingredients into a cohesive mask. The ingredients used for binding are egg yolks, pandas and bloods.

Egg yolks: - Are used in binding agents, stuffing kebabs etc.

Pandas: - Are used in preparation of fish meat, force meat, croquettes etc. Pandas are bread Pandas, flour panda, frangipane pandas'

Bread Pandas: - Is bread crumbs, boiling milk, salt and pepper

Flour Pandas: - Butter, flour, water and milk.

Frangipane Pandas: - Yoks, butter, flour, salt, pepper, grated nut-meg.

FATS AND OILS

Nutrientally used felt and in some form economically source of energy and add satiety value to the dish. They also contribute characteristics palatability quality of flavour and texture. They are popular used as cooking medium. Fat are solids at ordinary temperature when melt and heated those used in cooking are butter, marzine, lard, suet dripping and hydrogenated fat (like Dalda) Oils are liquids at ordinary temperature. But solidified at low temperature. The common used cooking oil is cotton seed oil, corn oil, safflower oil, soya bean oil, palm oil and salad oil, mustard oil

Salad oil is deodour vegetable oil used for salad dressing

Hydrogenation of oil

The conversation of oil into fats is brought about by the hydrogenation process this consists of treating oil under pressure at a suitable temperature with hydrogen in the presence of catalyst usually nickel under these condition the unsaturated fat acid present in the oil combined with hydrogen chemical process bring about a physical change and liquid oil become solid fat. The chief acids are unsaturated fatty acids are of oleic nature the varying consistency are due the process of hydrogenation begin stock at different stages.

Usage of Fats

Fats are used in cooking as a spread (all preserved are spread), shortenings for tempering as a salads dressing and as frying medium

Spread for example butter, margine and their function to add flavour nutritional value and satetity value to the food.

Shortening*:* Fats are used in confectionary to enrich the food and to impart to them short eating quality there effect is to break down the toughness of gluten so that instead of beign hard and tuff to eat food containing fats break of shorts and readily melt in the mouth. The factor to look for shortening are.

Creaming value: - It is the shortness or shorting power gives to the product shortness is necessary to baked biscuits cookies and pastries.

Stability: - It is the keeping quantity. If the stability is not good the keeping quantity of product decrease and the fat become rancid.

Consistency: - Hardness or softness is depending on purpose. Hardness is needed for puff pastries and softness in cake makings.

Tempering: - Use for tempering Indian food for special characteristics flavour.

Salad dressing: - Hot animal fat dressing which consists of bacon fat, vinegar and seasoning are used for green hot salads.

Cooked dressings: - Its cooked mixture of egg vinegar fat starch and seasoning.

French dressing: - It is an impulsion of oil vinegar or lime juice and seasoning.

Fat as frying medium

It functions in three ways:

1. It serves transfer for heat to the frying medium,
2. It adds nutritative value and
3. It adds flavour.

Fat use as frying medium should have following:-

1. A high smoked point.
2. A low congealing point.
3. A low moisture content.
4. High stability.
5. High expectable flavour.

Rendering of fat: - Its process or extracting fat from fatty tissues, a good supply of drippings can be obtained from rendering down suet (fat surrounding the kidney of cow) lard (pig) tallow (beef) etc can be done in two ways.

1. Cut the fat into small piece and place in on baking tin in a slow oven until the fat has melted and there are crisp brown pieces of tissues left strain through a fire cloth into a clear basin. Press the tissue to squeeze out all the fat.
2. Cut the piece of fat as above place in a pan without lid and with very little water boiled until water is evaporated then heat very gently until the fat has melted leaved only a crisp brown peace of tissue strain as before in both cases the temperature should not to be high or else fat will decompose.

Clarification of Fat: - Frying feel must be kept clean because particles of food such as bread crumbs lower the smoked point of fat. The dripping of roasting, frying, grilling and the fat from the top of the stews, soups, gravies, stocks etc. must be clarified before it's used for frying.

1. *To Clarified:* - Put a fat in a sauce pan without lid and cover with water.
2. *Bring to boil:* - Strain the fat to muslin and pour into clear basin leave until cold when fat will formed a hard layer top of the water and any impurities will either or left in the water or stock the bottom of fat layer lift up the cake of fat turn it, upside down and scrape

the bottom clean, the water left in the fat must be removed, melt fat in sauce pan and heat until its stop bubbling.

RAISING AGENTS OR LEAVENING AGENTS

Leavening is increase the surface area of tough or batter by creating within number of gas bubbles the function of the raising agent is to puff up the food so that it is spread and rise and becomes full of holes does making it light and not close and heavy. The holes made by the raising agents are retained during the process of cooking. The leavering of flour mixture process accomplished by the exposition of incorporated air and by internal production and expansion of water vapour and CO_2 gas when the product is heated the air expand and part of water vaporized the formation of CO_2 required the presence of suitable microorganism or chemical agent during the first part of heat gas production is accelerated and gas formed expand as a the temperature rise, gluten develops when moisture is added help to keep the raising agent with in till the foot sets. Does making it light and fluffy gluten is a sticky elastic substance which stretches when gas and air expand and prevent these from scaping. The air or gas does make whole in the mixture. Too much raising agents also raises the food rapidly and become heavy leavering action may be produced by physical chemical or biological means, the common leavering agents are:-

- Air,
- Steam and
- CO_2.

Air is introduced into the mixture through sifting mixing batter and incorporating the beaten egg white.

To some extent all flour mixture that a yeast leaven bread: quick breads, cakes and cookies depends on air for leavering but air is usually not sufficient you need other leavening agent as with the basic formula for shortened cake usually direct that some chemical raising agent we used although extensive creaming of fat and sugar is recommended for aeration this creaming action lead us to the formulation of air cells into which the CO_2 gas formed by the baking powder can defused for example when foam cake or angled food cake are heat the air trapped in the whole expand and volume of cake increases air contribution to the leveling of the finished product varies considerable air incorporated during mixing expands as it's worm in the oven and causes some increase in the volume of the baked product. The amount of air incorporated in determines by the following.

Amount of Manipulation: - That is although mixing generally increase more air in a product but it is not always true like in the case of beating egg whites. Use of manipulation to incorporate air to a optimum point causing a greater volume in the finished products beyond this point the cells walls in the form because less elastic either increase in beating or folding will causes loss air and reduce volumes optimum.

Viscosity batter: - The extensive creamy of fat and sugar is done to produce a form of gas in a solid although this a heavy firm compared to egg which firmed. It's every important because fine texture cakes results when fat, sugar air firmed has been beaten sufficient to produced many tiny air pockets. The viscosity of unbaked mixture varies with the temperature and proportion of ingredients it's difficult to cream a chilled fat to increase viscosity of the cooler fat makes its difficult to in cases air in the mixture so that with the same amount of worker less air is creamed mixture. On the other hand a much wamed (liquid) is less able to be trapped in air. In somewhat cooler less fluid mixture is extremely mixture with high portion of liquid is incapable in holding a large amount of air for longer period time.

Nature of Ingredients: - When the egg in a recipe is incorporated as an egg white the large amount of air help in the form contributes appreciable leavening as in angle cake or spoung whereas lesser amount of air will be contain in an egg yolk or whole egg formed.

Bench time: - The length of time lapsing during preparation of a product prior to baking also determines the amount of air available for leavening.

Steam: - Is an every present leavening agent even a small out of water in batter or dough causes an appreciable leavening action because volume of water expands 1600 time when it's converted into steam. During the process of baking although the steam produced during baking causes the mixture to expand steam alone cannot leave a mixture. Its action must be combined with that of Air, CO_2 some product like puffs depends entirely on steam produced testing baking to increase its volume.

CO_2: - The principal mean leavening flour mixture principal by the formation of CO_2 gas generated by the action of chemical leaveners or by biological needs by the help of yeast which produced the gas by its action on the sugar the chemical leaveners basically used are baking powders, baking soda or sodium carbonate (which depends on the presence of an acid ingredient) such as sour milk to give of CO_2.

Baking Powder: - This is produced by mixing an acid reacting material and sodium carbonate with the addition of corn starch and corn flour the acid ingredients tartaric acid or acid salts like sodium, potassium tartaric acid, and salt of phosphoric acid compound of a three types of baking powder.

1. *Fast Acting*: - Powder gives us most of the gases volume within the few minutes of contract with liquid.
2. *Slow Acting:* - Powders give up very little of the gas volume at low temperature they required heat of the oven to react completely.
3. *Double Acting*: - They are colder they become reacting at low temperature. and gives some smoothness and velocity to the batter but they do not go into complete reaction until they are exposed to high temperature these powder have two acid ingredients one is soluble in cool water and other is soluble in high temperature.

A baking powder should be so balanced that its baking soda and acid ingredients will formed a salt when the powder is combined with the liquid baking powder, also contain an inert filler usually cornstarch or powder calcium carbonate and filler act as buffer between the active ingredients and prevents them from reacting when exposed to moisture. It also served to standardized the strength of the powder to yield a standard amount of carbon dioxide, the weight of the soda is health constant while the weight of the difference acid components is varied act to the amount needed to release to necessary amount of CO_2 to standardized the powder the different of weight are charted by the use of fillers.

Fast acting chemical: Cream of tartor and tartaric acid.

Slow acting chemical: - A Hydrous mono-calcium Phosphates.

Double acting chemical: - Mono-calcium Phosphate, sodium, aluminum, sulphate with cream of tartar.

Baking Soda

Exact amount of soda must be used will revolt in edible product with yellow spot on the surface. Sour milk or butter milk are more frequently used as an acid ingredients when Sodium bicarbonate is heated it breaks down into sodium bicarbonate, water and CO_2. The residue of sodium carbonate in a flour mixture gives a disagreeable flavour so when soda is added in a suitable quantity of an acid is added so that a more mutal residue is formed. This is also a case with amino carbonate.

Yeast

Yeast is a microscope unicellular plant that reproduced rapidly under suitable condition of food warmed and moisture. SACCHAROMYCES CEREVICAE the particular strained used is baked product multiplies rapidly under controlled condition to released large quantity of CO_2. The yeast plant feeds on simple sugar and metabolized than CO_2, water and alcohol the levelling action of yeast is a brought after through fermentation. This take place when the enzymes zymase is released or extract from the yeast cell the action zymase convert sugar into alcohol and CO_2. The sugar require by the yeast is available from three sources:-

1. Sugar added in the mixing period
2. Sugar present as such in flour
3. Sugar released from wheat starch by enzymatic acting – that is yeast itself contains the enzyme sucrose need to split (sucrose to glucose and fructose) flour normally contains one to two per cent of monosolcarite glucose also that is available to yeast immediately.

In a yeast leaven flour mixture the CO_2 is retain in the gluten and acetone is given of during baking. The growth of yeast and its activates is graven by its temperature. That is yeast begin at 10° C (50° F) and multiplies rapidly a temperature ranging from 29° C to 35° C. The rise in temperature of yeast dough at its warms in the oven is execrated by released CO_2 until the tough approaches a temperature when yeast is killed at about. 60° C. In 5 minutes or 43°C in one hour. The fermentation process during proofing or raising period ultimately results in the release of alcohol CO_2 and water. This fermentation must be controlled to get desire texture and flavour. Now to control the gas production salt is added which retards the process fermentation must be stock in the oven by the high baking temperature before the tough becomes to porous form access amount of CO_2. Yeast market as Compressed yeast and Dry yeast.

Fig 3.1 The compressed yeast cake

Fig 3.2 The dry yeast

Compressed Yeast (Fig. 3.1)

Its moist mixture, yeast and starch the manufacture of yeast involves selection of strained of yeast that have a durable gas producing qualities the yeast is introduce into the solution of molasses and mineral salt and ammonia which permit to grow under very control condition after growth to ceases the yeast cell are separated from the solution by filtration or centrifugation mixed with a small amount of starch and compressed cake, its most of refrigerated in order to retard detoriation.

Dry Yeast (Fig. 3.2)

The main difference is dry yeast less moist and thus less susceptible to detoration during storage. The manufacturing of dry yeast storage similar to that of compressed yeast after yeast is washed and filtered its extruded in short noodle form an to a converted belt that passes through a dry. The drying cuts the moister content of the yeast to about 8% renders the yeast cell dormant and made refrigeration unnecessary the yeast cell are then mixed with corn meal and package. Dry yeast cell become inactive after prolonged storage has an expiry dated stamped on the package and should not be act certain species of bacteria under controlled condition of temperature and moisture grow and act on sugar breaking it down to CO_2 and hydrogen gas. These bacteria are used to liven the product are known as self-raising bread. Dry yeast is inexpensive.

FLAVOURING AND SEASONING

The taste and acceptability of food depends to a very great extent on the correct amount of flavouring and seasoning. These are variable ingredients and correct amount necessary for different dishes must be carefully studied to add just enough and no more should be the aim of ever cook, those which combined taste and smell essences cardomen, nutmeg saffron, are called flavouring. Those which enhance taste only are called seasoning for example:- red chilled, mustard, pepper. Condiments are aromatic substance added to food to improve its flavour.

The term seasoning used for substances which are added during cooking while condiments applied to those added at the table to food already prepared all condiment expect salt and salt peter are vegetable origin condiment are classified according to their dominant flavour into acid, aromatic bitter, salt, sweet etc.

1. **Acid**: The acid condiments are vinegar, lemon juice and tamarind.
2. **Bitter**: Pepper paprika, cayenne pepper, white pepper corn and green pepper corns.
3. **Aromatic**: Dill, anise, basil, cocoa, coffee, chervil, coriander, cumin, tarragon parsley, saffron, sage, thyme vanilla pots, orange, lemon jest.

Readymade condiments and proprietor sauces

- W. Sauces, Worcestershire, 8 to 8 sauce, mustard, soya sauces etc are readymade condiments.

Sweet condiments: is comports preserve fruits and candy peels.

Seasoning: The purpose of this is to enhance and accentuate flavours, specially flavour dominant in food or to create a dominant taste in bland food, in the west salt is the principal seasoning, in the east soya is the principal seasoning soya paste pepper is also thought as a seasoning but it basically a spices food extracts meat and vegetable extracts. Further served the purposes of seasoning. Since they are concentrates and can be preserved for a longer time. Asafoetida is a sold as a powder or in pieces and only minuet quantity are needs other seasoning gravy browned, gravy powder, gravy marmite and sodium, glutamate (it is also called ajinomoto), stock cubes.

EGGS

The basic principal of egg to cookery control around the ability of protein in both yolks and white to coagulated and when heated the thickening or coagulation of an egg mixture is brought about because protein molecules attracts and noted them in large quantity of water solid particles help suspended in the liquid results in jell formation. This quantity or eggs make them usable for thickening such food products as custards and puddings and for coating food materials as protein of the egg yolks differ from that of the white the temperature all which they coagulate also differ to.

Coagulation of egg protein

When heat is applied the egg white changes from a transparent vicious mask to a soft opaque (light cannot pass) material. If the egg white is heated pass the optimum coagulation temperature of 148° F or 68° C and white become tough and pours. Very high temperature cause the egg white to lose water shrink and toughen rather its becomes crumble in texture when heated beyond the optimum temperature the coagulation temperature will depend on the concentration or dilution of the egg and kind of material added. The dilution of egg protein raise the temperature at which the mixture thicken and concentration of egg protein lowers the temperature the addition of sugar to an egg mixture raise the temperature at which coagulation takes place addition if take lower the coagulation temperature. In a typical egg mixture curdling may result from stirred the protein gel hence it's better to add little salt before heating.

ACIDS

Any acidic material added to an egg mixture well to produce firm gel and lower the coagulation temperature prolong heating of acid mixture will result in peptization (a term used to indicate the up of a large aggregate molecules into smaller ones) of the protein and corresponding thinning out of mass.

Starch

Some food mixes like cream, pie-filling and cooked salad dressing make or the coagulation of the egg protein and the gelatinization of starch to bring about the thickness of a mixture. As the coagulation and gelatinization temperature differs a starch mixture to bring to its maximum thickness before adding the uncooked egg.

Uses of egg in cookery

Binding and coating: - Egg is used in food mixes like meat loaf, croquettes, medallions hamburger koftas etc. is distributed through the mixture upon heating the protein coagulates binding the food into a cohesive marks of desire firmed thus they retained their shapes during the cooking process the egg or egg batter helps, to give a coat to a food items and prevent them from disintegrating and given them protecting coating frequently an outer coating of flour, bread crumbs, cereals or butter is added to a food to enhance it appearance, texture or flavours and egg batter provide a binding and coating before crumbing. Egg batter also used for pan cakes.

Egg as a leavening agent: - Form is created when egg white is beat the form is made up of air bubbles surrounding by a thin elastic film of egg white when foam is incorporated into the mixture its provided leveling for such products as omelets, sponge cake, meringues when these product are heated air bubbles expand and the egg white film hardens the volume of an egg yolk increase when bitten and the presence of fat in the yolk makes it forming power considerable lower than that of a egg white.

Egg White Foam

It is used in many food to make them light fluppy and porous. An egg white Foam is colloid of bubbles of air surrounding by part of albumin that has been denature by the filling of the egg white. The denature albumin is stiff and gives stability to the foam, as egg white are bitten is loose is elasticity of some elasticity is necessary in an egg white foam. Which is used in some dishes as soufflés and cakes so that air cells can expand with of breaking down the cell walls the addition of sugar to egg white makes stable smooth foam is formed. One that will not collapse and drain quickly. Although more beating is required when sugar is added a more stable foam is formed. The sugar has to be added early in the heating process for over beating the egg white before adding sugar will cause drainage or leakage of egg white. The presence of even small amount of egg yolk or other food material containing fat such as milk oil cream or butter interference with the formation of the foam. Water added to egg white increase the foam but decreased this stability and egg white foam is formed and reaches greater volume more and quickly when egg whites are at room temperature rather than when they are refrigerated. A foam is be formed by beating air into an egg white with wire whisk a rotary beater or electrical mixture when an egg white foam is increasing in volume. The air bubbles become smaller and more evenly distributed the translucence change to an opaque whiteness and the elasticity of the foam decrease as it become stiffer egg white should be beaten only until peaks that's stand straight and bend slightly at the tips are formed. Egg white beaten to dry stage lack elasticity tends to break down in small try clumps and rapidly dimension became less in volume. Salt decrease the stability of egg foam. But limited amount of acid ingredients increase it.

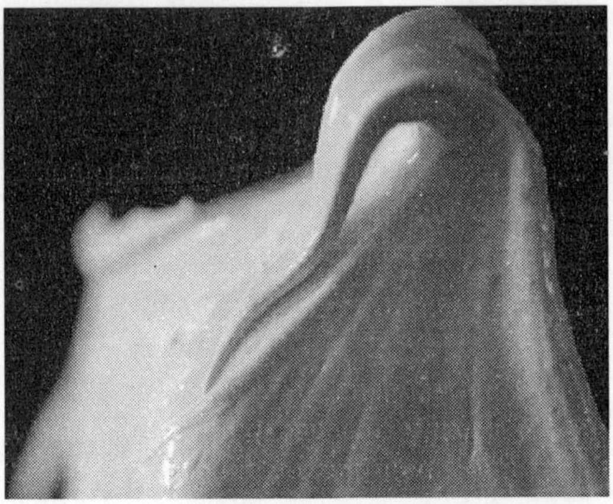

Fig 3.3 Meringues whipped to soft

MERINGUES

Soft Meringues (Fig. 3.3)

Soft Meringues have two table spoon of sugar for each egg white in confectionary and pastries. We use this as a toping to the filling while they are still not and baked at 375° F until the meringues reach a light colour. This yields a stable maring and reduces the amount of liquid leakage collecting under the meringues and the tendency of the meringues to spilt away from the pies. The liquid foam is due to the under coagulation of egg white or some times over coagulation also this is evidences by the formation of amber beads that frequently appears on the surface of the meringues.

Fig 3.4 The hard meringues

Hard Meringues (Fig. 3.4)

Have a much higher of position of sugar ¼ cups to egg white since sugar regards the denaturation of egg protein. A longer whipping time are required hard meringues can be shaped into objects such as basket, hearts, pie shells, or animal figures. They are baked for one and half hours at a very low temperature of 275° F.

Egg as an emulsifying agent: - They are used to form stable emulsion that in mayonnaise that is oil and vinegar separate out unless oil droplets are coated with the substance that keeps them from running together Egg yolks and as an interface among them. Eggs are also needed as emulsifier in ice-cream, cake and cream puffs.

Interfering substance: Beating egg white will act as interfering substance in mixtures such as sherbets, tiny bubbles of air trapped in the egg prevent ice crystals from coming together and creating large masses of icy materials, same thing happens in sugar candy here some time egg white and egg yolks added to sugar can be interference to the formation of large sugar crystal.

Eggs as clarified agent:- Egg albumins are collider matter the clarifying agent as raw egg white and shell which may be added to hot broths, stocks, coffee, wines, beers etc. when the proteins in the egg coagulated they trapped the loose particles in the liquid clarified it.

Clarified Agent

Are usually used in liquids to separate out impurities or unwanted matter or render the liquid clear.

Clarification of butter: Heat butter on a very gentle heat the butter melts and looks as clear as olive oil. White deposits forms of the bottle on the pan strain the clear butter for future.

Clarification of liquids or fruits juice: Most liquids can clarify by flittering fruits juices are clarified by light fermentation.

Clarification consommé: It is done with white of egg, lean beef (without fat) and vegetable out at into small dice or minced. Meat, egg white and vegetable are mixed with stock and whisked till the mixture reached boiling point lower the heat and simmer for ½ hours strained through a cloth without disturbing the raft.

Bindings Agents

They are used to whole to give shapes to those preparations which may otherwise break while cooking or handling. Some common binders are egg potato, corn, flour, gram flour. They are used for making cutlet Koftas tikkis etc. Binder should be used in such a manner they should not change the taste of the original dish.

HERBS

Types and Definition

Latin meaning "grass" defines as leaves and stem of soft steamed woody Plant Primarily grow in temperate climacteric can be basic of back to Egypt Greece and China. Herbs can be categorized as fresh, dried, pickle or frozen.

Fresh Herbs: As the name denotes are without alteration and freshly picked.

Dry herbs: Means the same as fresh expect the water has been removing to concentrate the flavour.

Pickle herbs: Are fresh herbs stored in brine.

Frozen herbs: May be either directly frozen 0° to 10° F or blanched Frozen.

SPICES

Types and Definition

The term 'spices' come from Latin and roughly translated with "fruit of the earth". Spices are distinguished from herbs and a derived from various parts of the plant, for example the bark of cinnamon, the buds of cloves, the flower of saffron, the fruits all of spices, the root of ginger, the seed of mustard. Spice can be as whole or ground categorized.

Whole spices are in their natural from seeds, nuts, barks, roots, flowers, leaves, buds or fruits advantages are long shelf life. Some spice contains antioxidants, components which slow down the removal of their essence by the introduction of oxygen. This anti oxidants are intact in whole spices allowing them to be stored for three to six months it is also easy to remove them from food when desire when left in food they provide interesting texture.

Ground spices another ones which are reduce to selected sizes by a food mill or grinder the advantages is to incorporate them in food more uniformly, disadvantage short shelf life.

WINES

It's a staple flavouring agent almost all culinary repertories. Wine is defined as a liquid Produce from Fermented Fruits, there are two basic categorized Table and Fortified.

Table wines are fermented Juice or Grapes.

Fortified Wines: are table wines which have had spirits added during or after fermentation in order to give them distinct flavour example sherry, Port, Marsala and Madeira.

VINEGARS

Is a technical a by-product of fermented wine the term vinegar come from French meaning "sour wine" commercially distilled vinegars generally content around 5% acidic acid which is what give vinegar.

Fig 3.5 The Cider Vinegar

Fig 3.6 The Distilled Vinegar

FLAVOUR AND CHARACTERISTICS

Cider Vinegar (Fig. 3.5)

Is made from apple native to America.

Distilled Vinegar (Fig. 3.6)

Is colourless and very strong it's used for Picking.

Malt Vinegar (Fig. 3.7)

Is made from molted barely and is caramel coloured used for Pickling and as a key ingredients worchietreshire sauces.

Rice Vinegars (Fig. 3.8)

Inherent to China and Japan can be red, white or black in colour.

Fig 3.7 The Malt Vinegar

Fig 3.8 The Rice Vinegar

Wine Vinegar (Fig. 3.9)

Can be derived from red white rose wine or sherry finest wine vinegar is made in "Oak Vats".

Flavored Vinegar

Herbs fruits or spice added used for cold dressing and special sauces example are rosemary, dill tarragon lemongrass, raspberry, rose pettle horseradish.

Fig 3.9 The different wine Vinegar

MARINATES

Types and Definition

It's a season liquid in which a product is soaked for either flavouring or tenderizing or both. There are three primarily type of marinates – cooked, raw and instant three primarily types are oil, acid and flavour.

BEST USES OF HERBS AND SPICES

Beef - Basil, Chives, Coriander, Dill, Garlic, Horseradish, Marjoram, Oregano, Parsley, Rosemary, Sage, Savory, Tarragon, Thyme.

Veal - Basil, Dill, Marjoram.

Lamb - Basil, Coriander, Dill, Garlic, Lemon, Balm, Marjoram, Mint, Oregano, Rosemary, Sage, Tarragon, Thyme.

Pork - Anise (seeds), Basil, Chives, Coriander, Dill, Garlic, Marjoram, Oregano, Rosemary, Sage, Tarragon.

Poultry - Anise (seeds), Basil, Borage, Chervil, Chives, Coriander, Dill, Garlic, Horseradish, Lemon, Balm, Marjoram, Oregano, Parsley, Rosemary, Sage, Savory, Tarragon, Thyme.

Fish - Anise (seeds), Basil, Borage, Chives, Dill, Fennel, Horseradish, Lemon, Balm, Oregano, Parsley, Rosemary, Sage, Savory, Tarragon, Thyme.

Shellfish - Basil, Chives, Dill, Marjoram, Oregano, Parsley, Thyme.

Cheese Dishes - Anise (seeds), Basil, Chervil, Chives, Dill, Oregano, Rosemary, Sage, Salad, Burnet, Tarragon, Thyme.

Egg Dishes - Basil, Chervil, Chives, Dill, Horseradish, Marjoram, Oregano, Rosemary, Sage, Savory, Tarragon.

Soups/Stews - Chervil, Chives, Cilantro, Dill, Fennel, Garlic, Marjoram, Oregano, Rosemary, Savory, Thyme.

Salads - Anise (seeds), Basil, Borage, Chervil, Chives, Cilantro, Dill, Fennel, Garlic, Lemon, Balm, Marjoram, Oregano, Brunet, Savory, Tarragon.

Potatoes - Basil, Chives, Fennel, Garlic, Horseradish, Marjoram, Mint, Oregano, Parsley, Rosemary, Sage, Savory, Tarragon, Thyme.

Tomatoes - Basil, Chives, Cilantro, Dill, Garlic, Marjoram, Oregano, Parsley, Sage, Tarragon, Thyme.

Carrots - Anise (seeds), Basil, Chervil, Chives, Dill, Gingerroot, Marjoram, Parsley, Savory, Tarragon, Thyme.

Spinach - Anise (seeds), Basil, Chervil, Chives, Dill, Marjoram, Rosemary, Tarragon, Thyme.

Desserts - Anise (seeds), Basil, Borage-flower, Coriander, Fennel, Lavender, Lemon, Balm, Mint, Rosemary.

Beverages - Basil, Borage flower, Coriander, Fennel, Lemon, Balm, Mint, Salad, Burnet, Savory, Thyme.

Breads - Anise (seeds), Basil, Chives, Coriander, Dill, Fennel, Garlic, Marjoram, Oregano, Parsley, Rosemary, Sage, Savory, Tarragon, Thyme.

Vinegar - Basil, Borage, Chervil, Chives, Coriander, Dill, Fennel, Garlic, Marjoram, Rosemary, Tarragon.

Pickles - Anise (seeds), Coriander, Dill, Tarragon.

Jams/Jellies - Lemon, Balm, Lavender, Mint, Rosemary, Sage.

HERBS AND SPICES

All spices (Fig. 3.10)

General Description

All spices are the dried, unripe berry of *Pimento dioica*, an evergreen tree in the myrtle family. After drying, the berries are small, dark brown balls just a little larger than peppercorns.

Geographical Sources

Allspice comes from Jamaica, Mexico, and Honduras.

Traditional Ethnic Uses

Allspice is used in Jamaican jerk seasoning and in Jamaican soups, stews, and curries. It also is used in pickling spice, spiced tea mixes, cakes, cookies, and pies. Food producers use it in ketchup, pickles, and sausages.

Fig 3.10 All spices in powder and Berry form

Taste and Aroma

Allspice is pungent and fragrant. It is not a blend of "all spices," but its taste and aroma remind many people of a mix of cloves, cinnamon, and nutmeg.

ANISE SEED (FIG. 3.11)

Fig 3.11 The Anise seed

General Description

Anise Seed is a gray brown oval seed from Pimpinella anisum, a plant in the parsley family. It is related to caraway, dill, cumin, and fennel.

Geographical Sources

Spain and Mexico.

Traditional Ethnic

Uses Europeans use Anise in cakes, cookies, and sweet breads. In the Middle East and India, it is used in soups and stews. Its licorice like flavour is popular in candies and Anise oil is used in liqueurs.

Taste and Aroma

Anise Seeds smell and taste like licorice.

BASIL (Fig. 3. 12)

General Description

Basil is a bright green, leafy plant, Ocimum basilicum, which is in the mint family.

Fig 3.12 The different varieties of basil

Geographical Sources

Basil is grown primarily in the United States, France, and the Mediterranean region.

Traditional Ethnic Uses

Basil is widely used in Italian cuisine and is often paired with tomatoes. It is also used in Thai cooking. The herb complements meat, vegetables, cheese, and egg dishes.

Taste and Aroma

Basil has a sweet, herbal bouquet.

BAY LEAF (Fig. 3.13)

General Description

Bay Leaves come from the sweet bay or laurel tree, known botanically as Laurus nobilis. The elliptical leaves of both trees are green, glossy, and grow up to 3 inches long.

Fig 3.13 Fresh bay leaves

Geographical Sources

Bay Leaves are grown in the Mediterranean region.

Traditional Ethnic Uses

Bay Leaves, a staple in American kitchens, are used in soups, stews, meat and vegetable dishes. The leaves also flavour classic French dishes such as bouillabaisse and bouillon.

Taste and Aroma

Bay Leaves are pungent and have a sharp, bitter taste.

CARAWAY SEEDS (Fig. 3.14)

General Description

Caraway Seed is actually the fruit of a biennial herb in the parsley family, known as Carum carvi. The seed is about 1/5inch long and tapered at the ends. The hard seed shells have five pale ridges.

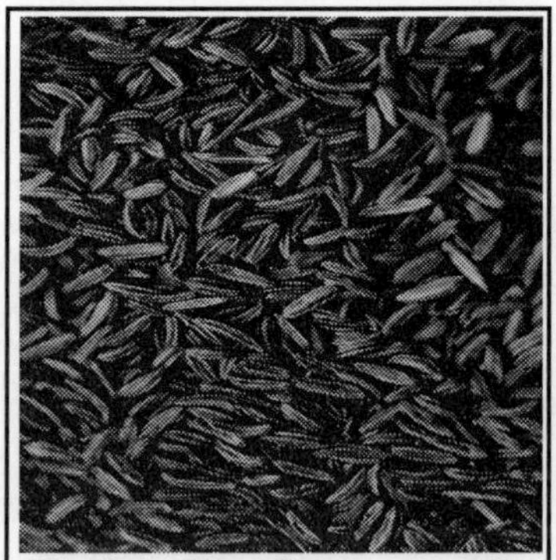

Fig 3.14 The Caraway seeds

Geographical Sources

Holland is the world's largest Caraway producer. It is also grown in Germany, Russia, Morocco, parts of Scandinavia, Canada, and the United States.

Traditional Ethnic Uses

Caraway Seed is a common flavouring for many kinds of rye bread. It is also used to flavour sauerkraut, sausage, cheese, cabbage, and soups.

Taste and Aroma

Caraway Seed has a pungent aroma and a distinctly sweet but tangy flavour.

CARDAMOM (Fig. 3.14)

Fig 3.15 The cardamoms pods

General Description

Cardamom is the ground seed of a tropical fruit in the ginger family known as Elettaria cardamom. The seeds are found in oval shaped fruit pods that are between 1/4 and 1inch long.

Geographical Sources

Cardamom comes from India, Guatemala, and Ceylon.

Traditional Ethnic Uses

In India Cardamom is traditionally used in curry blends, and in Scandinavian countries it is commonly added to breads; however, most of the world's Cardamom crop is used in Arabic countries as a flavouring for coffee.

Taste and Aroma

Cardamom has an intense, pungent, sweet flavour.

CAYENNE PEPPER (Fig. 3.16)

Fig 3.16 The cayenne pepper (Red)

General Description

Cayenne Pepper is made from the dried pods of pungent chili peppers. This fiery spice adds flair to dishes from Asia, the Americas, and the Middle East.

Geographical Sources

Cayenne Pepper comes from Central and South America and the West Indies.

Traditional Ethnic Uses

Cayenne Pepper is traditionally used in Mexican and Italian cooking.

Taste and Aroma

Cayenne Pepper has little aroma, but it is extremely hot to taste.

CELERY SEEDS (Fig. 3.17)

General Description

Celery Seed is the dried fruit of Apium graviolens, a biennial in the parsley family. This is the same genus and species used for growing table celery, although there are particular varieties that are used for the vegetable. The seeds are very small (about 1/16th of an inch), ovoid and light brown.

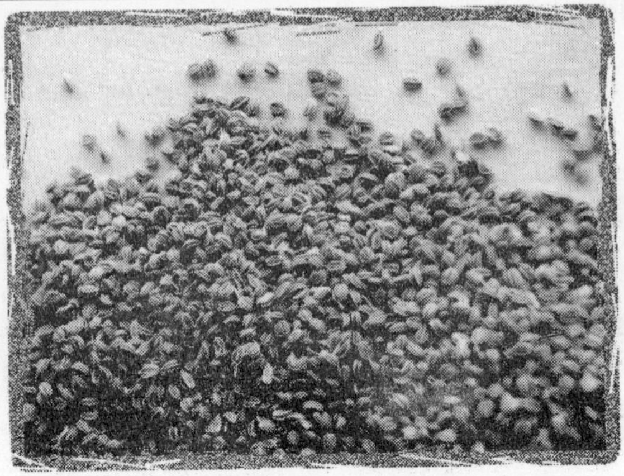

Fig 3.17 The Celery seeds

Geographical Sources

Celery Seed is grown in France and India.

Traditional Ethnic Uses

Celery or as the ancients called it "small age" has been used as a medicine since the time of the Greeks. In the middle Ages, it was discovered that cultivation produced a much superior plant. At that time people began to use it more widely as a vegetable. It was not until the 19th century that the seeds were used in recipes, appearing first in pickling recipes.

Taste and Aroma

Celery Seed tastes similar to table celery, with its warm, slightly bitter, aromatic flavour.

CHERVIL (Fig. 3.18)

General Description

Chervil is a light green, lacey, fernlike leaf of Annthriscus cerefolium, a low growing member of the parsley family.

Fig 3.18 The Chervil leaves

Geographical Sources

Chervil is grown in California and New Mexico.

Traditional Ethnic Uses

Chervil is one of the classic components of the popular French herb blend, fines herbs.

Taste and Aroma

The leaves of this aromatic and sweet herb bear a slight resemblance to parsley; however, the flavour is more distinctive with a trace of anise

CHIVES (Fig. 3.19)

Fig 3.19 The fresh Chives

General Description

Chives are the bright green, long, hollow, thin leaves of Alliums schoenoprasum, an onion like member of the lily family.

Geographical Sources

California.

Traditional Ethnic Uses

Chives are one of the herbs used in fines herbs, a traditional French herb blend. They also are great as a garnish.

Taste and Aroma

Chives have a mild, onion like flavour, with a hint of garlic.

CILANTRO (Fig 3. 20)

General Description

Cilantro is the leaf of the young coriander plant, Coriandrum sativum, and an herb in the parsley family, similar to anise.

Fig 3.20 The cilantro leaves

Geographical Sources

Cilantro is grown in California.

Traditional Ethnic Uses

Cilantro is traditionally used in Middle Eastern, Mexican, and Asian cooking.

Taste and Aroma

Cilantro's taste is a fragrant mix of parsley and citrus.

CINNAMON (Fig. 3.21)

Fig 3.21 The cinnamon bark

General Description

Cinnamon is the dried bark of various laurel trees in the cinnamomun family. One of the more common trees from which Cinnamon is derived is the cassia. Ground cinnamon is perhaps the most common baking spice. Cinnamon sticks are made from long pieces of bark that are rolled, pressed, and dried.

Geographical Sources

True Cinnamon is native to Sri Lanka. The Cinnamon used in North America is from the cassia tree which is grown in Vietnam, China, Indonesia, and Central America.

Traditional Ethnic Uses

Possibly most the common baking spice, Cinnamon is used in cakes, cookies, and desserts throughout the world. Cinnamon is also used in savory chicken and lamb dishes from the Middle East. In American cooking, Cinnamon is often paired with apples and used in other fruit and cereal dishes. Stick Cinnamon is used in pickling and for flavouring hot beverages.

Taste and Aroma

Cinnamon has a sweet, woody fragrance in both ground and stick forms

CLOVES (Fig. 3.22)

Fig 3.22 The cloves buds

General Description

Cloves are the rich, brown, dried, unopened flower buds of Syzygium aromaticum, an evergreen tree in the myrtle family. The name comes from the French "clou" meaning nail.

Geographical Sources

Cloves come from Madagascar, Brazil, Panang, and Ceylon.

Traditional Ethnic Uses

Cloves are used in spice cookies and cakes. Much of the world crop is used in Indonesia for Clove cigarettes, called "kreteks".

Taste and Aroma

Cloves are strong, pungent, and sweet.

CORIANDER SEEDS (Fig. 3.23)

General Description

Coriander is the seed of Coriandrum sativum, a plant in the parsley family. The seed is globular and almost round, brown to yellow red, and 1/5 inch in diameter with alternating straight and wavy ridges.

Fig 3.23 The coriander seeds

Geographical Sources

Coriander comes from Morocco and Romania.

Traditional Ethnic Uses

Coriander is used in Indian curries, gin, American cigarettes, and sausages.

Taste and Aroma

Coriander has a mild, distinctive taste similar to a blend of lemon and sage.

CUMIN (Fig. 3.24)

General Description

Cumin (pronounced "come in") is the pale green seed of Cuminum cyminum, a small herb in the parsley family. The seed is uniformly eliptical and deeply furrowed.

Fig 3.24 The cumin

Geographical Sources

Iran and India

Traditional Ethnic Uses

Cumin is frequently used in Mexican dishes such as chili con carne and hot tamales.

Taste and Aroma

Cumin has a distinctive, slightly bitter yet warm flavour.

DILL SEED AND WEED (Fig. 3.25)

General Description

Dill is a tall, feathery annual, Anethum graveolens, in the parsley family. Both Dill Seed and Weed (dried leaves) come from the same plant.

Fig 3.25 The dill seed

Geographical Sources

United States and India.

Traditional Ethnic Uses

Dill Seed and Weed are widely used in pickling as well as in German, Russian, and Scandinavian dishes.

Taste and Aroma

The Dill Seed flavour is clean, pungent, and reminiscent of caraway. Dill Weed has a similar but mellower and fresher flavour.

FENNEL (Fig. 3.26)

General Description

Fennel Seed is the oval, green or yellowish brown dried fruit of Foeniculum vulgare, a member of the parsley family.

Fig 3.26 The fennel seed

Geographical Sources

India and Egypt

Traditional Ethnic Uses

Fennel goes well with fish and is used in Italian sausages and some curry powder mixes.

Taste and Aroma

Fennel has an anise like flavour but is more aromatic, sweeter and less pungent.

HORSERADISH (Fig. 3.27)

Fig 3.27 The Horseradish root

General Description

Horseradish is a hot, pungent condiment made from a plant in the mustard family. The powdered form of Horseradish is made by grinding the root and drying in a gentle heat. Horseradish vinegar is the root combined with shallots, onions, garlic, and red pepper in vinegar.

Geographical Sources

Oregon

Traditional Ethnic Uses

It's most common use is as a condiment for roast beef, fish, and oysters.

Taste and Aroma

Hot and pungent.

JUNIPER BERRIES (Fig. 3.28)

General Description

Juniper Berries come from the juniper shrub, an evergreen in the genus juniperus, which grows in the Northern Hemisphere.

Fig 3.28 The Juniper berries

Geographical Sources

Europe and North America.

Traditional Ethnic Uses

Juniper Berries are used in Northern Europe and the United States in marinades, roast pork, and sauerkraut. They enhance meat, stuffing's, sausages, stews, and soups.

Taste and Aroma

Juniper Berries have a bittersweet aroma.

MACE (Fig. 3.29)

General Description

The nutmeg tree, Myristica fragrans, is special in that it produces two separate spices, nutmeg and Mace. Mace is the ground outer covering (aril) of the nutmeg seed. A piece of ungrounded Mace is called a blade.

Fig 3.29 The Mace

Geographical Sources

Indonesia, Grenada

Traditional Ethnic Uses

Mace is most popular in European foods where it is used in both savory and sweet dishes. It is the dominant flavour in doughnuts.

Taste and Aroma

Mace has a flavour and aroma similar to nutmeg, with slightly more pungency.

MARJORAM (Fig. 3.3)

General Description

Marjoram is the gray green leaf of Majorana hortensis, a low growing member of the mint family. It is often mistaken for oregano, although they are not the same plant.

Fig 3.30 The Marjoram leaves

Geographical Sources

United States and France

Traditional Ethnic Uses

Marjoram is used as a flavouring for meat dishes.

Taste and Aroma

Marjoram has a delicate, sweet, pleasant flavour with a slightly bitter undertone.

MINT (Fig. 3.31)

General Description

Mint is the dried leaf of a perennial herb. There are two important species, *Mentha spicata* L. (spearmint) and *Mentha piperita* L. (pepper-mint).

Fig 3.31 Different varieties of Mint

Geographical Sources

United States.

Traditional Ethnic Uses

Mint jelly served with lamb, sprinkled in peas, or in chocolate desserts.

Taste and Aroma

Mint is strong and sweet with a tangy flavour and a cool after taste.

MUSTARD SEEDS (Fig. 3.32)

General Description

Mustard Seed comes from two large shrubs, *Brassica juncea* (brown mustard) and *Brassica hirta* (white mustard), native to Asia. Both plants produce bright yellow flowers that contain small round seeds; brown mustard is more pungent than white.

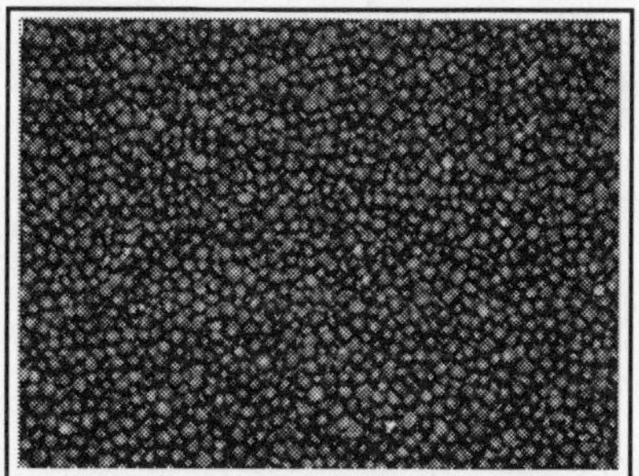

Fig 3.32 The Mustard seeds

Geographical Sources

Canada

Traditional Ethnic Uses

Mustard Seed's hot and spicy flavour enhances meats, fish, fowl, sauces, and salad dressings. Whole Mustard Seed may be used in pickling or in boiling vegetables such as cabbage or sauerkraut. Brown Mustard Seeds are an important flavouring in Indian dishes.

Taste and Aroma

Powdered Mustard has no aroma when dry, but a hot flavour is released when it is mixed with water.

NUTMEG (Fig. 3.33)

Fig 3.33 The Nutmeg

General Description

Nutmeg is the seed of Myristica fragrans, an evergreen tree native to the Molucca Islands. Interestingly, the tree produces both Nutmeg and mace, and grows up to 60 feet tall. Although the tree takes seven years to bear fruit, it may produce until the 90th year. Both spices come from the tree's fruit, which splits into a scarlet outer membrane, mace, and an inner brown seed, Nutmeg.

Geographical Sources

Nutmeg is grown in Indonesia and Grenada.

Traditional Ethnic Uses

Nutmeg is a mild baking spice and is used in sausages, meats, soups, and preserves. Nutmeg is commonly added to eggnog, puddings, and fruit pies. It is popular in The Netherlands and Italy, where it is used in vegetables, puddings, and stews.

Taste and Aroma

Nutmeg is more pungent and sweeter than mace.

OREGANO (Fig. 3.34)

Fig 3.34 The oregano leaves

General Description

Mediterranean Oregano is the dried leaf of Origanum vulgare L., a perennial herb in the mint family. Mexican Oregano is the dried leaf of one of several plants of the Lippia genus.

Geographical Sources

Oregano is grown in California and New Mexico, as well as the Mediterranean region.

Traditional Ethnic Uses

Oregano is the spice that gives pizza its characteristic flavour. It is also usually used in chili powder.

Taste and Aroma

Oregano has a pungent odour and flavour. Mexican Oregano is a bit stronger than Mediterranean Oregano.

PAPRIKA (Fig. 3.35)

General Description

Paprika is a spice which comes from a mild red pepper in the family Capsicum annum. It is a brilliant red powder and often used as a garnish.

Fig 3.35 The paprika chilies

Geographical Sources

The peppers used in Paprika are grown in Hungary, Spain, South America, and California.

Traditional Ethnic Uses

Paprika is the main flavour in Hungarian cooking, including dishes such as Goulash and Chicken Paprika's. In the United States, it is often used as a garnish on stuffed eggs, fish, and cheese and vegetable casseroles. Spanish paprika flavors shellfish, rice, and sausage dishes. In Morocco, Paprika is used in tomato dishes and salads.

Taste and Aroma

Paprika ranges from sweet and mild to hot. American Paprika is the blandest, while Hungarian Paprika has the greatest range of flavour.

PARSLEY (Fig. 3.36)

General Description

Parsley is the fresh or dried leaf of Petroselinum crispum, a biennial in the parsley family.

Fig 3.36 The parsley bunch

Geographical Sources

Parsley is grown in California.

Traditional Ethnic Uses

Parsley is most popular as a garnish and is an excellent breath freshener. It is high in vitamins A and C, and contains iron, iodine, and copper.

Taste and Aroma

Parsley has a light, fresh scent and flavour.

ROSEMARY (Fig. 3.37)

General Description

Rosemary is an herb in the mint family. It is a small evergreen shrub, Rosmarinus officinalis, whose 1inch leaves resemble curved pine needles.

Fig 3.37 The fresh Rosemary

Geographical Sources

Rosemary is native to the Mediterranean. Today it is widely produced in France, Spain, and Portugal.

Traditional Ethnic Uses

Rosemary is used primarily in Italy in lamb, pork, chicken, and rabbit dishes.

Taste and Aroma

Rosemary has a tea like aroma and a piney flavour.

SAGE (Fig. 3.38)

General Description

Sage is an herb from an evergreen shrub, Salvia officinalis, in the mint family. Its long, grayishgreen leaves take on a velvety, cottonlike texture when rubbed (meaning ground lightly and passed through a coarse sieve).

Fig 3.38 Fresh sage leaves

Geographical Sources

Sage is grown in the United States. It also is grown in Dalmatia and Albania.

Traditional Ethnic Uses

Sage enhances pork, lamb, meats, and sausages. Chopped leaves flavour salads, pickles, and cheese. It is one of the most popular herbs in the United States.

Taste and Aroma

Sage has a fragrant aroma and an astringent but warm flavour.

TARRAGON (Fig. 3.39)

Fig 3.39 Fresh tarragon

General Description

Tarragon is a small, shrubby herb, Artemisia dracunculus, in the sunflower family. Two species are cultivated, Russian and French. Leaves of the French variety are glossier and more pungent. Most commercial Tarragon comes from dried leaves of the French Tarragon plant.

Geographical Sources

Tarragon is native to southern Russia and western Asia. Today, its primary producer is France.

Traditional Ethnic Uses

Tarragon is commonly known as a flavouring for vinegar and is used in pickles, relishes, prepared mustards, and sauces. Tarragon also goes well with fish, meat, soups and stews, and is often used in tomato and egg dishes. Tarragon adds distinctive flavour to sauces.

Taste and Aroma

Tarragon has a slightly bittersweet flavour and an aroma similar to anise.

THYME (Fig. 3.40)

Fig 3.40 Fresh Thyme leaves

General Description

Thyme is the leaf of a low-growing shrub in the mint family called Thymus vulgaris. Its tiny grayish-green leaves rarely are greater than one-fourth inch long. For use as a condiment, Thyme leaves are dried then chopped, or ground.

Geographical Sources

Thyme is grown in southern Europe, including France, Spain, and Portugal. It is also indigenous to the Mediterranean.

Traditional Ethnic Uses

Thyme is often included in seasoning blends for poultry and stuffing and also commonly used in fish sauces, chowders, and soups. It goes well with lamb and veal as well as in eggs, custards, and croquettes. Thyme often is paired with tomatoes.

Taste and Aroma

Thyme has a subtle, dry aroma and a slightly minty flavour.

TURMERIC (Fig. 3.41)

General Description

Turmeric comes from the root of Curcuma long, a leafy plant in the ginger family. The root, or rhizome, has a tough brown skin and bright orange flesh. Ground Turmeric comes from fingers which extend from the root. It is boiled or steamed and then dried, and ground.

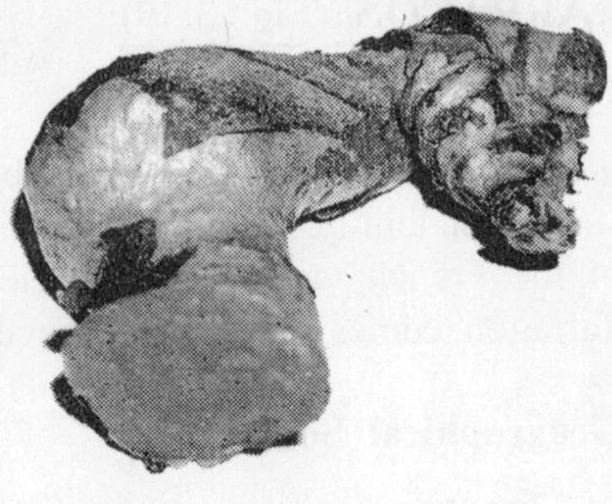

Fig 3.41 Fresh turmeric root

Geographical Sources

India is the world's primary producer of Turmeric. It is also grown in China and Indonesia.

Traditional Ethnic Uses

Turmeric is a necessary ingredient of curry powder. It is used extensively in Indian dishes, including lentil and meat dishes, and in Southeast Asian cooking. Turmeric is routinely added to mustard blends and relishes. It also is used in place of saffron to provide colour and flavour.

Taste and Aroma

Turmeric is mildly aromatic and has scents of orange or ginger. It has a pungent, bitter flavour.

VEGETABLES

It play a very important role in human diet. They provide vitamins and minerals as well as flavours which are not available in meats, cereals, dairy products and fruits. As a NATION the English do not possess a very good reputation for making the most of vegetables. It is not the vegetables that are at fault, for we grow the best in the world, but chefs so often do not realize how very important this branch of cookery is. We are inclined to exclaim in derision: "Why, she cannot even cook a potato! "But personally, I think a perfectly cooked potato is one of the signs of a good chef. The best chefs are those who are not afraid of taking trouble, and as a rule if the chef takes trouble over simple things like potatoes, he/she will with everything the undertakes.

Green vegetables should be cooked as fresh as possible; in fact, the sooner they are cooked after being taken from the ground the better. Remove any decayed or coarse leaves and cut across the stem of vegetables of the cabbage family. Wash well; put them in fresh cold water. Do not put salt in the water, for this kills some insects and they then remain in the vegetable: plain water will bring them out and you will find them in the bowl. Put them in boiling water with a teaspoon of salt to a quart of water, and if the water is very hand, add a pinch of bicarbonate of soda. As soon as the water boils again, remove the lid and boil quickly until they are done. Drain and press well with a wooden presser; this is very important as watery greens are most unpleasant.

Root vegetables and tubers must be well scrubbed before cooking, and very thinly peeled when peeling is necessary, except turnips which need to be thickly peeled. If you have a garden, however small, spare a corner for a little parsley, a root of tarragon, thyme, savory, sage and marjoram, and a few chives; and your savoury dishes need never lack flavour. It will be a source of delight, and add so much to the possibilities of your cooking, for it is often difficult to obtain fresh herbs in any city, and, when they are dried, the flavour is never the same.

Cabbages, savoys, brussels sprouts, and cabbage lettuce (ice berg) should feel from and hard to the touch when pinched in the centre. Leeks should be thick in the stem and very white. Small marrows are best for cooking as a vegetable; very large ones are coarse and only fit for preserves. Choose large Jerusalem artichokes; it is impossible to peel small ones a good shape. The latter are only fit for soup. White celery is preferable to the red, and looks more delicate when cooked. Turnips should be firm to the touch and heavy; when soft and spongy they are useless except for flavouring. Fresh asparagus is crisp and upright and the cut ends moist. Broad beans should be quite young. When not much larger than a six inch, they are most delicious. Spinach is a vegetable that should be cooked very soon after gathering. Fresh spinach is bright green without any sign of yellow in the leaves, and the stalks are crisp.

Here is a very nutritious and delicious way of cooking vegetables so that all the flavour and valuable mineral salts are retained. Any kind of vegetables can be used, either one kind or several combined. Cauliflower, cabbage, brussels sprouts, carrots, parsnips is all good cooked in this way; potatoes are not suitable. Prepare the vegetables in the usual way, washing them thoroughly but not drying them. They should, in fact, be quite wet. Allow 2 oz of butter or margarine to every pound or pint basin full of prepared vegetables. Put the butter in the casserole or saucepan and add a good seasoning of salt and pepper. Put in the vegetables and stir over very gentle heat until the butter has melted and the vegetables are well coated with it. Now cover very closely and cook until tender in a moderate oven or over gentle heat or they may be cooked with 1 oz of butter and about one inch of water in the bottom of the saucepan. The liquid is then served with the vegetable, or if preferred they can be drained and the liquid—which contains the salts—added to a soup.

FRIED VEGETABLES

This is an excellent way to dispose of left-over; mix together any kinds of cooked vegetables, with some potatoes among them. Potatoes, carrots and cabbage, or artichokes, carrots and potatoes are good mixtures. Chop finely the cabbage, or other green vegetable, mash root vegetables. Season with salt and pepper, and any kind of sauce or catsup. Form into round cakes and fry brown in a little dripping. Cooked artichokes are very good fried whole in butter or egg and breadcrumbs, so is cauliflower, divided into sprigs and fried in the same way.

Have vegetables dry, and dust with flour before putting them in the butter or egg. Some vegetables are excellent fried in fritter batter, if not already too well cooked. Sprigs of cauliflower, small pieces of well drained vegetable marrow or Jerusalem artichokes are good.

VEGETABLE PUREE

Prepare vegetables as for boiling, and then cut them up into small pieces. Any kind may be used, but be sure you have an onion among them—a cabbage heart, carrot and turnip mix well.

Wash and put them quite wet into a stew pan. Add a good ounce of butter to a pint of cut vegetables. Cover closely and cook very gently until the vegetables are tender. The water from the vegetables should be sufficient moisture, but they must be over low heat and looked at now and then to see that they do not stick to the pan. Now rub through a sieve, season well with salt and pepper, and add enough milk to make a consistency as thick as Devonshire cream. Serve very hot.

Note: This makes a nice surround for a dish of mince or a hash

Types and Description

Cabbage family

To cabbage is one of the cheapest as well as one of the most plentiful of vegetables, and is obtainable all the year round; but it is most delicious in late spring and early summer. Like all green vegetables, the sooner it is cooked after cutting, the better. Cabbage is very wholesome, and is invaluable as a blood purifier. For those who find cabbage indigestible, it should be put into fast boiling water, and as soon as the water comes to the boil again it should be strained off and the cabbage covered with fresh boiling water. This method also takes away the strong taste of winter cabbage.

The savoy cabbage has closely wrinkled leaves and a very compact heart which is sometimes almost white. It makes an excellent vegetable dish and the delicate heart can be shredded into salad as a faint pineapple flavour and are deliciously crisp. Savoys, spring greens and turnip tops follow the general rules for cooking cabbage.

TO BOIL

Time: 20 to 30 minutes. Temperature: 100°C boiling. one cabbage enough for 2 to 6 persons, according to size.

Remove the outside and discoloured leaves and the hard centre of the stump, cut large cabbage in halves or quarters. Small spring cabbages only need cutting across like Brussels sprouts. Look the cabbage well over for insects and wash well. Then leave it in cold water for half an hour before cooking. Drain well. Put it in a saucepan of fast boiling water with a good teaspoon of salt to a quart of water, see the cabbage is well covered, bring quickly to the boil again, and boil well with the lid off until it is quite tender or when the cabbage has boiled for a few minutes, drain off the water and cover again with boiling water, add salt and boil until tender. This is a little more trouble, but the result makes it worthwhile. Remove all scum as it rises. Drain well and press out the water with a wooden presser. Get it as dry as possible, but be quick doing this as it must be served very hot. Turn it into a hot vegetable dish that has a strainer. Score it across with a knife to make serving easy, and serve at once. If liked, a little hot butter seasoned with salt and pepper may be mixed with the cabbage.

Head cabbage: Regular cabbage light green white or dark in colour (Fig. 3.42).

Red cabbage (Fig 3.43): Identically to a green cabbage should have a solid heavy head. Good for boiling, steaming, frying, braising and sautéing. It is excellent stuff used for salad and Cole slaw. Although generally pickled, red cabbage may be cooked in the same way as green cabbage.

Choose when young before the heart is too hard when pickled cabbage is termed Sauerkraut. That cabbage is not cooked so long it because a limp crisp texture is required for sauerkraut.

Chinese cabbage (Fig 3.44): Long loosely pet leaves. This mild flavour cabbage used in oriental cooking.

Savoy cabbage (Fig 3.45): Has yellowish crinkled crimpy leaves, mild flavour, stored at 32° F don't freeze at room temperature its wilts.

Fig 3.42 Head cabbage

Fig 3.43 Red cabbage

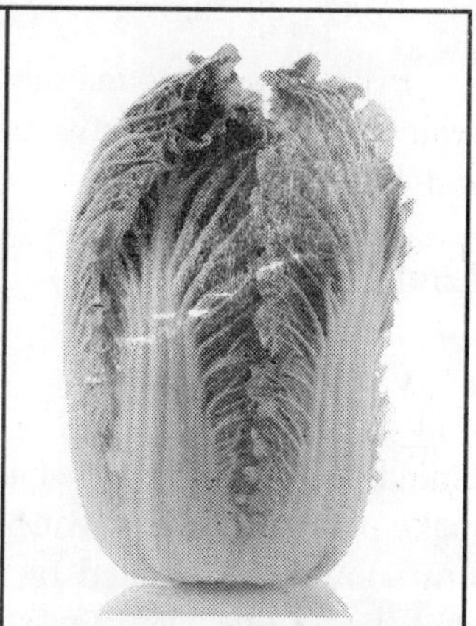

Fig 3.44 Chinese cabbage

Brussels sprouts (Fig 3.46): Miniature cabbage like bright and green cabbage. name after the Belgium city. A very useful vegetable, as both the sprouts growing on the main stem and tops can be used. The sprouts should be firm and round like a tiny compact cabbage. If loose and soft they lose their shape while cooking and the appearance of the dish is spoiled, and the flavour is not so good. They are one of the best winter vegetables to grow as they do not take up a great deal of room and pay so well for browing.

Fig 3.45 Savoy cabbage

TO BOIL OR STEAM (BRUSSELS SPROUTS)

Time: about 30 minutes to steam—15 to 20 minutes to boil. 1½ lb. enough for four persons.

Trim off the outside and discoloured leaved, and cut the stalk quite short; then make a slit across the stalk as you would in a cabbage. Wash them and look them over well for insects, let them remain in cold water for half an hour, then drain. They may be streamed or boiled; if steamed, place them in a steamer over boiling water, sprinkle with salt, and steam until tender; or cook in boiling

Fig 3.46 Brussels sprouts

water without a lid and allow a teaspoon of salt to a quart of water. Be careful not to overcook or the colour and flavour will be spoilt. They should be tender but whole and a rather bright green. In very frosty weather they may need a little more cooking. When done, drain well, press lightly to retain their shape, and serve very hot. They are improved if tossed in a little hot butter, allowing 1 oz. To a pound of sprouts.

TO FRY

Time : 20 minutes. Temperature: moderate.

Brussels sprouts may also be fried. Choose little hard buttons, boil them first for then minutes, drain well and dry gently in a cloth. Flour them. Then dip in beaten egg and seasoned breadcrumbs and fry in boiling fat.

Cauliflower (Fig. 3.47)

Come from the Latin termed meaning cabbage flower, stalk flower. A very highly esteemed vegetable that may be boiled and served with white sauce, but May also be used to make many kinds of savoury dishes. Choose them with a hard firm flower surrounded by fresh green leaves. Beware of a cauliflower that has been stripped of its leaves. You may be quite sure that those leaves were yellow and wilte3d, and of all unwholesome food perhaps a stale cauliflower is the most dangerous. The young leaves that grow immediately round the flower are very good when served as greens by themselves.

Fig 3.47 Cauliflower

A good quality cauliflower will have curdily creamy white in colour with only small amount of spotting and spackling. No sign of growth of smaller flower should be there. The following should be there in mind while purchasing cauliflower:

1. Yellowish curd is indicative of poor growing condition and poor handling and edging.
2. Texture of curd should not look like rice.
3. Loose open flower should show over maturity.

Preparation of cauliflower

- It can be served boil with butter steamed, puree for sauce and soups, raw in salads or used for gratinate.
- Soak the head in cold water in one hour this gave freshness and it's also remove insects.
- Avoid over cooking it become mushy.
- If cooking with hard water adds fresh lemon juice to hard water, high alkalis turn flower yellow and soft.

- Never used soda in cooking cauliflower.
- Adding milk to cooking water heightens the colour and gave some sweatiness.

TO BOIL

Time: 15 to 25 minutes according to size.

Cut off the thick part of the stalk and most of the leaves. Cut the stalk across two or three times. Wash well and look carefully for green caterpillars, for nature has made them in appearance very like the pale green stalk. Put the cauliflower in a bowl with enough cold water to cover it well and leave it for half an hour before cooking. Then put it in a saucepan of fast boiling water with a teaspoon of salt to a quart of water. The cauliflower should be put in flower downwards, so that it may not be discoloured by the scum. Boil gently until tender but unbroken. Drain without pressing and serve with white sauce.

Kohlrabi (Fig. 3.48)

Light green to white colour round or globular leaves similar to turnips leaves. Terms kohlrabi in German meaning cabbage turnip can be cooked like spinach best steamed peeled and cut into juliennes. First Cole slaw is made with kohlrabi. That is why Cole comes from kohlrabi.

Fig 3.48 Kohlrabi

Broccoli (Fig. 3.49 and 3.50)

Green cauliflower deep green in colour with deep green or purplish steam or purplish flower. Compact yellow flower in buds indicates old tough broccoli. Versatile vegetable can be used similar to cauliflower, steamed, puréed and baked in casserole and raw used for salads. The difficulty in properly cooking broccoli is protecting the colour and texture of blossoms end. Since Florists cook faster than stalk.

Fig 3.49 Green Broccoli

Fig 3.50 Purple Broccoli

BROCCOLI (WHITE)

White broccoli is similar in appearance to cauliflower; in fact, few people know the difference. It is a more hardy vegetable. It is cooked in exactly the same way as cauliflower.

BROCCOLI (Purple Sprouting) : Time: about 20 minutes.

A delicious vegetable, very prolife. When the purple sprouts are young, they taste very like asparagus. Cook the sprigs, cutting away any hard stalks. Put in boiling water with a teaspoon of salt to a quart of water; boil with the lid off until quite tender. Drain, press and serve very hot.

STALK VEGETABLES:

Stalk vegetables are plant steams that are high in cellulose fibers. Stalk vegetable should be young these includes asparagus, celery Boak Choy

Asparagus (Fig. 3.51)

Asparagus is a delicious vegetables but somewhat expensive unless it is home grown. It is not difficult to cultivate and needs little attention once it is established. The last week of May and the first weeks of June are the cheapest times for purchasing. It should be cooked as soon after cutting as possible—though it may be kept for a few days in a cold place if its stalks only are put in water. When stale it looks wilted and droops and should be avoided as it is then almost flavourless.

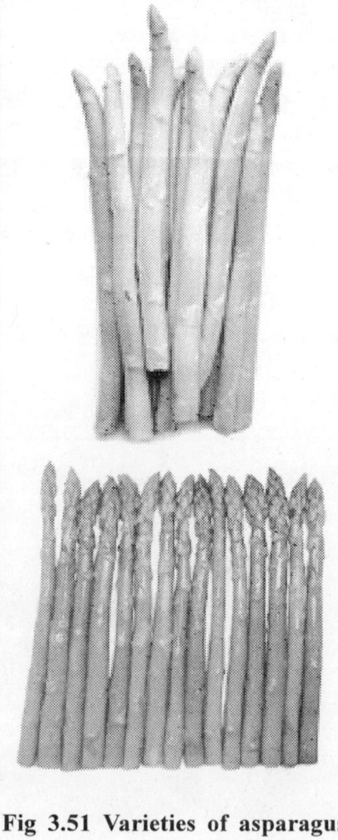

Fig 3.51 Varieties of asparagus

TO BOIL

Time: 20 to 30 minutes according to size. Temperature: very moderate.

An asparagus saucepan is very deep with a fitment inside whereby the stalks are in the water while the tips rise above so that they are streamed; but it can be cooked in a small kettle that has a drainer in it, or a large saucepan. To prepare it for cooking, cut the stalks all one length, a length that your saucepan or kettle will accommodate easily. Then scrape the white part of the stalk; be careful not to injure the heads. Put them into cold water as you do them. When finished, gather into bundles, with the stalks all one end, and tie with a piece of tape; do not use string. Put into boiling water with a teaspoon of salt to a quart of water and boil gently until the green part is tender. When done, lift it out gently and remove tape; if you have not a strainer in the stew pan, use a fish slice. Serve on a folded dinner napkin or on a strainer in a hot tureen, with the stalks all at one end. Serve liquid butter separately or vinaigrette sauce. Asparagus is also very good cold with mayonnaise or oil and vinegar dressing. Be careful not to overcook or the tips will be broken.

There is of two types White or green in colour. Both are vast in their taste and texture. White are more expensive because it shielded from the sun to retain its white colour. It cannot be eaten raw because it should be too tough should be partly peeled before cooking. Fresh asparagus should straight stock and compact pointed tip. Soft tip not acceptable. The bottom of the stalk should be kept them with towel highly perishable.

Preparation of Asparagus:

- Whole stalk near the bottom and bend the stalk. Otherwise the base becomes tough and inedible.
- Peeling is necessary for white not for green.
- Cook by placing stem down with in boiling water to protect buds from over cooking.

Celery (Fig. 3.52)

Member of parsley family. There is two types

1. Golden heart
2. Pascal

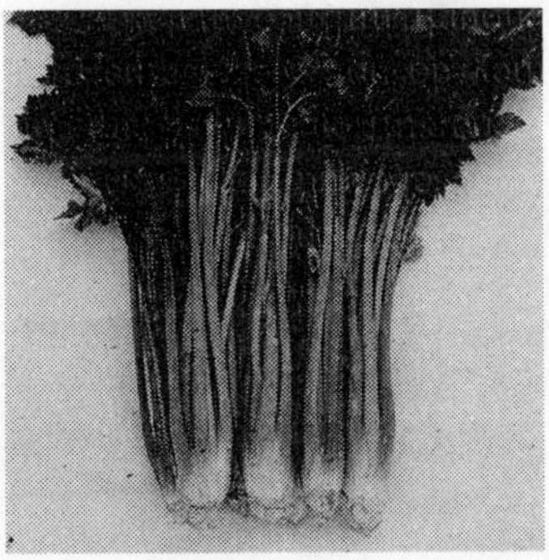

Fig. 3.52 Golden heart and Pascal Celery

Golden heart is white Pascal is more popular used. Light or dark green in colour stalk of good quality. Fresh celery will break with snap. Used in making soups, stocks or used in raw salad (only tender stalks are used)

To serve raw

Celery is generally eaten raw and is considered at its best after a touch of frost. Choose heads of medium size and remove the outside stalks. Well wash the white centre and examine well, for the little red celery worm is often found near the heart. Let the celery remain in the coldest possible water for half an hour before serving, then serve in a celery glass or any wide mouthed glass vase or large tumbler half full of cold water.

To serve hot

Celery is an extremely nice and wholesome vegetable. It may be boiled and served with white sauce or braised or cooked au gratin. It adds flavour to a vegetable stew or casserole—makes excellent soup and delicious sauce.

Boiled celery

Large Heads celery—1/2 pint White Sauce.

Time: 30 to 45 minutes. Enough for 4 to 6 persons.

Remove outside sticks of the celery, well wash and cut in small lengths. Put it in boiling water, boil for five minutes then drain off the water. Then just cover with milk and simmer until tender. Drain off the milk and use it to make white sauce. Put the celery in a hot tureen and pour and sauce over.

Fig 3.53 Swiss chard

Swiss chard (Fig. 3.53)

Dark green vegetable with crinkle leaves and firm white stalk leaf may be cooked like green and stem like celery. Native to Mediterranean region.

Bok Choy (Fig. 3.54)

Resemble to Swiss chard and celery the names means white vegetable sometimes called white mustard cabbage large leafy green vegetable with long white stalk used in oriental.

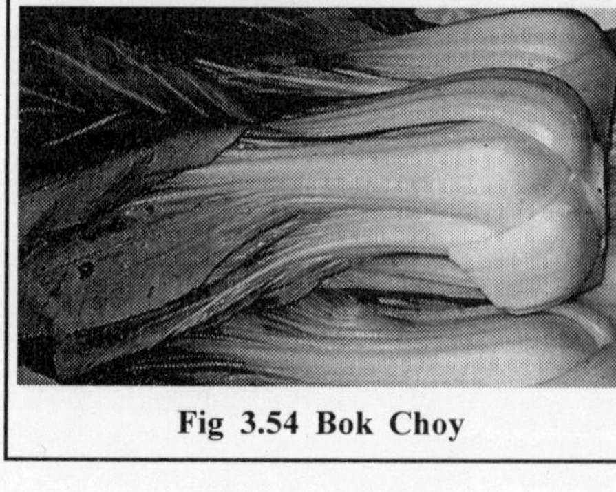

Fig 3.54 Bok Choy

LEAFY VEGETABLES

Spinach (Fig. 3.55)

When fresh is it crisp dark green leaf in colours (Fig 3. 55).

For preparing

Being it washing thoroughly became 2 to 3 times. Cooks very easily so used short cooking methods. Usually is cook with liquid which clings to the leaves after washing. It is versatile vegetable can be served steamed, creamed buttered or eaten raw.

Fig 3.55 Spinach leaves

To Boil

Pick all the leaves from the stalks and put them in a bowl of cold water, wash well, but handle gently as they are easily bruised. Take them out, leaving the grit at the bottom of the bowl. It will be necessary to wash spinach two or three times in this way, as, growing so near the earth, it is usually full of grit.

Put it into a saucepan with a teacup of boiling water to 2 lb. of spinach, add a good pinch of salt and boil gently until tender—about ten minutes. Turn it into a colander and press as dry as possible. Then chop it or rub it through a sieve, put it in a clean saucepan with 1 oz. Of butter or margarine and a sprinkling of salt and pepper. Make very hot and serve. It can be served if preferred without being chopped or sieved.

Kale (Fig 3.56)

As hardy curled leaves which are deep green in colour can be used steamed and raw in garnished.

Collards (Fig 3.57)

Bright green with crispy leaves cooked with pork and famous in South Asia.

Fig 3.56 Kale leaves

Fig 3.57 Collards leaves

Fig 3.58 Sorrel leaves

Sorrel (Fig 3.58)

The sorrel should be young and freshly gathered, otherwise it is bitter. It may be cooked in the same way as spinach.

Narrow pointed leaves in the shape of arrow head can be prepared like spinach.

Salad greens

Salad greens are types of lettuce or lettuce of all types sorrel endives grow has bunch like head. Yellowish white used in green salad. A vegetable with two distinct varieties—cabbage lettuce is shaped like a small cabbage, and the cos is a tall lettuce. The latter is tied up to blanch. Lettuces are invaluable for salads either alone or in conjunction with other vegetables. The shredded heart of a savoy cabbage may be used as a substitute when lettuces are rare. For recipes. Lettuces may also be cooked like spinach, but will only need five minutes boiling.

Witloof chicory: also called as Endives (Fig 3.59)

This is also known as Belgium Endives. White tightly folded plant that grows upright in thin elongated stocks. Crisp with tender leaf.

Different types of lettuce

a. Crisp head (iceberg) (Fig 3.60)

Used in salads and sandwiches they are crisp and sweet tasting

b. Butter Head (Boston Bibb) (Fig 3.61)

Loose over lapping leafs are light green and inside leafs are inner are light yellowish, soft pliable leafs with buttery flavour.

Fig 3.59 Witloof chicory

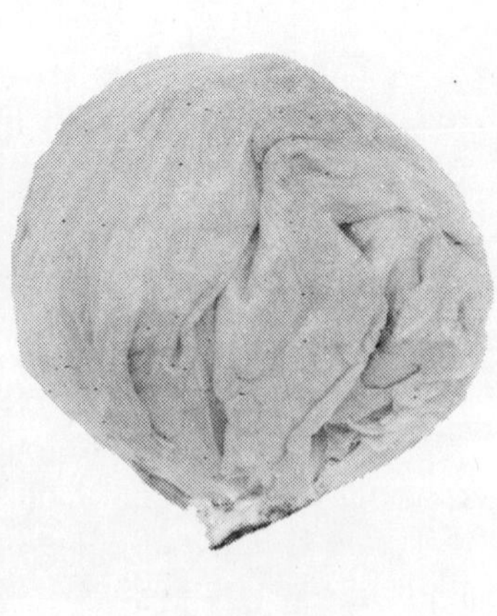

Fig 3.60 Iceberg lettuce

Fig 3.61 Butter head lettuce

*c. **Romaine (cos)*** (Fig 3.62)

A long leaf shape head of lettuce has long narrow edges leaves. Outer leaves are dark green, inner leaves are golden yellow, sweet, tender and crispy (Fig 3. 62).

b. Leaf lettuce

Oak lettuce, lollorossso, pink are grown in oaty.

Chicory (Fig 3.63)

Chicory belongs to the endive family. It is blanched and cooked in the same way as seakale.

Dandelions (Fig 3.64)

Nowadays we realize that the young leaves of the dandelion are very good in salad, and that it is also a wholesome spring vegetable. Remember, however, that only the very young leaves must be used, as the older, larger leaves taste very bitter. A very good home-made wine can be obtained from dandelion leaves and instructions for making it will be found in the preserves section. Dandelions are perhaps best in a mixed salad; to serve as a vegetable they should be cooked as follows

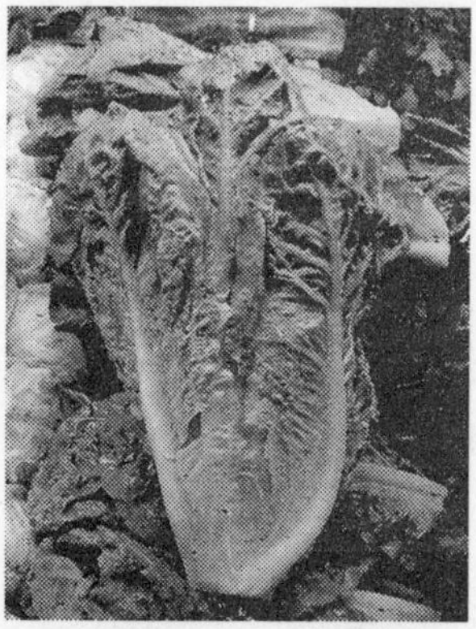

Fig 3.62 Butter Romaine lettuce

Fig 3.63 Chicory lettuce

Fig 3.64 Dandelions leaves

Nettles (Fig 3.65)

In spring the young shoots of the nettles form a very wholesome vegetable. They may be cooked as spinach and country-dwellers should be able to obtain them easily

Fig 3.65 Nettles leaves

Sea-Kale (Fig 3.66)

Fig 3.66 Sea-Kale

A delicious vegetable, very welcome in spring, as it comes before asparagus, when growing it is covered with earthenware pots to blanch it.

SEEDS, EDIBLE PODS AND YOUNG SHOTS

Peas (Fig 3.67)

The shells should be bright green, and the peas of medium size. Do not shell until just before cooking as the skims soon harden when exposed to the air. The shells, when quite young, make as appetizing soup. Stewed until tender and rubbed through a sieve they may also be used to thicken a mixed vegetable soup or meat stew. When green peas are too old they are only fit to serve as purees when they make a good surround for hashes and made dishes.

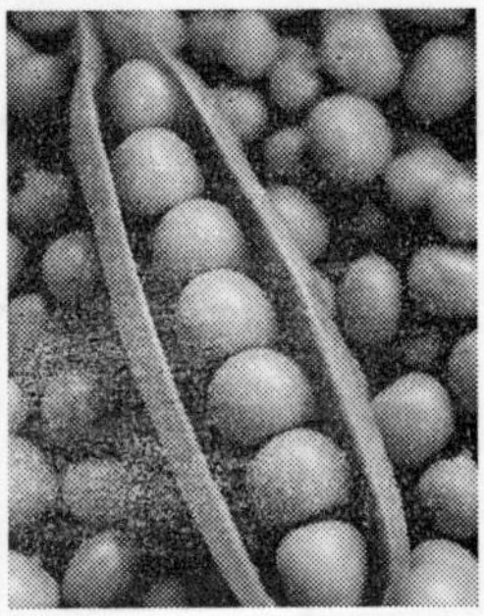

Fig 3.67 Peas in pods

Should be well filled and should snap easily. yellowish pods indicate edging mildewed swollen or spackled pods to be avoided.

Boiled Green Peas

Pint shelled Green Peas—Salt and Pepper—small teaspoon Sugar—1 oz. Butter—sprig of Mint, if liked.

Time: 20 to 30 minutes according to size. Temperature: moderate.

Shell the peas, wash them in cold water, and drain them in a colander. Put them in a saucepan with the salt and mint and sugar with enough boiling water to cover them. Bring to the boil, remove any scum and then boil gently until they are tender. Drain the water; add a sprinkling of pepper and the butter. Make very hot and serve. Young peas will not need sugar.

Snow Peas (Fig 3.68)

Mange touts: this type of peas spit in very early stages of development when peas within the pod is very small. The entire pod is tender and edible and used in oriental cooking (Fig. 3.68).

Fig 3.68 Snow peas

Beans Sprout (Fig 3.69)

Can be sprouts of any germinated bean most commonly sprouts of moong or soy. They are golden cream or white coloured with tendrelling like appearance should be crisp and have moist tips.

DRIED VEGETABLES

Beans

Dried beans consisting of haricot, butter or Lima beans, and flageolets are very nourishing. They are cheap and most useful when fresh vegetables are both scarce and dear. They should be soaked in cold water overnight to soften them, then washed and cooked in fresh water until tender. They will need two to three hours cooking.

Fig 3.69 Beans sprouts

Beans edible Seeds

I) Soya beans (Fig 3.70)

Native to china but largest producer is U. S. Used for making of oil, food production for animal feed, yellow or black in colour.

Fig 3.70 Soya beans

II) Haricot beans (kidney beans white in colour) (Fig 3.71)

First cultivated in Aztec Indians of south America, black bean, lima beans, peazean beans, black eye bean, Pinto beans(two coloured kidney beans).

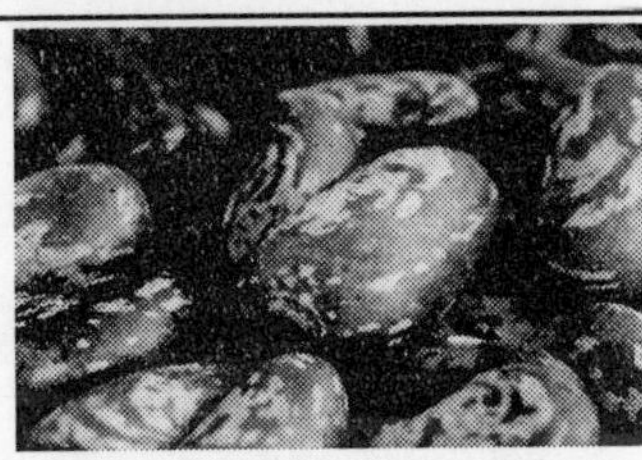

Fig 3.71 Haricot beans

III) Fava Beans (Fig 3.72)

Also called as broad beans.

IV) String Beans (Fig 3.73)

Grows along straight pods. Green or yellow in colour.

V) Lima beans (Fig 3.74)

Flat kidney shaped beans. A popular south U. S. A dish called Succotash is a combination of Lima and corn kernel.

Fig 3.72 Fava beans

VI) French Beans (Fig 3.75)

These are the dwarf beans, sometimes called kidney beans. They may be cooked whole when young after removing the stalks and tips; if fully grown they will need to have the stringy edge removed and should then be sliced in thin strips the length of the bean. As you slice them, put them into cold water. Then drain them and put them into a saucepan of boiling water with

Fig 3.73 String beans

Fig 3.74 Flats beans

Fig 3.75 French beans

a good teaspoon of salt to a quart of water. Let the water boil quickly, removing the scum as it rises. Keep the lid off and dish them up as soon as they are tender. If overcooked they lose their lovely green colour. Serve very hot as soon as they are done. It is an improvement to toss them in a saucepan with 1 oz. Of hot butter and a sprinkling of salt and pepper before serving them.

Vii Scarlet Runner Beans

These are a coarser type of bean than the French bean, and they are never cooked whole, but are sliced after stringing and then cooked in the same way as French beans. They are of excellent flavour. A very useful vegetables, they seem to grow almost anywhere and are very prolife.

Corn

There is about two hundreds variety corn. Sweet corn is the variety which is commonly used in kitchen. these is picked when than kernels are white in colour look like soft and milky. Numbers of by products are corn starch, corn meal and corn syrup.

VEGETABLES FRUITS

Cucumber (Fig 3.76)

Botanically considered a berry originated in Thailand. Green, white, yellow, short, thin, long stubby. Smooth skin, rough skin, early maturing; late maturing etc. latest in European and English is seedless variety 2 to 2 ¼ inch diameter. Eaten raw cooked and pickled in salad, sandwiches or garnished. Cucumbers are generally served raw, but many people find them indigestible in this way. They are, however, very good steamed or fried, but they are tasteless if boiled

Fig 3.76 Cucumber

To Serve Raw

Choose a firm straight cucumber of medium size, if flabby it is stale. Peel and slice very thinly with a cucumber or vegetable cutter. Serve in a glass or cucumber dish with vinegar or oil and vinegar dressing. Raw cucumber dressed with vinegar is the usual accompaniment to boiled salmon. Raw cucumber is said to be more easily digested if eaten with the peel on, but this sometimes has a bitter taste.

Okra (Fig 3.77 and 3.78)

It is also called *Gumbo.* Originated in Africa with the name of guin gumbo/kingumbo. Too selected the tips to be snap. It is popular ingredients in creole style cooking. It give out polyscride gum which is a natural thickening agent in a gambo. Its goods in soup and stews. Cooking its longer period destroyed the colour and makes its sticky. Choice of:

Fig 3.77 Variety of okra

Green variety: strong, robust plants having green fruits (Fig 3.77)

Red variety: has red stem and unusual red fruits (Fig 3.78).

Fig 3.78 Variety of okra

Egg plant/aubergine/Brinjal

Originated in India but best know in oriental cooking and meditation cooking. Large vegetable in light in weight. heavy denotes seedy. It is never eaten raw but can be eaten marinated. Has a bitter flavour so soaked briefly in salted water.

Peppers

Classified into two categories mild sweet peppers include bell pepper the hot pungent group includes chili, pimento and cayenne pepper.

Squash (Fig 3.79)

Gourds' that are eaten for their meat or flesh (Fig 3.79).

Fig 3.79 Squash

Summer Squash (Fig 3.80)

Yellow crook neck or zucchini are also called marrow /courgette 98% edible (both skins and seeds are edible).

Winter Squash (Fig 3.81)

Acorn and butter nuts squash skin and seeds are in edible a corn is large but looks like a nut.

Pumpkin (Fig. 3.82)

Belongs to the same family as the melon and vegetable marrow, but is very much larger. It is very little used in this country, but may be cooked in the same way as vegetable marrow. Bright orange squash. seeds of pumpkin are good roasted popular ingredients for pies and custard.

Fig 3.80 Different varieties summer Squash

Spaghetti squash (Fig. 3.83)

Cucuzzi/calabash/Suzza Melon are the other names bright yellow in colour after cooking. The flesh of skin looks like a spaghetti.

BULBS

Stems holding a food reserve in a flashy over lapping leaves. Onion, shallots and garlic.

Fig 3.81 Winter Squash

I) Onions :

Sold after drying a very wholesome vegetable. If you sit down when peeling them, the fumes will not affect the eyes as they do if you stand over them. After peeling them, wash your hands in cold water and the smell of the onion will disappear.

II) Scallion (Fig 3.84)

Any shoot from the white onion variety pulled before the bulb has been formed. Its includes green onions, shallots and leeks.

I) Green onions (Fig 3.85)

Harvested young tender green top can be eaten along with mature bottom bulb.

Fig 3.82 Pumpkin

II) Shallots (Fig 3.86)

These are bulb which grows in cluster. They are tinny spherical and bit elongated. They have dry papery skin.

Fig 3.83 Scallion

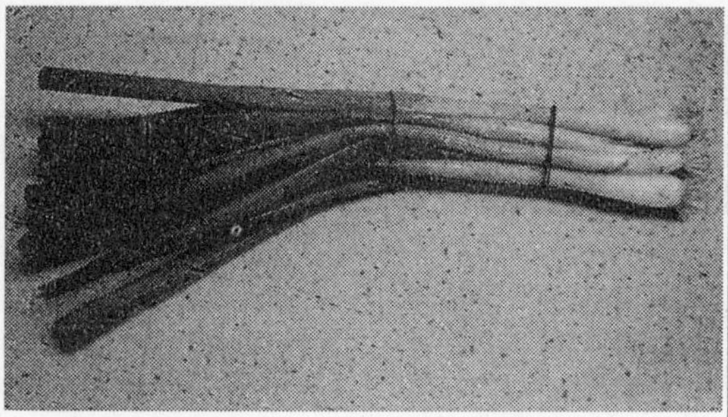

Fig 3.84 Scallion

Fig 3.85 Green onion

Fig 3.86 Shallots

III) Leeks (Fig 3.87)

Looks like over grown scallion flat green leaves and a white stock. Use to flavour stocks, soup. The leek is similar is flavour to the onion, but very much milder. When well grown it is thick and white. Leeks make excellent soup; they are also a good vegetable and most useful for flavouring stews and other made dishes. When preparing leeks great care is needed to remove the grit, for as in the case of vegetables that are earthen up to blanch, the earth penetrates into the leaves

Boiled Leeks: —to—Leeks according to size—teaspoon Salt —boiling Water—teaspoon Lemon Juice (optional).

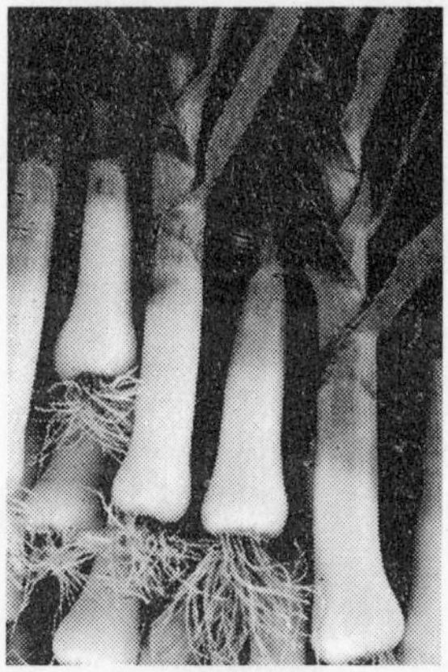

Fig 3.87 Leeks

Trim the root off the leeks and remove the outside leaves and cut away most of the green part, then split them down one side to enable the water to get to the centre. Wash the leeks under a tap, then put them in a bowl of cold water, allowing them to remain for at least a quarter of an hour. Then put them in a fresh bowl of water, and leave until they are to be cooked. Have ready a saucepan of fast foiling water with a teaspoon of salt to a quart of water, and boil with the lid off until tender. Drain and press. Serve with plain hot butter or white sauce. A teaspoon of lemon juice added to the water helps to keep the leeks white.

Fig 3.88 Chives

IV) Chives (Fig 3.88)

Tiny onions whose roots and tops are used greens are pencil thin they can be purchased freshed.

Fig. 3.89 Garlic

V) Garlic (Fig 3.89)

Great flavouring agent with medicinal value. each Segment called clove.

Tomatoes (Fig 3.90)

Native to Peru brought to America by the Spanish. Tomatoes are berries usually red but can be yellow. extremely versatile vegetable fruit eaten raw in salad and fried made into soup and sauces. Used mostly in Italian, Mexican, Indian and Caribbean cuisine.

Tomatoes impart flavour to so many dishes, and are the mainstay of many others. They can be bought so cheaply now, that they are more of a necessity than a luxury, and they can turn a few scraps into a fresh and attractive dish.

Fig. 3.90 Tomatoes

Edible Fungi Mushrooms

They are not vegetable they are edible fungi. They are over 38 thousands kinds of mushrooms. Three quarters are edible they are cultivated indoors and sold fresh. They should be refrigerators unwashed and covered so that they can be breath. French name of mushroom is Champignon. Though edible and very valuable in cookery these are really members of the fungus family. In late summer, especially if the nights are dewy, the wild one are often very plentiful and are far superior in flavour and texture to those which are cultivated. They may be distinguished from poisonous kinds of fungi by the mushroom smell and pinky brown colour when fresh. They can be easily peeled which is not the case with other fungi

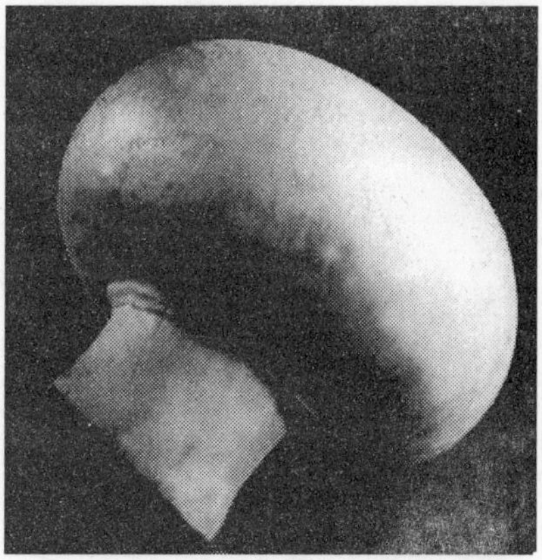

Fig 3.91 Champignon de Paris

Champignon de Paris (Fig 3.91)

Cultivated most of him in USA of white in colour.

Chanterelle (trumpet) (Fig 3.92)

Grown in trumpet climate like Japan, India and USA.

Fig 3.92 Chanterelle

Enoki (Fig 3.93)

This is new variety looks like a beans sprouts with a cap.

Fig 3.93 Enoki

Morel (Fig 3.94)

Sponge mushroom yellow brown in colour called Gucchi in India. Most desirable extremely costly can be purchased dried or fresh.

Cepe (Fig 3.95)

Some time called King bolete or Poicino large mushroom with caps. Shape like a ham burger bun this club shaped stem bulb like base.

Truffles (Fig 3.96)

Tubers of varieties of edible fungi grown near the root of oak tree not fungi visible from above the ground. Special dogs and pigs are used to find them. Two most varieties are period which is black truffle from France and Pidemontese which is white from Alba Italy very expensive.

Bearing the rich musk and flavour of their underground origins, truffles have long reigned as one of the earth's richest culinary treasures. Highly esteemed food stuff, is rounded of variable size and irregular shape.

Truffles are a rare and delicate type of edible mushroom that grow in Perigueux, Bergerac in France, Italy, and Sardinia- called everything from a black diamond to a princess, the truffle

Fig 3.94 Morel

Fig 3.95 Cepe

Fig 3.96 Varieties of truffles

has long reigned as the jewel of haute cuisine, a magical ingredient that classifically trained chefs have elevated to the ultimate luxury, truffles are prized around the world for their heady culinary power.

The world's best know truffles are white truffle from Italy and black truffles "Black Diamond" from France are considered to be best in the world due to their intense flavour and aroma. There are 70 varieties of truffles, 32 which found in Europe.

White Truffles (Fig 3.97)

Fig. 3.97 White truffles

Also termed to as Alba or piedmont truffles, can be four to five times of even best black truffles. Italy's white truffles, Tuber Magnatum, is a relative newcomer on the scence, having been discovered a mere two hundred years ago or so. White truffles are faintly golden, beige or pale brown, with lighter tan or cream-coloured flesh marked by thin pale veins. It tasting like "the perfect marriage between a clove of garlic, shallot and Parmesan cheese". It's always consumed raw over various dishes of risotto and pasta. It loses all flavour when cooked. White truffles are also known as Tuber Magnatum it means the name Magnatum refers to the rarity and costliness. White truffles season runs from early January with late November and December being the peak.

Black Truffles - The Black diamond of Franc Cookery (Fig 3.98)

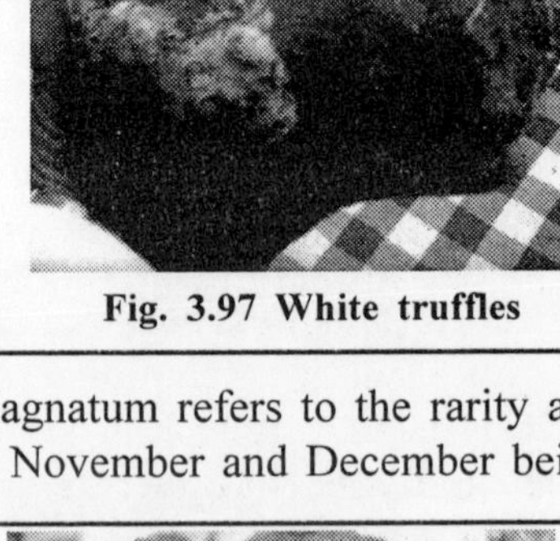

Fig. 3.98 Ripe Black truffles

Although it is often called the Pe'rigord truffle. Black truffles have an earthy intense somewhat winy fragrance. Black Truffles called the queen of truffles that mainly found in France and also found in Spain, particularly in the Catalonian region, all the way down to Valencia. It grows four to five inches underground generally in Oak Forests. They usually range from dark brown to black in colour, depending on how mature they are:

"Coal black means a ripe truffle". The flesh inside is grey or purplish black with white veins running throughout it. As shown in picture

Black truffles are found season from late November through March and are usually at their best from December to March.

Where Truffles Grows

Oak trees are one of the favourite host trees for truffle but many other broad leaves trees including poplars, pine trees and certain fruit or nut trees. Such pieces of truffle which are Himalayan Ones are grown under pine trees. They are grown under the soil near the roots of these trees.

How Truffles Grows

Truffles grows over a period of about six to eight months, with most types, other than summer truffles, maturing in the late of summer with all that said, truffles are anything's but predictable. No one really knows why truffles appear year after year under the same trees.

TRUFFICULTEURS (Fig. 3.99)

Truffle hunters usually work alone, in the dark night. He might have trained pigs rather than dog's. In the early times female pigs were used to hunt for truffles, as the pungent odour the truffles is similar to that of male pig.

Fig 3.99 The truffle hunt

How to used Truffles

- Fresh white truffles should never be cooked. They should be warmed, through gentle heat brings out their intoxication fragrance but too much will destroy it. That is why white truffle are usually shaved or grated over a plate of warm pasta or risotto dishes.
- Black truffles can be served raw, slices paper thin and incorporated into salad. But their flavour is usually enhanced when they are warmed or cook. Long cooking is not generally advised because it will mute the flavour.

Storing Truffle with their suggestive measure

- Ideally, truffles should be used within a day or so of purchase, but, properly stored, they will keep for longer:-
- Shell life of White truffles: Three to four days
- Shell life of Black truffles: - Up to two weeks.
- Storing truffles in rice in a tightly sealed jar is often recommended, but it is not actually a good way to keep them.
- For one thing, truffles need to "breathe" If they are kept in an airtight container they may be rot.
- Furthermore the rice will draw out moisture so they may dry out.
- The best way to store truffles is wrapped individually in paper towels in a card board box, in the coldest part of the refrigerator.
- Fresh black truffles can be frozen (Fig. 3.100).

Fig 3.100 Frozen truffles

SPECIALTY VEGETABLES

Artichoke (Fig. 3.101)

Fig. 3.101 Artichoke

Resemble a thistle with thick over lapping leaves tip with thorn. Usually dark green inside the covering of the leaves is the heart. Which is surrounded by fine hear like growth called choke. The base of each leaves and heart is only edible portion. Cook artichoke are eaten by stripping the cook artichokes are eaten by stripping the cook leaves and eating the bottom of them dip in appropriate sauces such as hollandaise and vinaigrette. When the heart is exposed it can be removed and eaten. When cooking adds a little lemon juice to help retain colour can also be stuff with sea food and neat mixture.

The globe artichoke is not very generally used in our country. It is very pretty when growing, resembling a huge green and purple thistle with beautiful grey-green foliage. The edible parts are the fleshy succulent portions at the root end of the leaves and the cup-like base from which the flower leaves grow. These artichokes are generally boiled and served with oil and vinegar dressing or vinaigrette sauce, sometimes with hollandaise sauce. They may be served hot or cold. They are also stuffed and baked. The bottoms may be fried, fricasseed, or served filled with herb forcemeat. Globe artichokes are generally eaten with the fingers.

To Boil

Time: about 45 minutes. Allow 1 for each person.

Choose artichokes that are young and green; when they become purple they are not so tender. Remove the hardest leaves at the base, and then cut a small piece off the top, to open the centre. Wash them very thoroughly and let them lie in cold water for about half an hour before cooking. Then put them in a colander, run some cold water over them, and leave them to drain, turning them upside down so that the water drains out of them.

To a large saucepan rather more than half full of boiling water, add a tablespoon of lemon juice and a teaspoon of salt. Put in the artichokes, flower end downwards, and when the water comes to the boil again let it boil rapidly for a few minutes; this improves the colour. Then boil gently until the artichokes are so tender that the leaves can be easily pulled out. Take them out of the water, drain them very thoroughly, remove the soft flower centre and serve on a napkin with hot liquid butter, lemon or hollandaise sauce.

Rhubarb (Fig. 3.102)

Rich dark red colour with coarse folly edge very large green leaves resemble elephant ears have a tart flavour only the stalk is edible. The leaves are bitter from oxcligic acid and can proved fatal eaten in quantity used for pudding pies, tarts. jams and jelly (Fig. 3.103).

Fig 3.102 Rhubarb

Jerusalem artichoke (Fig. 3.103)

Irregular shaped white or purple in colour looks like knobby potatoes have a nutty flavour prepared in the same manner as the potatoes.

Fig 3.103 Jerusalem artichoke

Japanese /Chinese artichoke (Fig. 3.104)

White tuber without skin small oblong ring like shaped.

Gardens beets /table Beets (Fig. 3.105)

Thicken lower part of the stem and upper part of the root. Best eaten boiled.

Carrot

Carrots are nourishing, containing both sugar and starch; they are indispensable for flavouring many kinds of made dishes. They are invariably served with boiled beef, and when served as vegetable, parsley sauce is served with them or hot butter and chopped parsley. There are two types

1. Early summer (yellowish orange) (Fig. 3.106).
2. Winter summer (reddish orange) (Fig. 3.107).

Fig 3.104 Japanese/Chinese artichoke

Fig 3.105 Garden Beets

Fig 3.106 Early summer

To Boil

Time: young carrots about 45 minutes—old carrots 1 ½ to 2 hours.

Very young carrots only need to be washed and brushed before cooking, but old carrots must be lightly scraped from the top downwards. Do not scrape off more than is absolutely necessary, as the red outer portion of the carrot is the best part. Young carrots are cooked whole, but old ones should be cut in pieces. Put them in boiling water with a teaspoon of salt to a quart of water and boil quickly with the lid on until they are quite tender. Ser with parsley sauce, white sauce.

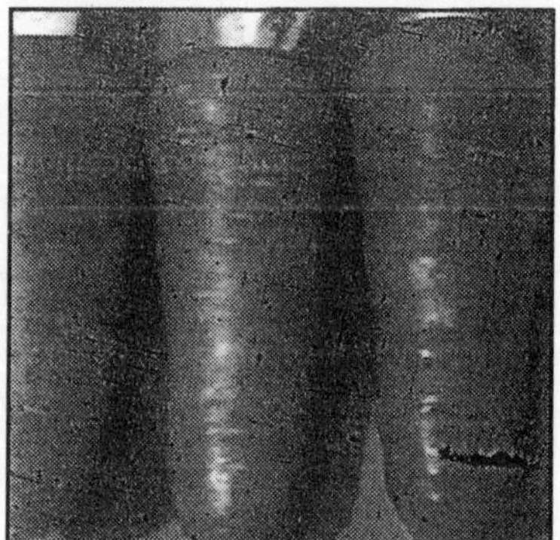

Fig 3.107 Winter summer

Celeriac (Fig 3.108)

It is a variety of celery also knows as a celery root. Needs to be peeled. Pale brown in colour. A vegetable with the flavour of celery but the shape of a turnip. The root is the edible part.

Fig 3.108 Celeriac

BOILED CELERIAC

Two Celeriac Root—large teaspoon Salt—pint White or Hollandaise Sauce.

Time: about 1 hour. Temperature: moderate. Enough for 4 persons.

Well brush and wash the roots, remove the outside skin, cut out any brown parts, then cut the root into cubes. Put them in a saucepan of boiling water that will well cover them, add the salt and boil gently with the lid on until quite tender. Drain and serve with white or hollandaise sauce

Fennel (Fig 3.109)

Leafy bulb with pour white greenish white bulb base green upper stalks and grass green fern like shout. All parts are used. Seeds are used in India and for making sausages and bread.

Fig 3.109 Fennel

Water chestnut (Fig 3.110)

Flattish round tuberous root stalk used mostly in oriental cooked caned.

Fig 3.110 Water chestnuts

Parsnip (Fig 3.111)

Look like white carrot. A wholesome and nourishing vegetable that should be more used. The flavour is improved by frost. They are cooked in the same way as carrots. When large they should be cut in quarters or wedges before cooking.

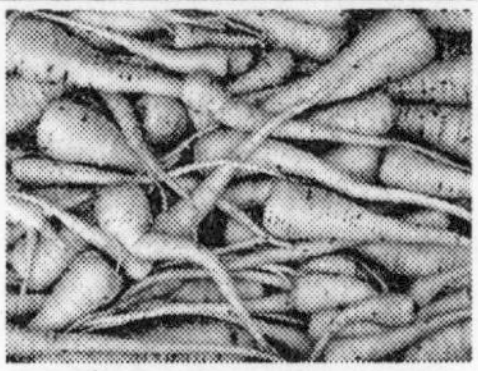

Fig 3.111 Parsnips

Reddish

Round red bulb variety also is available as red and white long pointed tips.

Garden Turnips (Fig 3.112)

Flat semi long too long white fleshed which sometimes have coloured head.

Fig 3.112 Garden turnips

SWEDES (Fig 3.113)

Similar to turnips but larger and sweeter. They may be cooked in the same way.

Adzuki Bean (Fig 3.114)

Varieties include Japanese Red, Chinese red, Adzuki Express (Johnny's Selected Seeds), Takara (Japanese import), and Minoka (Minnesota Agricultural Experiment Station). Compared to other beans, adzuki beans have a slightly sweet flavour. The plant grows 1 to 2 feet high with leaves resembling those of Southern peas. The plant yields yellow flowers that are followed by a cluster of smooth, short, cylindrical pods containing seeds two to three times larger than mung beans. The seeds are primarily dark red, but can include green, straw-colored, black-orange, and mottled seeds. The seeds are round with a protruding ridge (seed scar) on the side.

Fig 3.113 Swedes

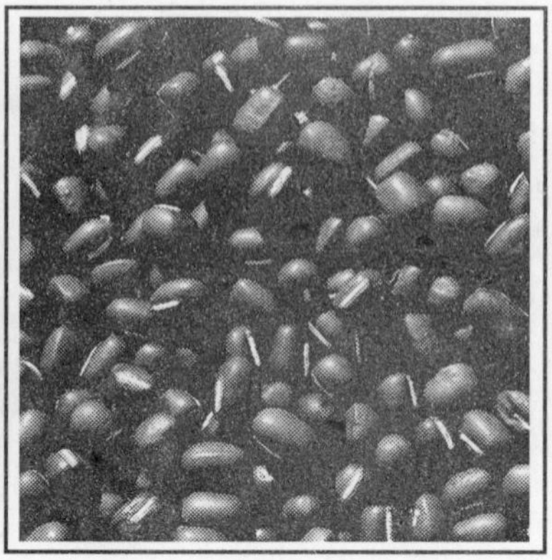

Fig 3.114 Adzuki beans

Fig 3.115 Baby corn

Baby Corn (Fig. 3.115)

There are special varieties especially for baby corn such as Baby and Baby Asian. You can also grow regular sweet corn to pick young, any well adapted sweet corn cultivar would work but some buyers prefer cultivars that produce longer ears. You may also want to choose varieties that bear more than one ear per stalk. Silver Queen, Early Extra-Sweet, Early Sunglow, How Sweet It Is, and Kandy Korn are typical varieties used for baby sweet corn. Keep in mind that the Baby and Baby Asian varieties are different than the sweet corn varieties that are just picked young

Tomatillo (Fig. 3.116)

Fig 3.116 Tomatillo

Varieties: Little breeding work has been done on the tomatillo. The only known cultivar is "Rendidora," from Mexico, although growers have attempted to improve on it by their own selection. Little has been accomplished, however, so tomatillo remains a crop with great variablility in plant habit, fruit size, earliness, and other characteristics. Tomatillo is primarily a self-incompatible, out-crossed plant, although some selfing is known to occur.

The tomatillo is of Mexican origin and is related to the husk tomato. It is an annual low growing, sprawling plant usually not more than two feet high. The tomatillo has small, sticky, tomato-like fruits enclosed in papery husks. They are 1 to 3 inches in diameter and green or purplish in colour

Fig 3.117 Daikon

Daikon, Lobok, Oriental or Chinese radish (Fig. 3.117)

Varieties include Mino Spring Cross (spring cultivar), Summer Cross No. 3, Chinese White (cylindrical), Chinese Rose (round), Celestial (cylindrical), and Tokinashi (a good all season cultivar).

Oriental radishes have extremely large roots. The Sakurajima variety, one of the largest, weighs up to 50 pounds. Most are in the 1 to 2 and a half pound class at full maturity. It is quite common for the leaf spread to be more than 2 feet. The leaves differ from spring radish types by being greatly notched and spreading from the tops of roots in a rosette fashion. Some varieties form large round to top-shaped roots, while others are cylindrical in shape.

Napa Cabbage, Chinese Cabbage, Celery Cabbage, Pe-tsai (Fig. 3.118)

Varieties include the Che-foo types: Wong Bok, Wintertime, Tropical Pride, Spring Giant, Tokyo Giant, and the Chihili types: Michihili, Jade Pagoda, Market Pride, Shantung, and Shaho Tsai.

There are two principal forms of Napa cabbage. The "Che-foo" type (also known as Chiifu or Wong Bok, and sometimes Napa) develops a compact; often drum shaped head that is slightly taller than it is wide. It has numerous broad, soft light green leaves. In the retail trade, Napa or Nappa is usually understood to be this type.

The "Chihili" type—forms a cylindrical head about three times as tall as it is wide. It has narrow, somewhat coarse, leaves that are darker green than those of the Che-foo type

Fig 3.118 Varieties of Napa cabbage

SALSIFY (Fig. 3.119)

Salsify is often called the oyster plant, as it has a decided oyster flavour. It is a neglected vegetable that should be more used. It is very good boiled and served with white sauce, and can also be served au gratin or fried.

Salsify is often called the oyster plant, as it has a decided oyster flavour. It is a neglected vegetable that should be more used. It is very good boiled and served with white sauce. and can also be served au gratin or fried.

Boiled Salsify: — 200 gram, Salsify—teaspoon, Vinegar or Lemon Juice.

Time: about one hour. Temperature: moderate. Enough for 4 to 6 persons.

Fig 3.119 Salsify

Scrape the roots lightly, just to take off the outside skin. Have by your side a bowl with a quart of water and a teaspoon of vinegar or lemon juice in it, and drop the salsify into this as you scrape it, to keep it a good colour. Put the roots in boiling water with a teaspoon of salt, and boil quickly until quite tender. Drain them and serve with white sauce.

BEETROOTS (Fig. 3.120)

Fig 3.120 Varieties of beet root

There are mainly two varieties of beetroots, the globe (turnip shaped) and the long beetroot which is shaped like a carrot. In some places, beetroots are usually sold ready cooked. When choosing them, remember that the deeper they are in colour the better the flavour will be. The turnip-shaped ones are the easier to cook as they do not require so much room, and beetroots need such very careful handling, for if the skin is broken and the red juice escapes the beetroots will be pink instead of red. So do not scrub them when cleaning them. Let them soak first in cold water and them remove any earth as gently as possible, being careful not to break the skin or the roots.

To Bake

Time: 2 to 3 hours. Temperature: Gas. Electricity. 375° F.

Beetroots may be baked; many cooks prefer this way as there is less chance of the juice escaping. But as they need two to three hours baking, it is not economical unless the oven is in use for other cooking.

To Boil

Time: 1 to 3 hours according to size and age. Temperature: moderate.

Wash the beetroots very carefully, being careful not to break the skin or the roots. Put them in a stew pan or kettle and well cover with cold water. They should be allowed plenty of room. Bring to the boil and then boil gently until they are done. When cooked sufficiently they will fee tender to the touch; they much on no account be tried with a fork. They may be served cold with vinegar dressing or served hot as a vegetable with while or lemon sauce.

POTATOES (Fig. 3.121)

Native to Andes mountain of South America called PAPAS by Indian called Patatas by Spanish. As there are numerous varieties of potatoes, both floury and waxy in texture, the kind to choose is just a matter of taste. But the time to cook varies according to the variety, for whilst some kinds boil easily without breading, other kinds break and become soppy almost as soon as they boil, and for these steaming is undoubtedly the best method. Old potatoes have more starch than they have lost the moisture and will observe other flavour easily they are best used in making potatoes, pan cakes, stews and salads. Low starches have a more moist crisper flesh it hold it shape in boiling.

High starch potatoes variety makes mashed and French fry. The mealy texture causes them to fall apart when boil.

The potato is a starchy, tuberous crop from the perennial Solanum tuberosum of the Solanaceae family. The word potato may refer to the plant itself as well. In the region of the Andes, there are some other closely related cultivated potato species. Potatoes are the world's fourth largest food crop, following rice, wheat, and corn.

To determine the starchy content of potatoes

Rub to cut half together. If they are stick together they are high in starch.

The method to tell mealy potatoes to waxy potatoes is to put them in a brine solution. A waxy potatoes will float and mealy will settle because of dense mask.

Types of potato

For culinary purposes, potato varieties are often described in terms of their waxiness. The distinction arises from the comparative ratio of two potato starch compounds: amylose and amylopectin. Amylose, a long-chain molecule, disintegrates easily when cooked in water, and lends itself to dishes in which the potato is mashed; varieties containing higher amylopectin content are classified as waxy. Since amylopectin is a more branched and stable molecule, waxy varieties are preferred in dishes where the potato is expected to retain its shape.

Culinary uses

Potatoes are prepared in many ways: skin-on or peeled, whole or cut up, with seasonings or without. The only requirement involves cooking to break down the starch. Most potato dishes are served hot, but some are first cooked then served cold, notably potato salad and potato chips/crisps.

Common dishes are: mashed potatoes, which are first boiled (usually peeled), and then mashed with milk or yogurt and butter; whole baked potatoes; boiled or steamed potatoes; french-fried potatoes or chips; cut into cubes and roasted; scalloped, diced, or sliced and fried (home fries); grated into small thin strips and fried (hash browns); grated and formed into dumplings, Rösti or potato pancakes. Unlike many foods, potatoes can also be easily cooked in a microwave oven and still retain nearly all of their nutritional value, provided that they are covered in ventilated plastic wrap to prevent moisture from escaping—this method produces a meal very similar to a steamed potato while retaining the appearance of a conventionally baked potato. Potato chunks also commonly appear as a stew ingredient.

Potatoes are boiled between 10 and 25 minutes, depending on size and type, to become soft.

Varieties of potatoes

Potatoes have been bred into many standard or well-known varieties, each of which has particular agricultural or culinary attributes. Varieties are generally categorized into a few main groups—such as russets, reds, whites, yellows (also called Yukons) and purples—based on common characteristics.

Popular varieties (cultivars) include:

Belle de Fontenay	BF-15	Bintje	Cabritas	Camota
Chelina	Chiloé	Cielo	Clavela Blanca	Désirée
Fianna	Fingerling	Flava	Golden Wonder	Jersey Royal
Kerr's Pink	Kestrel	King Edward	Kipfler	Maris Piper
Nicola	Pachacoña	Pink Eye	Pink Fir Apple	Red Pontiac
Rooster	Russet Burbank	Spunta	Yukon Gold	

Classical preparation of potatoes

1. **Allumettè**: Cut of match sticks shapes, fry in deep fat with a pinch of salt.
2. **Anna**: Cut in cyclinder shapes slice is rounders, well wash, dry on cloth. Set them in layer a special pan with clarified butter cook in the oven when half done turnover to colour both side.
3. **Berny**: Potatoes croquettes combines with chop truffles shape like apricot, egg washed them and rolled in slice almonds deep fat fry.
4. **Boulanger**: Slice onions and potatoes cooking in butter add the potatoes after words season, moisture in consommé. Cook in the oven.
5. **Bretonné**: Cut in large dices, cooked in consommé with onions, little chop garlic and diced tomatoes.
6. **Byron**: Pomme macarie, hollow the top, sprinkle with shredded cheese cover with cream.
7. **Châteaux**: Shape like a large olive. Blanch them in roasted to nice brown colour in butter.
8. **Crème**: Cooked in water, peel slice, moisten with milk and butter and salt cook and add cream while serving.
9. **Croquettes**: Shapes as fancy, coated egg with bread crumbs and fry it in deep fat.
10. **Dauphine**: One part of choux paste without sugar, two part dutch potatoes, shapes as cocks eggs and bread crumb and fry.
11. **Dauphi Noise**: Cut in raw slices cook in oven with milk grated with gruyere cheese.
12. **Duchesse**: Cooked as puree thicken with yolks of eggs
13. **Aufour**: Large potatoes for baked in the oven served with skin.
14. **Lyonnaise**: Sauté potatoes mix with onions called a'la' layonnaise
15. **Menth**: Same as Anglase add mint.
16. **Mousseline**: Mash potatoes with whipped cream.
17. **Marquis**: Its pomp duchesse mixed with reduced tomatoes sauce.
18. **Noisettè**: Cut with round scoop like a size of hazel nut cook the same as chaute potatoes
19. **Normandè**: Slice and cook with onions, white of leeks toasted in butter add a little flour with mix seasons, place in gratinated dish, brown.
20. **Paysanne**: slice thickly cooks in butter with consommé, shredded garlic, sorrel and chervil.

Carlingford
Skin: White
Flesh: White
Shape: Oval

Delaware
Skin: Cream
Flesh: White
Shape: Oval

Desiree
Skin: Pink
Flesh: Yellow
Shape: Long Oval

Eureka
Skin: Cream
Flesh: White
Shape: Oval

Kestrel
Skin: White, Blue Eyes
Flesh: Cream
Shape: Long Oval

Kipfler
Skin: Pale Yellow
Flesh: Yellow
Shape: Elongated

Mondial
Skin: Pale Yellow
Flesh: Pale Yellow
Shape: Oval

Nadine
Skin: Cream
Flesh: White
Shape: Short Oval

Royal Blue
Skin: Purple
Flesh: Yellow
Shape: Long Oval

Ruby Lou
Skin: Dark Pink
Flesh: White
Shape: Oval

Fig 3.121 Different varieties of potatoes

STANDARD RECIPES OF POTATOES

Potatoes Baked in their Jackets

Time: 1 to 1 ½ hours according to size.

Temperature: Gas, Electricity. 450° F. Allow 1 or 2 for each person.

1. Choose large potatoes of uniform size and scrub them quite clean. Put them into a hot oven. They will need about an hour.
2. To try them, piece with a thin skewer.
3. As soon as they are done, make a slip in the skin at one end to let the steam escape.
4. If liked, a piece of butter that has been seasoned with pepper and salt can be inserted. Serve on a folded table napkin in a vegetable dish.

Potatoes Baked in Milk

Time: 30 to 45 minutes. Temperature: Gas. Electricity, 425° F. enough for 4 persons.

Ingredients	*Quantity*
Potatoes	750g
Milk	250ml
Salt and pepper	15g
Butter	50g

1. Choose small potatoes, boil and drain them. They should be tender, but not at all broken.
2. Well butter a square baking dish and put the potatoes in it, close together. Season the milk and pour it over them.
3. The milk should not be more than half-way up the potatoes.
4. Put the remainder of the butter on the top of the potatoes in small pieces, and bake until brown.

Boiled Potatoes

Time: about 30 minutes according to be kind of potato.

1. Potatoes may be boiled with or without their skins. Choose those of about the same size.
2. Wash and brush them until quite free from earth, then peel them as thinly as possible—a potato knife, which can be bought for a few pence, makes this easy. Remove any black specks, and put the potatoes in a bowl of cold water as you peel them.
3. When they are to be cooked, drain them, put them in a saucepan of cold water, and add a sprinkling of salt. Cover, bring to the boil quickly, and let them simmer until tender.

4. To try when sufficiently cooked, pierce them with a skewer or knitting needle. Then tilt the lid, and carefully drain off all the water.
5. Let the pan stand at the side of the stove with the lid tilted. Shake the pan gently and when they are quite dry, serve in a hot tureen. Potatoes do not improve with keeping, so time them, if possible, to be done just as they are required.

To Boil Potatoes in their Jackets

1. Prepare but do not peel them. Cook in the same way.
2. Then when done peel them as quickly as possible, putting them into a hot tureen as you peel them—or they may be served in their jackets.

Steamed Potatoes

Time: about 30 minutes

1. Every chef should realize that a steamer is a necessity in a kitchen, and by no means a luxury, for it economizes in fuel and space.
2. It is very difficult to boil potatoes that break easily— and these are the best kind.
3. But if steamed, they cook perfectly, and require very little attention once they are put in.
4. Potatoes may be steamed either in their skins or when peeled. They are more nourishing when cooked in their skins, for then their valuable salts are not lost, and this method is also more economical, as the skins can be removed without wasting any of the potato.
5. Choose potatoes of equal size scrub them thoroughly clean, put them in a steamer over fast-boiling water, put on the lid, and keep the water boiling until they are done.
6. Then take off the lid, put the saucepan at the side of the stove until the potatoes have dried.
7. Peel them, putting them back into the steamer as you do them back into the steamer as you do them, to keep hot. Potatoes should, if possible, be served as soon as they are done.
8. If kept waiting long, or if over-cooked, they lose their floury appearance, and their flavour is not so good.
9. A very good substitute for a steamer is a colander.
10. Prepare the potatoes and put them in a colander, put this on a saucepan containing boiling water, put the lid over the potatoes in the colander, keep the water boiling well underneath.

Fried Potatoes

1. These are the most difficult for the beginner. But the trouble generally is the same as with fish—the potatoes are not dried.
2. If fried while wet, they will never be crisp. Another important point is to have plenty of fat; the potatoes must be well covered. Either a very deep frying pan or a saucepan should be used.

3. Well wash the potatoes and peel them. Then cut into squares or thick slices. As you cut them, put them in cold water that has a little salt in it. Leave them in this until you are almost ready to fry them.
4. Then drain and dry them in a soft cloth. Put into hot fat, a few at a time—use a basket if you have one—and cook until tender.
5. Now take them out. Boil up the fat in the pan until a thin smoke rises and put in some more potatoes and fry a golden brown. Drain and serve.

Potato Chips

1. These are cooked in the same way, but cut in very thin slices.
2. This is easily accomplished with the tin cutters. The potatoes should be well dried.

Potatoes Fried in Batter

1. Potatoes may also be fried in batter. Peel and cut them in cubes, and dry well in a cloth.
2. Have ready a pan of hot fat, and as soon as the thin blue smoke rises, dip each piece of potato in batter, then drop it in the fat, fry a golden brown, drain and serve very hot.

Note: The batter should be a thick fritter batter.

Mashed Potatoes

1. Steam as many potatoes as required. As soon as they are cooked, rub them through a sieve, or mash with a fork.
2. Put into a saucepan with seasoning of salt and pepper. Add 1 oz. Of butter and a tablespoon of milk to every pound of potatoes.
3. Beat till smooth, and stir over hot water or gentle heat until very hot. Pile in a tureen, smooth with a fork, and serve.

Potato Aigrettes

Time: 30 minutes. Temperature: Moderate. Enough for 4 to 6 persons.

Ingredients	*Quantity*
Potatoes	750 gram
Eggs	4 no.
Butter	50 gram
Salt and pepper	15 gram
Oil	500 ml

Method

1. Steam the potatoes and rub them through a sieve.
2. Add the butter, melted, and a good seasoning of salt and pepper.
3. Whip the yolks and whites of the eggs separately. Beat the yolks into the mashed potato, and then add the stiffly whipped whites.
4. Heat some fat until a thin blue smoke is rising from it. Then drop the potato mixture in, in small tablespoons, and fry until it is a golden brown.

Potato Balls

Time: 10 minutes. Temperature: Moderate. Enough for 4 persons.

Ingredients	*Quantity*
Potatoes	750 gram
Eggs	4 no.
Grated processed cheese	50 gram
Salt and pepper	15 gram
Oil	500 ml
Milk	50 ml
Breadcrumbs	100 gram

Method

1. Rub the potatoes through a sieve. Season them with salt and pepper.
2. Stir in the milk and grated cheese, then half the well beaten egg
3. Form into balls or croquettes and dust them with flour.
4. Leave them for an hour or more. Dip in beaten egg, then in breadcrumbs, and fry a golden brown in boiling fat. Drain and serve.

Buttered Potatoes

Time: 15 minutes. Temperature: Moderate. Enough for 4 persons.

Ingredients	*Quantity*
Potatoes	500 gram
Parsley	20 gram
Butter	50 gram
Salt and pepper	15 gram

Method

1. Well butter a fireproof dish. Cut the potatoes in slices.
2. Put in a layer of potato slices, then some scraps of butter and repeat until all are used. Season each layer with salt and pepper.
3. Bake in a moderate even until lightly brown, sprinkle with chopped parsley, and serve.
4. The top layer may be covered with grated cheese before baking.

Duchesse Potatoes

Time: about 20 minutes. Temperature: Gas, Electricity, 450° F.

Ingredients	*Quantity*
Potatoes	500 gram
Butter	50 gram
Salt and pepper	15 gram
Milk	100 ml

Method

1. Mash the potatoes and rub them through a sieve, sprinkle well with salt and pepper, add the butter (melted), and the milk.
2. Stir over gentle heat for five minutes to mix the ingredients well.
3. Cool, and when only just warm, force it through a forcing bag into heaps on a buttered baking dish, or it may be put in little rocks with a fork.
4. Brown in a quick oven, pile on a doily and serve as hot as possible.

Potatoes With Lemon

Time: about 10 minutes. Temperature low. Enough for 4 to 6 persons.

Ingredients	*Quantity*
Potatoes	500 gram
Butter	50 gram
Salt and pepper	15 gram
Béchamel sauce	100 ml
Lemon	2 no
Chopped parsley	20 gram

Method

1. Cut the boiled potatoes into slices. Put them in a saucepan with the white sauce, the parsley, butter and a good sprinkling of pepper and salt.
2. Heat slowly. Squeeze over them the juice of half a small lemon, and serve hot. This is very good with veal.

Potatoes Lyonnaise

Time: 10 to 15 minutes. Temperature: moderate. Enough for 4 persons.

Ingredients	*Quantity*
Potatoes boiled cold	500 gram
Butter	50 gram
Salt and pepper	15 gram
Shredded onion	100 gram

Method

1. Make the butter quite hot in a frying pan, put in the shredded onion and cook until it is brown and tender. It should be only a light brown, not dark.
2. Now remove the onion with a fish slice, draining it from the butter and leaving as much butter in the pan as possible.
3. Brown the potato slices in the butter and sprinkle them with salt and pepper. Put the onion back in the pan and reheat it with the potatoes. Serve hot.

Potatoes Maitre D'hôtel

Time: about 20 minutes. Temperature: Moderate. Enough for 4 persons.

Ingredients	*Quantity*
Potatoes	500 gram
Butter	50 gram
Salt and pepper	15 gram
Milk	100ml
Chopped parsley	20 gram
Egg yolk	4no
Lemon juice	10ml

Method

1. Peel the potatoes and put into cold water, drain them and cut into balls with a cutter, or into cubes.
2. Boil them in slightly salted water until tender.
3. The drain and and put them in the heated milk and leave at the side of the stove.
4. Cream the butter, add to it the egg yolk, and beat together to mix. Stir in gradually the lemon juice, chopped parsley and a seasoning of salt and pepper. Strain the milk from the potatoes, put in the butter mixture.
5. Stir a minute. Turn out, and serve.

Potato Sauté

Time: about 10 minutes. Temperature: Moderate.

Ingredients	*Quantity*
Boiled Potatoes	500 gram
Butter or dripping of Bacon	50 gram
Salt and pepper	15 gram
Milk	100ml
Parsley	

Method

1. Cut the potatoes into rather thick slices, and sprinkle a little salt and pepper over them.
2. Fry in hot fat, browning them on both sides. Place on a hot dish, sprinkle with very finely chopped parsley and serve.

Spanish Potatoes

Time: about 30 minutes. Temperature: Moderate. Enough for 4 to 6 persons.

Ingredients	Quantity
Potatoes	500 gram
Butter	50 gram
Salt and pepper	15 gram
Milk	100ml
Tomatoes	50 gram

Method

1. Steam the potatoes, rub them through a sieve, then season well with salt and pepper.
2. Slice the tomatoes and simme3r them gently with the butter until tender. Then rub through a sieve.
3. Mix the tomato puree with the mashed potato, add the cream. Stir over gentle heat until the mixture is very hot. Pile on a hot dish and serve.

GUIDELINES FOR PROPER DONENESS OF VEGETABLE

1. Don't over cook the vegetables.
2. Cook vegetables as close to the service as possible. Remember they continue to cook when hold hot.
3. If you have to cook a head undercooked vegetable slightly .This will allow some holding time or reheating.
4. When precooking for reheating the vegetables soak the vegetable in ice water to stop cooking process.
5. Cut uniform size piece to ensure even cooking.
6. Vegetable with tough and tender parts needs special attention.
   a) Peel stem of asparagus
   b) Peel and split stem of broccoli
   c) Score the base and stem end of Brussels sprout.
   d) Special care for buds of broccoli and asparagus for extended heat.
7. Your aim is to hence the fresh crispy flavour of vegetables. Not diminish it.

TIPS ON HOW TO PRESERVE THE NUTRIENT CONTENT OF VEGETABLES

Vegetables is no doubt the best food we can eat to live a healthy and active life. Vegetables are eaten in a variety of ways as part of main meals and as snacks. The nutrient content of different kinds of vegetables differs considerably. The leafy vegetables are green because of the presence of *chlorophyll*, a nutrient that can remove toxin from our body. The yellow/orange colour of fruits and vegetables is due to *carotenoids* which has a strong anticancer effect. The red/blue colour of vegetables is due to *anthocyanins* a potent antioxidant.

HOW TO CHOOSE VEGETABLES

- Avoid damaged, wilted, and bruised vegetables because they have like loss their nutrients.
- Leafy vegetables should be crisp, firm, and of a good colour, and root vegetables should be firm and free of brown marks.
- Avoid insect infected vegetables.

Tips on how to preserve the vitamin and mineral content of vegetables

- If the vegetable require peeling, peel it very thinly as there are vitamins and minerals under the skin which could easily be removed. Young potatoes, carrots, and other vegetables often do not require peeling and can be served with their skins on. It is important to soak it in water with salt to for a minute then place it under running water while cleaning it with your hands to remove remaining dirt and chemicals. The salt does not only clean your vegetable but it can also enhance the taste of the vegetable. Do not soak the vegetable in water for a long time because it will cause water-soluble vitamins and minerals to be lost.
- Prepare vegetables just before cooking to prevent the destruction of vitamins by enzymes. They can be places in a plastic bag in a cool place to prevent the oxidation of vitamins.
- Cook the vegetables in the minimum amount of boiling water. Placing them in boiling water destroys enzymes, and so helps to preserve the vitamins. They should be cooked for the minimum time, with a lid on the pan.
- When vegetables are just tender, they should be drained and served immediately. If kept hot, there will be further losses of vitamin C.

PRINCIPAL STORAGE OF VEGETABLES

- Potatoes should be stored in a dark, cool, dry place to prevent them from becoming moldy, and to stop them sprouting in warmth. Most root vegetables should be stored in a same way.
- Leaf vegetables lose vitamin C and water rapidly during storage and should be stored for the minimum time in a cool place, in a plastic bag

FLAVOURING AND SEASONING (Fig. 3.122)

The human body indentifies basic taste sensation through tongue there are four major sensations: - Sweet, Sour, Bitter and Salty.

Taste Sensation of the five sensive that human have smell and taste are directly related. They are detached simultaneously because the mouth and share the same air way. The 18th Century French Gastronome name "Brillat Savarin". In lighting the tissue of taste and smell when it stated that "Smell and taste formed a single sense of which the mouth is the Laboratory and nose is the Chimney and or to speak more exactly of which ones serves that the tasting of actually body and other for savoring there gasses.

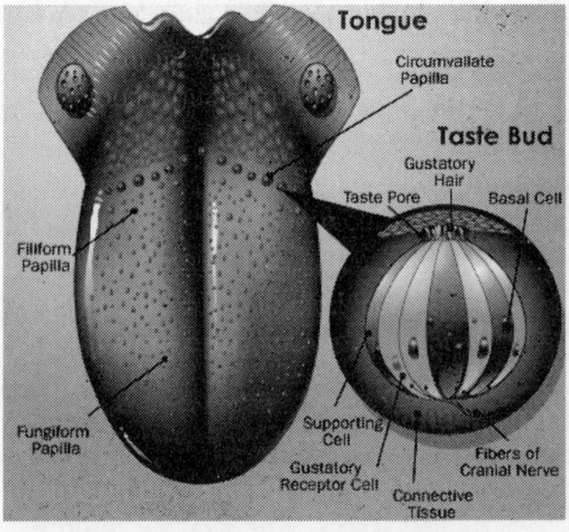

Fig 3.122 The taste sensation of tongue

Sweet sensation come form sugar and sweetens. These are detective at the tip of the tongues, it also a primary sensation that the body Prefers. The body within limit will tolerate the over abundant the sweet substance and allow you to swallow when some is extremely sour, bitter or salty is eaten by the body that Protests. The body persuades it as a potentially toxic danger and the result is one enability to sallow easily.

Sour sensation come from acid and the detective all the sides of the tongues citreous juices such as lemon or lime, tomato products, Vinegar are all acidic foods the tongue reacts in varying degreing depending on the concentration a small amount pleasing concentration may the mouth to pucker.

Salty sensation comes from sodium chloride and other salt and some sodium glutamate and Potassium chloride this sensation is detective at the front of the tongue salt is an essential nutrients and desirable in small quality over used of salt result in psychological need to drink large quantity of water causing a loss of appetite.

Bitterness is the reaction to alcholide which are bitter this sensation is detective at the back of the tongue Tannin and Caffeine are example of bitter alcolides. Although the body react high concentration of alcolides. We have got used to low concentration is coffee and tonic water.

Temperature Effect Sensibility to Taste

Foods that are hot or too cold seem to used flavour only because our taste buds cannot easily detect flavour at extremely temperature. It's important that the taste sensation of various compound are consideration when seasoning and flavouring of that food mixing, which matching the sensation is truly exciting and challenge. Seasoning and flavouring what stimulate the taste sensation therefore the culinary need to understand the difference between seasoning and flavouring.

SEASONING TYPE AND DEFINITION

Can be defining as the enhancement of the natural flavour of food without drastic alternation of its flavour salt. In its various forms is a primary seasoning agent there are two type of salt seasoning available.

Rock Salt: It's mixed formed deposits on land this salt is very coarse in nature and is often refined and sold as table salt normally idonized added in it.

Sea Salt: It's Produce by evaporate of sea water. Its impured salt containing natural idonized or other compound from the two primary salts they are also derived flavour of salt and soya.

Flavour Salt: Are refined salt combine with other natural flavouring garlic salt, celery salt and season's salt are example of flavouring salt. These salts can be used in cooking and work well in many names.

Soy: In its various forms paste and sauce come from orient where it is derived from soya bean fermented in brine it is dark in colour in liquid form it can provide a very subtle seasoning however it will alter the colour of food because of it dark colour. Soy contain varies in it salt content. Add less than recommended by a recipe and taste before adding more.

MSG (Mono Sodium Glutamate or Agi-no-moto): An example of second source of seasoning is MSG or the sodium salt of Glutamate acid that is a white powder compound produced naturally by both plants and animals. The MSG which is used in today's kitchen may be derived from a number of natural sources including wheat gluten, seaweed and beat or cane sugar it's extracted through a Process of Fermentation and drying which result in fine white crystal know as MSG. It's only a slight salted tastes its purpose is to bring out a natural flavour of the food even those MSG is sodium it's contains only one-third of the Sodium of natural salt. Mono Sodium Glutamate is very common in oriental cooking and it used properly may reduce need for salt.

Characteristics

Salt like Sugar is a crystal which dissolve in water this enable it to blend in most food. Easily and quickly but not with fat. Salt has an incredible capacity to absorb water when place in food can draw out water in turns penetrate into the food where water was once. The withdrawing or water can enhance the natural flavour of the food and examples of this practice when a piece of fish is like salted before begin taken in the oven. Although the heat from the oven draws much of the moisture out of the fish the salt, aids this process and can be tasted throughout the Fish. In salt cured country Ham, the salt act as prescribed by drawing almost all of the moisture from the ham this helps to eliminate bacterial growth. Salt has to be used in restrain it's incredible absorbed Property can completely dry out the Product it too much salt is exposed to the Product from two long to recover food which has too much salt added is very difficult and often impossible.

Some Basic Guidelines for Seasoning Foods are:

1. Seasoning as well as flavouring is indented to enhance the main ingredients. Not to hide its flavour or cover up Poorly Prepared Food.
2. Most seasoning or liquid product are done towards the end of cooking process. Special a liquid will be reducing.
3. Liquid that reduces cause seasoning to concentrate intensity the seasoning taste gain the write balance of seasoning.
   A) Cook your liquid product for 3 quarter of your total cooking time.
   B) Taste in to see what seasoning if any is needed.
   C) Add a small amount of seasoning and allow the liquid to finished cooking remember you can always add more if needed.
   D) Taste again and adjust seasoning if needed.
4. When preparing solid peace of food it's best to seasons at the beginning of the cooking process this allows the seasoning to be absorbed and blend into food it's also allowed time for the seasoning to bring out the natural flavour of the food itself.
5. Because salt draws water out when attenting to brown meats it may not be advantages to salt the meat before cooking the water extracted by the salt may retard the browning process.

6. Seasoning may also be added after cooking this can be very effected if the cooked food has little flavour of its own. French fries are simple and but classic example many people enjoy and french fry more for the salt than from the Potatoes.

As an opposed to seasoning, is the addition of new flavour to a food. This result in alteration of the original natural flavour .The various types of flavouring agent can be categorized as spices herbs, concentrate flavouring agents, wines, vinegars and marinated, without flavour there is little distinction from one recipe to the next it's the flavour in most cases which define the international cuisines. The Chilli Pepper of Moscow, the fermented soya bean sauce of Far East, turmeric and cardamoms mixture of India curry, as well as the oregano and basil flavour of tomato sauce of Italy will provide strong flavour.

It should be noted there are dominated flavour and under tones. The dominant flavour should be limited to one or two elements such as main ingredients and possible one additional ingredients or flavouring agent. Any additional flavouring should be fined subtle. So as not to take away attention from the dominant flavour of a particular recipe may called for five to six herbs or spices one or two of them should be dominant the other agents should combined to form under tones there under tones may offer not be recognizable .Yet persistent enough in the overall flavour to be classified as "secret" ingredient.

Texture

It is term used to describe the capabtlity of finished product in which sequence ingredients are added to the dishes and what different methods are used for cooking and which effect the resulting of final product. The texture when related to food is not accumulated itself. There are several characteristics which are given below:

1. **Visual Appearance**: The appearance of objects is given by the way in which the first foods its size shape and distribution of cells are very important. The colors of food, the holes in sponge item are evenly distribution.
2. **Touch illusion**: It exploits the sense of touch which should be exactly desire by a particular dish.
3. **Sense of Soft**: The texture of the food should be according to their normal softness for example cake sponge should not be hard.
4. **Mouth feel**: Its shows the product physical and chemical interacting in the mouth. It's evaluate from initial perception on the palate to first bite through mastication to swallowing and after taste mouth feel is often related to a products, water activity make it hard or crisp the products having lower water activities and soft products having intermediate to high water activities.

VARIOUS TEXTURE OF FOOD

Firm and Close: The texture of food is very firm and close according to the end product of the food. For example the holes made by the raising agent are many but equally distribution of mixing is very important.

Short and Crumble: This is closely related to firm and close but more fat is added in this for example Nan-Khatai.

Fluffy and Harmonious: The food product is a homogenous blend of evenly incorporated air molecules and hence the final products is firmed and texture; but not hard and tough .Also it is neither too soft like a Pastry or Sponge and Cake for example: Medira cake.

Flakey: This caused by method of adding fat. The layer formed by air pockets in cased of thin crisped layer.

Incorrect Texture

(A) **Sturdy**: Sturdiness is caused by if you added two much liquid or through incorrect mixing. Sturdiness is also come if two little fat is added to mixture.

(B) **Chapped**: It's through unevenly mixing. In some parts wholes are large and uneven and food is sunk in the centre. This is done when we added too much leaving agent to the mixture.

(C) **Tough**: It's a very common fault when we all too much liquid to the mixture or added less fat to the mixture or put too much liquid or two much pressure while mixing.

VEGETABLE CUTS

The vegetable cut selected for a particular dish must complement the dish it is being used for. For example, a robust casserole would require larger pieces than a light consommé. Many other loose descriptions exist, e.g. strips, bite-sized pieces, chunks, and slivers. The following are the traditional cuts used in the hospitality trade

Batons

"Sticks" of vegetables around 12mm/½ -inch thick and up to 7.5cm/3-inches long. Usually cut before cooking.

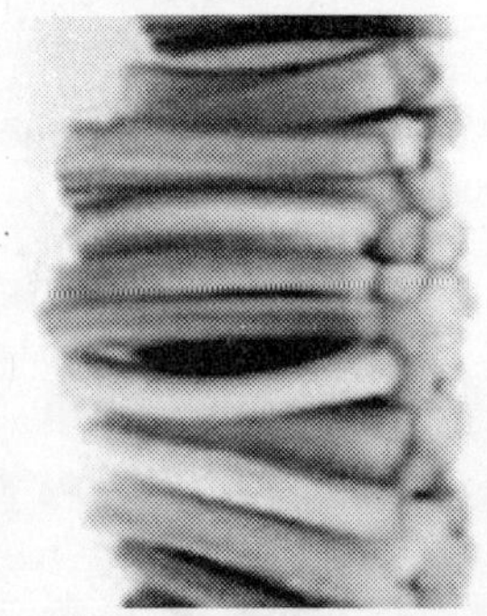

Batons

Brunoise

A very fine dice up to 2mm/1/12th inch square. Usually cut before cooking. Often used as a garnish.

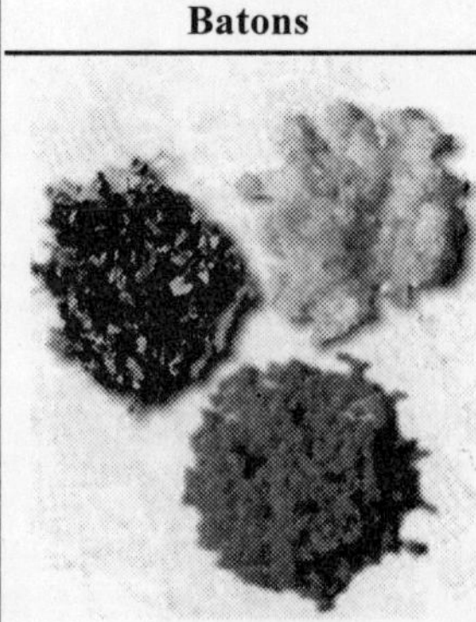

Brunoise

Chips/French Fries/Crisps

Chips and Fries are "sticks" of vegetables between 5cm/2-inches and 10cm/4-inches long and up to 2.5cm/1-inch thick. Crisps are very thin slices no thicker than 6mm/¼-inch. Both are cut before cooking and are usually deep fried until crispy.

Chunks

A piece of cut vegetable larger than 3.75cm/1¾-inches. Usually cut before cooking.

Cubes

Pieces of vegetables from 12 mm/½ -inch to 36 mm/1½-inches square. Can be cut before or after cooking.

Dice

Pieces of vegetables between 6 mm/¼-inch and 12 mm/½ -inch square. Can be cut before or after cooking.

Grated

Thin pieces of vegetables created using a grater. They can be any length depending on the vegetable used but are always wafer thin.

Chips/French Fries/Crisps

Chunks

Cubes

Dice

Grated

Julienne

Mashed

Juliénne

Strips of vegetables usually 3mm/ [1 inch square up to 5 cm/ 2-inch long standard. Often a mandoline is used for accuracy. Often used as a garnish.

Matchsticks

Mashed

Vegetables which have already been cooked until soft then further broken down with a fork or masher.

Matchsticks

Thin "sticks" of vegetables no thicker than 6mm/¼-inch square and 5cm/ 2-inches long

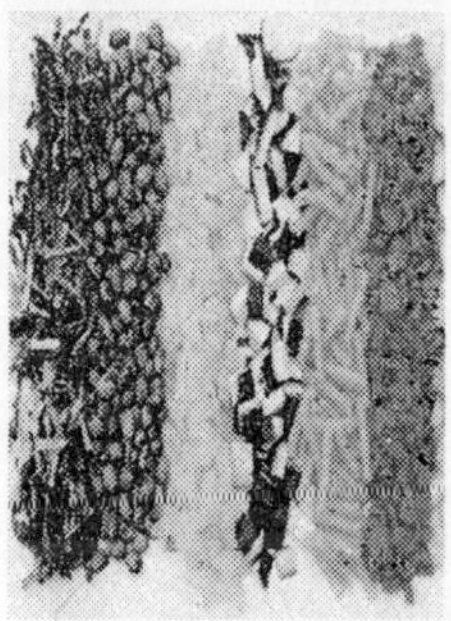

Paysanne

Paysanne

Very thin slices of vegetables no larger than 6mm/¼-inch square. Most often used as a garnish This cut may be squares, triangles, circles or half-rounds. In order to cut economically, the shape of the vegetable will decide which shape to choose. All are cut thinly, about 1–2mm thick.

Purée

Purée

Vegetables which have usually already been cooked until soft then mashed then made smooth by rigorous beating or passing through a sieve. With some vegetables a food processor can be used.

Shred

Vegetables cut into thin strips generally no wider than 6mm/¼-inch. Usually done before cooking.

Slices

Vegetables cut into similar size flat pieces. Can be lengthways or width ways, from 6mm/¼-inch to 2.5cm/1-inch thick.

Slices

Shred

Sulfrino Balls

Sulfrino vegetable balls are made with a very small melon scoop, sometimes called a Parisienne scoop, up to 12mm/½-inch in diameter. Most usually used for garnishes.

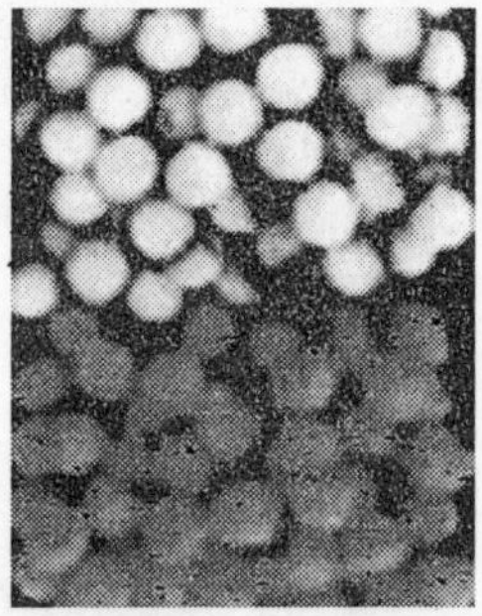

Sulfrino Balls

Mirepoix

A mixture of roughly-chopped vegetables used as a base for sauces or to enhance the flavour of meat, fish and shellfish dishes. Normally onion, celery and carrot are used and these are slowly cooked in butter until they are very tender. Thymeand bay are often added.

Mirepoix

Matignon

Roughly cut vegetables cooked in butter with ham, thyme and bayleaf, finished by deglazing the pan with a little Maderia.

Matignon

Chiffonade

Finely sliced or shredded green leafy vegetables, usually lettuce or spinach, used as a base, garnish or in soups.

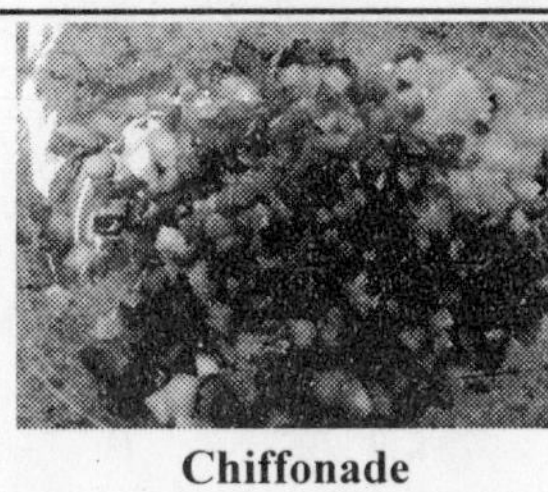

Chiffonade

LEARNING OUTCOME

For the preparation of good, tasty and colorful dishes, it is essential to have a basic knowledge of the raw materials, their characteristics and the special part they play. This knowledge helps to substitute materials when necessary, or rectify the texture and taste if something goes wrong. Also it helps to improve the quality and get standard end product. To prepare good tasty colorful food its essential to have basic knowledge of raw material their characteristic and the part they play this knowledge help to substitute material when necessary rectified the texture and taste if something's goes wrong it also help to improve the quality of the end product. Herbs and spices play a vital role in commercial kitchen .It is very important to know the description and there uses. Vegetables provide vitamins and minerals as well as flavours which are not available in meats, cereals, dairy products and fruits. Vegetables are eaten in a variety of ways as part of main meals and as snacks. The nutrient content of different kinds of vegetables differs considerably. The leafy vegetables are green because of the presence of *chlorophyll*, a nutrient that can remove toxin from our body. Flavouring and seasoning play a very important role in commercial cooking .Seasoning can be define as the enhancement of the natural flavour of food without drastic alternation of its flavour salt. The vegetable cut selected for a particular dish must complement the dish it is being used for. For example, a robust casserole would require larger pieces than a light consommé.

LESSON END ACTIVITY

- Collect the different herbs and spice and paste in your journal.
- Collect the pictures of English vegetables and paste in your journal.
- Bring carrot, beans, cabbage and onion from the market and cut with the following method:

   i) Julienne
   ii) Chiffonade
   iii) Mireporx
   iv) Burnoise
   v) Slices
   vi) Shred
   vii) Dices
   viii) Cubes

QUESTIONS FOR DISCUSSION

1. Describe the characteristics of the various raw materials.
2. Explain the uses of salt and the different types of salt.
3. Explain the different uses of fats and oils.
4. What are the different raising agents?
5. Define sweetening with different types and it's used.
6. Explain the different types of thickening agents.
7. Explain the process of hydrogenation of oil.
8. Explain the different usage of fats and oils.
9. Explain the following terms:

   i) Rendering of fat,
   ii) Baking powder,
   iii) Baking soda,
   iv) Viscosity batter.

10. Define yeast and its types.
11. Describe the used of egg in cookery.
12. Define herbs and spices.
13. Explain the following terms:
    i) Meringues
    ii) Types of vinegars
    iii) Marinates
    iv) Binding agents
14. Which herbs and spices are best used for the following items :
    i) Veal
    ii) Lamb
    iii) Pork
    iv) Beef
    v) Egg dishes
    vi) Fish
    vii) Breads
    viii) Beverages
    ix) soups
    x) Carrots
15. Explain the following herbs and spices with their traditional ethnic used and with their taste and aroma:
    i) Anise seed
    ii) Basil
    iii) Caraway seeds
    iv) Cayenne pepper
    v) Chives
    vi) Coriander
    vii) Thyme
    viii) Rose marry
    ix) Fennel
    x) Horseradish
    xi) Mace
    xii) Clove
    xiii) Mint

xiv) Oregano

xv) Paprika

xvi) Tarragon

16. Explain the different varieties of cabbage.
17. Name the 20 vegetables with its types and its boiling techniques.
18. Name the five dried vegetables beans with their used.
19. Name the different varieties of squash.
20. Explain the different varieties of bulbs vegetables.
21. Name and explain the any five specialty vegetables.
22. Name the 20 varieties of potatoes and 10 classical potatoes preparation with their ingredients.
23. Write the guidelines for the proper doneness of vegetable.
24. Write the tips on how to preserve the vitamin and mineral content of vegetables.
25. Explain the major areas of taste of human tongue with the help of tongue diagram.
26. Explain the seasoning and its types with their characteristics.
27. Write the basic guidelines for seasoning foods.
28. Explain the term texture and its various types.
29. Explain the different cut off vegetables.
30. What is the temperature effect on the sensibility of taste.

STATE TRUE AND FALSE

- The foundation ingredients cannot be liquid or a solid
- It's essential to have complete and proper knowledge ingredients to prepare a colorful dish.
- Salt has physical effect gluten of floor in reasonable quantity
- Too much liquid make food not soggy as in case of water cakes or pudding
- Sugar is also used as a preservative.
- Binding Agent_are used to form a mixture of ingredients into a cohesive mask
- The conversation of oil into fats is brought about by the hydrogenation process.
- The chief acids are unsaturated fatty acids are of oleic nature.
- The extracting fat from fatty tissues is called rendering of fat.
- The common leaving agents are air, water and CO_2.

- Yeast is a microscope unicellular plant
- The taste and acceptability of food depends to a very great extent on the correct amount of flavouring and seasoning.
- Any acidic material added to an egg mixture well to produce firm
- Soft Meringues have four table spoon of sugar for each egg.
- A longer whipping time is required hard meringue
- The time required for soft boiled eggs about to 10 minutes
- The time required for hard boiled eggs about to 15 minutes
- Frozen herbs may be either directly frozen 0 to 10° Fahrenheit
- Some spice contain antioxidants, components which slow down the removal of their essence by the introduction of Oxygen
- Cider Vinegar is made from potatoes.
- Allspice is pungent and fragrant.
- Bay Leaves are grown in the Mediterranean region.
- Caraway Seed has a pungent aroma and a distinctly sweet but tangy flavour
- Chives have a mild, onion like flavour, with a hint of garlic.
- Mace is more pungent and sweeter than nut Meg.
- Broccoli available in market in 4 colours.
- Okra is also available in red colour.
- Enoki is a variety of tomatoes
- Black truffles called the black diamond from France.
- Paysanne very thin slices of vegetables no larger than 6mm/¼-inch square.

KEY TERMS

- Acid
- Aroma
- Coagulation
- Flavour
- Flavouring
- Leaveners
- Meringues
- Mineral
- Raw material
- Seasoning
- Sensation.
- Taste
- Vegetables
- Vitamin
- Yeast

Chapter 4

Methods of Cooking

After studying this chapter, the student must know :

- Principles of cooking food
- Types of fuels
- Various methods of cooking
- Effect of food on heat
- Ways to leading the decomposition of food
- Solving difficulties
- Cooking effects on food
- Food for health

PRINCIPLES OF COOKING FOOD

Those substances which produce energy on burning in presence of oxygen are termed as fuels (not in case of electricity). Fuel is any material that is burned or altered in order to obtain energy and to heat or to move an object. Fuel releases its energy either through a chemical reaction means, such as conduction, or nuclear means, such as nuclear fission or nuclear fusion. An important property of a useful fuel is that its energy can be stored to be released only when needed, and that the release is controlled in such a way that the energy can be harnessed to produce work. Thus a fuel is a substance that release unable energy through an oxidation reduction, reaction with an oxidizer.

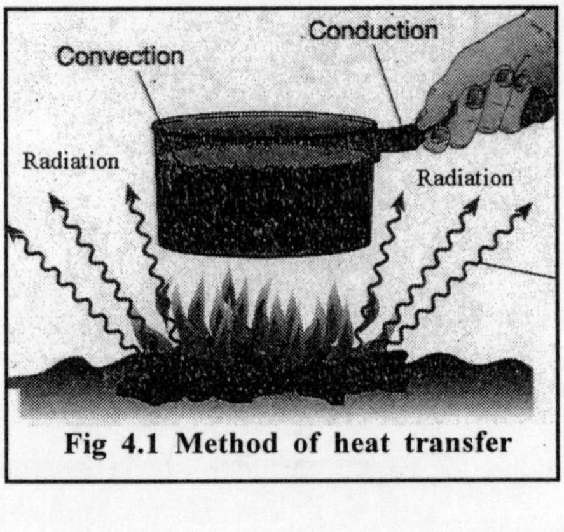

Fig 4.1 Method of heat transfer

There are three methods of heat transfer:

1) Conduction
2) Radiation
3) Conventions.

1. Conduction

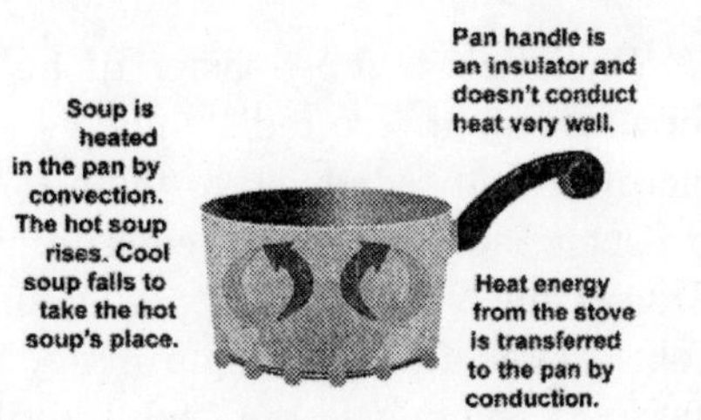

Fig 4.2 The method of conduction heat transfer

Conduction is the transfer of heat by direct contact of particles of matter. The transfer of energy could be primarily by elastic impact as in fluids or by free electron diffusion as predominant in metals or phonon vibration as predominant in insulators. In other words, heat is transferred by conduction when adjacent atoms vibrate against one another, or as electrons move from atom to atom. Conduction is greater in solids, where atoms are in constant contact. In liquids (except liquid metals) and gases, the molecules are usually further apart, giving a lower chance of molecules colliding and passing on thermal energy. Example: putting your hand on a stove burner. The amount of energy transferred depends on how conductive the material is. Metals are good conductors, so they are used to transfer energy from the stove to the food in pots and pans. Air is the best insulator, so good insulating products try to trap air and not allow it to move.

2. Convections

Fig. 4.3 The method of convection heat transfer

Convection is the transfer of heat energy through a moving fluid at various temperatures. It is mainly a combination of diffusion and the bulk motion of molecules. When the mass of the fluid is in contact with a hot surface, its molecules expand and scatter, causing the mass of fluid to become less dense. When this happens, the fluid is displaced vertically or horizontally while the cooler fluid gets denser and sinks. Thus the hotter volume transfers heat towards the cooler volumes of that fluid. Example: holding your hand over a stove burner. In meteorology, we speak of convection predominantly as that caused by rising currents of warm air. We refer to all other mass motions of air as advection.

There are two types of Convective Heat Transfer:

a. **Natural Convection**: Is when the fluid motion is caused by the density variations that result from the temperature distributions in heat transfer and gravitational forces. These variations in density can be described by buoyancy forces (body of force proportional to density gradient), thus buoyancy is the driving force for natural convection. The change in density of the boundary layer while heating will cause the fluid to rise and be replaced by a cooler fluid. Example: Transfer of heat from hot water to a radiator in a room.

b **Forced Convection**: Unlike natural convection, forced convection is not related to the use of heat transfer between fluids but rather an external source such as pumps and fans. It creates an artificially induced convection current

3. Radiation

Radiation is the transfer of heat energy through empty space. All objects with a temperature above absolute zero radiate energy at a rate equal to their emissivity multiplied by the rate at which energy would radiate from them if they were a black body. No medium is necessary for radiation to occur; radiation works even in and through a perfect vacuum. The energy from the Sun travels through the vacuum of space before warming the earth. Example: heat felt when standing away from a large fire on a calm night. Everything that has a temperature above absolute zero radiates energy. Radiation is not "felt" until it is absorbed by a substance. It does not require a medium to transfer energy through as do conduction and convection

TYPES OF FUELS

1. Gas fuel.
2. Solid fuel.
3. Electricity.
4. Liquid fuel.

1. Gas fuel

Natural gas is a mixture of hydrocarbons mainly methane that is extracted from underground reserve natural gas is compressed natural gas or liquid petroleum gas or propane.Its contains at least 90% of propane 2-5% of butane and higher hydrocarbons and the balance of ethane and propane. Most fuel gases are composed in whole or in part of the combustibles hydrogen, carbon monoxide, methane, ethane, propane, butane, and oil vapors and, in some instances, of mixtures containing the inverts nitrogen, carbon dioxide, and water vapour

Benefits of gas fuel

- Generally produce much less CO_2
- The heating capacity is not limited as compare to electricity
- Generally it is much cheaper than portable electric heater
- Less pollution
- Doesn't leave residue after use
- Easy to handle
- Controllable through regulation.
- is the most economical energy choice
- is a highly reliable

Disadvantages

- Not available at every time
- Leakage of gas can be dangerous

- It comes under fertile fuel which can be going finish one day.
- Produce combustible gasses
- Managing the gas is difficult and its needs regular serviced from time to time.
- Needs to store at safe place

2. Solid Fuel

Solid fuel refers to various types of solid material that are used as fuel to produce energy and provide heating, usually released through combustion. Solid fuels include wood (see wood fuel), charcoal, peat, coal, hexamine fuel tablets, and pellets made from wood (refer wood pellets), corn, wheat, rye and other grains. Solid-fuel rocket technology also uses solid fuel (refer solid propellants). Solid fuels have long been used by humanity to create fire. Coal was the fuel source which enabled the industrial revolution, from firing furnaces, to running steam engines. Wood was also extensively used to run steam locomotives. Both peat and coal are still used in electricity generation today.

The use of some solid fuels (example. coal) is restricted or prohibited in some urban areas, due to unsafe levels of toxic emissions. The use of other solid fuels such as wood is increasing as heating technology and the availability of good quality fuel improves. In some areas, smokeless coal is often the only solid fuel used. In Ireland, peat briquettes are used as smokeless fuel. They are also used to start a coal fire.

Fire wood: It should be well seasoned (left to dry for at least two summers). Hard wood contain more energy than soft wood and burns longer and more staidly but it also harder to light.

Coal: its hard block mineral used as a fuel.It has high energy content than wood. It can be burnt in a slow combustion. Mostly use in barbeque for grilling food.

Benefits of coal:

- Wood and coal are easily available almost everywhere wood is economically to use.
- Produce the least amount of CO_2 when comparisons with solid other fuel.
- No heavy cost of installation

Disadvantages:

- You need space to stored wood or coal.
- Difficult to maintain the temperature.
- Leave ashes after burning
- Solid fuel are less energy efficient as compared to electric and gas
- They produce higher amount of combustion gases that needs chimney
- The smoke from wood and coal fire contributes to air pollution.
- And then, ecological problems: the burning of coal is very polluting. Like oil, coal contains sulphur that gives off sulphur dioxide when it is burnt. In the atmosphere, this becomes

sulphuric acid, by oxidation, an irritant for the lungs and the main component of "acid rain", so harmful to forests. The burning of coal also gives off oxides of nitrogen (No2). Several efficient processes exist for sulphur and nitrogen cleaning of gas emissions from the burning of coal. Action can be taken both upstream, before burning, or downstream, by treating the fumes. In the latter case, the proportion of So2 can be reduced by 90% and that of nitrogen oxides by 80%.

3. Electricity

Source of electricity which cannot be heard, smell, tasted, seem or felt. It is very safe source of energy.But its misuses cause's serious injuries or can kill. It cannot be stored other than in battery.

Benefits:

- It is available almost everywhere
- Sometimes it is also generated from renewable source such as solar, hydro wind.
- Electricity does not produce pollution.

Disadvantages:

- Heating with portable electric heater can be relatively expensive.
- Power plants that generate electricity by burning fossils fuel produce considerate amount of air pollution.
- If there is any power cut cure cannot do everything.
- Heavy installation cost involved.

4. Liquid fuel

Liquid fuels are those combustible or energy-generating molecules that can be harnessed to create mechanical energy, usually producing kinetic energy; they also must take the shape of their container. Most liquid fuels, in widespread use, are or derived from fossil fuels; however, there are several types, such as hydrogen fuel (for automotive uses), which are also categorized as a liquid fuel. It is the fumes of Liquid fuels that are flammable instead of the fluid.

Fossil fuels: Fossil fuels are also generally liquid fuels. The most notable of these is gasoline. Although unproven, it is generally accepted that they formed from the fossilized remains of dead plants and animals by exposure to heat and pressure in the Earth's crust.

Gasoline: is the most widely used liquid fuel. Gasoline, as it is known in United States and Canada, or petrol in India, Britain, Australia, New Zealand, South Africa and many English-speaking countries, is made of hydrocarbon molecules forming aliphatic compounds, or chains of carbons with hydrogen atoms attached. However, many aromatic compounds (carbon chains forming rings) such as benzene are found naturally in gasoline and cause the health risks associated with prolonged exposure to the fuel.

Production of gasoline is achieved by distillation of crude oil. The desirable liquid is separated from the crude oil in refineries. Crude oil is extracted from the ground in several processes, the most commonly seen may be beam pumps. To create gasoline, petroleum must first be removed from crude oil.

Gasoline itself is actually not burned, but the fumes it creates ignite, causing the remaining liquid to evaporate. Gasoline is extremely volatile and easily combusts, making any leakage extremely dangerous. Gasoline for sale in most countries carries an octane rating. Octane is a measure of the resistance of gasoline to combusting prematurely, known as knocking. The higher the octane rating, the harder it is to burn the fuel, which allows for a higher compression ratio. Engines with a higher compression ratio produce more power (such as in race car engines). However, such engines actually require a higher octane fuel

Kerosene: It is paraffin oil comes from petroleum which is used as fuel.

Benefits:

- It is cheaper source of energy.
- Easily available in market.
- Does not leave any ash.
- It should be easy to transport
- Easy to store
- It should be cheap
- Easily available
- It should be moderate ignition temperature
- It should not leave any residue or ash.
- It should not produces any poisonous gases

Disadvantages

- It has low energy efficiency.
- It produces bad smell of burning.
- It stored in available in air light container.

METHOD OF COOKING

Food preparation is an important step in meeting the nutritional needs of the family. Food has to be pleasing in appearance and taste in order to be consumed. Foods like fruits, vegetables and nuts can be eaten raw but most foods are cooked to bring about desirable changes. The process of subjecting food to the action of heat is termed as cooking

A) Boiling

Food's cooked surrounding by boiling or simmering liquid.Only sufficient liquid and no more

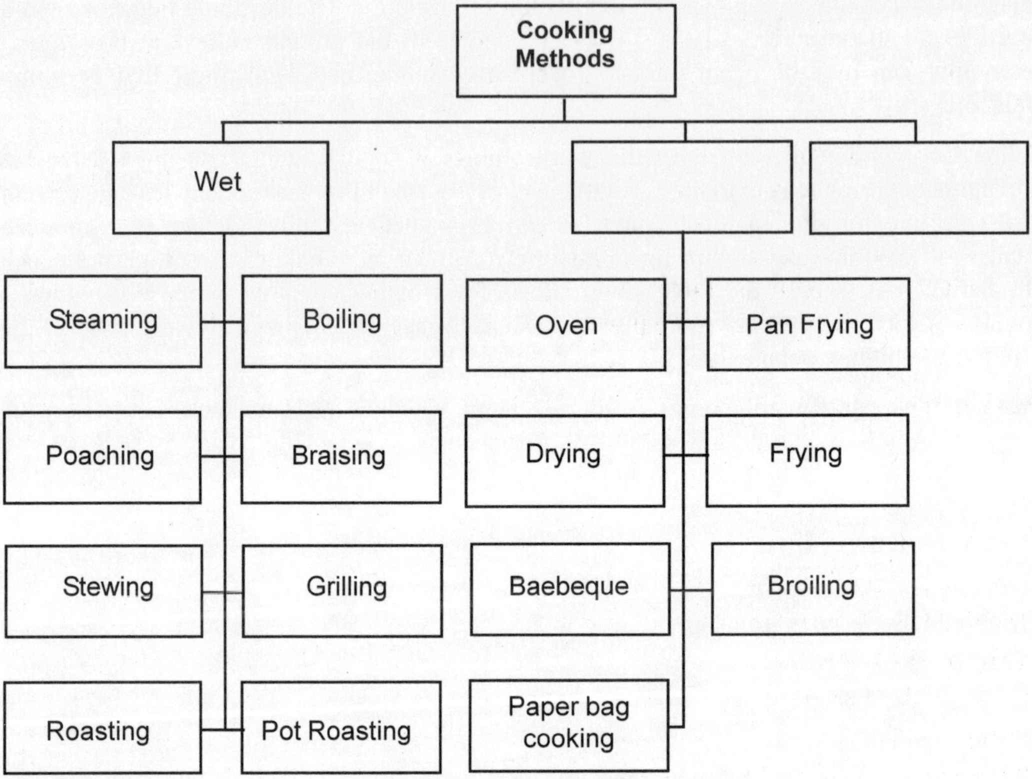

Fig 4.4 Different methods of cooking's

should be used. Gently boiling helps to breakdown tuff fibers, structure of certain food which would be less tender. Is the cooking of food in liquid at boiling point. This could be water, milk or bones stock. Boiling of eggs shown in Fig 4.5. Boiling is a method of cooking foods by just immersing them in water at 100° C and maintaining the water at that temperature till the food is tender. Rice, egg, *dal*, meat, roots and tubers are cooked by boiling.Generally speaking vegetables grown above the ground are cooked in boiling salted water and vegetable grown below the ground are started with cold water with expections of new potatoes and baby carrots.

Fig 4.5 The Boiling of Egg

Advantages

1. Helps to break the tuff fibers.
2. Nutritious, well flavoured stock can be produce.

3. It is appropriate for large scale cookery and is economic on fuel.
4. Simple method - It does not require special skill and equipment.
5. Uniform cooking can be achieved.

Disadvantages

1. Continuous excessive boiling leads to damage in the structure and texture of food.
2. Loss of heat, liable nutrients such as B and C vitamins if the water is discarded.
3. Time consuming - Boiling takes more time to cook food and fuel may be wasted.
4. Loss of colour - water soluble pigments may be lost.

Methods of Boiling

There are two ways of boiling :

1. Place the food into boiling liquid, reboil, than reduce the heat for gentle boiling to take place, thus is know as simmering.
2. Cover food with cold liquid, bring to the boils, then reduce heat to allow food to simmer.

B) Poaching

Cooking slowly in minimum amount of liquid which will never be boil but will be never boil but will be under boiling point.The cooking of food in the required amount of liquid at just below boiling point. Poaching of prawns in poaching liquid as shown in Fig. 4.6. This involves cooking in the minimum amount of liquid at temperatures of 80° C-85° C that is below the boiling point. Egg and fish can be poached.

Advantages

1. Easy to digest.
2. Safe to eat
3. A suitable tender texture
4. No special equipment is needed.
5. Quick method of cooking and therefore saves fuel.
6. Poached foods are easily digested since no fat is added.

Fig 4.6 The Poaching of Prawns in Liquid

Disadvantages

1. Poached foods may not appeal to everybody as they are bland in taste.

2. Food can be scorched if water evaporates due to careless monitoring.
3. Water soluble nutrients may be leached into the water.

Method of poaching

There are two ways of poaching :

1. **Shallow poaching** : Foods example cuts of fish and chicken to be cooked by this method are cooked in a minimum liquid that is water, stock, milk or wine.The liquid should never be boiled.
2. **Deep Poaching**: Eggs are poached through this method.Eggs are cooked in approxiametly 8cm of gently simmering water.

C. Stewing

Fig 4.7 Stewing of vegetables

This is a very gentle method of cooking in a closed pan using only small quantity of covered with liquid, the food should not more than half covered with liquid. Stewing is the slow cooking food cut into pieces and cooked in the minimum amount of liquid (water, stock or sauces); the food and liquid are served together. Stewing is done in electric steamer as shown in Fig. 4.7 It refers to the simmering of food in a pan with a tight fitting lid using small quantities of liquid to cover only half the food. This is a slow method of cooking. The liquid is brought to boiling point and the heat is reduced to maintain simmering temperatures (82°C – 90°C). The food above the liquid is cooked by the steam generated within the pan, apple, meat along with roots, vegetables and legumes are usually stewed.

Advantages

1. Tenderized tough food.
2. Slow cooking result in very little evaporation
3. Loss of nutrients is avoided as water used for cooking is not discarded.
4. Flavour is retained.

Disadvantages

1. The process is time consuming and there is wastage of fuel.

D. Steaming

The food to be cooked surrounding by steam from fast boiling water (the food can be kept in a perforated plate with holes or basin). So that boiling water doesn't come contract with food. Meat and vegetable cooked by steaming as shown in Fig. 4.8. It is a method of cooking food in steam generated from vigorously boiling water in a pan. The food to be steamed is placed in a container and is not in direct contact with the water or liquid. *Idli* is made by steaming. Vegetables can also be steamed.

Fig 4.8 The Meat and vegetable cooked by steaming

Advantages

1. Less chance of burning and scorching.
2. Texture of food is better as it becomes light and fluffy. *Example* Idli.
3. Cooking time is less and fuel wastage is less.
4. Steamed foods like idli and udappam contain less fat and are easily digested and are good for children, aged and for therapeutic diets.
5. Nutrient loss is minimized.

Disadvantages

1. Steaming equipment is required.
2. This method is limited to the preparation of selected foods.

E. Braising

Combining method of roasting and stewing in a pan with a light fitting lid the meat should be sealed by browning on all side. Braising of bones as shown in Fig. 4.9. Braising is a combined method of roasting and stewing in a pan with a tight fitting lid. Flavourings and seasonings are added and food is allowed to cook gently. Food preparations prepared by combination methods are:

Uppuma - Roasting and boiling.

Cutlet - Boiling and deep frying.

Fig 4.9 The Braising of bones

Vermicilli payasam - Roasting and simmering

Fig 4.10 The Broiling of vegetable

F. Broiling

Cooking on direct heat on a hot metal griddle or pan with no oil is used. Broiling of vegetable as shown in Fig. 4.10

G. Grilling

Cooking by dry heat the food is either cook on a hot iron griddle or under hot grill bar or between hot grills bars. Grilling of beef steak in griddle as shown in Fig. 4.11 Grilling or broiling refers to the cooking of food by exposing it to direct heat. In this method food is placed above or in between a red hot surface. Papads, corn, phulkas, chicken can be prepared by this method. Grilling can be done in followings ways :

Fig 4.11 Grilling of beef steak

1. Grilling over heat.
2. Griliing under salalamander or hot grills bars.
3. Grilling between hot bars.
4. Infrared grilling.

Advantages

1. Enhances flavour, appearance and taste of the product.
2. It requires less time to cook.
3. Minimum fat is used.

Disadvantages

1. Constant attention is required to prevent charring buring.

H. Baking

The food to be cooked in surrounding by hot air is closed in oven. The action of dry heat is modified by steam while arises from food while cooking. In this method, the food gets cooked in an oven or oven like appliance by dry heat. The temperature range maintained in an oven is 120° C-260° C. The food is usually kept uncovered in a container greased with a fat coated paper. Bread, cake, biscuits, pastries and meat are prepared by this method.

Advantages

1. Baking lends a unique baked flavour to foods.
2. Foods become light and fluffy – cakes, custards, bread.
3. Certain foods can be prepared only by this method – bread, cakes.
4. Uniform and bulk cooking can be achieved. Example. Bun, bread.
5. Flavour and texture are improved.
6. Variety of dishes can be made.

Disadvantages

1. Special equipment like oven is required.
2. Baking skills are necessary to obtain a product with ideal texture, flavour and colour characteristics.
3. Careful monitoring needed to prevent scorching.

I. Paper bag cooking

Food is highly sealed in oil greased proof paper or foil. No steamed escaped during cooking and maximum natural flavour and nutritive value is retained.

J. Roasting

The term roasting was originally applied to the cooking of large pieces of meat, on a turning spit over an open fire. Roasting on lamb is shown in Fig. 4.12. In this method food is cooked in a heated metal or frying pan without covering it. *Example* Groundnut. The three types of roasting are as follows :

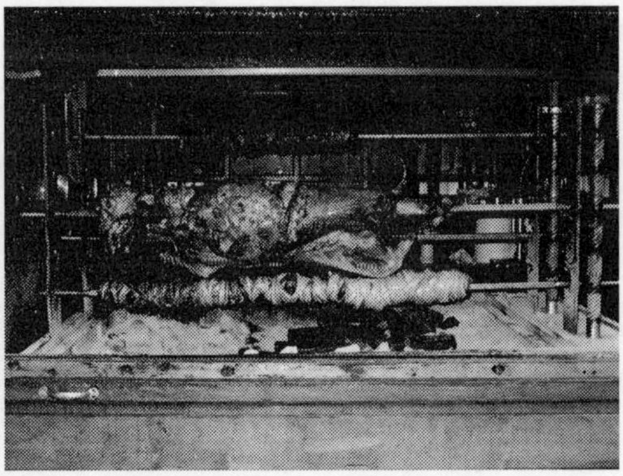

Fig 4.12 Roasting of lamb

1. **Spit roasting** : Food to cooked in direct contact with clear bright fire. The food is often basted with fat to avoid is getting dry turned to insure even cooking.The food cook in this manner has special flavour and which is very desirable.
2. **Oven roasting**: Done in closed oven with fat the food is cooked in a oven.Intially the oven is kept very hot for the meat to get coloured and later the heat is reduce and than meat is cooked slowly this doen for the meat cooked throughly.

3. **Pot roasting** : It is done from the small joints of meat and if an oven is not available a thick heavy pan is essential. First the joint of meat is brown in pan with some of fat and after browing little of water to cooked that meat.Than pan is than covered with lid and cooked on slow fire until the meat is cooked.

Advantages

1. Quick method of cooking.
2. It improves the appearance, flavour and texture of the food.
3. Spices are easily powdered if they are first roasted.

Disadvantages

1. Food can be scorched due to carelessness.
2. Roasting denatures proteins reducing their availability.

K. Sautéing

Sautéing is a method in which food is lightly tossed in little oil just enough to cover the base of the pan. The pan is covered with a lid and the flame or intensity of heat is reduced. The food is allowed to cook till tender in its own steam. The food is tossed occasionally, or turned with a spatula to enable all the pieces to come in contact with the oil and get cooked evenly.

The product obtained by this method is slightly moist and tender but without any liquid or gravy. Foods cooked by sautéing are generally vegetables which are used as side dishes in a menu. Sautéing can be combined with other methods to produce variety in meals.

Advantages

1. Takes less time.
2. Simple technique.
3. Minimum oil is used.

Disadvantages

1. Constant attention is needed as there is chance of scorching or burning.

L. Frying

In this method, the food to be cooked is brought into contact with larger amount of hot fat. When food is totally immersed in hot oil, it is called deep fat frying. Samosa, chips, *pakoda* are examples of deep fat fried foods. In shallow fat frying, only a little fat is used and the food is turned in order that both sides are browned. Example Omlette, cutlets, parathas.

There are two types of frying methods:

1. **Shallow fat frying**: In this method food is impressed in little fat.
2. **Deep fat frying** : In this method food is impressed in large quantity of fat.

Advantages

1. Very quick method of cooking.
2. The calorific values of food are increased since fat is used as the cooking media.
3. Frying lends a delicious flavour and attractive appearance to foods.
4. Taste and texture are improved.

Disadvantages

1. Careful monitoring is required as food easily gets charred when the smoking temperature is not properly maintained.
2. The food may become soggy due to too much oil absorption.
3. Fried foods are not easily digested.4. Repeated use of heated oils will have ill effects on health

M. Microwave Cooking

Microwaves are electromagnetic waves of radiant energy with wave lengths in the range of 250 × 106 to 7.5 × 109 angstroms. The most commonly used type of microwave generator is an electronic device called a magnetron which generates radiant energy of high frequency. A simple microwave oven consists of a metal cabinet into which the magnetron is inserted. The cabinet is equipped with a metal fan that distributes the microwave throughout the cabinet. Food placed in the oven is heated by microwaves from all directions.

Moist foods and liquid foods can be rapidly heated in such ovens. Food should be kept in containers made of plastic, glass or china ware which do not contain metallic substances.

These containers are used because they transmit the microwaves but do not absorb or reflect them.

Advantages

1. Quick method – 10 times faster than conventional method. So loss of nutrients can be minimized.
2. Only the food gets heated and the oven does not get heated.
3. Food gets cooked uniformly.
4. Leftovers can be reheated without changing the flavour and texture of the product.

5. Microwave cooking enhances the flavour of food because it cooks quickly with little or no water.

Disadvantages

1. Baked products do not get a brown surface.
2. Microwave cooking cannot be used for simmering, stewing or deep frying.
3. Flavour of all ingredients do not blend well as the cooking time is too short

EFFECTS OF HEAT ON FOOD

Undesirable effect of our cooking

Proteins: - get denatured toughens or become string and ultimately disintegrates.

Vitamins C, vitamin B and thyme are destroyed and leached fruit and vegetable soften two much and unpalatable flavour are lost and changed and destroy muscles fabric and connective tissues becomes specially dry and hard and there is general loss of nutrient flavour form texture and colours.

Red colour changed to dirty blue or people colorific pigments become yellowish or dark green white become goes to grey and yellow

Food is composed of the following five nutrients mainly carbohydrates, fats, proteins minerals and vitamins.

The action of heat in protein:-

It coagulates and sets when heated the white of an egg is an example the coagulation process help in keeping the nourishing within the food its sealed in by the formation of a coat on the outside and increases digestibility. The protein, of meat is myosin, of egg is ovalbumin, of wheat is gluten and of pulp is legumen, is coagulated by heat. Protein gets denatured on heating sometime, its desired or some times its not coagulation follows denaturalization is caused by structure alteration that is when the structural organization is distracted during cooking the protein of the muscles fiber start to coagulated and toughen and at the same time collagen is hydrolyzed and soften the characteristics colour of the meat is caused by the muscles pigment called mioglobin heat brings about colour change from pink brown or grey the surface of the cooked meat browns as a result of partial break down of proteins, fats and pigment etc. Mioglobin is similar to hemoglobin when it under goes oxidation with chlorites or nitrates the iron portion changes to difference valence that is from pheros to ferric and the colour changes to desire red colour to brown.

Connective tissue: There are two connective tissue proteins.

1. Collagen
2. Elastin

Collagen is a structural protein knows as white connective, tissue, collagens fibers are arranged parallel to each that or may run remendelle in all directing each collagen molecules consists of three fibers gelatin molecule on heating the three trends of collagen will be separated two individuals gelatin strength. It's this conversion of gelatin that causes less tenders cuts of meat to increase in tenders when cooked very slow in moist heat hence when boiling protein food such as meat and fish put them in hot water when roasting meat put them in an even which is fairly hot and then reduce the heat.

Elastin: is made up of very strong and elastic blanch fiber since elastin extremely restinance to change by heat or acid neglezable to change occur on heating. It only shrinks on normal temperature.

Action heat on carbohydrates

Starch granules do not dissolve readily in cold water but form suspension when granules heated in water or placed in hot water they begin to swell at a temperature know as the gelatinization temperature on further heating the granules becomes to swell as the starch changes absorbs moisture and begins to uncoil from the lightly packed configuration eventually the starch changes absorb so much water as they uncoil that the water is bound into a vicious paste no discernable granules remaining its form a solid when cold but transfer into a gel with water trapped in the starch changes this process its form as gelatinization of starch the starch chain is also vulnerable to dry heat it breaks down and fragment produce is dextrin dry heat decomposition of starch produces. The familiar toasting colour sweetish in colour and the crust of bread when sugar is heated by itself or in a highly concentrated solution the dry sugar melts to colorless liquids that soon began to develop a brown colour. It undergoes a complex decomposition process a darkening of colour associated with a pleasant yet pungent aroma and slightly bitter taste. On further heating the pleasing characteristic of caramel aroma changes to that of brown sugar and becomes a hard carbon like mask with a disagreeable flavour the chemical changes that occur are the sucrose, molecules is hydrolyzed to glucose and fructose and these monosaccharide are partial decomposed with the evolution of water into acidic form of sugar. The change sucrose to glucose fructose is to invert sugar. The presence of invert the solubility of sugar increase and its tends to recrystallised very slowly. In version raised the boiling point and lower the freezing point of sugar solution of invert sugar is highly more digestible and absorb sugar on boiling is passes through regular stages before it becomes caramelized at 163° C it passes through the following stages.

Small thread	102° C
Large thread	103° C
Pearl thread	106° C
Soft bowl	114° C
Heard bowl	120° C
Soft crack	143° C
Hard crack	156° C
Caramel crack	163 to 177° C

EFFECT OF HEAT ON FAT

Fat are triglycerides :- Fats are used as cooking medium fats melt when it come in contact with heat, cooking oil and fat is decomposed in the cooking process and this decomposition leads to distortion in cooking quality if the oil is kept in used for a long time at temperature in the region of 230 to 260° C melt oils will emit a thin blue haze which is a sign of that decomposition is started as the oil is used for looking detoration caused a study decreased in the smoke point until the smoke point falls below the temperature of cooking.

Ways leading to decomposition:

Pyrolysis is or thermal break down is the action of heating the oil whether not it is in contact of food causes the breakdown of the molecular structure.

1. **Oxidation:** Reaction of hot oil surface with oxygen in the air causes the molecular break down and ultimately the development of rancidity this stage occur whenever oil is heated.
2. **Hydrolysis:** - It is break down by water expected from food as water is boiled in large quantity from food while frying some of the water will tend to decompose the fat.
3. **Reaction with food residue**: - Any food fragment left in the oil after cooking will undergo chemical reaction particular in the oil is heating again without the residue been removed.
4. **Reaction with metal:** - Metals like cooper and alumni reacts with acid expelled with Food and act as a catalyst on oxidation and break down and decomposes the fat.

Triglycerides under goes hydrolicellis and pyrollesis as the cases may be break down into glycerol and fatty acid the glycerol freed by liquid hydrolysis on further pyrolysics is decomposed thought dehydration. Than a Caroline the decomposition is the product is the volatile irrupting compound its formation is know by the acrid fumes coming out from the heated fat if we continued to heat the fat at the smoked point the fat polymerizes and the polymeric decomposition products increases the vecoity of the medium and

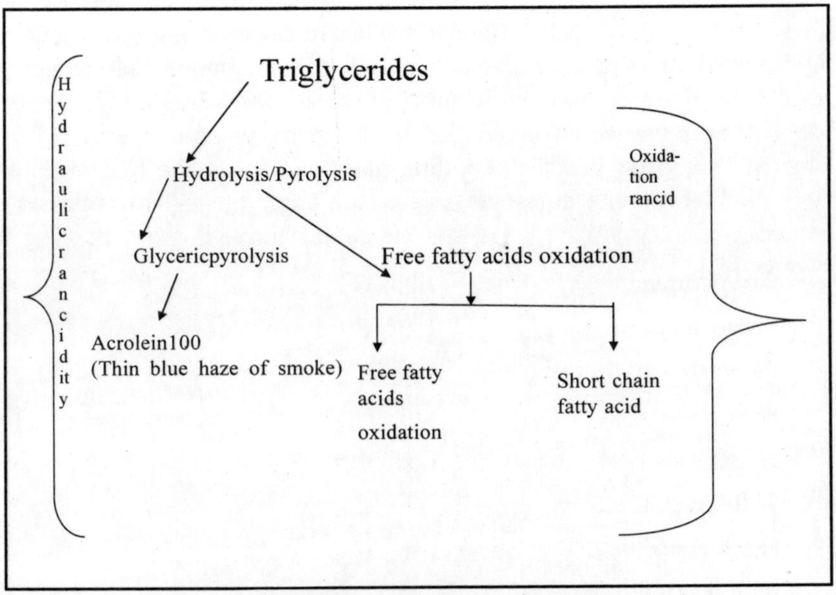

Fig 4.13 The Effect of heat on fat

it becomes thick gummy and frothy and is no longer fit for use with continues uses fat detroy because of excess temperature moisture air and presence of carbonized crumbs and small residues of food to appoint when it will just bubbles in the pan too weak to perform the function of frying.

Action of heat on minerals

There is no appreciable loss of minerals due to cooking accepting when the cooking liquor is thrown out some mineral are made readily available by cooking.

Action of heat on vitamin

Vitamin C is only vitamin which becomes unstable when heated although care full cooking help to retain some of it vitamin A and Vitamin D are not destroyed during cooking if cooked at high temperature for example baking of biscuits and manufacture of breakfast cereals by addition of baking soda.

SOLVING DIFFICULTIES

In the main, therefore, this section sets out to solve cookery difficulties by stating briefly and concisely cause and effect-or, more correctly, effect and cause.

Here you will find a lifetime of experienced condensed into a few pages of helpful fact. Queries sent from every type of cook the world over are here set down plainly and answered in language that a child of ten could understand. Master the points explained here, and –although you may know little of the academic side of the chemistry of cookery- you will be practically equipped to grapple with the day-by-day problems of the kitchen. In short, you will be well on the way towards becoming an excellent and practical cook. The heights you reach will be bounded only by your ambition and your diligence in following these instructions. But before concerning ourselves with specific reasons of failure in the various branches of cookery we will consider briefly the various methods of cooking bringing to light the "reasons why that lie behind them". For cookery most decidedly is a very exact science. To obtain results you must follow the rules. Details may vary-but the principles behind the method never. Once these principles are thoroughly understood, cooking becomes a pleasant task without thought of failure.

RETAINING FLAVOUR

To return first of all to our definition of the aim and object of cookery. "To retain nourishment and flavour… or to extract it." There is in meat- one of the main forms of food in this country- a large proportion of albumen which hardens, just as the white of an egg does, when it comes in contact with heat. That is why, when we want to keep the flavour in meat, we put it into boiling water, causing the albumen on the outside to harden and so form a protective jacket that will prevent the goodness escaping. If, however, we continued this process of fast cooking, the whole of the joint would harden and would be most indigestible, if not uneatable.

Therefore, the wise cook slackens the heat as soon as the water has boiled for two or three minutes, allowing is just to simmer gently until the food is tender. Remember that "to simmer" means that the water should be just moving gently, not bubbling fast or rising in the saucepan. The same principle applies to roasting, baking, and frying. With all these methods our desire is to keep in the goodness. It is there of no use to put food into a lukewarm oven, under a cold grill or in a cold frying pan. Inevitably the result would be tasteless meat because the thin coating of albumen would not be given an opportunity to form.

The oven must be the correct heat when the food is put in. Similarly, the grill or the frying pan must be made hot first. Then the juices will be sealed inside, the outside nicely browned, and the inside moist and tender. For this reason we do not stick a fork in meat when turning it while grilling or frying as the fork would pierce the albumen and allow the juices to escape. The exception to this rule is salt meat. If it were put in boiling water the salt would be all sealed inside and the meat made hard in consequence. So we put salt meat in cold water. Now for the contrast. When we wish to extract flavour and goodness we put meat in cold water and simmer it the whole time until the meat is quite flavourless and devoid of nourishment. This method applies to the making of beef-tea, stock, broth or soup.

RULES FOR FRYING

The first principle applies when frying food covered in egg and bread crumbs or batter. If the fat is not hot enough the egg will not solidify. Instead, it will mix will the fat and the result will be flabby, patchy fish or meat. If, on the other hand, the fat is boiling, the albumen in the egg will at once form a coating just as it does in meat.

But remember that fat - unlike water - is not at boiling point when bubbling and spluttering. It is just when these finishes - when the fat becomes still and blue smoke begins to raise that the boiling point is reached. Deep fat frying is always to be recommended for any food covered with egg and breadcrumbs. It is absolutely necessary when batter is the covering. With this style of frying the whole object is covered at once. Therefore, being entirely coated with its protective jacket, it cannot absorb the fat it is fried in and become greasy. Do not imagine that deep fat frying is expensive. On the other hand, it is really economical; for if the fat is carefully strained after using (keeping the fat that fish has been fried in separate), it can be used many times. Whereas, if only a small quantity of fat is used, the little that remains is generally not considered worth saving.

Deep fat frying also has the advantage that it needs so little attention as the food is not inclined to burn, the temperature being even all over. This method is used for all kinds of food encased in egg and breadcrumbs or batter, such as cutlets, fish, fritters and beignets. With potato ribbons, cubes or chips, and all other small pieces, a frying basket should always be used. For shallow- or dry frying, as it is sometimes called-very little fat is used. Indeed, with meat that has a fair proportion of fat or an oily fish such as a kipper, little or no fat is needed. But the pan must be quite hot when the meat or fish is put in and the food should be turned, so that each side is quickly browned. Then the heat can be reduced and a moderate heat maintained until it is sufficiently cooked.

Sautéing is really only another form of frying, generally used for food that has already been cooked, such as potatoes. They are just tossed in very little fat until delicately brown. Grilling or broiling in these days of gas and electric grills is one of the easiest ways of cooking and certainly one of the most nourishing. The action of direct heat seals up the juices immediately and an appetizing meal can be produced in a few minutes. Braising is one of the best methods of cooking for the chef who has to practice economy. It really combines the principles of both roasting and stewing and has the advantage of making cheap cuts of meat or old birds delicious and tender.

The meat is first browned in a little fat and then placed in a stew pan or casserole on vegetables. A little water or stock is added, the lid is put on, and the food is left to cook in the steam, the vegetables imparting flavour to the meat. Incidentally the casserole is a boon to the busy chef. Not only is it easily kept clean, but also the food can be served it, thus saving all the brother of dishing-up. Add to that the fact that the modern casserole is decorative as well as useful. The glass ones have the advantage that you can see how the dish is progressing without constantly lifting the lid. The only precaution necessary is to abstain from putting the dishes into cold water while they are hot. They are ideal for braising and for stews and made-up dishes of many kinds. You can also use them for cooking pies and tarts.

Roasting and baking are practically the same process nowadays; the main point is to keep the oven scrupulously clean. If a dish boils over or spills, make a point of cleaning out the oven before anything else is baked. The flavour of uncovered baked food is so easily spoilt. Steaming is an economical method of cooking. The nourishment is kept in the food and the cost of fuel is minimized, especially with a two- or three-tiered steamer, which only needs a gas or electric ring to cook a whole dinner. Stewing requires a low heat and slow simmering to make tough meat tender. The cheapest cuts can be cooked in this way and, if vegetables are added to the meat, a one-pot dinner that needs very little attention is procured. The usual fault is to add too much water. As the liquor is served with the meat it should be strong and good.

OBTAINING LIGHTNESS

In many branches of cookery lightness is of paramount importance - especially with soufflés, many puddings, pastry, and various types of cake and small cakes. To obtain this lightness it is essential that air is beaten into the mixture. Then, when these air bubbles come in contact with heat, they will expand and cause the mixture to rise. With a soufflé, for example, just as long as the dish remains hot (with the air bubbles expanded) the lightness is there. Directly the soufflé cools or comes in contact with very cold air it falls. The necessary air-lightness can be beaten into the white of eggs much more easily than into the yolks or any other ingredient. That is why, when we particularly want lightness, we separate the yolks from the whites and then beat them stiffly, which just means as full of air as possible. Now you see what makes the soufflé rise and the necessity for a hot oven so that the lightness you have introduced may remain.

Exactly the same principle applies to cakes. When they should be particularly light we beat the whites and yolks of eggs separately. In the case of sponge cakes that require this lightening we beat the eggs over warm water. The action of the heat causes big bubbles to rise. Try beating your eggs over cold water as an experiment and you will find that the air-bubbles are absent as there is no heat present to expand them.

Puff pastry is another example of the necessity of introducing air into the paste. That is why it is necessary to roll in short rolls, with a gentle action so as not to break the air-bubbles which can be clearly seen on the pastry. It explains, too, why we must never roll right to the edge of the pastry. That would mean that the bubbles would burst and the lightness be lost.

Similarly, we put puff pastry into a very hot oven to expand the air in it and make the pastry light. Now think a minute and you will realize the effect of opening the oven door before your cake or pudding has risen! Remember that effect is increased if you shut the door with a bang!

A practical appreciation of the common-sense reasons that lie behind these principles makes cookery so much more interesting. It is also so much easier to remember these points when one realizes that they are not just fads without any real justification. So much for the practical and scientific principles of cookery. They are essential—but not sufficient of themselves to make the perfect cook. She must at the same time keep several secondary objects always in view. First she must strive to make her handiwork give pleasure to the eye, garnishing her dishes simply in a way that adds to their appearance. Equally she must season her food with care and discretion so that it appeals to the palate. And, lastly, she must practice economy in the best sense of that misused word-spending every penny of her allowance to the utmost advantage and allowing no waste in here household. And the more she studies her subject the more she will find that cookery is not merely a household duty. It can be at the same time, an absorbing hobby and, unlike many pastimes; its cope will increase with the years and its interest last a life time.

COOKING EFFECT ON FOOD

The first, to retain the flavour and nourishment of food. The second, to extract it. There you have the fundamental difference between the various forms of cookery in a nutshell.

Most emphatically, the preparation of food is not a haphazard task. The old adage, "A good cook is born, not made, "has probably done more harm than good. Chefs with a bent for cooking have taken their gift for granted and not troubled to improve it. On the other hand, Chef who dislikes it has never faced the fact that cookery- like any other art based on science-can be learnt. There is no magic about the process. There are, however, very definite principles, every one of them bases on scientific fact.

SOUP

When bone stock is greasy and a bad colour: Fat or marrow was left on the bones and the stock was not skimmed when it came to the boil, causing the scum to boil down into it and spoil the colour.

When stock reduces too much: The lid did not fit well and so much steam escaped.

If stock turns sour twenty-four hours after it was made. It was either left in the saucepan all night or covered when put away.

When stock that should be clear is cloudy. Probably

(1) it was cooked too quickly—stock needs long slow simmering;

(2) or it was not skimmed sufficiently;

(3) or it was stirred when being strained. It is necessary to be very careful not to disturb the sediment.

When a thick soup is lumpy

The thickening was put in carelessly. Thickening can be added in the form of a roux (that is, flour and butter kneaded or cooked together). If thickened with flour, milk or water, the ingredients must be mixed very smoothly and a little hot soup added before they are stirred into the soup.

When artichoke soup is grey instead of a creamy white—Probably an iron saucepan has been used. Or the artichokes were not put into water that contained either a little lemon juice or vinegar directly they were peeled.

When soup that contains haricot beans or lentils is not smooth.—It was boiled too fast and the cereal did not soften. Or after the soup was sieved, it was not stirred when reheated and the puree did not mix properly with the stock.

When soup that contains rice has a slightly burnt taste though it does not appear to have "caught." –Probably a few grains of the rice stuck to the bottom of the saucepan and burnt because it was not stirred sufficiently.

When soup containing egg has curdled.—The soup boiled after the egg was added. When an egg is added to soup, the pan should either be taken off the stove or stood at the side. Mix the egg with a little milk and add it very gradually, stirring all the time, and on no account allow it to boil. Soup that contains cheese is also liable to curdle. Unless you are an expert cook, it is wiser to serve grated cheese separately on a small dish or plate on a dish paper. Alternatively, it may be put in the tureen and the soup poured gradually on to it.

When tapioca has been used as a thickening and has not softened sufficiently- Flake tapioca should have been used and sprinkled into the soup whilst boiling and the cooking continued until it was soft and transparent.

When a vegetable puree is too thick- The fault lies in too many vegetables having been allowed in proportion to the amount of stock or milk, or the soup cooked too quickly and so reduced. To remedy this, thin down with stock or milk and reheat, stirring all the time, and a good smooth puree with result.

When a curry soup is too hot—too much has been added, the quality varies and of some kinds less is required. Add more stock or milk and a little butter.

FISH

When boiled fish breaks while being dished up—

(1) It has been cooked too long or too fast. Boiling is not suitable for small pieces of fish; they should be steamed.

(2) The boiler did not have a drainer. If you do not posses one, tie the fish in a piece of muslin, then it can be lifted out easily.

When steamed fish breaks and lacks flavour

(1) The water boiled too fast under it.

(2) It was kept waiting. The water should boil gently and the fish must be served as soon as it is done.

When boiled salt fish is hard and very salt—it was not soaked sufficiently before it was cooked. Leave it in cold water for at least six hours, changing the water several times.

When grilled fish is broken

(1) The beat was too great.

(2) The fish was turned carelessly. Wait until it looks cooked on one side, and then turn very carefully with a broad fish slice.

(3) Broken fish can also be caused by the fish sticking to the grid-iron. Make sure that the grid-iron is quite dry, and grease it well before the fish is put on.

When grilled fish is dry

(1) It was not brushed over with butter or oil, as it should have been.

(2) It was a dry kind of fish (such as red mullet) and should have been wrapped in well greased paper before cooking.

When fish is grilled in paper and the paper burns.—Great care is needed when cooking fish in this way. The grill must be made red hot, the fish put under and them the heat reduced so that the flame cannot touch the paper.

When baked fish is dry

(1) there was not enough fat to keep it moist.

(2) The oven was too hot. Baked fish needs basting while cooking, unless it is wrapped is very well-greased paper.

When a fish soufflé falls at once and is heavy and stodgy.—The water boiled –it should only simmer. But be sure to see that it does simmer all the time, for it will also be heavy if it stops cooking at all.

When fish fried in egg and bread crumbs tastes greasy and is patchy in appearance.—The cause may be due to any of the following reasons:

(1) It was not dried sufficiently; this is the most frequent cause of all because so few cooks realize it importance.

(2) It was not floured after being dried.

(3) The egg was not beaten enough; it must be beaten until yolk and white are thoroughly mixed.

(4) The fish was not completely covered with the beaten egg. Use a pastry brush.

(5) The fat was not hot enough; wait until the fat ceases to bubble and a little thin blue smoke rises before putting in the fish.

(6) There was not enough fat to cover the fish.

(7) It was not drained either on a sieve or soft paper.

MEAT

When boiled salt beef is tough—It was either put in hot water instead of cold, or it was allowed to boil when it should only have simmered gently.

When braised meat is undergone, although plenty of time has been allowed and it has not stopped simmering—It was the saucepan which was at fault. The lid did not fit closely, so the steam escaped and therefore the meat did not get cooked right through. When roast meat is tough—The wrong kind of joint has probably been chosen, inferior joints are not suitable for roasting. The cheaper cuts should be braised, stewed or baked in a casserole.

When a join is dry.—It was not basted sufficiently or it was too lean and needed extra dripping for basting.

When meat, though not overcooked, is lacking in flavour.—The oven was not hot enough when it was put in, therefore the albumen in the meat did not coagulate and the juices escaped, together with the flavour.

When boiled meat is tasteless though cooked gently.—Too much water was probably used. There should only be just enough to cover the meat. Also some kinds of root vegetable such as carrot or turnip should have been cooked with it and a tiny bunch of sweet herbs.

When the stuffing in a joint is not done, although the joint was allowed the usual time and temperature.—If a joint is stuffed it requires longer than an unstuffed one. For a 4 lb joint allow twenty minutes more gentle cooking.

When the crackling of pork is hard and uneatable.—It was not brushed over with salad oil before it was cooked. This makes it crisp and delicious.

When a grilled steak or chop is black outside and blue inside. – You know that the grill was too fierce. Light the grill several minutes before you need it; experience of your own stove will tell you how long are necessary. See that it is quite red. Brown the meat on one side and then turn and brown the other so as to seal up the juices. Lessen the heat and turn two or three times while the meat finishes cooking.

When grilled meat is dry though apparently not overdone.—You have either stuck a fork into the meat and the gravy has escaped, or you put it under fierce heat while dry and lean. If you do not possess grilling tongs use two forks or a palette knife. A fork can be used if it is put into the fat only. When lean meat is to be grilled it should first be brushed over with liquid butter or dripping.

When grilled meat is touch.—Either it was too fresh. Only prime cuts such as rump or fillet steak, loin chops or cutlets really grill well. To make a steak very tender, first beat it well with a rolling pin, then pour a little best salad oil over the meat and leave it for about an hour before cooking. Do not buy meat that is too fresh; ask for grilling steak and your butcher will know what you require.

POULTRY AND GAME

When poultry or game lacks flavour:

(1) The oven was not hot enough when the bird was put in, and the goodness escaped instead of being sealed in the bird.

(2) It has been overcooked.

When a bird is dry:

(1) It was not larded. All poultry and game, but not water fowl, are improved by the breast being covered or larded with fat bacon. It is a good plan, too, to put a piece of butter or dripping inside the bird before it is cooked

(2) you neglected to baste sufficiently. Baste well every quarter of an hour for a large bird like a turkey, every ten minutes for a small bird. A piece of greased paper placed over the bird when it is brown enough also helps to keep it moist.

When steamed chicken or turkey is not sufficiently cooked although given the full time.—

(1) The water under the steamer was not kept boiling all the time.

(2) More water was needed and the water that was added was not actually boiling, and so checked the cooking.

(3) The lid did not fit closely. A piece of greaseproof paper placed under the lid, which is then shut tightly, will remedy this defect.

When steamed or boiled chicken or turkey is a bad colour.—It was not rubbed over with a slice of lemon before it was cooked. (When choosing a chicken or fowl for boiling chooses one with white flesh and legs. It will be more satisfactory than a game bird.) Wrapping a bird in buttered paper before cooking also keeps it white.

When braised poultry is touch.—It was allowed to cook too fast; braising is a long, slow method of cooking.

When roast game is tough.—It was probably too fresh or not young enough for roasting. Choose a young enough for roasting.

When a roast hare (of rabbit) is tough and dry.—It was too old for roasting and not basted sufficiently. Hare must be quite young for this method of cooking and as the flesh is dry and lean it needs to be well basted.

When jugged hare (or rabbit) is tough and flavorless.—It was snot cooked sufficiently or slowly enough. Long slow cooking will make an old hare or rabbit tender. Both need a good deal of seasoning, savoury herbs and a little bacon.

SAUCE

When white sauce is lumpy.—The fault was in the mixing. Butter and flour must be cooked gently to a perfectly smooth paste before any milk is added—then the milk stirred in gradually and kept perfectly smooth. Lumpy sauce may be strained and reheated.

When sauce that should be white has a fawn tint. –The butter and flour was cooked over too great heat and just began to brown, thereby causing the discoloration.

When onion sauce lacks flavour.—The onions were overcooked or cooked in too much water; they should be strained as soon as they are tender and only enough water used to cover them while cooking.

When bread sauce is flavourless though clove and onion were added.— The flavourings were not allowed to infuse long enough; the clove, mace and onion are put in the milk, which should be stood at the side of the stove or over very gentle heat until it is well flavoured.

When bread sauce is thick like porridge.—Either too many breadcrumbs have been used or it has been cooked too long and the milk has dried up.

When cranberry sauce is lumpy.—It should have been rubbed through a sieve and then reheated.

When a sauce curdles.—This often occurs in sauce that contain eggs. The reason is that the sauce was allowed to boil. This kind of sauce should be made in a double saucepan and never allowed to boil after the eggs have been added. Another cause is adding acid, such as lemon juice or vinegar, too quickly.

VEGETABLES

When boiled green vegetables are a bad colour.—

(1) They were not put into boiling water, or

(2) The lid was kept on while they were cooking, or

(3) They were overcooked all green vegetables should be served as soon as they are ready.

Winter cabbage or savoy sometimes has a strong, unpleasant flavour.—You can prevent it by blanching your vegetable first. Have ready a kettle of boiling water, as well as the fast boiling saucepan into which you put your cabbage. Then, as soon as your vegetable boils, strain off the water and re-cover it with fresh boiling water from the kettle.

When green vegetables are soppy and unpleasant in flavour.—They were boiled too long or not pressed. They should be strained as soon as they are sufficiently cooked, then pressed with a wooden presser or an inverted saucer. Brussels sprouts need to be shaken afterwards to separate them, otherwise they lose their character.

When boiled potatoes are broken and soppy.— They were cooked too fast or too long. Boiled potatoes need slow boiling, and they should be strained a few minutes before they are done, them left to finish in their steam and shaken once or twice to make them floury.

Potatoes do not break if steamed. A colander makes a good substitute for a steamer; place it over a saucepan so that the holes are below the saucepan rim; cover the potatoes with the lid.

When mashed potatoes are lumpy.—They have not been mashed sufficiently. A sure way is to rub them through a sieve or put them through a potato masher before adding butter or milk; this is especially necessary when cold cooked potatoes are being used.

When fried potatoes are greasy.—They were too wet when put in the fat. Lightly press them in a cloth before cooking and be sure the fat is hot enough and that there is plenty of it. Deep frying is best for potatoes.

When Jerusalem artichokes are a bad colour.—A little lemon juice or vinegar was not added to the water into which they were put after peeling.

When (1) leeks, or (2) spinach are gritty. – (1) Leeks should be slit down one side and held under a tap to wash out all grit. The earth in which vegetables of this type are planted is inclined to get between the leaves. (2) Spinach also needs very careful cleaning, for the leaves are so near the ground that they are invariably gritty. Wash the spinach in several waters, rinsing out the bowl each time.

When vegetable marrow is watery.—It was not drained sufficiently; after straining, stand the colander over a saucepan, cover with a lid, and leave it at the side of the stove until the water has ceased to drip.

When the skins of broad beans are tough.—The beans were too old. When cooked in their skins they should not be much larger than a sixpence. If they are older they are best skinned and served as a puree.

When the flower of a boiled cauliflower is not white.—It was put stalk downwards in the water and the scum settled on the flower. Had it been head downwards, this could not have happened.

EGGS

When the white of a boiled egg is solid although the egg was newly laid and should therefore have been creamy.—The water boiled too fast. Gentle heat should always be employed for cooking eggs, except when you wish them to be hard boiled. For soft boiling, the water should just boil gently. (When coddled the whites always remain creamy).

When a poached egg is broken and not a good shape.—

(1) You probably cooked it without a proper poacher and the water boiled too fast. Or

(2) You broke it straight into the pan. Break the egg into a cup, give it a little swing round and drop it gently into water that is simmering; move the water with a spoon so that it flows over the egg and causes the white to cover the yolk. Take out very carefully with a slice.

When the white of a poached egg is not perfectly white.—The egg was probably not new laid. A few drops of vinegar added to the water would have helped to keep it a good colour. Make sure, too, that you always use a scrupulously clean pan.

When scrambled eggs stick to the pan though plenty of butter was used.—The butter was not melted first as it should have been—before the eggs were put in.

When fried eggs are hard and not appetizing in appearance.—

(1) They have been cooked too quickly.

(2) Something else such as bacon was cooked in the pan first, and that had browned the pan a little. Always use a perfectly clean pan. Pour into it a little of the fat from the bacon if you wish (you can use other fat if you prefer) and make it hot before dropping in the egg. In this way there will be no unpleasant discoloration of the white.

When an omelet is dry and very fluffy.—You will know you have beaten the eggs too much. Eggs for omelets need very little beating. Beat yolks and whites together and then only lightly if you prefer a moist omelet. Separately but still only enough to froth them if you prefer the lighter kind.

If an omelet breaks when it is folded after a filling has been added. – You will know it was cooked too long and had become crisp at the edges.

When however long you whip whites of eggs they will not stiffen:

(1) The eggs were stale or too fresh. Eggs should be new laid, but not just laid. The white of an egg that has only been laid a few hours is almost as difficult to whip as a state one.

(2) The basin you used was not perfectly dry. The least drop of moister such as water or milk will make it impossible to whip stiffly. Whipping can even be spoiled by a wet fork.

STEAMED PUDDINGS

When a steamed pudding containing baking powder or bicarbonate of soda is heavy and stodgy.—You either made the mixture too wet or you did not put it in the steamer as soon as it was ready. These "lightening" begin to lose effect as soon as they are mixed with moisture. The water must be boiling in the saucepan and the steamer ready before you wet the dry ingredients and mix the pudding.

When a steamed pudding is heavy although breadcrumbs are the chief ingredients.—The pudding cloth was too tight and there was not enough room for the mixture to swell. If your basin is full, make one or two pleats in the cloth when putting it on.

When a pudding containing spices or other flavouring in powder form is well flavoured in some portions, and in others not at all.—They were not properly mixed with the other dry ingredients. To remedy this always mix these small powders—also "lightening" powders with the flour and then put them through a sieve. Liquid essences should be added to liquid ingredients such as eggs or milk. This will distribute the flavour evenly.

When a pudding sticks to the cloth.—You forgot to put a piece of greaseproof paper on top of the pudding before you put the cloth on.

When a pudding breaks while being turned out. —The basin was not thoroughly greased. To ensure that every part is covered, use a brush and melted fat. Do not be in a hurry to turn the pudding out. If, after removing the cloth, you wait a minute or two until some of the steam has escaped, the pudding will shrink from the sides of the basin.

When a steamed pudding is soppy.—Although only the necessary amount of moisture was used in the making, the pudding was cooked in a saucepan and the water found its way in. When steaming a pudding without a steamer it should be raised well above the level of the water on a stand or inverted saucer.

FRYING

When pancakes or fritters are heavy.—

(1) The batter had not been beaten sufficiently. The word "batter" means "to beat," and beating is therefore the main point.

(2) The fat was not hot enough. A thin blue smoke should be rising when your fritters are put in.

(3) The batter was used directly it was made. It should stand for one hour.

When pancakes or fritters are tough. Too much batter was poured into the pan at once, and so they took too long to cook. The bottom of the pan should only be covered thinly.

When a pancake breaks when being turned. You have not had enough practice in the knack of "tossing". Some cooks never learn this art. Turning is made easier if the edges of the pancake are loosened from the pan as soon as it begins to set. Use a flat slice with which to turn.

When a pancake sticks to the Pan.—You were too sparing with the fat.

When fritters are patchy in appearance and the batter does not entirely coat the fruit:

(1) The batter was not made thick enough. It should drop, not pour from a spoon.

(2) The fruit was too wet. Tinned fruit should be drained before it is put in batter.

When fritters are flabby instead of crisp and dry.—The fat was neither hot enough nor deep enough. A thin blue smoke should be rising and the fat is deep enough to cover the fritters completely. Also be careful not to overcook. Take a fritter out as soon as it is golden brown.

PASTRY

When pastry is sticky and therefore difficult to roll out.—You will know that you have made it too wet or mixed it in a very hot kitchen or with hot hands. Pastry should be just wet enough to roll easily, but not in the least sticky. Add the water very gradually—you can put in more but you cannot take any away! Mix it in as cool a place as possible, mix with a knife and do not handle it more than absolutely necessary—if you have naturally hot hands—wash them in hot water a few minutes before you start. See, too, that all the utensils are quite cold. Pastry can easily be spoilt if a bowl fresh from a hot water washing is used

When pastry is touch.—You made it too wet or used damp flour. Keep flour in a very dry place.

Why pastry is heavy.—Perhaps you used the rolling pin with a heavy hand—pastry must be rolled lightly with short rapid movements. Perhaps you rolled out all the air, by rolling right off the pastry instead of stopping before you came to the end. Always roll forwards all the time—not backwards and then forward—and remember if you roll off the edge you naturally force the air out. Your object must be to keep it in. Puff pastry will not rise if the oven is not sufficiently hot; the temperature must be 5000° F. when it is put in; 450° F. is sufficient heat for short pastry.

When short pastry is heavy though made with baking- powder. –It was not put in the oven as soon as it was mixed. Pastry that contains baking powder or self-raising flour must be put in the oven as soon as possible after it is made. If it stands any time after mixing. Before cooking, it will not rise.

When short pastry is lumpy and has a spotty appearance. The fat was hard and did not mix well with the other ingredients—a fault which most frequently occurs with dripping. To prevent this, keep the fat in a warm place for some time before using it or beat it until creamy. Do not go to the other extreme and make it warm enough to be oily.

When the pastry has fallen in a fruit tart so that it is soppy underneath.—Four different causes may account for this state of affairs.

(1) There was not sufficient fruit to hold up the pastry.

(2) The fruit had been stewed first and it was still warm when the pastry was put on. (The steam in that case had melted the fat in the pastry, and caused it to fall before the heat of the oven had set it.

(3) Too much juice or water had been put in the dish, or

(4) A centre funnel had not been used so that the steam could not escape.

SWEETS

When a jelly will not turn out, but breaks in the process:

(1) The mould was not rinsed out with cold water or brushed over with salad oil.

(2) The mould was shaken vigorously whilst the jelly was being turned out, instead of being dipped in warm water.

When a cream that contain gelatin or isinglass has a jelly top and a solid base when turned out, instead of being all of the same consistency.—The mixture should have been allowed to stand before being put in the mould until it was quite cold and just beginning to set. You should stir it, too, several times while it is cooling.

When the fruit in a jelly all rises to the top of a mould.—A layer of jelly should have been put in the mould and allowed to set before any fruit was added to it.

When milk puddings that contain eggs curdle in the baking.—The oven was very hot and the mixture boiled. A very slow oven is needed-about 325° F.

When puddings containing a cereal are milky at the top and solid at the bottom.—The pudding was not stirred when it had been cooking for a little while and the cereal remained at the bottom.

When a junket curdles and will not set.—The milk was made too hot, it must be only just Luke warm.

When a rice cream is too dry and the rice not soft and creamy

(1) The saucepan was not buttered before the rice was put in.

(2) It was cooked too quickly and the milk evaporated.

When custard flavoured with lemon peel has a slightly musty taste.—You forgot to wash the lemon or wipe it with a cloth.

When cream will not whip, however much it is beaten. – It was too new or too warm. Cream for whipping is best a day old and keeps it in a very cold place if possible.

When cream suddenly turns to butter when it is being whipped.—The whipping was too vigorous and too prolonged. As soon as it begins to thicken, watch it carefully and stop directly it is thick enough.

When treacle sticks to be scale.—The scale should be well floured, then the treacle will come away easily. If it is wanted for some dish that will be spoiled by even a suspicion of flour, weigh the cup or whatever you wish to put it in then pour in the treacle and weigh again.

FRUIT

When a salad is the dried fruits are still dry and tough.—You will know you did not soak them long enough. They should have been put in cold boiled water for twenty-four hours.

When stewed dried fruits, such as apricots and pears, are lacking in flavour.—Either you used too much water or the fruits were stale and out of season. Most dried fruits best in autumn, but the flavour can always be improved by adding lemon juice or rind. With prunes, put in a few of the kernels.

When rhubarb is acid, although cooked with a good deal of sugar.—Add a pinch of bicarbonate of soda; very much less sugar will then be needed, for it reduces the acidity.

When rhubarb loses its shape and colour.—It was put in cold water and cooked too long, probably in a sauce pan. To remedy this, put the rhubarb in a pie dish or casserole and pour hot syrup on it. Then cook in the oven.

When apples in a pie have remained in slices and are rather hard. –They were sliced too thinly-thin slices take a long while to soften. Cut the apples in small pieces. Slices are suitable for a flan.

When applies burst while baking.—A slit was not cut round the middle, just through the skin.

When fruit flavoured with lemon rind is bitter.—The white pith was not taken away—only the yellow part of the rind must be used.

When bananas or apples in a salad have turned a bad colour.—You will know it was caused by a steel knife; always use a stainless one.

When stewed apples "fall" and have more the appearance of apple sauce. –You did not slice them thinly enough; if sliced very thinly, they will keep their shape when cooking.

CAKES

When cakes are heavy

(1) Wet fruit is often the reason. Buy good fruit, then it will not need washing. Just put it on a sieve and rub it with a little flour,

(2) Damp flour is another possible reason, especially if you are using the self-raising kind. Always keep flour in a dry place.

(3) Or perhaps you were too anxious about your cake and opened the oven at intervals to have a peep at it, often shutting the door with a bang. Opening the oven lowers the temperature so quickly—you can see this for yourself if your oven is fitted with a thermometer—whilst a bang of the door causes a sudden draught and a beautifully risen cake immediately falls down. Therefore, do not look at your baking more often than is absolutely necessary, especially when it has only been in for a short while. Most kinds of cake are safe for at least a quarter of an hour. When you must open and shut the oven do so as gently as possible.

(4) Finally—and perhaps most likely of all—the cake contained baking powder and you did not put it into the oven directly after mixing it. The "lightening " of baking powder or cream of tartar or bicarbonate of soda begins to lose effect, directly they are mixed with any moisture. So do not mix a cake until the oven is ready to bake it.

Sometimes a cake appears excellent from the outside, but when cut it is almost hollow inside

(1) This may be caused by the oven being too hot at the start, making the cake rise too rapidly and then fall.

(2) Perhaps, on the other hand, it had too much baking powder or other "lightening" which caused the same result. **Sometimes a chocolate cake**

An unpleasant spotted appearance.—Then you will know that the chocolate has not been properly mixed with the other ingredients. The safest plan is to melt it in the milk, if you are using milk, or grate it and beat it into the butter.

When small cakes will not rise.—The oven was not hot enough when they were put in.

When cakes of the "Queen Cake" variety are gritty, instead of smooth and spongy.—they were not beaten sufficiently. With cakes of this kind, sugar and butter must be beaten to a soft cream and the whole mixture when ready must be a smooth even batter, without any suspicion of a lump.

When a cake sticks to the tin.—Either the tin was not sufficiently greased or it was not perfectly dry when greased.

When all the fruit sinks to the bottom of a cake.—Either the mixture was not stiff enough or the fruit was too heavy and sticky. Cherries and raisins should be cut in halves or quarters and lightly floured before being added to the other ingredients. Candied peel and almonds should be sliced finely before being added.

When a dripping cake is spotty and not of even texture.—The dripping was hard and would not mix well with the flour. It should first have been made slightly warm and beaten until creamy, before being rubbed into the flour.

When a flavouring of orange or lemon rind gives a cake a slightly bitter taste.— You will know some of the white pith has been included. Only the yellow part of either orange or lemon peel should be used for flavouring.

When a cake, though containing several eggs, is not light,—It was not beaten sufficiently. Cakes that depend upon eggs for their lightness need to be well beaten to aerate the mixture.

When a yeast cake is heavy.—You may be almost sure that your ingredients and utensils were very cold and the yeast would not work. When using yeast would not work. When using yeast everything should be slightly warm. Alternatively, the cause might be that you left the dough to rise in a very draughty place, or did not give it sufficient time to rise.

When some parts of a cake are spicy and well flavoured, and others not.—The dry ingredients were not thoroughly mixed before the moisture was added to bind them together.

When a large, rich cake is not done in the centre, yet overcooked on the outside.—The oven was kept at too great a heat. A large cake should be put in a hot oven, but as soon as it begins to brown the heat should be reduced to very moderate. Long, slow cooking is necessary. A rich cake weighing about 4 lb. Will need about four hours baking to cook evenly right through.

When rock cakes appear to be anything but rocks when taken from the oven.—The reason is either that the mixture was too moist or the oven not hot enough. Rock cake mixture should be very stiff and placed on a baking tin in little rough pieces with a fork. The oven must be 425° F otherwise the fat in the cakes will melt before the mixture has had time to set.

When almond icing is not smooth.—The icing sugar was not rubbed through a fine sieve or the ingredients were not well blended. It should be kneaded in much the same way as shortbread.

When almond icing shows through the white icing on a cake.—The white icing was put on before the almond icing was firm, or it was not put on thickly enough. On rich dark cakes it is wise to add a second coating.

When royal icing has not a smooth surface:

(1) The sugar was not rolled and then finely sifted, or

(2) the white of egg was added too quickly. To spread use a warm stainless knife, dipping it is boiling water when it needs reheating.

When glace icing is dull.—It was made too hot; especially is this the case with chocolate icing. Which should be only lukewarm.

When fancy icing loses its pattern.—The icing was not firm enough.

When boiled icing is lumpy.—The syrup was poured too quickly on to the white of egg.

When shortbread is rough in texture.—

(1) The flour, sugar and rice flour were not sifted;

(2) it was not kneaded sufficiently. It should be worked until it will roll without cracking or breaking.

When shortbread is greasy. –The butter was warmed so gradually that it softened without getting greasy. In warm weather it will not need warming at all. Kneading will soften it sufficiently.

When shortbread lacks the butter flavour.—The necessary pinch of salt was omitted.

When shortbread or biscuits rise in bubbles, instead of keeping flat and smooth.—Self-raising flour has been used; always use plain flour for shortbread and biscuits, and prick well before baking.

When shortbread or biscuits are brown and dry. — The oven was too hot and dried up the butter. The temperature should not be more than 350° F.

SWEET MAKING

When uncooked sweets are rough and coarse in texture.—This icing sugar was not fine enough. It pays to buy best quality sugar—but even then it must be rolled and sifted until it is as fine as flour. It is impossible to obtain smooth sweets with lumpy sugar. Good results will only be obtained by careful sieving.

When uncooked sweets have an eggs flavour and the real flavouring used seems lost.—This happens when an egg is not quite fresh; so-called "cooking" eggs must not be used for uncooked candies—they must be new laid.

When uncooked sweets are hard and rocky, although the usual amount of white of egg has been used.—This also is due to the staleness of the eggs; the white of a fresh egg makes almost twice as much when shipped as a stale egg does.

When sweets have a common appearance and do not taste as if made with good ingredients.—Too much colour and also too much flavouring have been used; be sparing with both. In the case of nut sweets, one nut may not have been quite good—and this can easily spoil a whole batch.

When the sugar while boiling granulates on the sides of the saucepan.—You will know the flame is too high.

When toffee that should be clear granulates when poured into a tin.—You will know that it should not have been stirred while it was cooking. Never stir boiled sweets unless you are directed to do so in the recipe. Another cause for granulation may be that you added the batter to the hot syrup in one piece, instead of adding a small portion at a time.

When toffee is very dark in colour and rather blackish in taste.—It boiled too fast and too long. Toffee must not boil beyond 300° F. If you are cooking without a thermometer, take it off the stove as soon as it is brittle, when a little is tested in cold water.

When toffee that should be brittle is soft and sticky.— It is a sure sign that it was not boiled to the right temperature. Toffee will not be brittle if boiled under 290° F and must be brittle when tested in cold water. Toffee that is intended to be the soft kind will only form a hard ball that could not be broken only stretched.

When toffee sticks to the saucepan or burns.—The heat under it was too great. If you are boiling on a gas ring that will not keep alight when turned very low, use an asbestos mat under the saucepan. Also be sure that you use a thick saucepan—toffee is sure to burn in a thin onc.

When caramels are hard and brittle, instead of soft and creamy. –They have been boiled to a toffee degree; the proper heat for caramels is 254-270° F, according to the variety.

When fudge refuses to granulate and remains a solid toffee.—You did not work the fudge enough. It must be well stirred with a wooden spoon while it is cooking.

If fudge is clear instead of being an opaque candy.—You will know you did not stir it sufficiently or else you boiled it too rapidly.

PRESERVES

When jam, jelly, or marmalade turns mouldy:

(1) The fruit was gathered on a wet day.

(2) It was over-ripe.

(3) The jar was not dry and warm as they should have been.

(4) The preserve was not made airtight.

(5) The jars were stored in a damp place.

When preserves ferment:

(1) They were not cooked sufficiently.

(2) They were stored in too warm a place, probably near hot water pipes.

When jars crack as the preserve is put in.—They were very cold and the sudden heat was the cause. Make jars quite warm and pour the preserve in gradually.

When preserves granulate and become very hard and sugary.—They were over-cooked—not a bad fault. The remedy is to turn the jam, jelly or marmalade into a saucepan and bring it to the boil. It will then be as clear as before. It is best to do this with each jar, as it is used, as granulation will take place again very shortly.

When preserves will not set:

(1) They were not sufficiently cooked or, probably, not boiled fast enough. Especially with jams that only require short boiling, you must make sure that the cooking is fast and furious. Do not stiffen with gelatine unless you are using the jam at once. Preserves with gelatine added to them will not keep long.

(2) The fruit was too wet.

(3) Ripe fruit was used when unripe was given in the recipe.

When preserves waste in the cooking.—The fruit boiled too fast before the sugar was added.

When drawing juice for jelly, the liquid dried up, with the result that a very small quantity of juice is obtained in proportion to the quantity of fruit used.—The water round it boiled too fast or the oven was too hot. It is best to draw off the juice from time to time as it flows, and so save it evaporating.

When jelly is cloudy. –The fruit was pressed when the juice was strained off. It should be allowed to drip without being touched.

When the peel in marmalade is tough:

(1) It was not soaked long enough before it was cooked.

(2) It was not cooked until tender before the sugar was added.

(3) It was not cut finely.

(4) the marmalade boiled too fast and the intense heat caused the rind to become hard.

When pickles turn mouldy.—They were not corked tightly and made airtight.

When pickles of the chutney variety taste slightly burnt. –They were not stirred sufficiently during the cooking and consequently some stuck to the bottom of the saucepan.

When pickles taste bitter.—A metal pan or spoon was probably used in the making, which produced a poison, making the pickles quite unfit for food. Use an enameled or earthenware pan when preparing pickles, and always stir or pack with wooden spoons.

When pickles go mouldy at the top, though quite good underneath.—There was not sufficient vinegar—the vegetables must be well covered.

When bottled fruit becomes mouldy:

(1) It was kept in a damp place.

(2) The water or syrup did not completely cover the fruit.

(3) The bottles were not sterilized long enough.

(4) There was a crack or a flaw in the bottles.

(5) The bottles were not screwed down tightly.

(6) The rubber ring was faulty.

When wines turn sour:

(1) They were put into damp bottles or old corks were used.

(2) They were stored in a warm place. The temperature should not exceed 60° F

(3) When wine is cloudy with sediment at the bottom, it was bottled too soon.

FOOD FOR HEALTH

Food is composed of several groups of substances which combine to provide the needs of the human body. These groups include Proteins, Carbohydrates. Fats and Vitamins. Minerals, Salts and Water also form part of the food we eat.

Proteins are the nourishing types of food which help to repair the worn tissues of the body and which assist in the growth of children. Protein foods include meat, fish, eggs, milk and cheese, nuts, peas, beans and lentils.

Carbohydrates are the starch and sugar foods which include wheat, bread, rice, macaroni, tapioca, maize, sugar and honey. They provide body heat and muscular energy. We should avoid eating too great a quantity of such foods, as an excess will result in a tendency to put on unwanted weight, and, instead of energy, case a feeling of tiredness and lassitude.

Fats are also a source of energy. Fat is stored in the liver, the muscles and in the tissues just under the skin where it forms a protection against cold and acts as a support for certain organs of the body. Fats should not form too large a part of the diet, especially in older people, as they may cause indigestion by preventing the gastric juices from reaching the other foods in the stomach.

Mineral Salts are contained in all foods in their raw condition, but are often lost through refining or incorrect cooking. It has been estimated, for example, that potatoes lose 17 per cent of their mineral salts when they are peeled and boiled. Iron is a mineral which should have an important place in the diet, as it is necessary for creating blood, and it is contained in egg-yolk, liver, red, meat, prunes and spinach.

The fourth group of substances contained in foodstuffs is called Vitamins, a word which comes from the Latin word which comes from the Latin word "vila" meaning "life." Vitamins cannot be seen, smelled or tasted and even the greatest scientists have not yet found out exactly what they are or how they work. The six best known vitamins are called by the first six letters of the alphabet, A, B, C, D, E, and F. These vitamins are contained in our everyday food and it is most important that we should eat a large enough quantity of certain foods on account of the particular vitamin which they contain and its value in preventing diseases, and in promoting the work of certain organs. Vitamins help the other food groups to nourish the body.

Vitamin A is found in greens, liver, egg-yolk, milk and in butter made from the milk of grass-fed cows. It helps us to be free from colds and other germs. Children, especially, should eat foods containing Vitamin A as it increases growth and assists bone formation.

Vitamin B is found in yeast, beans, lettuce and brown or whole meal bread, which contains the germ of wheat. Vitamin B helps babies to grow, improves appetite and strengthens nerves.

Vitamin C is found in most fresh fruit and vegetables, especially in tomatoes, oranges, lemons and grapefruit, also in raw spinach. Keeps the blood in a healthy condition, preventing scurvy, and other skin troubles.

Vitamin D is found in milk, cod-liver oil, egg-yolk, and is also very largely formed in sunlight. This vitamin helps in the formation of children's bones and is very valuable in preventing the disease called rickets; it also prevents the decay of teeth.

Vitamin E is found in wheat germ, fresh lettuce, water – cress and egg-yolk and in fresh meat. Foods containing this vitamin are valuable for creating mental vigour.

Vitamin F, found in the same foods as Vitamin B, has the same qualities and is said to prevent certain skin diseases.

LEARNING OUTCOME

The foundation of any cooking is you should know the principles and heat transfer method of cooking. Fuel is any material that is burned or altered in order to obtain energy and to heat or to move an object. Fuel releases its energy either through a chemical reaction means, such as combustion, or nuclear means, such as nuclear fission or nuclear fusion. The three method of heat transfer are conduction, convention and radiation. There are different types of fuels such as gas fuel, solid, electricity and liquid fuel. The foremost important aspect of cooking is you should now the different method of cooking. The process of subjecting food to the action of heat is termed as cooking. The cooking method is divide into three Wet, Dry and Microwave. It is very important we should know the different cooking method with their advantages and disadvantages and it proper temperature.Effect of cooking on food such as **Vitamins C, vitamin B and thyme** are destroyed and leached fruit and vegetable soften two much and unpalatable flavour are lost and changed and destroy muscles fabric and connective tissues becomes specially dry and hard and there is general loss of nutrient flavour form texture and colours. The action of heat on protein it coagulates and sets when heated the white of an egg is an example the coagulation process help in keeping the nourishing within the food it's sealed in by the formation of a coat on the outside and increases digestibility. How different way to leading the decomposition of food Pyrolysis is or thermal break down is the action of heating the oil whether not it is in contact of food causes the breakdown of the molecular structure. Now the major part come from last section of this chapter sets out to solve cookery difficulties by stating briefly and concisely cause and effect-or, more correctly, effect and cause. Food is composed of several groups of substances which combine to provide the needs of the human body. These groups include Proteins, Carbohydrates. Fats and Vitamins. Mineral Salts and Water also form part of the food we eat.

LESSON END ACTIVITY

- Take a water in pan boil some eggs and vegetable at one time on item and shows the effect of heat transfer on these products
- Collect more information on such fuel which helps to reduce fuel consumption and make our environment eco-friendly.
- Bring Carrot, eggs, aniseed, tomatoes, potatoes from market and do all the method of cooking one by one.
- Bring some spinach, eggs, lemon, mutton what are the effect on these product when we over cooked these food items.
- Collect the information on different food material with their composition how much they provide vitamins, minerals and carbohydrates.

QUESTIONS FOR DISCUSSION

1. Describe the principles of cooking.
2. Explain the three methods of heat transfer.
3. Describe the types of fuels with their advantage and disadvantages.
4. Describe the wet method of cooking.
5. Describe the microwave cooking.
6. Describe the moist cooking method.
7. Difference between broiling and braising.
8. Difference between steaming and stewing.
9. Difference between boiling and broiling.
10. Explain the effect of heat on food minerals.
11. Describe the ways to decomposition of food.
12. Explain how we retain the flavour of the food.
13. What are basic rules for frying.
14. Explain the cooking effect on food :

    i) Cakes

    ii) soup

    iii) meat

    iv) Fish

v) Sauces

15. Write a short not on food for health?

STATE TRUE AND FALSE

- Food is composed of several groups of substances which combine to provide the needs of the human body
- Fats are also a source of energy.
- When almond icing is smooth. That means the icing sugar was not rubbed through a fine sieve or the ingredients were not well blended
- When a pancake sticks to the Pan.—it means you added too sparing with the fat.
- Principles of cookery said not to, to retain the flavour and nourishment of food
- Reaction of hot oil surface with oxygen in the air causes the molecular break down
- Boiling temperature is below than 90° C.
- Braising and boiling is same thing.
- Starch granules dissolve easily in cold water
- Collagen is a structural protein.
- Moist foods and liquid foods can be rapidly heated in such ovens.
- Sautéing is a method in which food is lightly tossed in little oil just enough to cover the base of the pan.
- In steaming less chance of burning and scorching.
- Poaching temperature is above 100° C.
- Fossil fuels are also generally liquid fuels.
- Production of gasoline is achieved by distillation of crude oil.
- Natural gas is a mixture of hydrocarbons mainly methane that is extracted from underground reserve.natural gas is compressed natural gas or liquid petroleum gas or propane.
- The use of some solid fuels (example. coal) is restricted or prohibited in some urban areas, due to unsafe levels of toxic emissions.

KEY TERMS

* Caramelize	* Liquor	* Retaining
* Fluid	* Molecules	* Steak
* Gasoline	* Oxidation	* Toughens
* Liquid	* Preserves	* Triglycerides

5

Kitchen Organization and Management

After studying this chapter, the student must know

- Kitchen organization chart
- Duties and responsibilities of kitchen staff
- Kitchen equipment and tools
- Safety precaution of handling equipments and tools.

Kitchen Organization Chart

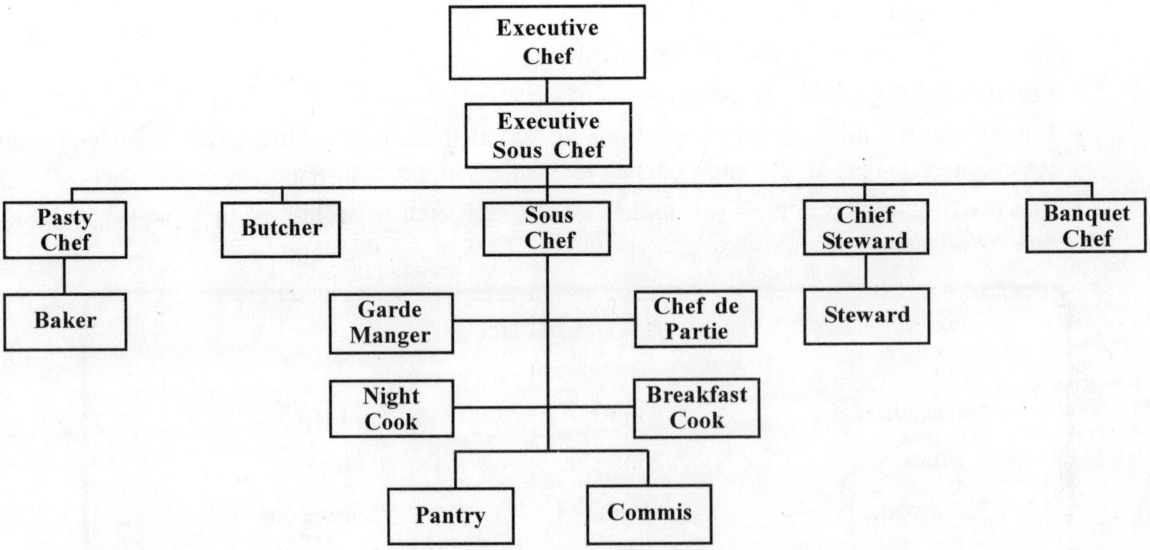

Fig 5.1A The kitchen organization of small hotel

TYPICAL FRENCH ORGANISATION CHART

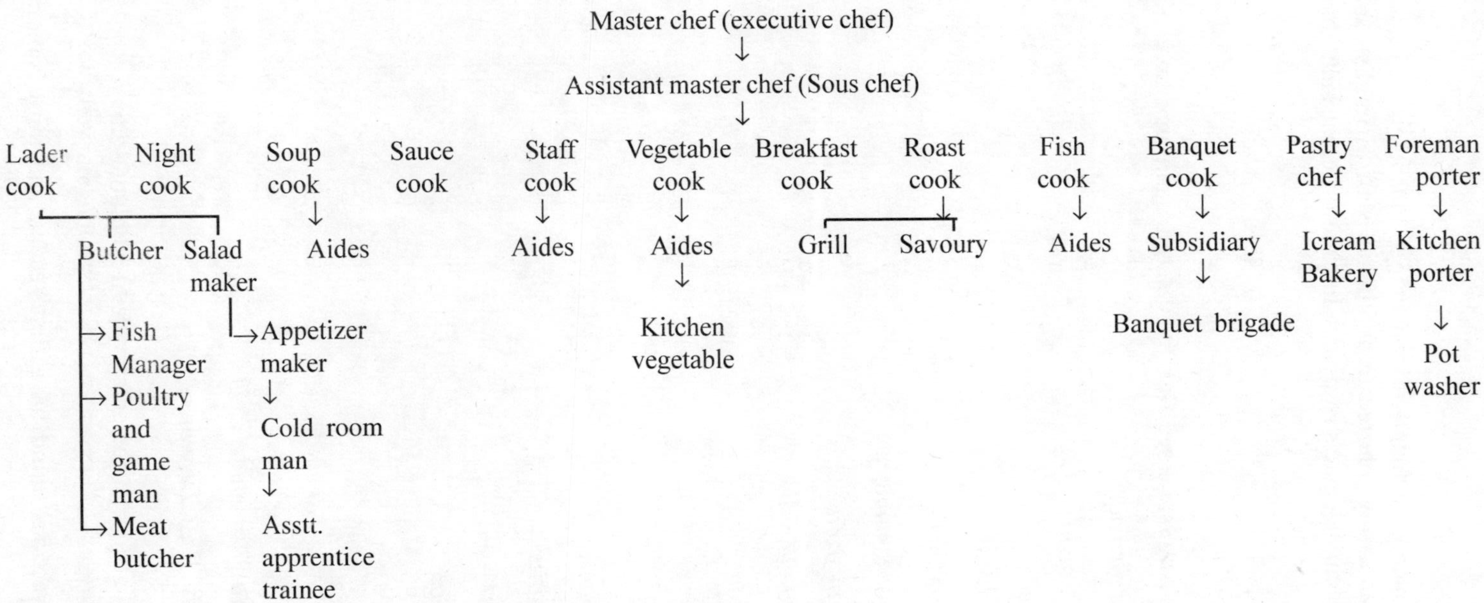

Fig 5.1b The typical French kitchen organization

KITCHEN ORGANIZATION

Brigade de cuisine is a system of hierarchy found in restaurants and hotels in France that employ extensive staff and are commonly referred to as kitchen staff in English speaking countries. This structured team system delegate's responsibilities to different individuals that specialize in certain tasks.

Kitchen Organisation

This is the partie system devised by **Auguste Escoffier** for a large traditional hotel Kitchen

La Brigade de Cuisine - the Kitchen Brigade

1. Head Chef — *Chef de Cuisine*
2. Second Chef — *Sous Chef*
3. *Chef de Partie* — *Section Heads*
4. Larder Cook — *le Garde-Manger*

These three chefs come under the Garde-manger

- Cold Work Chef — *le Chef du froid*
- Hors d'Oeuvre Cook — *le Hors d'Oeuvrier*
- Butcher — *le Boucher*

5. Sauce Cook — *le Saucier*
6. Roast Cook — *le Rôtisseur*
7. Fish Cook — *le Poissonnier*
8. Vegetable cook — *l'Entremettier*
9. Soup Cook — *le Potager*
10. Pastry Cook — *le Pâtissier*
11. Baker — *le Boulanger*
12. Relief Cook — *le Tournant*
13. Staff cook — *le Communard*
14. Night or Duty Cook — *le Chef du Nuit ou le Chef de Garde*
15. Breakfast Cook — *le Chef du Petit Dejeuner*
16. Carver — *le Trancheur*
17. Grill Cook — *le Grillardin*
18. Assistant Chefs - Commis - big sections could have first second and third commis

19. Apprentice - l'Apprenti
20. *Subsidary Departments under the Chef de Cuisine*
    Kitchen Clerk or Announcer - Aboyeur
    Scullery - Plongeur
    Kitchen Porter
    Stillroom
    Plate Room (Silver)
    China Pantry
    Stores

DUTIES AND RESPONSIBILITIES OF KITCHEN STAFF

Executive Chef

The executive chef is in charge of everything related to the kitchen, including menu creation, staff and business management aspects. While the position requires extensive cooking experience and often involves actively cooking, the staff of benefit, it also involves a high level of management and business skills of the kitchen. They can also be referred to as the "chef" or "head chef". Although "head chef" may seem redundant, the word "chef" has come to be applied to any cook, kitchen helper or fast food operator, making the distinction necessary.

Responsibilities of Executive Chef

- Full supervision of kitchen brigade
- Kitchen staff recruitment and training
- Menu planning
- Supervision of inventory and stock control
- Maintaining budgetary targets
- Supervision of health and safety (HACCP).

Sous Chef

The sous-chef de cuisine (Deputy-chef of the kitchen) is the direct assistant of the executive chef and is second in command. He may be responsible for scheduling, and filling in for the executive chef when he or she is off-duty. The Sous Chef will also fill in for or assist the chef de partie (line cooks) when needed. Smaller operations may not have a sous chef, while larger operations may have multiple. The term "sous-chef" is pronounced like "sous chef". Some sous chefs act as an expeditor. This means that they serve as the liaison between the restaurant's customers and its line cooks. They deal with complaints regarding food quality. They also are in charge of coordinating cooking so that the wait staff delivers all food to the customers in a timely fashion and so that everyone sitting at a table is served at the same time.

Responsibilities of Sous Chef

- Supervising the kitchen staff
- Preparing and cooking meals to order
- Demonstrating cooking techniques and proper equipment usage to the kitchen staff
- Some menu planning
- Some ordering of food and kitchen supplies

Chef de Partie

A chef de partie, also known as a "station chef" or "line cook", is in charge of a particular area of production. In large kitchens, each station chef might have several cooks and/or assistants. In most kitchens however, the station chef is the only worker in that department. Line cooks are often divided into a hierarchy of their own, starting with "First Cook", then "Second Cook", and so on as needed.

Chef Saucier (sauce chef)

Is responsible for all sautéed items and their sauce. This person prepares sauces, stews and hot hors d'oeuvres and sautés food to order. Although it is the highest position of the station cooks, the saucier is still considered subordinate to the chef and the sous-chef.

Chef Entremetier

Prepares hot appetizers and often prepares the soups, vegetables, pastas and starches. In a full brigade system a potager would prepare soups and a legumier would prepare vegetables. Chef Entremetier is also responsible for peeling and cutting vegetables.

Chef Garde Manger (Larder)

Is a French term meaning "keeping to eat" or "keeper of the food", refers to the task of preparing and presenting cold foods. These typically include such food items as salads, hors d'oeuvres, cold soups, aspics, and charcuterie. Larger restaurants and hotels may have the need for the garde manger to perform additional duties, such as creating decorative elements of buffet presentation like table arrangements and edible centerpieces made from materials such as ice, cheese, butter, salt dough or tallow. In most modern kitchens however, the garde manger is synonymous with pantry chef, having duties focusing on salads, soups, cold food items, and dessert platings. It is usually the entry-level line cook position within a restaurant.

Chief Butcher

Is responsible for the preparation of meat. The butcher has the techniques of cutting, slicing and removing the bones from the meat.

Chef Poisonnier

Prepares fish dishes and often does all fish butchering as well as appropriate sauce. This station may be combined with the saucier position.

Chief Steward

Is responsible for the washing of dishes and cleanliness of the kitchen and looking for the good hygiene.

Pastry Chef (Pâtissier)

Is a station chef in a professional kitchen, skilled in the making of pastries, desserts, and other baked goods. The responsibilities of a pastry chef can include duties such as menu planning, costing, and ordering. Day-to-day operations can also require the pastry chef to research recipe concepts and develop and test new recipes. The pastry chef is often in charge of the dessert menu, which besides traditional desserts may include dessert wines, specialty dessert beverages, and gourmet cheese platters.

Chief Baker

Is responsible for the supervision of the baker staff as directed by the Pastry Chef Supervisor. Assists in the preparation and cooking of all bakery products, follow the HACCP procedures as set by the company.

Chef Tournant

Is responsible to replace those who are absent. Have to know a bit of all work to be able to replace them.

Kitchen Assistants

An apprentice or (commis) in larger kitchens would work under a chef de partie or station chef in order to learn the station's responsibilities and operation.

- A communard would be in charge of preparing the meal for the staff during a shift. This meal is often referred to as staff or family meal.
- The escuelerie-dishwasher is the keeper of dishes, having charge of dishes and keeping the kitchen clean

EQUIPMENT AND TOOLS

Kitchen equipment is expensive and to justify the expenses, it is essential that maximum use be made of it. This can be done only if the equipments work efficiently and this depends upon the care and maintenance. The type of fuel is to be used is an important factor. Though solid fuel and oil both have their place under certain circumstance, for professional cookery the choose lies between electricity and gas. The routine used, care and cleaning of all items of equipment are important and this should be appreciated and understood.

When selecting equipment, capacity, trade name, good quality, simple design and easy to clean should be the criteria. The purpose and price is also considered.

Kitchen equipment may be dividing into various categories as given in Fig. 5.2.

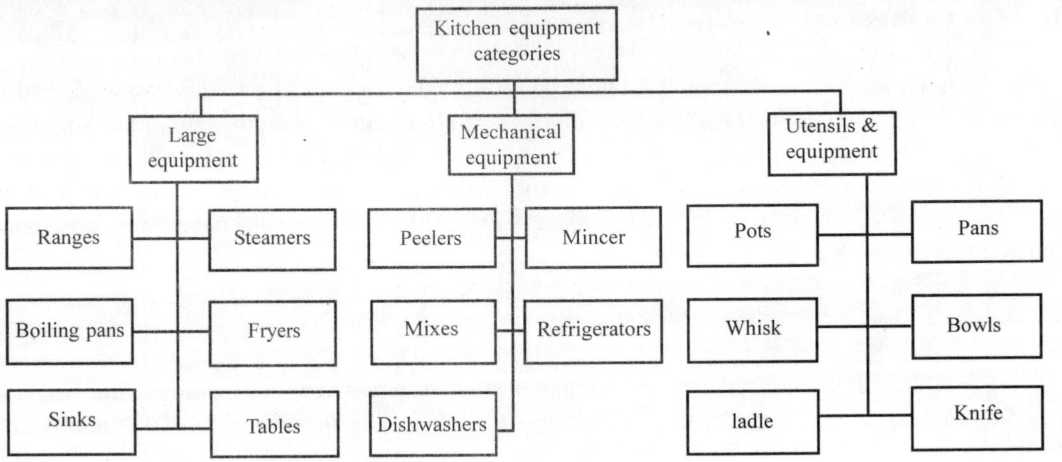

Fig 5.2 Various categories of kitchen equipment

Equipments

A) Steamers (Fig. 5.3)

Steaming ovens that work from a main stream supply need little maintenance electric steamer shown in Fig 5.3. The door controls should be greased occasionally. The Steamers trays and runners should be washed in hot detergent water.

Fig 5.3 Electric steamer

B) Deep fat fryers (Fig. 5.4)

Modern fryers are heated by gas or electricity. Most incorporate a thermostatic control in order tom save the fuel and prevent overheating.Deep fat fryer with two columns one for vegetables items to fry and one for non vegetable items to fry as shown in Fig 5.4.

Fig 5.4 Deep fryer with two columns

Fig 5.5 The Bain Marie

Fig 5.6 Salamander

C) Hot cup boards and Bain-marie (Fig. 5.5)

Hot cupboards are (commonly referred to in the trade as the hot plates) are used for heating plates and serving dishes and for keeping food hot. Care should be taken to see that the amount of heat fed into the hot cupboards and a thermostat is necessary in maintain this.An electric bain-marie as shown in Fig. 5.5.

D) Grill and salamander (Fig. 5.6)

The salamander, heated from above, probably cause more wastage of fuel than any other item of kitchen equipment, through being allowed to burn unnecessarily for long unused periods. Most salamanders have more than one set of heating elements or jets, and it is not necessary to have them all turned on. Salamanders are heated by gas or electricity or a combination of the two. Electric type salamander as shown in Fig. 5.6.

E) Sinks (Fig. 5.7)

Different materials are used for sinks according to the purpose for which they are intended.

- Heavy galvanized iron pot wash
- Stainless steel for general purpose
- Glazed earthen ware for general light purpose.

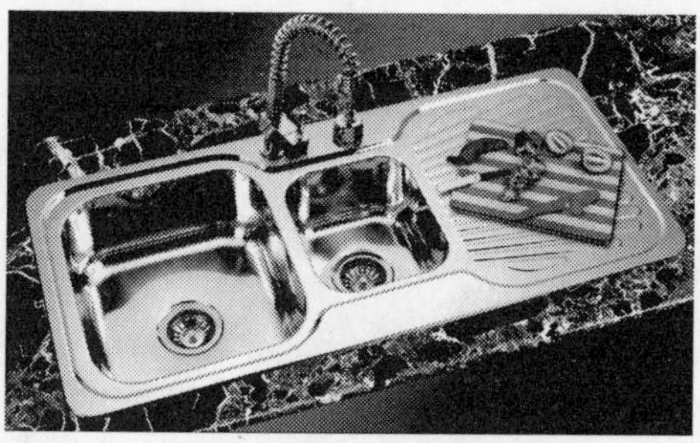

Fig 5.7 Stainless Steels Sinks

F) Tables (Fig. 5.8)

Stainless steel tables are used in hotel industry, should be washed with hot detergent water, rinsed with hot water and dried. Stainless Steel table as shown in Fig 5.8

G) Potato peelers (Fig. 5.9)

Potatoes should be free of earth stones before loading into the machine; otherwise damage to the machine will result. Before any potatoes are loaded, the water spray should be turned on and the abrasive plates set in motion. Different types of potatoes peeler are as shown in Fig 5.9

H) Food slicers and choppers (Fig. 5.10)

Food slicers available are both manually and electrically operated. They are labour saving devices, which can be dangerous if not operated with care. Because, of this, the working instructions should be placed in a prominent position near the machine. Electric Food slicers are shown in Fig 5.10

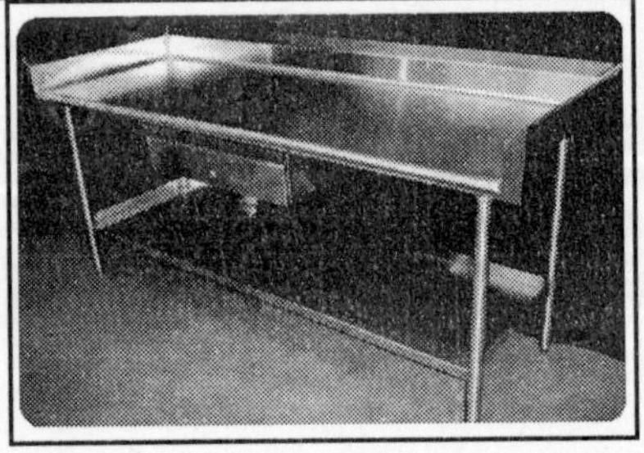

Fig 5.8 Stainless Steel table

Fig 5.9 Different types of potatoes peeler

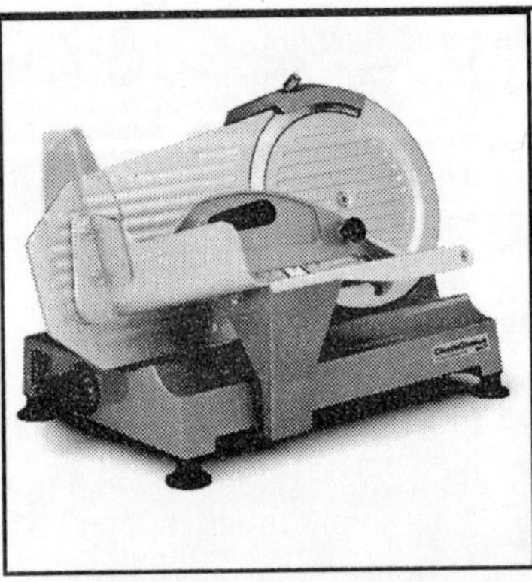

Fig 5.10 Electric Food slicers

I) Ranges (Fig. 5.11)

A range can be used to do almost any type of cooking. Ranges may be either gas or electricity operated. Gas range with oven and salamander as shown in Fig 5.11.

J) Ovens (Fig. 5.12)

There are many types of oven.Range ovens have been traditionally and versatile piece of production equipment in most food service operations.Many ranges have ovens beneath them. Pan, steamer, oven, or warmer. Electric oven as shown in Fig 5.12

Fig 5.11 Gas range with oven and salamander

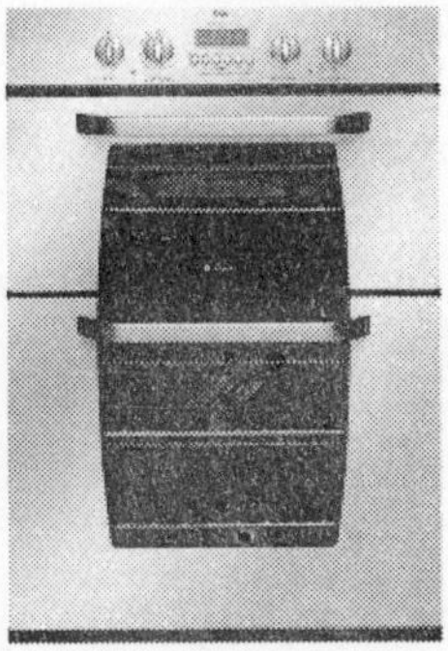

Fig 5.12 Electric oven

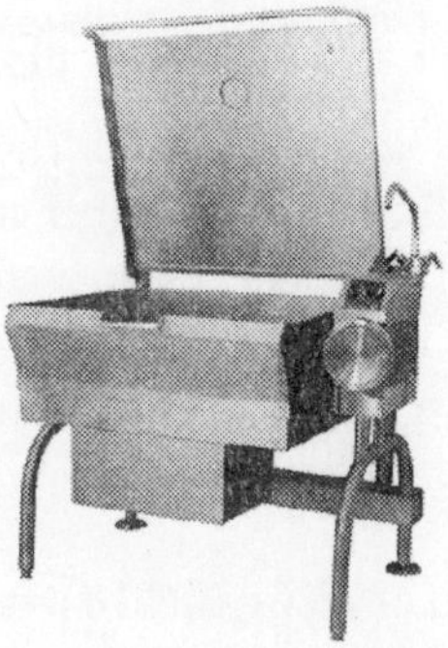

Fig 5.13 Electric Tilting pan

K) Tilting braising pans (Fig. 5.13)

A tilting braising pan is flat – bottomed and can be used as a kettle, griddle, fry pan, steamer, oven, or warmer/service. Electric Tilting pan as shown in Fig 5.13

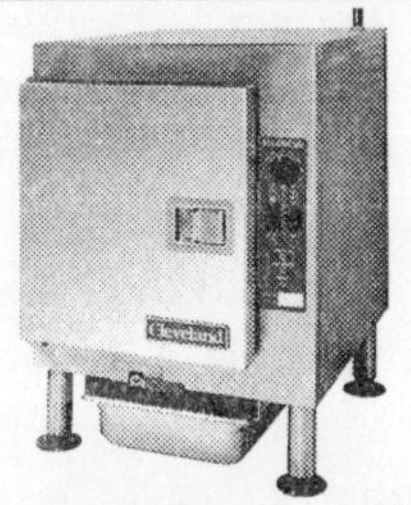

Fig 5.14 Electric steamer

L) Steamers (Fig. 5.10)

Steaming ovens that work from a main stream supply need little maintenance electric steamer shown in Fig. 5.14. The door controls should be greased occasionally. The Steamers trays and runners should be washed in hot detergent water.

Fig 5.15 Deep fryer with two columns

M) Deep fat fryers (Fig. 5.15)

Modern fryers are heated by gas or electricity. Most incorporate a thermostatic control in order tom save the fuel and prevent overheating.Deep fat fryer with two columns one for vegetables items to fry and one for non vegetable items to fry as shown in Fig 5.15

J) Hot cup boards and Bain-marie (Fig. 5.16)

Hot cupboards are (commonly referred to in the trade as the hot plates) are used for heating plates and serving dishes and for keeping food hot. Care should be taken to see that the amount of heat fed into the hot cupboards and a thermostat is necessary in maintain this.An electric bain-marie as shown in Fig 5.16

Fig 5.16 Bain Marie

K) Grill and salamander (Fig. 5.17)

Fig 5.17 Salamander

The salamander, heated from above, probably cause more wastage of fuel than any other item of kitchen equipment, through being allowed to burn unnecessarily for long unused periods. Most salamanders have more than one set of heating elements or jets, and it is not necessary to have them all turned on. Salamanders are heated by gas or electricity or a combination of the two. Electric type salamander as shown in Fig 5.17

Mixers (Fig. 5.18)

A mixer is a kitchen appliance intended for mixing, folding, beating, and whipping food ingredients. Mixers come in two major variations, hand mixers and stand mixers. A hand mixer, as the name implies, is a hand-held mixing device. It typically consists of a handle mounted over a large enclosure containing the motor, which drives one or two beaters. The beaters are immersed in the food to be mixed. A stand mixer is essentially the same as a hand mixer, but is mounted on a stand which bears the weight of the device. Stand mixers are larger and have more powerful motors than their handheld counterparts. They generally have a special bowl that is locked in place while the mixer is operating. Heavy duty commercial models can have bowl capacities in excess of 100 quarts (95 L). Typical home and commercial models are equipped with bowls of around 4 quarts (4 L). A typical home dick stand mixer will include a wire whip for whipping creams and egg whites; a flat beater for mixing batters; and a dough hook for kneading.

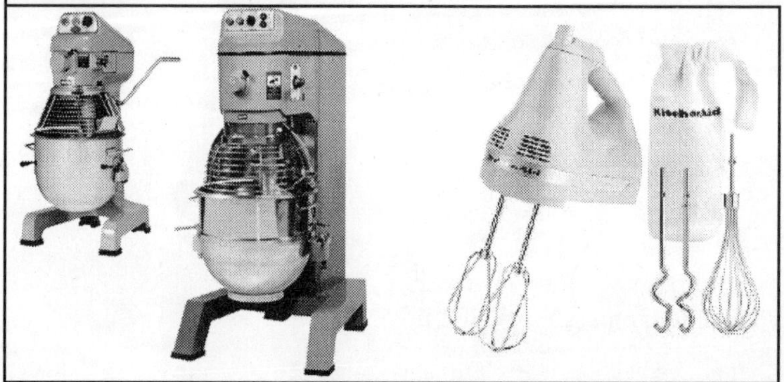

Fig 5.18 Mixers

Fig 5.19 Varieties of blender

Blender (Fig. 5.19)

A blender or liquidizer is a kitchen appliance used to mix ingredients or puree food. The blending container can be made of glass, plastic, or stainless steel, and often has graduated markings for approximate measuring purposes. At the top of the container is a lid to prevent ingredients from escaping during operation. At the bottom is a serrated blade assembly, sometimes removable for cleaning purposes.

REFRIGERATORS (Fig. 5.20)

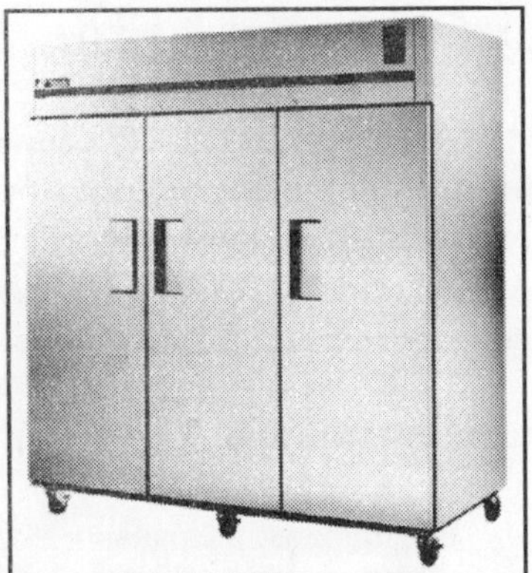

Fig 5.20 Three door refrigerator

A refrigerator (often called a "fridge" for short) is a cooling appliance comprising a thermally insulated compartment and a mechanism to transfer heat from it to the external environment, cooling the contents to a temperature below ambient. Refrigerators are extensively used to store foods which deteriorate at ambient temperatures; spoilage from bacterial growth and other processes is much slower at low temperatures. A device described as a "refrigerator" maintains a temperature a few degrees above the freezing point of water; a similar device which maintains a temperature below the freezing point of water is called a "freezer". Freezers keep their contents frozen. They are used both in households and for commercial use. Most freezers operate at around -18°C (0°F)

UTENSILS AND SMALL EQUIPMENTS

Cookware and Bake ware

Cookware and bake ware are types of food preparation containers commonly found in the kitchen. Cookware comprises cooking vessels, such as saucepans and frying pans, intended for use on a stove or range cook top. Bake ware comprises cooking Vessels intended for use inside an oven. Some utensils are both cookware and bake ware.

Braising pans and roasting pans (Fig. 5.21)

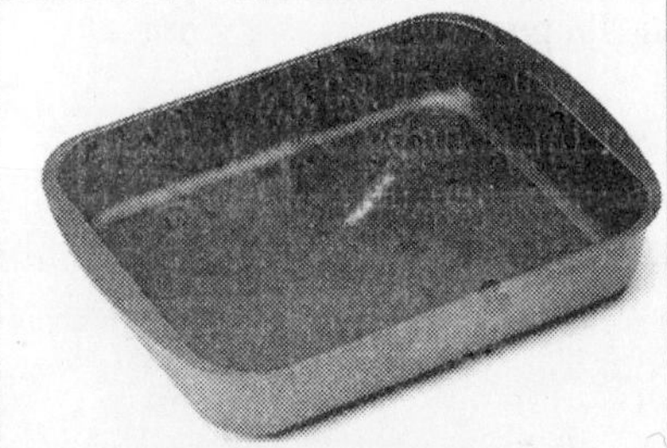

Fig 5.21 Roasting pans

Braising pans (also known as braisers and roasters) are large, wide and shallow, to provide space to cook a roast (chicken, beef, or pork). They typically have two loop or tab handles, and may have a cover. Roasters are usually made of heavy gauge metal so that they may be used safely on a cook top following roasting in an oven. Unlike most other cooking vessels, roasters are usually oblong or oval. There is no sharp boundary between braisers and roasters - the same pan, with or without a cover, can be used for both functions.

Casserole pans (Fig. 5.22)

Fig 5.22 Casserole pans

Casseroles pan (for making casseroles) resemble roasters and dutch ovens, and many recipes can be used interchangeably between them. Depending on their material, casseroles can be used in the oven or on the stovetop. Casseroles are commonly made of glazed ceramics or pyrex.

Dutch ovens (Fig. 5.23)

Fig 5.23 Dutch oven

Are heavy, relatively deep pots with a heavy lid, designed to re-create oven conditions on the stovetop (or campfire). They can be used for stews, braised meats, soups, and a large variety of other dishes that benefit from low heat, slow cooking. Dutch ovens are typically made from cast iron, and are measured by Volume.

Large and small skillets (Fig. 5.24)

Fig 5.24 Skillets

Frying pans, fry pans, or skillets provide a large flat heating surface and shallow sides, and are best for pan frying. Fry pans with a gentle, rolling slope are sometimes called omelets' pans. Grill pans are fry pans that are ribbed, to let fat drain away from the food being cooked. Fry pans and grill pans are generally measured by diameter (20–30 cm).

Saucepans (or just "pots") (Fig. 5.25)

Fig 5.25 Saucepans

Are vessels with vertical sides about the same height as their diameter, used for simmering or boiling? Saucepans generally have one long handle. Larger pots of the same shape generally have two handles close to the sides of the pot (so they can be lifted with both hands), and are called sauce-pots or soup pots (3–12 liters). Saucepans and saucepots are measured by volume (usually 1–8 L). While saucepots often resemble dutch ovens in shape, they do not have the same heat conduction characteristics.

Sauté pans (Fig. 5.26)

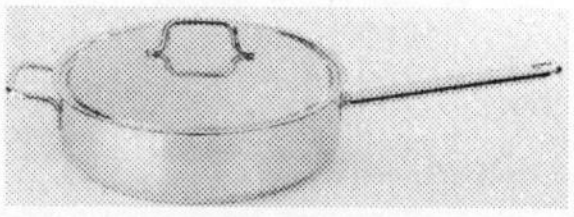

Fig 5.26 Sauté pans

Sauté pans are used for sautéing, have a large surface area, like a fry pan, but with vertical sides, to prevent food from escaping during cooking.

Stockpots (Fig. 5.27)

Fig 5.27 Varieties of stock pots

Stock pots are large pots with sides at least as tall as their diameter. This allows stock to simmer for extended periods of time without reducing too much. Stockpots are typically measured in volume (6- 36 L). Stock pots come in a large variety of sizes to meet any need from cooking for a family to preparing food for a banquet. A specific type of stockpot exists for lobsters, and an all-metal stockpot usually called a caldero is used in Hispanic cultures to make rice.

Woks (Fig. 5.28)

Wok is typically lens-shaped. This allows a small pool of cooking oil to be heated to a high heat using relatively little fuel, while the outer areas of the wok are used to keep food warm after it has been fired in the oil. In the Western world, woks are typically used only for stir-frying, but they can actually be used for anything from steaming to deep frying.

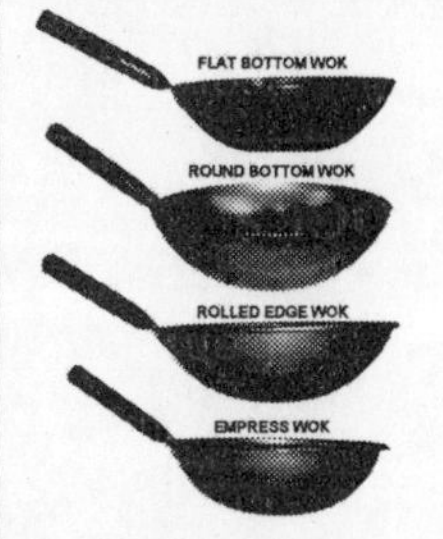

Fig 5.28 Varieties of wok

Baking pans (Fig. 5.29)

Baking pans are designed for use in the oven (for baking) and encompass a variety of different styles of bake ware such as cake pans, pie pans, and loaf pans. These are often made from light or medium gauge metal. The longest lasting baking's sheets and pans are made with heavy-gauge steel or aluminum. They are heavier in Weight which helps in heat distribution evenly and prevents the metal from warping.

Fig 5.29 Baking trays

Cake pans (Fig. 5.30)

Cake pans include square pans, round pans, and specialty pans such as angel food cake pans and spring form pans often used for baking cheesecake.

Fig 5.30 Cake pans

CUTTING, MASHING, GRATING AND GRINDING TOOLS

Cutting (Fig. 5.31)

A chef's knife, also known as a French knife, is a cutting tool used in food preparation. It is the primary general-utility knife for most Western cooks. A chef's knife generally has a blade eight inches (20 cm) in length and 1 and a half inches in width, although individual models range from six to 14 inches (15 to 36 cm) in length (Fig 5.31).

Grater (Fig. 5.32)

Grater is a kitchen utensil used to grate foods into fine strips or crumbs. Several types of graters have different sizes of grating slots, and can therefore aid in the preparation of a variety of foods. They are commonly used to grate cheese and lemon or orange peel (to add zest), and can also be used to grate other soft foods. They are commonly used in the preparation of toasted cheese, welsh rarebit, and macaroni and cheese (Fig 5.32).

Fig 5.31 shows the different Knifes
From Top Left: cleaver, utility knives (next two), slicer, flexible slicer, scimitar, Serrated slicers (pointed and round-tipped)
From Bottom Left: French knives (first three in row), Boning knife, granton-style edge French knife, paring knife, tourné knife

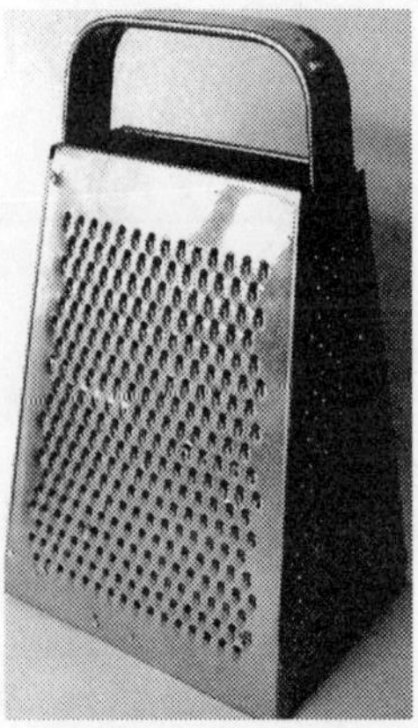

Fig 5.32 Grater

Fig 5.33 Chinois

Fig 5.34 Beater

Chinois (Fig. 5.33)

Chinois fits on top of a deep container and mashes food when pressed through it (Fig 5.33).

Egg-beater (Fig. 5.34)

Egg beater used to beat mixture vigorously and homogenize (Fig 5.34).

Mortar and pestle (Fig. 5.35)

Mortar and pestles is a tool used to crush, grind, and mix substances. The pestle is a heavy stick whose end is used for pounding and grinding, and the mortar is a bowl. The substance is ground between the pestle and the mortar (Fig 5.35).

Fig 5.35 Mortar and pestle

Potato masher or bean masher (Fig 5.36)

Potato masher is a food preparation utensil used to crush soft food for such dishes as mashed potatoes, apple sauce, or refried beans.

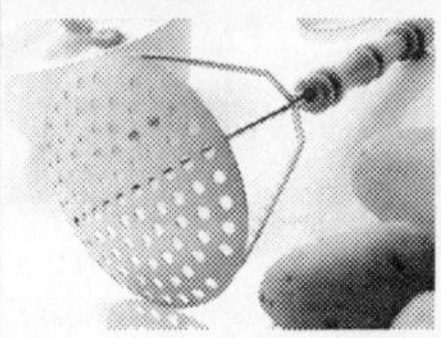

Fig 5.36 Potato masher

Meat mallets (Fig. 5.37)

Meat mallets tenderize or flatten meat. Made from wood or metal, they are typically two-sided, one flat with slight bumps, and the other with more pronounced protrusions. Meat mallets can be made from wood, plastic, or steel, but their use has lessened with the invention of cube steak machines and other electric tenderizers. Meat mallets can also be used to crush ice (Fig 5.37).

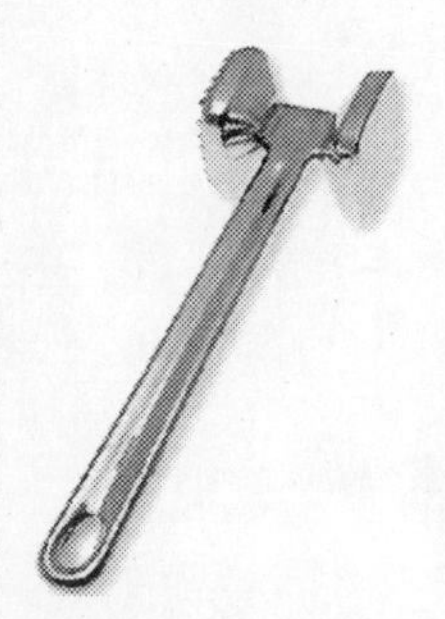

Fig 5.37 Meat millet

Vegetable Peelers (Fig 5.38)

A peeler is a metal blade attached to a metal, plastic or wooden handle that is used for peeling vegetables, frequently potatoes. There are two main varieties, the 'Yorkshire' (or sometimes called a Lancashire peeler) design involving the blade as an extension of a handle, in much the same way as the blade is attached to a knife. The second variety more closely resembles a safety razor (sometimes it is called a Y-peeler (due to its shape), Rex peeler, yoke peeler, or speed peeler), with the blade perpendicular to the handle, is used with a similar action to a razor, shaving off skin in strips parallel to the handle. Most speed peelers have an 'eye gouger' beside the blade, a loop of metal used to dig out eyes and blemishes from the potato. Peelers can be used on citrus fruits, asparagus, eggplant, tomatoes and even mushrooms.

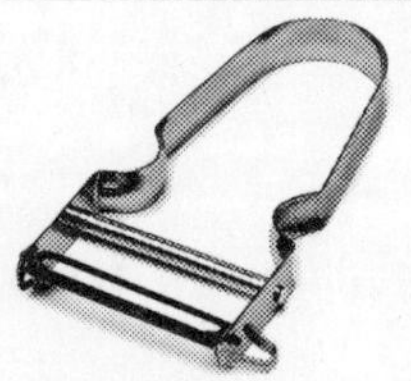

Fig 5.38 Vegetable peeler

Safety precaution while handling equipments and tools

Before operating any machinery workers should:

- Get trained in their use.
- Wear any personal protective equipment provided by your employer.
- Use any machine guarding provided.
- Always ask for help if you are not sure how to do something.
- Be aware that age restrictions exist for workers under the age of 18 from using or cleaning certain equipment.
- Follow the manufacturer's instructions for machine use and cleaning.
- Follow the general recommendations below to identify and avoid potential hazards associated with kitchen machinery.

Mincers, choppers, dicers, slicers:

- Always use push sticks or tamps to feed or remove food from these types of machines.
- Do not use your hands to feed smaller pieces of meat through slicers.
- Make sure you are using any machine guarding that is provided to prevent access to cutter blades. Do not bypass safety guards.
- Do not open up or put your hands into an operating machine to stir contents or guide food.
- Turn off and unplug the machine before disassembling and cleaning.

Food processors, mixers

- Do not attempt to remove items (for example, a spoon that falls into the mixture) from dough while the machine is mixing.
- Do not open up the lids of processors to stir contents while food is processing.
- Make sure the processor is off before opening the lid or adding items.
- Turn off and unplug machinery before cleaning or removing a blockage.
- Use any machine guards provided.
- Do not wear loose clothing or jewelry that could become caught in machinery.

Microwaves

- Microwave ovens in poor repair may omit radiation.
- Make sure the microwave is located at approximately waist level and within easy reach, to provide for ease in the lifting of hot foods.
- Follow manufacturer's instructions for operating microwave ovens.
- Cover foods cooked in microwaves to avoid splattering.

- Use caution when opening tightly covered containers. Open containers away from your face because they may be under pressure and could be extremely hot.
- Use appropriate personal protective equipment such as hot pads when removing foods from microwave.
- Make sure door seals are in good condition and free from food or grease buildup.
- Do not use a microwave if it has a door that is damaged or doesn't lock properly. Damaged ovens may emit harmful radiation.
- Do not microwave metals, foil, or whole eggs.
- Keep the interior of the microwave clean to avoid splattering and popping.
- If you notice any sparking inside the microwave, immediately turn off the microwave, unplug it, report it to the supervisor, and do not use it.
- Be advised that microwaves may interfere with the workings of pacemakers.
- Be aware that food cooked in the microwave can remain hot long after the microwave turns off.

Steamers/Pressure Cookers

- Do not open the door while the steamer is on, shut off the steam, and then wait a couple of minutes before releasing the pressure and opening.
- Clear the area around the steamer before opening.
- Open the steamer door by standing to the side, keeping the door between you and the open steamer.
- Use oven mitts to remove hot trays from the steamer.
- Place hot, dripping steamer trays on a cart to transport. If trays are carried by hand, they will drip on floors and create a slip hazard.
- If a steamer is stacked, remove the tray from the top steamer first, then the lower one, to prevent burns from rising steam.

Pressure Cookers

- Shut off the steam supply and wait for the pressure to equalize before opening the lid of the pressure cooker.
- Stand to the side and open the pressure cooker away from yourself, keeping the open lid between you and the pressure cooker.

Coffee Makers

- Do not place hot coffee makers close to the edge of counters where people passing by may come in contact with them.
- Check to make sure the coffee filter is in place before making any coffee.

- Do not remove the filter before the coffee has stopped dripping.
- Never stick your fingers into the chamber of a coffee grinder to get beans to drop into the grinder; tapping on the outside of the container will encourage beans to drop into grinder.

LEARNING OUTCOME

Organization play a very vital role in the development of any organization.It is very important to know about the hierarchy structure of any organization before want to accomplished any goals.In kitchen organization Brigade de cuisine is a system of hierarchy found in restaurants and hotels in France that employ extensive staff and are commonly referred to as kitchen staff in English speaking countries. This structured team system delegates responsibilities to different individuals that specialize in certain tasks.

Kitchen equipment is expensive and to justify the expenses, it is essential that maximum use be made of it. This can be done only if the equipments work efficiently and this depends upon the care and maintenance. The type of fuel is to be used is an important factor. Though solid fuel and oil both have their place under certain circumstance, for professional cookery the choose lies between electricity and gas. The routine used, care and cleaning of all items of equipment are important and this should be appreciated and understood. Very important aspect you must know the safety and precautions to handle that tools and equipment.

LESSON END ACTIVITY

- Collect the brands name information related to kitchen equipments available in India.
- Collect the information and do market survey on famous equipment company and collect the details information regarding equipments and tools.
- Collect the information related to latest equipments and tools.
- Go through the different five star hotels in your place and collect the information which kitchen equipment brand is mostly used in the industry.
- Collect the information related to the Kitchen organization chart of any six five stars hotels and how they do manipulate their work.

QUESTIONS FOR DISCUSSION

1. Draw a kitchen organizational chart of 5 star hotels?
2. Explain the term Kitchen organization?
3. Draw a kitchen organization chart which divided by Auguste Escoffier?

4. Describe the duties and responsibilities of Executive chef and sous chef?
5. Explain the classification of kitchen equipments and tools?
6. Describe in details about the large equipments which are used in kitchen?
7. Describe in details about the small equipments which are used in kitchen?
8. Describe in details about the mechanical equipments which are used in kitchen.

STATE TRUE AND FALSE

- Brigade de cuisine is a system of hierarchy found in restaurants and hotels in France
- Head chef is also called as chef de cuisine
- Souf chef is also called chef de partie.
- le Trancheur is called soup chef
- Full supervision of kitchen brigade is a work of commis.
- Kitchen equipment are less expensive
- Classification of kitchen equipment divided into eight parts
- Refrigerators come in large equipments
- Food slicers are only manually operated
- Tilting pan is also known as braising pan
- Most freezers operate at around -18°C (0°F)
- Braising pans and roasting pans both are same thing.
- A chef's knife, also known as a French knife.
- Mortar and pestles is a tool used to crush, grind, and mix substances

KEY TERMS

* Chef
* Delegati
* Equipments
* Executive
* Hierarchy
* Mallets
* Management
* Mortar
* Pestle
* Precautions
* Supervisions
* Tools

Chapter 6

Stocks

After studying this chapter, the student must know:

- Introduction
- Definition, meaning and its elements
- Types of stocks and its preparations
- Preparation of stocks components
- Method of preparation of stocks
- Evaluating quality of stocks and its flavouring
- Flavouring of stocks
- Savoury aspic and jelly
- Conveniences bases and glazes

STOCKS

According to Laures stock also termed "Fond" is a liquid base for making a saucer stew or braised dish.

"*Stock to a cook is voice to a singer.*" - *Anon.*

One of the first lessons of any cooking course is learning how to make stocks. Stocks form the basis of most sauces and soups. Stock is a broth liquid containing the juices of meat, bones or vegetables that have been extracted by long, slow cooking. Stocks are the foundation for many soup recipes, and are a wonderful way to use leftover meats and vegetables.

Flavour, body and clarity are the characteristics of a good stock and of the three; flavour is the most important. To get a good flavour a high proportion of ingredients to water is used. The most flavorful stock is achieved by just covering the bones, shell, or vegetables with water. Chicken and vegetable stocks are the easiest to prepare and are the mildest in flavour and have become one of the most popular stocks to use in just about anything including fish soup and beef stew.

Cooking times for stocks varies. Once all the flavors and goodness have been extracted from the meat bones and vegetables the stock must be strained. In a stock meat adds flavour whilst the bones add body. Bones from joints such as the knuckles or shoulder contain gelatin, which gives a stock body and a rich smooth texture.

Today, ready-made stock and stock cubes consisting of dried, compressed stock ingredients are readily available. These are commonly known as bouillon cubes (or ox cubes, after a common brand of stock cube sold in Britain) or cooking base.

STOCK / FOND

The worl fond come from the world foundation just has foundation is the base for a house fond is the base much a cooking almost every culinary preparation required a fond for all practical Purpose stocks and fonds have the same meaning.

Fond is the result of extraction and concentration of taste and nutrients this is done by using liquid as a base with a variety of food stuff.

Four elements of a fond

1. Nourishing elements including meat bone fish head fish trimming and vegetable of acceptable quality.
2. Aromatic and spices from the mireporx, bouquet garni, herbs and roots.
3. Liquid such as water, wine, remouillage (Second Bouillon) or consommé.
4. Seasoning, this salt only normally salt should not be used in stock. One ounces per gallon of reduce stock will enhanced its flavour (in small amount salt can served to extract protein from fish and meat, givening the final sauces shine and falvoured.) If the stock is too made into a glazes. The salt must be omitted or the concentration will be too salty.

Types of Stock

There are three basic types of stock / fond

1. White Stock (Fond Blanc)
2. Brown Stock (Fond Brun)
3. Vegetable or nutrial stock (Fond mairge)

The classification refers in general to the content and preparation method of the stock not necessary to colour. A white stock made from beef and beef bone will be slightly brown in colour but its white stock nonetheless due to the method of preparation.

White Stock

White Stock is made with white meat or beef, beef bones, Chicken carcus and aromatic vegetable. The bones and meats put in cold liquid and slowly brought to a boil. The flavouring mixture (base of diced vegetable) and occasionally pork fat is sweated in suitable fat and then added to as liquid before it's develops any colour. The mixture is reduced to a simmer to finishing cooking. This stock is used for white sauce, blanquettes. Fricassee and Poached chicken dishes.

Brown Stock

Brown Stock is made from beef veal and poultry meat and bones. The bones are roasted till golden in colour not burn the mixture is added when the bones are three quarter roasted, tomatoes product may also be added at this time when the bones and mixture are golden in colour, cold liquid is added and the mixture is slowly brought to a boil then reduce to a simmer to finish cooking. This stock is used for brown sauces and gravies, braised dishes and meat glaze.

Vegetable Stock

It's basically a nutrial stock composed of vegetable and aromatic herbs sauté gently in butter cooked in a liquid. This is literally new type of stock which is gaining popularity. It uses has been limited to vegetarian cooking and veloutes.

*Fish Stock (***Fome de Poision***)*

Fish Stock (*Fome de Poision*) is categorized separately from the other basic stock because of limited usages. The basic of fish preparation is the fumet or fond. It has been said the all fish produced a fumet but not all fumet are equal some fish produces better quality stock than other. The results from some fish are stocks that are to gelatins. Fish which are oily yield stocks that have a bitter or that is milky.

Classical preparations calls from the bones of a specific fish ex. Dogger, Soul, Turbot, and Brillare recommended for their superior flavour. The most important thing is that the fish should be fresh and flesh should be white.

A few guidelines are listed below:

(i) Don't use trimming from oily fish, salmon, mackerel etc.

(ii) Flounder or lemon soul will work for soul fume.Halibut for turbot and striped bass for grilled.

(iii) Sometimes complementary juices of oyster, mussel or clam are added to fish. This liquid should not be reduced; it is used as an additive only.)

iv) Fish stock is cooked for a very short time. The fragile soft bone of the fish does not require longer cooking time. Long cooking time also caused harsh flavour develops in the stock.)

PREPARATION OF STOCK

Stock is a base from which you will create a wide variety of dishes. So the stock must be right. You must start with the quality ingredients.

Six steps in Produces a Stock are:

(i) Start with a cold liquid.
(ii) Allow natural clarification to occur.
(iii) Skim carefully.
(iv) Simmer don't boil.
(v) Straining
(vi) Colouring

(i) Cold liquid to start

Beginning with the cold liquid prevents the sealing of the items. This makes it possible to reduce the flavour of the food and entrance the liquid. This is a form of cooking by inter change. The flavours of the meat, bones poultry etc. are transferred to the liquid to surrounded them. This interchange occurs weather the bones and vegetables are browned or not when they are brown additional flavour is added. This is caused by the caramelization of natural sugar which occurs during browning. It's adds a richness of flavour and colour not achieve otherwise.

(ii) Natural Clarification

A high quality stock has a clear clean appearance. This requires that if be clarified. Passing the stock through a sieve is not what we are talking about here. It is the removal of the small minute particles which form during the cooking process. Albumin is a protein found in muscle, blood, milk, egg white and many vegetables tissues such as leeks. It is soluble in only cold water. Albumin is valued for its property of clarification by coagulation. By forming a mass when exposed of heat, the better the removal of cloudiness from liquid.

Bringing the stock slowly to a boil gives the albumin time to past into the solution. As the protein coagulated they attract particles in the liquid similar to a magnet. However as with magnet when disturb that will drop the particles.

Do not wash your bones or meat prior to cooking stock. Fresh meat and bones do not need to be washed. Also do not bring the stock to a boil and then throw away the first boil. All the clarifying elements and light aromatics are than wasted. This reduces the flavour and increases the chance of producing cloudy stock.

Cloudiness normally is the result of stock being boiled too long and fast over high heat. This extended boiling breaks down the texture of bone fibers. When this happens particles become blended and suspended in the liquid. This makes it difficult to clarify. A slightly amount of cloudiness is normal in the stock. The lack of blood in the bones used in stocks creates a lack of albumin there is not sufficient protein to attracts all the particles. After removing every particle of fat, strain the liquid through a linen cloth. Be careful not to press it through. If it is still cloudy, the best way to clear it is with an egg; it must be a fresh one. To clarify one quart of stock, you will need the white and shell of one large egg. See that the shell is quite clean before you break it up into small pieces and put it in a bowl with the white of the egg. Then add one teaspoon of cold water and whisk until the mixture is quite frothy. Heat your stock—it must not boil, remember—and then stir in the eggshell mixture thoroughly. Bring your soup to boiling point, and strain it again through a jelly bag or a piece of linen.

(iii) Skimming/Depouiller/Ecremer

As the stock, the albumin rise to the top of the pot. It is important to remove all of it. This removal is called skimming that is carefully lifting fat and scum from the surface.

The mirepoix of vegetables is finely cut for the best flavour extraction. This end the aromatics flavour on the top of the pot. This can make it difference to skim properly. To make it easier to skim add the mirepoix and aromatics has about ¼ of the cooking time has lapsed. The largest accumulation of fat and scum will occur in the early cooking of the stock. Once the mirepoix and aromatics are added do not skim unless necessary. Let the stock cook undisturbed.

(iv) Simmering

This simple operation is often misunderstood in proper application of it. Generates most of the burn stocks or sauces. Simmering is when liquid is hot enough to form small bubbles get rise from the bottom of the pan.The bubbles break before the top surface of the liquid. As they rise and break a small disturbance occurs. When the temperature is too high, this turbulence is too great. When the temperature is too high this turbulence is too great, if the temperature is too low, there is little or any movement in the liquid. Simmering is correct when it creates a slight roll in the liquid

Simmering is important in the cooking of stocks and sauces when the slightly role is simmer is not present, the coarser particles will settle at the bottom of the pan. These create an insulating layer between the heat and the stock and its starts burning. When it burns it imparts an unwanted flavour. Too much action in the liquid also harms. The heavy rolling action of a high boil will break up the scum and fat. This makes it difficult to skim. It also doesn't allow the albumin together the fine particles.

(v) Straining

Strain your stock into a bowl directly it is made. It must never be left in a metal stock-pot. If you want it to keep a few days, take out the vegetables. Then, as soon as it is cold, remove the fat. Some cooks imagine that if the fat is left on the stock it will keep longer. I have proved the reverse. Stock, closely covered with fat, soon turns sour. It helps to keep stock fresh if it is brought up to boiling point every day. Always provide, too, a net cover to protect your stock-bowl, especially in hot weather; it keeps the flies away. Naturally, it must be washed out in hot water every time it is used. Whatever type of soup you are making, beware of too much seasoning. Salt and pepper can always be added, but they cannot be taken away. It is always better to use spice and herbs with discretion. One flavour should never predominate.

(vi) Colouring

The appearance of soup is almost as important as the taste, and we must remember to appeal to the eye as well as the palate. White soup must be white or creamy. That means taking care that nothing goes into the stock-pot that will discolour it. Nothing is more unappetizing than a grey soup—or, incidentally, a greasy one. If white stock has become dislittle browning and turn it into a brown soup instead of a grey one.

THICKENING OF SOUPS

Thick soups should be of the consistency of rich cream. Avoid making them too thick, especially if they are white, and be sure that they are perfectly smooth. If through careless mixing the liquid has become lumpy, it should be rubbed through a sieve and then reheated. Soups are thickened by the vegetables cooked in them being rubbed through a sieve or by a flour and butter thickening. First-class professional cooks always thicken with brown or white roux, a mixture of cooked flour and butter thickening. First class professional cooks always thicken with brown or white roux, a mixture of cooked flour and butter. This adds both richness and flavour, and is infinitely better than raw flour. For some reason, many women imagine that roux is difficult to make. It is really quite simple.

For white roux, melt two ounces of butter in a saucepan, and blend with it very gradually two and a half ounces of flour. Stir slowly until your mixture is a thick smooth past. When it leaves the sides of the saucepan it is ready. Brown roux is exactly the same mixture, cooked—stirring all the time, remember—until it turns brown. Half the quantity will thicken a quart of soup, and if the remainder is put in a jar it will keep for some days. The making of roux is only the first step; if your soup is to be perfect, it must be carefully added. First, put the roux into a basin and add a little hot soup. Add more soup in small quantities until the liquid is quite thin, when it is ready to stir slowly into the soup. If you add your roux direct to the soup it is almost impossible to keep the liquid smooth. Remember to be as sparing with your thickening as you are with the seasoning.

Rich cream soups are thickened with egg yolks and cream. Great care must be taken that they do not curdle. When the soup is ready, take it off the stove, mix the egg yolks and cream together, add a little hot—but not boiling—soup to them. Then stir the mixture into the soup. Stir while it cooks for two or three minutes, but it must not boil, or it will curdle. See that your soup is hot if it is meant to be a hot soup—and icy cold if it is a cold soup. For the good cook and the discerning guest, soup to be perfect must be of the right consistency, colour, flavour and temperature. Properly served soup is the perfect beginning to a well-planned meal.

Re-Mouillage

Re-Mouillage means "second wetting". After draining away the first stock, more water is added and the mixture is simmered again. These extract additional flavour of the elements. This yields a weak stock but in richer than water. The re-mouillage if often used as the liquid for making a new stock thereby yielding a richer stock.

Second stock

When fresh meat has been used for making stock, quite a useful stock—known as second stock—can be made. Throw away the cooked vegetables and put the meat and bones back in the stew pan with a fresh lot of vegetables, celery, onion, carrot, turnip, etc. Add a bunch of fresh herbs (or half a teaspoon of dried ones in a muslin bag), a clove, six peppercorns, a scrap of mace, and a teaspoon of salt. Pour over a quart of water, simmering for three hours. If you want a thick soup, remove the herbs and spices and rub the vegetables with the stock through a wire sieve. When cold, remove the fat and you have quite a palatable vegetable soup. Or strain the liquid clear from the vegetables into a bowl. Remove the fat when cold and the stock can be used as a foundation for any kind of soup which does not depend entirely on stock for its flavour.

PREPARATION OF STOCK COMPONENTS

The preparations of some important stock components are given below:

Preparation of Mirepoix

Mirepoix

Yield	200ml
Onions, peeled and chopped	100 gram
Carrots, trimmed and chopped	50 gram
Celery, trimmed and chopped	50 gram

Method

- Cut the vegetables into an appropriate size based on the cooking time of the dish

Preparation of White Mirepoix

White Mirepoix

Yield	approx. 200 ml
Onions, peeled and chopped	50 gram
White portion of leeks, trimmed and Chopped	50 gram
Parsnips, trimmed and chopped	50 gram
Celery, trimmed and chopped	50 gram
Mushroom trimmings	25 gram

Method:

- Cut the vegetables into an appropriate size based on the cooking time of the dish.

Preparation of Matignon

Matignon

Yield	200ml
Onions, peeled and diced small	50 gram
Carrot, trimmed, peeled and diced small	50 gram
Celery, trimmed, peeled and diced small	50 gram
Mushroom, diced small	25 gram
Bacon or ham, diced small or minced	25 gram

Method:

- Cut all the vegetables and the bacon or ham into a neat, small dice and combine. Sweat in whole butter.

Preparation of Sachet d'epices

Sachet d'epices

Yield	¼ cup
Parsley stems, chopped	5 gram
Thyme leaves	3 gram
Bay leaf	1 no
Cracked black peppercorns	5 gram
Garlic clove crushed	5 gram

Method:

- The above ingredients are placed into a 4" square of cheesecloth and tied into a sack.

Preparation of Stocks

Recipe of White Stock (Chicken, veal and Beef)

White stocks	Yield 15gallon

(i) Bone cuts small	60 LB
(ii) Cold water	18 Gallon
(iii) Mireporx (diced)	
Onions	3 LB
Carrot or Parsnip	3 LB
Celery	3 LB
Leeks	2 LB
(iv) Butter	1 LB
(v) Thyme	1 tbsp
(vi) Bouquet Garni	1 large
(v) Bay leaf	10-15

Method of preparation

1. Place bones in stock pot and water with cold water.
2. Bring slowly to a boil and skin the scum.
3. Sauté mireporx in butter until golden.
4. Add sauté mireporx and aromatics to stock.
5. Simmer 5-6 hours for Chicken and 8-10 hours for veal.
6. Pass through a fine strainer, label, cool refrigerate.

A tall narrow pot correct ration of bones to water and the method of flavouring such as bouquet garni contribute to a good stock. Quite surfaces with rising bubble indicate correct temperature.

Brown Stock (Fond Brun) (Beef and veal)

Yields	15 gallons
1. Bones (Cut small)	60 LB
2. Tomato Product	Optional
3. Mireporx (Diced)	
Onions	3 LB
Carrot or Parsnip	3 LB
Celery	3 LB
Leeks	2 LB
4. Butter Thyme	1 tbsp
5. Bay leaf	10-15

Method of preparation:

1. Place bones in a roasting pan and brown in a 350° F oven.
2. When bones are ¾ done place mireporx over the bones and finish browning (Fig. 6.2).
3. When browned remove bones and place in a stock pot (Fig 6.3).
4. Remove the fat from the roasting pan deglazed roasting pan with water, add mireporx with aromatic and add to the stock pot (Fig 6.4).
5. Add remaining cold water or re-mouillage to cover the bones.
6. Bring to a boil reduce to a simmer and skim (Fig 6.4).
7. Simmer for 8-10 hours.
8. Pass through a fine strainer label, cool and refrigerate (Fig 6.5).

Fig 6.1 The bones are placed in roasting pan

Fig 6.2 When bones are ¾ done than we added mireporx

Fig. 6.3 Roasted bones are places in nstock pots

Fig 6.4 The mire porx, water and bouquet garni is added

Fig 6.5 The scum are coming in the stock

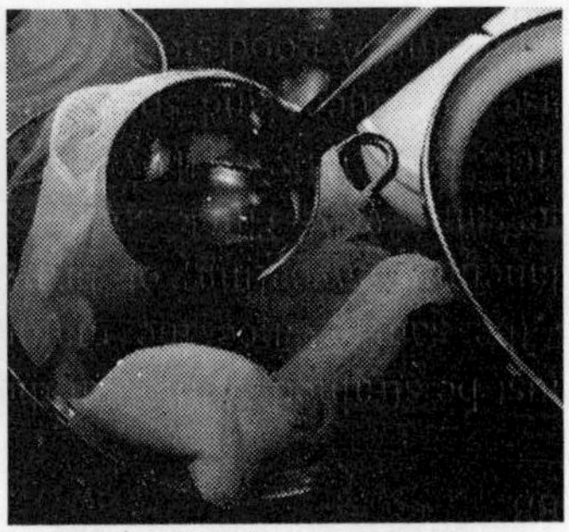

Fig 6.6 The straining of stock with muslin cloth

Fish Stock (Fumet de Poisson)

Yield	3 gallon
Fish bones with heat	12 LB
Cold Water	3½ gallon

Mireporx (Diced)	
Onion	8 Oz
Celery	4 Oz
Leeks	4 Oz
Butter	2 Oz
White Wine (Chablis)	1 Qt (Quest)
Bay leaf	2 No.
Parsley	As needed
Thyme	One good pinch

Method of Preparation

1. Clean bones and head in cold running water break the large bone remove any black skin, blood clots and gills.
2. Sauté mireporx and aromatics in butter.Cover and let sweat in their own juices.
3. Add fish bones, cover and let sweat for a few minute.
4. Add white wine and cover with cold water.
5. Bring to a slow boil and simmer uncovered up to 45 minutes.
6. Pass through a fine strainer, label, cool and refrigerate.

Preparation from Stock

Essences:

Essences are stocks made in a concentrated flavour. Essence is made in the same manner as a stock but with less liquid. Essence is used to boost the flavour of a stock, soup or sauce. The addition of this concentrated flavour is meant to enhance the already good flavour of the items. The best essences are made from highly flavoured items such as celery, truffles, mushrooms, morels etc.

Glaze/Glace

Its unity the principal strength and flavour of the ingredients in the stock. They have been reduced to the consistency of syrup. These distinguish them from essence which is only extraction of the flavour of the product being used. The various glazes of meat, fish, poultry and game are widely used in modern cooking.

Glazes serve four basic purposes in cooking:

1. Glace gives a brilliant shine and moist cooking to a finished dish.
2. They are re-enforcing the quality and tone of a sauce.
3. Glazes strengthen the flavour and body of a preparation made from a weak stock.
4. Glazes can act as sauces when properly buttered and creamed to match this dish they are to be used with.

Recipe of meat Glace (Yield 1 QT)

Good rich brown stock: - 1 gallon = 4 QT = 16 Cup

1. Place brown stock in a heavy bottom stock pot, cook over moderate heat allowing it to reduce.
2. After a suitable amount of reduction has occurred, strain the stock into smaller pat, contains this process as the reduction progress.
3. Skim the stock carefully throughout the process. This will determine the quality of glace.
4. As the stock reduces, gradually reduce the heat. When the reduction is nearly complete, it must be over a very moderate heat to prevent scorching.
5. The glace is ready when it adheres to the back of the spoon. It should be glossy, translucent, syrupy coating. This stage is normally reached after the reduction of 2/3 or ¾ of the original quality.

Fish essence Yield 1 QT

Ingredients

Clean head bone and trimmings	4.5 pounds
Butter	3.5 Ounce
Slice onions	4.5 ounce
Mushroom trimmings	11 ounce
Parsley stalks	2 ounces
Dried white wine	8 ounce
Clean fish stock	3 pints
Lemon juice	1 number
Salt	pinch

Method:

1. Melt butter, add onions, mushroom trimmings and parsley stalks and swet without colouring.

2. Add the fish bones and trimmings.Cover and allow to swet gently for 15minute.
3. Add the wine and reduce by half uncovered
4. Add the fish stock, lemon juice and salt
5. Bring to boil, skim carefully and allow to simmer gently for 15 minutes
6. Strain to a fine strainer and cool.

VEGETABLE STOCK

Water or Liquor in which vegetables have been boiled—2 lb.

Mixed Vegetables	2 oz.
Dripping	1 teaspoon
Salt	1/4 lb.
Lentils	100 gram
Peppercorns	10 gram
small bunch fresh Herbs	10 gram

Methods:

1. Soak the lentils overnight in sufficient water to cover them (save the water).
2. Any kind of raw vegetable and vegetable trimmings can be used for this it will depend upon the season; in any case; a good variety is best.
3. Carrot, turnip, onion, leeks, a shallot, parsnip, asparagus stalks, cauliflower, lettuce, celery may all be used.
4. Be sparing with parsnips and turnips as their strong flavour is liable to predominate.
5. If celery is out of season, use a pinch of celery seed.
6. Well wash the vegetables, cut them in small pieces and drain them.
7. Melt the dripping in a stew pan, put in the vegetables and fry until they are well browned.
8. Add the water from the lentils and simmer ten minutes.
9. Then pour in the water and bring to the boil.
10. Skim well, add the lentils, peppercorns, celery seed and herbs tied in a muslin bag and the salt.
11. Simmer gently for three hours. Then strain for use.
12. Vegetable stock will not keep long; in summer it should be used either the day it is made or the following day.
13. If using the water in which vegetables have been boiled, be sure it is free from soda.
14. The lentils may be omitted if all vegetable is preferred—or the water in which rice has been boiled can be substituted.

VEGETABLE STOCK (WHITE)

Water	2 oz.
Pearl Barley	1 ½ lb.
Vegetables, such as Carrot, Turnip, Celery, Parsnip	4oz.
Onion	2 oz.
Butter or Margarine	2oz
White Peppercorns	10 gram
Sprig of Parsley	10 gram
Thyme and Marjoram	5 gram
Salt	5 gram

Method:

1. Wash and cut up the vegetables.
2. Melt the butter in a stew pan, add the vegetables, cover and cook for ten minutes.
3. Add the other ingredients and bring to the boil Skim.
4. Then simmer for three hours. Strain and use.
5. Do not use any vegetable that will discolour the stock, such as asparagus stalks.

EVALUATING QUALITY OF STOCK

A good stock is evaluated by flavour, colour, aroma, and clarity.

Flavour - If the correct procedure and ratio of bones, mirepoix,and aromatics to liquids has been followed, the flavour should be well balanced, rich, and full-bodied.

Colour - White stocks and fish fumet should have a very light colour that turns translucent. Brown stocks are a deep amber or brown because of the roasting process.

Aroma - The aroma should be appealing but not over pungent. When stock is reboiled it should be tested for sour taste and smell.

Clarity - Most stock, with the exception of vegetable essences and fish fumet, should be almost crystal clear when hot. This is maintained by proper simmering. Never allow the stock to boil continuously, and also skim the stock during the cooking process. Skimming removes the impurities that are trapped by the coagulated albumen that rises to the top during the cooking process.

FLAVOURING

Many kinds of vegetables are used to flavour stock, and in most cases the parts not suitable to be served as a vegetable are quite good for the purpose; for instance, the outer leaves of celery, trimmings of mushrooms, stalks of asparagus, all add flavour to the stock, also the water in which such well-flavoured vegetables as onions, leeks, asparagus, celery, etc., have been boiled, should either be added to the stock-pot or used as a stock for other soups. Herbs also form valuable flavouring; always use fresh ones whenever you can, as they are so much milder and more delicate in flavour than dried ones. A bunch of herbs for the stock-pot consists of a tiny sprig each of plain or lemon thyme, marjoram, basil, tarragon and parsley. A bay leaf is valuable too, and a small piece of lemon rind may take the place of lemon thyme. They should be tied in a bunch or put in a little muslin bag with the spices; then they can easily be removed when the stock is sufficiently flavoured.

If you use dried herbs, be very sparing with them, as the flavour is more concentrated. Celery seed is quite a good substitute for celery, when the former is out of season. When using spices—such as cloves, mace, etc.—we need to be careful, also, as it is so easy to spoil the flavour by adding just a little too much.

Savoury Aspic and Jelly

Jellies are highly clarified and concentrated forms of stock. Through reduction it is possible for the cook to concentrate the natural gelatin. Contained of stock creating the jelly. These are used to quote cold foods providing moisture, protection and flavour for the product. These jellies gain the quality from the flavour of the stock used. It is the quality of the jelly. Development of a high amount of gelatin needed for a jelly calls for some special ingredients. Calf's feet and pork rind are both used. They are high in natural gelatin. The goal is to make a jelly which will set without the use of added gelatin. This also gives / yields a jelly which is soft in consistency.

COURTBOUILLON

Is not actually is a stock preparation however it is used in a simpler manner.It's a flavorfully poaching liquid used for fish and shell fish and some other items such as sweet breads.

A courtbouillon is made up of three elements:

1. Aromatic and spices
2. Salt
3. Liquid.

The flavour of bouillon is created when fish is poached in it. Basic guidelines for using court bouillon are given below:

- Always prepare in advance.The time for poaching is less than ½ hour.
- Whole fish should be emerged in cold court bouillon and then brought to a poaching temperature.
- When poaching is in small amount of liquid.The mireporx is placed under the strainer.In a pan enough liquid to cover one third of the pieces of fish. Fish cooked in this manner should be frequently basted to prevent drying.

- Court Bouillon for lobster will be at a full boil.When the lobster is emerged.This is also used for small or medium fish.
- Fish which is served cold is cooled in the court bouillon.This will improve the flavour of the fish.
- Shell fish are always cooled in the court bouillon, be carefully about over cooking.

Recipe for court Bouillon

1. Plain Court Bouillon: The quantity of court bouillon is determined by the amount of fish been cooked. It is composed of salted water,1quart of milk, per quart of water and some thin slices of peeled lemon in case of (turbot and soul)
2. Just salted water for sea bass
3. Salted water, carrot, parsley, bay leaf, thyme and vinegar for large salmon trout.
4. Water, wine and aromatic for pike, trout, elle and salmon.
5. A matelotes preparation uses red wine instead of white wine.

Convenience bases and Glazes

Stocks which are the base of classic sauces take time to prepare it are necessary to have bones and trimming to make a stock. In a classical kitchen this is not a problem since the ingredients and man power is easily available but in today's kitchen meat, poultry, fish is often bought ready to cook. The elements for stock are not available. The staff is also smaller particularly in restaurants. This factor makes the production of stock difficult. This difficult situation has created a market for bases. They are concentrated stock which are granular and paste on form when diluted in water they become like fresh stock. Many contain high levels of salt and MSG which can yield a salty stock. They should be used with discretion. Although there is no substitute but if you must choose, choose carefully. Glazes are true reduction without sodium additives.

LEARNING OUTCOME

Stocks form the basis of most sauces and soups. Stock is a broth liquid containing the juices of meat, bones or vegetables that have been extracted by long, slow cooking. Stocks are the foundation for many soup recipes, and are a wonderful way to use leftover meats and vegetables. A stock is a flavorful liquid made by gently simmering bones or vegetables in a liquid to extract their flavour, aroma, colour, body, and nutritive value. Stocks are the foundation for many soup recipes, and are a wonderful, efficient and economic way to use leftover meats and vegetables. The classification refers in general to the content and preparation method of the stock not necessary to colour. A white stock made from beef and beef bone will be slightly brawn in colour but its white stock nonetheless due to the method of preparation. Flavour, body and clarity are the characteristics of a good stock and of the three; flavour is the most important. Cooking times for stocks varies. Once all the flavors and goodness have been extracted from the meat bones and vegetables the stock must be strained. Although the ingredients may vary, the basic preparation for making various stocks is the same. Once the major flavour ingredients have undergone any preliminary steps such as blanching, sweating, or browning, all stocks, essences, fumets, and *court bouillons* are prepared the same way Thick soups should be of the consistency of rich cream. Avoid making them too thick, especially if they are white, and be sure that they are perfectly smooth Stocks are used as base for sauces and soups, as base for stews and braises, and as a cooking medium for vegetables and grains. A good stock is evaluated by flavour, colour, aroma, and clarity. Many kinds of vegetables are used to flavour stock, and in most cases the parts not suitable to be served as a vegetable are quite good for the purpose; for instance, the outer leaves of celery, trimmings of mushrooms, stalks of asparagus, all add flavour to the stock, also the water in which such well-flavoured vegetables as onions, leeks, asparagus, celery, etc., have been boiled, should either be added to the stock-pot or used as a stock for other soups.

LESSON END ACTIVITY

- Collect the different types of bones from the butcher shops Such as chicken, mutton, beef and fish.Prepare three types of stocks.
- Bring root vegetable and prepare the vegetable stock according to the standard recipe given above.
- Bring two piece of fish.You have to boil one piece of fish in water and other in court bouillon and check the difference between those preparation.

QUESTIONS FOR DISCUSSION

1. Define stock and its elements.
2. Why we need stock in our kitchen?
3. Describe the types of stocks.
4. Explain the role of stock in food preparation.
5. Describe the six basic steps of stocks preparations.
6. Describe in details about the thickening of soups.
7. Explain the term Re-Mouillage.
8. What are the different preparation stocks components?
9. Describe the recipe of white stocks with their method.
10. Describe the recipe of brown stocks with their method.
11. Describe the recipe of vegetable stocks with their method.

12. Describe the recipe of Fish stocks with their method.
13. Explain the different preparation from stocks.
14. Explain the quality for evaluating good stocks.
15. Explain the term glazes with their preparation of basic method.

STATE TRUE AND FALSE

- White stocks can be made from any bones.
- White stocks can be made without browning of the bones.
- Chicken bones can be used for making brown stocks.
- Fish stocks can be made only by fish bones and seafood shells.
- Flavour,body and clarity can be a character tics of good stocks
- Court bouillon is a flavoured poaching liquid.
- Jellies are highly clarified and concentrated forms of stock
- Essences are stocks made in a concentrated flavour.
- Re-Mouillage means "second wetting.
- Rich cream soups are thickened with egg yolks and cream.
- A high quality stock has a clear clean appearance.
- Cloudiness normally is the result of stock being boiled too long and fast over high heat.
- Simmering is when liquid is hot enough to form small bubbles get rise from the bottom of the pan

KEY TERMS

* Aspic	* Mireporx
* Drippings	* Simmering
* Essence	* Stockpots
* Glazes	* Stocks

Chapter 7

Soups

After studying this chapter, the student must know

- Introduction, types and definition
- Classification of soups
- Soups and its types with their preparation
- Specialty soups - national and regional types
- Quality of soup
- Garnishes of soups
- Soups and its recipe

SOUPS

It took almost a century to bring soups to perfection on it is today. Modern cooking has replaced the heavy dishes of the past with simpler ones. George Auguste Escoffiér, the master of the world cuisine in the late 19th and 20th century believed that soups and the stocks they are based upon where of utmost importance in modern cuisine. The role of soup has remained unchanged in the last 10,000 years. Good soup is still the ultimate food for stimulating our appetite, nourishing our bodies and sustaining our spirits. The soup must be in harmony with the whole menus.

Among all items making up the menu of a dinner, soups required the most attention. The good or bad impression that they make on the guest affect the success of an entire meal that follows.

The word 'soup' comes from the Latin 'suppare', which means 'soaking', and once described a dish of meat or vegetables that was soaked in the liquid in which it was cooked. Stock is the foundation of all good soups. Soups are made from meat stock. Meat stock is a broth made by cooking meat with water and it requires long, slow cooking. Beef, veal, lamb or chicken can be cooked separately or in combinations. Soups are served all over the world, and they are wonderful time-savers and appetite satisfiers. Soup may be served as an appetizer, to stimulate the appetite, or it may be served as the main dish of the meal. If the soup to be served is a hot soup, it must be served piping hot. If it is to be a cold soup, it must be served icy cold.

Types and Definition

Soups of the old classical kitchen were complete dishes in themselves containing apart from the liquid and garnish, a wide variety of meat, poultry, game and fish. It is only the liquid part of the classical dishes which retains the name "Soup" today. Their preparation is much more simplify taking almost 100 years to arrive at the state of perfection they have reached today.

Classification of Soups

Thin	Thick	Specialty
Broth, Consommé, Essence and Jellied Soups	Purees, Coulis, Bisqué, Vegetable Soup, Cream Soups, Veloute Soups	National Regional Soups Cold Soups.

Clear Soups

Clear Soups prepared in the same manner whether made from meat, poultry, game, fish, shellfish, turtle or vegetables. Consommés are one of the sub categories always classified, sometimes thicken with tapioca. They normally inclined a light garnish matching the character of consommé. Broth is another sub category; they are not clarified like consommé. Their cleanness comes from very careful cooking. The last two sub categories include all kinds of essences and chilled jellied soups.

Thin clear soups are a good first cause. They stimulate the appetite. Their preparation is more time consuming especially the ones requiring clarifications.

Broth

The term broth and bouillon means the same. The flavour of the soup comes from long simmering of all ingredients together in one pot and assortment of separately cooked foods may be added at various times during cooking, depending on the cooking requirements of the individual items. All ingredients should finish cooking at the same time. The plain unclarified broth from cooking meat, fish or vegetable is used instead of water or white stock for cooking certain dishes and for the preparation of soups and sauces.

Common addition to broth include sherry, madeira, lemon, hot pepper sauce, red wine for beef and white wine for veal. Pasta and rice may also be used but may cloud the broth and should be cooked separately and then added.

Broth can be accompanied by baked, toasted or fired croutons which are bread crust sometimes rubbed with garlic, grated parmesan or swiss cheese. The selection of what is rubbed on it would depend on the nature of the broth. Common garnishes broths are chopped or finely minced fresh herb. This includes chervil, chives, scallions and others.

Consommé

Fig 7.1 The consommé juliennes

Consommé is a concentrated thin clear soup made from meat, poultry or fish. The word has the same origin as consummate meaning to bring to a completion or to perfection. A consommé is cooked long enough for most of the nutritive properties of the ingredients to be extracted into the liquid. In most general sense consommé is a meat poultry or fish stock, which has gone through a special clarification process served hot or cold and normally at the beginning of the dinner meal. Consommé is the most sophisticated of all stocks based on soups.It is made by reducing veal, beef, chicken, or fish stock. The liquid is than clarified enriching with nutritive and aromatic substance producing a transparent sparkling liquid. This soup may be garnished in many different ways depending on the base of the from which is it made.

Preparation Consommé:

1. **<u>The Stock</u>**: - Beef and Chicken are the most common however; fish and games are becoming popularity. Consommé stock made richer with pieces of meat also added to the stock pot along with bones.
2. **<u>Clarification</u>**: - The term "Consommé double" describes the process whereby the meat or fish flavour is extracted twice. First when making the stock and second while clarifying the consommé. It is the clarification that makes it a true consommé. The process is simple, well flavoured fat free stock is brought slowly to a boil while a clarification mixture is whisked in. As the albumin in the egg whites and the ground meat in the clarification mixture cooks, it expands and rises to the top of the stock. It forms a gray froth of coagulated proteins which forms a bitter. This is called a raft. The consommé is left to simmer for approximately an hour. The mixture is not allowed to boil once the raft formed. The strong rolling action would break the raft a parts. This allows the impurities to percolate through the filter leaving the liquid consommé crystal and sparking.
3. **<u>Flavour and Colour</u>**: - While the egg whites clarify the liquid, they also absorb flavour ground and finely chopped vegetables are added to the stock. They provide flavour to the consommé and body to the raft. Brown meats which are in character with the consommé are added. The blood in the meat and flavour and act as a clarifying agent. Sherry or Madeira can be added before serving. Meat consommé' should be darker than that of chicken or fish.

4. **Thicking Consommé**: - Consommé are thickened naturally by their gelatin contents. The gelatin content of consommé gives it a smooth texture. When hot and sets it when chilled to a shivering jelly.

   Consommé may also be thickened with egg yolk, fresh cream, tapioca and arrowroot. The use of these thickeners would depend on the type of consommé being prepared

5. **Garnish**: - Garnish is added just before serving the soup so that it does not cloud the soup. No ingredient should be longer than the size of peas and all cut garnishes should fit within the bouillon spoon, chopped herbs, small quenelles, pasta, burnoise of vegetables and royals are appropriate garnish. A table spoon per serving is sufficient.

6. **Accompaniments**: - Would accompaniments for consommé are cheese straws, wafers, small puffs or Paté aur choux. The accompaniments should not corporate with the consommé.

Basic Clarification

Process for Consommé yield approx 1 Gallon.

• Egg Whites	3-4 eggs
• Lean Ground Meat	1 Pond (lb)
• Mireporx finely diced including white of leeks and Parsley stems	1/2 lb
• Small onions caramelized and spiked with cloves	1
• Crushed tomatoes	8 oz
• Defatted Cold old jellied white stock	1 gallon and 1 Quart
• Salt and Pepper	To taste

Method of Preparation

1. In a stainless steel bowl whip egg white until frothy.
2. Add ground meat, mireporx onion and tomatoes and let it marinates for two hours.
3. Stir the clarification mixture into cold stock in the stock pot.

   Note: It is best to use a stock pot with a drain spigot. This allows the draining of the consommé for straining without disturbing the raft.

4. Place stock pot on a moderate fire in a way that it will not boil too quickly.
5. With a spatula stir the mixture from time to time prevent it sticking to the bottom.

   Note: Under the influence of that, the albumin from the meat and egg dissolved in Cold water stock will coagulate and expands in volume rising and accumulating on the surface of the stock in the form of a raft.

6. When the stock comes to first boil gently, lower the heat and with the ladle make a vent/ hole in the solid clarification fitter or raft.
7. Simmer the consommé for 40-60 minutes to extract all the flavours fully.

Fig 7.2 The straining of the consommé

Fig 7.3 The hole making process in consommé

8. To strain, place damp cheese cloth over a fine mash strainer and ladle the consommé in to it.
9. Once drained if not used immediately, rapid cooling is needed to prevent fermentation.
10. When Cool cover, label and refrigerated.

Special Factors for Making Consommé Soup

Since consommé soups contained milk and cream. Curdling is a common occurrence. Heat of cooking combined with natural acidity of the ingredients is the cause. Consommé soups are thickened with some types of starch that is roux. There are three steps to avoid curdling.

1. To thicken the milk before adding it to the béchamel.
2. Whenever possible suet the vegetable in butter. This removes the natural acidity and neutralizes the enzymes of the vegetables. If it is not suitable to sweat the vegetables, blanch then in boiling salted water.
3. Always boil the milk or cream before adding to the hot soups never after.

Essences

Essences are a derivation of the mentioned consommé with special flavoures. The flavour comes from the extract of aromatics and flavourful herbs, plants, vegetables or fungi's. The most common essences are Celery, Tarragon, Truffles and Tomatoes.

There are also special consommé flavoured with wines usually fortified wines. That is added at the last minute just before serving.

Jellied soups

Jellied soups are only appropriate for serving warm season or in warm region. Most clear soups are jellied with the addition of little unflavoured gelatin.

Note:- It should be served piping hot if they are hot soups and absolutely chilled if cold soups.

Thick Soups

Is termed used for soups served at the substantial first course of a meal or as the main dish. They are not necessary thickened, they made with stocks of any character such as meat, fish, shellfish, poultry or vegetables. To the stock are added ingredients given them there particular taste and usually heavy consistency.

There are several kinds of thick soup. The soup liaison binding or thickening may be from a variety of sources. It can come naturally from the major ingredient of the soup or from the farinaceous ingredient such as roux, rice, pasta, bread etc. Many thick soups are bound with the liaison of cream before serving. It will be divided into 4 sections:-

A. Puree, Coulis and Bisques
B. Veloute Soups
C. Cream Soups
D. Vegetable Soups

A. PureT, Coulis and Bisques

Pureé

Purees are either purees of starchy vegetables or leguminous plant. The liaison is achieved naturally from the vegetable purees using seeds such as beans and lentils and starchy vegetables need additional thickening agent. Vegetable such as carrot, celery, broccoli, pumpkin must have some thickening agent. Among the classical pureed soups are Vichyssoise, Potage Crecy (Carrot thickened with rice) and Potage St. Germaine (Split peas flavored with ham).

Coulis

Coulis is the term best use for purees poultry, game, shellfish, and fish. Today it is sometimes being used for fruits and non-farinaceous vegetables also.

Bisque

Bisque is a creamy puree that concentrated the essence of single ingredients into a rich performed soup. The thickening agent is rice or crust of bread fried in butter. Traditionally the base of bisque has been shellfish. This is cooked with mire poix. Shellfish bisque follows a classical preparation.

1. The principle ingredient is often sautéed and flambéd. This is especially true, if live shellfish is used.
2. Fish stocks and aromatics are added along with rice or thickening.
3. When all the ingredients are cooked, the bisque is pureed. This was previously done by motor and pestle but today it's done with food processor with bladder.
4. The bisque is then sieved before returning to that for simmering. The second heating the marriage flavour.
5. It is finely enriched with cream which gives it the characterize of velvety texture which is truly a bisques.

Bisque is seasoned with cayenne pepper enriched with shellfish butter. There are best garnish with the item that represent the base like for shell fish bisques use small shell fish like shrimp, crab or lobster meat. Tiny quenelles may also be used. Bisque is mostly served with fried croutons.

Veloute Soups

The foundation of these soup is always veloute sauces, one whose preparation is in harmony with nature of ingredients of soup have been prepared.This means using either meat or vegetable,poultry game or fish shell fish stock in preparation. In addition with finale liaison of veloute soup 5 to 6 cup of egg yolk per cup of heavy cream for each quart of veloute soups.In cream soups only heavy cream is used these soups always composed of four items.

The base of the veloute soup should be in harmony with the nature of ingredient of the soup being prepared. In addition, the final liaison in veloute soup is 5-6 egg yolks per cup of heavy cream for each quart of veloute soup. Velouté soup is a lighter richer soup than broth, potages and purée soups. These soups are made using a blond roux and white stock with a few base vegetables for flavouring.. The base vegetables are diced and sweated in fat until softened, but not coloured. The flour is then added and a blond roux is made. The well flavoured white stock is added and, after bringing to the boil, the soup is simmered for 40-50 minutes. The type of stock used will depend upon the type of soup that is being prepared. For example, if a chicken velouté is being prepared, then chicken stock is used and diced chicken will be added for garnish just before service. After being simmered, the soup is passed through a fine strainer, reheated, and then checked for consistency and flavour. To finish the velouté soup, cream or milk is often added just before service and an appropriate garnish is added.

1. Puree of main flavour/ingredients
2. An ordinary meat, game, poultry, vegetable or fish veloute this should be prepared a little thinner than usual.
3. An liaisons composed of eggs yolks and cream
4. A garnish in keeping with nature of the soup.

Cream Soups

Cream soups are based on Béchamel where as veloute soups are based on veloute sauce. A cream soup is a smooth, rich soup that has a definite main ingredient and flavour. It is a soup that has been made from another base soup. For example, it can be made from any of the three following methods, a potato base that is finished with milk to create a creamy texture; a puree base that is combined with a thin, béchamel sauce to create a creamy based soup of a lighter texture than full puree soup; and a veloute base that is finished with the addition of a cream and egg yolk liaison to create a creamy rich soup (care must be taken when adding the liaison).

Cream Soup

The preparation is same like veloute but has some following differences:-

1. The main difference is that one is Béchamel base another is veloute soup.
2. In cream soup the correct consistency of soup is obtained by adding boiled milk or light cream instead of broth.
3. Cream soups are not finished with egg cream liaison.
4. Consommé soups are not buttered but finished with heavy cream.
5. The same garnish as veloute applies to cream soup.

Vegetable Soups

Any soups containing one or more vegetables cut in dices brunoise, juliennes, chiffonade or paysanne and eaten with the liquid they have flavoured, is classified as vegetable soups or potage. Flour thickening may be used in certain cases. However vegetables soup is usually made of clear broth in which potatoes and other ingredients such as tomatoes etc. give the broth a certain thickness. The preparation of a basic vegetable soup should be as follows:-

1. Ingredients are cut into similar shape and sizes.
2. Braised vegetables well in butter. This expels their moisture and acidity while saturating them in butter.
3. Add liquid and simmer until solid ingredients are tender and broth is well flavoured.

Specialty Soups

This category includes soup of a specific, national or regional origin. Which do not easily fit into other classification. A good example of this is "American Chowder" another is "Hungarian Goulash".

NATIONAL AND REGIONAL TYPES

America

Is known for chowder, Gumbo, Oyster Stew, she Crab soup and Philadelphia pepper pot.

- ***Chowder***

Premier American soup chunky hearty soups. They are sometimes full of good things that they are more like stews than soups. Most are based on fish, shell fish or vegetable and contained pork, potatoes and milk or cream.

- ***Gumbo***

Pride of the state of Louisiana.Its tale its name from an African word okra.This ingredients gives a charactertics of galantines texture.many gumbo are roux based but the term roux used takes new meaning in Louisiana, Creole and Cajun communities.In this communities the roux is made with flour and fat are cooked much longer at high temperature so that roux is very closed to turn burned. Boil and steamed rice is the usually accompliments of gumbo.

Austria

Kuhlsuppe (Cabbage soup). Cabbage braised in lard, roux added to a stock season and add caraway seeds. Garnish with smoked sausages.

France

Petit Marmite, Bouillabaisse, French Onion Soup, Marsellaise

Hungary

Goulash Soup. To gives this soup a real taste used Hungarian Paprika its has its own distinctive flavours.

Greece

Avgolemono is a soup made up of rice cooked in meat broth.finished well with well beaten egg and lemon juice.

India

Mulligatawny is a creamy of lentil soup.

Italy

Minestrone

Russia

Borscht (Beet soup containing beef and duck meat).

Scotland

Scotch broth (Mutton broth is thickened with Barley), Cock a leekie

Chinese

Wanton soup it can be served fried separately starters with sweet Chili sauce,egg drop soup and hot sour

England

Oxtail Soup

COLD SOUPS

This is the special category because of this grouping of soup is served differently from others. It is served well chilled in chilled cups or bowl. The popularity of cold soup is popular in USA in recent years as the American dying public has become willing to experiment with new trends as the population moved to hotter climates. Many soups which are prepared hot can be served cold by simply chilling them and making miner alteration in structure or flavour. Many purees can be served chilled if they are made with little or no butter and thinned with cream after chilling. Jelly consommé was addressed in the section of clear soups, because the method of preparation is so closely tied to the preparation of hot consommés.

Some hot soups that can be served cold cream of water cress, lobster, bisque and Borsht, Vichyssoise.

Vichyssoise:- Combination of leek and Potatoes.

Gazpacho: - Specialty Spanish Soup.

Fruit soups: are famous in Scandinavia and are favorite breakfast items in Japan.

QUALITY OF SOUPS BASED ON

There are three factors on which the standards of quality are based.

Thickness: - Consistency should be like cream or syrup. It should coat the back of the spoon.

Texture: - Should be smooth, creamy, and velvety with no lumps or graininess. The soup must disappear completely on the palate.

Taste: - Should have a distinct delicate flavour of the main ingredient. Cream Princess should have the flavour of asparagus and chicken.

Garnishes for Soups

The garniture of soups may take many forms, major ingredients like the vegetables in clear soup are often considered garnishes such as Meat, Poultry, Seafood, Barely and Rice can be used as garnish for soups. Consommé like Celestin or Burnoosé are often named after their garnish. Vegetable cream soups and velouté are usually garnished with carefully cut pieces from which they are made.

Soup are often finished with some types of garnishes what type depends on the nature of the soup and the recipe whatever should chosen as a garnish every effort is should be made to have it act as a meaningful part of the soup and not just add as a sluff.

Common Garnish

1. **Croutés and croÊtons**: Croutes are made from flute or baguette is a long thin French bread. The crust of the bread is used only and cut into pieces about 1-½ long buttered and dried in the oven.
2. **CroÊtons**: CroÊtons are prepared in two ways. The most popular croutons for fresh onion soup which is made using the thin slices of fresh bread. The Slice is sprinkled with clarified butter topped with grated cheese and then dried and toasted in oven.

   The croutons commonly used for pureed soups in made from a loaf of white bread. The leaf is diced small and then fried in clarified or butter and then dried and browned in the oven.
3. **Eggs Royale:** Eggs can be whisked through a china cap (Conical strainer beater) into boiling soups for garnish.

Royale is a complex egg preparation used in soup garnish usually for a broth or consommé. For a plain Royale 1 egg and 3 egg yolk are beaten add one cup of consommé or milk is added. It is poached in a buttered deep dish in a Bain-marie like custard. Then they chilled completely in a refrigerator. After which they are cut by small cutters.

Other Garnishes: Pasta is a popular garnish. Vermicelli, Alphabets Pasta and small Ravioli (Pocket pasta) are commonly used.

Profit roles are interesting items and they are like a bowls size of peanuts. They made out of choux paste. They can be filled with meat or vegetable puree and served plain like croutons.

Quenélles are garnish for soup. Vegetables cut in different shapes and forms cooked in salted water and quick chilled after cooking.

Toppings: Toppings of the soup must be done with care they should be placed on the soup just at service so that they will not sink or loose, there fresh appreance, there flavours must be accompliment with that soup. Clear soups are generally served without topping with an exception of sprinkling of chervil, finely chopped chives, parsley or herbs. Thick soups especially those that are all one colour have often decorated with toppings Example of some toppings is:

- Fresh herb
- Toasted slice
- Almonds or hazelnuts
- Toasted bread
- Coconut
- Sieved Egg yolk and Sliced Egg white
- Grated Parmesan cheese.
- Toasted Croutons
- Sour or Whipped Cream.

Cheese Diamonds

Flour—4 tablespoon, Grated Cheese—1oz. Butter—1 oz, Yolk of Egg—1 no, 2 teaspoon Lemon Juice, Pinch of Cayenne Pepper, Salt and Mustard.

1. Rub the butter into the flour, add the cheese and seasoning, and mix well.
2. Beat the egg yolk, add to it a dessert-spoon of cold water and the lemon juice, stir this into the flour, and knead to a paste.
3. Roll out and cut in small diamond shapes. Bake a golden brown.

Parmesan Fingers

Grated Parmesan cheese—4 Oz., Butter —1 oz., Flour—few grains of Cayenne Pepper

- Mix all these ingredients together and knead to smooth dough. Cut into thin strips and bake a golden brown in a moderate over.

Devilled Biscuits

Spread a thin layer of curry paste on plain cheese biscuits, make very hot and serve with game or curry soup.

Service of Soup: The standard portion size for a soup is 6 oz in a soup as part of the meal. As a main course the portion should be about 10 oz in a deep soup plate or soup tureen. Serve soup cold in a chilled bowls. Served hot soups piping hot in hot cups or bowls.

STANDARD SOUPS RECIPES

Artichoke Soup

Ingredients	*Quantity*
Jerusalem Artichokes	500 gram

White stocks	1 litre
Milk	250 ml
Onion	80 gram
Butter	20 gram
Lemon juice	20 ml
Salt and pepper	10 gram

Fig 7.4 The Artichoke soup

Method

1. Put the lemon juice or vinegar into a basin of cold water.
2. Wash the artichokes, peel and put them at once in the acid water in order to keep them white.
3. Melt the butter in a stew pan and as soon as it is hot, drain the artichokes well and add them to the butter with the onion peeled and sliced.
4. Sprinkle with salt and pepper and cook gently for five minutes; to not cook quickly as they must not brown at all.
5. Add the stock gradually and simmer gently until the vegetables are quite soft.
6. Rub through a sieve, return to the stew pan and add the milk.
7. Taste to see if sufficiently seasoned. Bring to boiling point and serve.

Cream of Asparagus

Ingredients	*Quantity*
Asparagus	500 gram
Butter	30 gram
Flour	30 gram
Vegetable stock	200 ml
Pepper corns	6no
Salt	10 gram
Milk or clean	80 ml

Fig 7.5 Asparagus soup

Method

1. Cut off the tips of the asparagus and put them in enough boiling water to cover them; add a pinch of salt and boil gently until tender but unbroken (they will take about ten minutes), strain and reserve them.

2. Well wash the asparagus stalks, cut them in short lengths, put them in a stew pan with the water in which the points were cooked, the salt, the peppercorns tied in a piece of muslin and the stock.
3. Boil gently for half an hour Strain through a sieve and rub as much of the asparagus through as possible.
4. Melt the butter in a stew pan, add the flour and stir over gentle heat until it is a smooth paste.
5. Then add the soup gradually and continue stirring while it boils gently for five minutes.
6. Cool a little, then add the cream or hot milk and the asparagus tips. Make very hot and serve.
7. A little cream is a great improvement to this soup; if a gill is though too expensive, whip a tablespoonful and floats a teaspoonful of it on each soup cup.
8. If fresh asparagus is too expensive, the tinned variety may be used. In this case the liquor from the tin may be used. In this case the liquor from the tin may be used as additional flavouring.

Beetroot Soup

Ingredients	*Quantity*
Beetroots	350 gram
Onion	30 gram
Flour	30 gram
Butter	30 gram
Celery	40 gram
Vegetable stock	1litre
Cream	50 ml

Fig 7.6 The beet root soup

Method

1. Boil or bake the beetroots if they are not already cooked.
2. Wash the celery and peel the onion and beetroots.
3. Cut all the vegetables in small pieces, make the butter or dripping hot in a saucepan, put in the prepared vegetables and cook gently for three or four minutes.
4. Add the stock, stir for a minute, then simmer slowly until the vegetables are soft and pulpy; about one and a half hours.

5. Rub all through a sieve. Return the soup to the stew pan, mix the milk with the flour, and add the milk gradually being careful to keep it quite smooth.
6. Stir this into the soup and continue stirring until it has boiled for five minutes.
7. The addition of two tablespoons of cream after the soup has ceased boiling is a great improvement.

Bouillabaisse Soup

Ingredients	*Quantity*
Fish/seafood	250 gram
Onions	60 gram
Butter	20 gram
Shallot	30 gram
Bay leaf	2 No.
Tomatoes	250 gram
Lemon	20 ml
Parsley	30 gram
Fish stock	500 ml
Salt and pepper	10 gram
White wine	10 ml

Fig 7.7 The bouillabaisse soup

Method

1. Remove all skin and bones from the fish and cut it into small pieces.
2. If fresh tomatoes are used, slice them and cook gently in a small saucepan until soft, then rub them through a sieve.
3. Peel and chop and onions and shallot.
4. Melt the butter in a stew pan, put in the onions and shallot and fry until nicely browned.
5. Add the pieces of fish, bay leaf, tomato pulp, pepper and salt and the lemon.
6. The addition of a wineglass of white wine is a great improvement. Cover with the stock and boil gently for ten minutes. Sprinkle in the parsley just before serving.

Boulongne Soup

Ingredients	*Quantity*
Cauliflower	350 gram

Onions	80 gram
Bread slices	4 no
Ham or Bacon	30 gram
Salt and pepper	15 gram
milk	100 ml
water	100 ml
butter	20 gram

Method

1. Remove all but the very small leaves of the cauliflower round the flower.
2. Wash and put into boiling water with a teaspoon of salt and boil until tender, about twenty minutes.
3. Peel and slice the onions.
4. Melt the butter or dripping in a stew pan, and when hot put in the onions, cover closely and cook gently for five minutes.
5. Then add the cauliflower cut in pieces, the bread in small pieces, the ham, pepper and the water in which the cauliflower was boiled.
6. Simmer all together for an hour, and then rub through a coarse sieve with a wooden spoon. Add the milk, bring just to boiling point, and serve.

Breton Soup

Ingredients	*Quantity*
Cabbage	200 gram
Carrot	50 gram
Turnip	50 gram
Leek	30 gram
Celery	20 gram
Onions	30 gram
Parsley	20 gram
Thyme	5 gram
Marjoram	5 gram
Butter	20 gram

White stock	1litre
Chicken (boiled)	75 gram
Salt and pepper	15 gram

1. Peel the onions and turnip, scrape the carrot and well wash all the vegetables.
2. Take the heart of the cabbage—it should be a small one—and cut it in shreds; chop the onions, leek and celery; cut the carrot and turnip into dice.
3. Heat the butter in a stew pan, put in the vegetables, sprinkle with salt and pepper (unless the broth is highly seasoned) and fry gently for five minutes.
4. Add the stock and the herbs tied in a piece of muslin.
5. Simmer gently until the vegetables are tender.
6. Take out the herbs and serve with toast cut in tiny squares.

Broad beans soup

Ingredients	*Quantity*
Broad beans	350 gram
Vegetable stock	1litre
Onion	30 gram
Bouquet garni	10 gram
Butter	20 gram
Flour	30 gram
Milk	250 ml
Salt and pepper	15 gram

Method

1. Put the beans in boiling water and boil until tender, strain, cool in cold water and remove the skins.
2. Put the beans in boiling water and boil until tender, strain, cool in cold water and remove the skins.
3. Put the skinned beans in a stew pan with the onion peeled and sliced, the herbs and the stock.
4. Simmer until the onion is tender.
5. Then take out the bunch of herbs and rub beans and stock through a sieve. Return to the saucepan.
6. Add the butter, the flour mixed with the milk, and season to taste with salt and pepper. Stir while the soup boils for five minutes, and then serve.

Bruges Soup

Ingredients	*Quantity*
Celery	250 gram
Vegetable stock	1litre
Sago	2tbsp
Yolk	1no
Milk	100 ml
Tarragon Vinegar	10 ml
Salt and pepper	15 gram

Method

1. Cut the celery in small cubes and put it with the stock into a stew pan, simmer for ten minutes, add the sago and boil gently for fifteen minutes.
2. Cool a little until it has gone off the boil.
3. Then beat the yolk of egg, mix the milk with it and stir this in.
4. Make very hot; add seasoning of salt and pepper, if required.
5. Drop in the vinegar and serve. Only the heart of the celery may be used for this soup, but the outside sticks make excellent material for flavouring stock or for a soup that is sieved before serving.

Brussels Sprout Soup

Ingredients	*Quantity*
Brussels sprouts	200 gram
Vegetable stocks	1litre
Milk	100 ml
Corn flour	20 gram
Nutmeg grated	5 gram

Fig 7.8 The Brussels sprouts soup

Method

1. Trim and wash the sprouts, put them in a pan of boiling water with a small teaspoon of salt and the bicarbonate of soda, bring to the boil, and boil for five minutes; remove any scum.

2. Then strain in a colander. Put the stock in a stew pan; when it boils, put in the sprouts and boil until they are quite soft—about ten minutes.
3. Then rub them through a sieve. Return the puree and stock to the stew pan.
4. Mix the corn flour to a very thin paste with milk
5. Stir it into the soup and continue stirring until it has boiled for five minutes. Season to taste with salt and pepper.
6. Add the nutmeg and the remainder of the milk. Make very hot and serve.

Cabbage Cream Soup

Ingredients	*Quantity*
Cabbage	350 gram
Milk	100 ml
Water	30 ml
Butter	20 gram
Onion	50 gram
Tapioca or Roux	20 gram
Salt and pepper	15 gram
Cream	50 ml

Method

1. Remove the outer leaves from the cabbage, well wash and slice the remainder, peel and slice the onion. Put them into a saucepan with 3 pints of water and a teaspoon of salt.
2. Boil until the vegetables are quite soft—i.e. 25 minutes. Skim well. Rub vegetables with the water through a sieve.
3. Return to the stew pan, sprinkle in the tapioca, add the butter and milk, season to taste with salt and pepper and simmer for a quarter of an hour.
4. Take the pan off the stove and, if available, stir in one or two tablespoons of cream, which is a great improvement.
5. Make very hot and serve. Another soup of special benefit to children, which in addition forms a nourishing supper.

Calf's Foot Soup

Ingredients	*Quantity*
Calf's Foot	300 gram
Lemon rind	20 gram

Ham or bacon	50 gram
Thyme	2 gram
Marjoram	2 gram
Peppercorns	5 gram
Mace	2 gram
Carrot	50 gram
Onion	100 gram
Milk	120 ml
Egg	1 No.
Parsley	10 gram
Water	200 ml

Method

1. Well wash the calf's foot and cut it in pieces, put them in a stew pan with a small strip of lemon rind (the yellow part only), the ham—or, failing this, a good teaspoon of salt—the herbs, mace, peppercorns and the vegetables cut in small pieces, 3 pints of water and the milk.
2. Bring to the boil and skim well. Then simmer very slowly for three hours. Strain into a bowl and leave until next day.
3. Bring to the boil and skim well. Then simmer very slowly for three hours. Strain into a bowl and leave until next day.
4. Remove all fat, put the jelly in a stew pan with a few pieces of the meat cut in very small pieces, bring to the boil, then take off the stove.
5. Beat the yolk of an egg with a tablespoon of milk, stir a little of the hot broth into it, then put it in the stew pan and make very hot, but do not let it boil. Sprinkle with chopped parsley and serve.

Note: If a thicker soup is preferred, mix a tablespoon of plain flour with water to a thin paste, stir in and boil while stirring for five minutes before the egg yolk is added. Pea-flour can be used in place of plain flour; in this case the egg yolk can be omitted. Simmer very slowly, using a low gas or low temperature mark on electric stove. If allowed to boil, the soup will reduce too much and not be enough when done. This soup has a high nutrition value, and is easily digested. It is particularly good for invalids and delicate people, and when cold will form a thick jelly which is equally delicious. The long, slow, cooking brings out its goodness to the full. It also has the advantage of being very cheap to prepare.

Cauliflower Soup

Ingredients	*Quantity*
Cauliflower	500 gram
Vegetable stock	1 litre
Milk	200 ml
Salt and pepper	10 gram
Grated cheese	50 gram

Method

1. Wash the cauliflower and break into small sprigs. Keep four sprigs for garnish. Put the remainder in a stew pan with the vegetable stock and simmer until the vegetable is quite soft, about 20 minutes.
2. Rub through a sieve, season to taste, and add the boil milk. Boil the cauliflower reserved for garnish in a little salted water until tender but unbroken. Make the soup very hot, and serve with a sprig of cauliflower in each cup or plate. Grated cheese in a very good accompaniment.

Cauliflower cream soup

Ingredients	*Quantity*
Cauliflower	500 gram
Tapioca	30 gram
Butter	20 gram
Milk	200 ml
Water	100 ml
Salt and pepper	20 gram
Egg	1 No.
Cream	50 ml
Castor sugar	20 gram

Fig 7.9 The cauliflower cream soup

Method

1. Well wash the white part of the cauliflower; it is important that it should be very fresh, and have a good hard flower. Put it into a saucepan containing. 1 ½ pints of boiling water; add the salt.

2. Cover, and as soon as it boils uncover, skin and boil until cover the cauliflower, but the cauliflower can be broken in pieces if necessary.
3. Strain off the water into a bowl and rub the cauliflower through a hair sieve. Put the water into the saucepan, and when it boils sprinkle in the tapioca and simmer gently for ten minutes.
4. Make the milk hot and add, also the sugar and the cauliflower puree. Stir until it reaches boiling point.
5. Melt the butter. Beat the egg yolk and add the melted butter and cream.
6. Mix a little of the soup with it and stir well to mix. Then add to the soup. Stir until very hot, but not boiling, and serve at once, in soup.

Fig 7.10 The celery soup

Celery Soup

Ingredients	*Quantity*
Vegetable stocks	1litre
White celery	350 gram
Milk	200 ml
Onion	50 gram
Butter	30 gram
Salt or pepper	15 gram

Method

1. Remove the outer leave of the celery, wash the white part thoroughly and cut it in small pieces. Peel and chop the onion.
2. Melt the butter in a stew pan, put in the onion and celery, and toss over gentle beat for five minutes, but do not let it acquire any colour.
3. Add the stock, season with salt and pepper and simmer gently until the celery is quite soft.
4. Rub through a sieve, return to the pan and add the milk. Make very hot and serve. Two tablespoons of cream added with the milk is a great improvement.

Chestnut Cream Soup

Ingredients	*Quantity*
Chestnuts	350 gram
Vegetable stock	1litre

Onion	20 gram
Butter	20 gram
Egg	2 No.
Cream	100 ml

Method

1. The water in which either veal or fowl has been boiled is excellent for this soup. Peel the chestnuts; the easiest way to do this is to make a small cut on the flat side of the nuts with a penknife and to put them in a hot oven until the skins crack and open, when they can be quite easily removed.
2. They take five to ten minutes, according to the heat of the oven. Peel, slice and fry the onion in the butter without letting it colour at all.
3. Add the peeled chestnuts and the stock and boil very gently until the chestnuts are quite soft, then rub all through a sieve.
4. Put this puree in a double saucepan with hot water in the bottom container. Beat the egg yolk with the cream and stir in.
5. Cook for five minutes. The water under the puree should just simmer, not boil rapidly. Serve very hot with fried croutons.

Chicken soup (cold)

Ingredients	*Quantity*
Chicken broth	1 liter
Carrot	20 gram
Leek	30 gram
Onion	30 gram
Bay leaf	2 No.
Parsley	20 gram
Clove	5no
Lemon juice	20 ml
Egg	2 No.
Cream	100 ml

Method

1. Put the chicken broth in a stew pan. Prepare and cut up the carrot and leek. Add them

to the broth, also the onion stuck with a clove, the bay leaf and parsley, and boil until the broth is reduced to about a quart.

2. Strain into a bowl, stir in the strained lemon juice and leave until quite cold. Remove any fat.
3. Reheat in a double saucepan. Whisk the egg yolk, mix the cream with it, put it in the soup, and whisk while it is cooking for three minutes, but do not let it boil. Pour into soup cups and put in a cold place—a refrigerator, if possible –until cold and set.

   Note: If, when the broth is cold, it is not sufficiently jellied, dissolve one teaspoon of powdered gelatin in the broth when reheating.

Chicken Soup (Brown)

Ingredients	*Quantity*
Roast chicken bones	500 gram
Onions	30 gram
Celery	20 gram
Parsley	20 gram
Thyme	10 gram
Peppers corns	5 gram
Flour	30 gram
Butter	20 gram
Finally chopped chicken	20 gram
Salt and pepper	15 gram

Method

1. Remove any meat from the carcass, chop finely and reserve. Break up the bones and put them in a stew pan with the giblets. Add 1 quart of cold water.
2. Bring very slowly to boiling point. Bring very slowly to boiling point. Then simmer slowly for one hour. Do not let it boil fast.
3. Now add the onion peeled and sliced, the celery chopped, parsley, thyme, peppercorns and a teaspoon of salt. Simmer one hour longer.
4. Strain off the broth, leave until cold, then remove any fat.
5. Melt the butter in a small pan, sprinkle in the flour and stir whilst it cooks gently for five minutes.
6. Mix a little of the stock with it and then stir into the remainder of the stock. Add a few drops of browning.

7. Bring to the boil and simmer for ten minutes. Add the chopped chicken and serve.

Note: One or two tomatoes when available are an improvement; add them with the onions.

Green Pea Soup (Thick)

Ingredients	*Quantity*
Green peas	350 gram
Vegetable stocks	1 litre
Milk	300 ml
Mint	30 gram
Butter	20 gram
Flour	20 gram
Salt and pepper	15 gram

Fig 7.11 Green pea soup

Method

1. Shell the peas. Well wash the pods and put them in a stew pan with the stock. Simmer for twenty minutes.
2. Strain and return the stock to the stew pan, put in the peas and mint, and simmer until tender. Then rub through a sieve. Add to this puree the butter, the milk mixed with flour and a good seasoning of salt and pepper.
3. Stir while it boils for eight minutes. Serve very hot with fried croutons.
4. A little cream, though it is not necessary, is a great improvement to this soup and should be added just before serving.

Green Pea Soup (Clear)

Ingredients	*Quantity*
White vegetable stock	1litre
Mint	30 gram
Green peas	100 gram
Sugar	10 gram
Salt and pepper	15 gram

Method

1. Put the peas into boiling water with the sugar and mint and boil gently until tender—about fifteen to twenty minutes according to the age of the peas.
2. Then strain. Bring the stock to the boil, add the peas, boil for one minute and serve.
3. Season with salt and pepper if the stock was not already seasoned.

Haricot Bean Soup

Ingredients	*Quantity*
Haricot beans	100 gram
Tomatoes	150 gram
Butter	20 gram
Vegetable stocks	1litre
Salt and pepper	15 gram
Bread slice	2 No.
Onion	50 gram

Method

1. Wash the haricots, put them in a basin, and well cover with cold water and leave to soak until next day.
2. Put the tomatoes in a pot, cover with boiling water, and leave for a few seconds, then take out the tomatoes and skin them.
3. Peel and chop the onion. Put the tomatoes and onion in a stew pan with an ounce of dripping, and fry for five minutes.
4. Add the stock, and the beans, but not the water in which they were soaked.
5. Boil very gently until the beans are tender.
6. Season with salt and pepper to taste, if the broth was not already seasoned.
7. Rub through a sieve, reheat, and serve very hot with little cubes of bread fried in the remainder of the dripping.

Jardiniere soup

Ingredients	*Quantity*
Carrots	100 gram
Turnips	100 gram

Onions	50 gram
Cabbage	50 gram
Tarragon	10 gram
Sugar	10 gram
Vegetable seasoned stocks	1 liter

Method

1. Scrape the carrots, peel the onions and turnips, and cut all the vegetables into cubes or fancy shapes, leaving the little onions whole.
2. Shred the cabbage and chop the tarragon. Put all into a stew pan with the sugar and the stock, and simmer slowly till the vegetables are tender and serve hot.

Lobster Soup

Ingredients	*Quantity*
Lobster (tinned)	250 gram
Butter	20 gram
Tomatoes	100 gram
Mushrooms	50 gram
Bread crumbs	20 gram
Fish stock	1litre
Milk	50 ml
Salt and pepper	15 gram

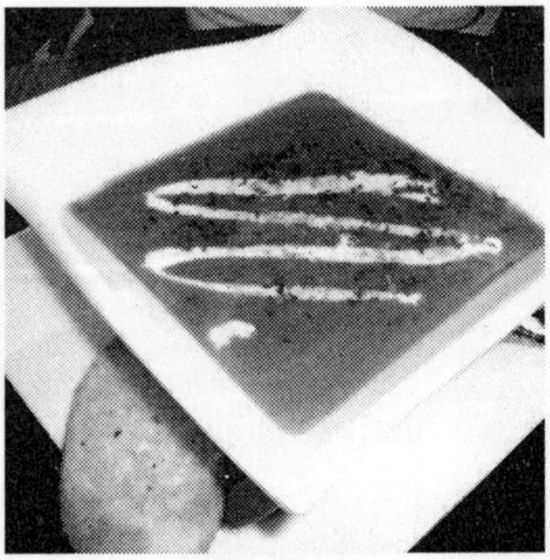

Fig 7.12 The Lobster soup

Method

1. Drain off of liquor from the lobster and cut the fish in very small pieces.
2. Slice the mushrooms and tomatoes and cook them in the butter for then minutes, then rub them through a sieve.
3. The mushrooms should be quite small fresh ones before they have become brown.
4. Add the puree to the fish stock, season with salt and pepper if necessary.
5. Make the milk hot and pour it on the breadcrumbs.
6. Beat for a minute, and then add them to the stock. Simmer for fifteen minutes. Add the pieces of lobster and the liquor. Make very hot and serve.

Milk Soup

Ingredients	*Quantity*
Milk	450 gram
White onion	50 gram
Celery	20 gram
Butter	20 gram
Parsley	20 gram
Salt and pepper	15 gram
Water	200 ml

Method

1. Peel and chop the onions, wash the celery and cut it in small pieces.
2. Put them in a stew pan with the butter and cook gently for five minutes, add ½ pint of water and simmer for half an hour, or until the vegetables are quite tender.
3. Make the milk hot, and stir in, season with salt and pepper.
4. Bring to the boil, add the parsley and serve very hot.

   Note: If a thicker soup is preferred, sprinkle in a tablespoon of flaked tapioca when the water is added.

Mushroom Cream Soup

Ingredients	*Quantity*
Mushrooms	500 gram
Butter	20 gram
Vegetable stocks	1 liter
Flour	30 gram
Milk	150 ml
Salt and pepper	15 gram

Fig 7.13 Mushroom soup

Method

1. The mushrooms should be freshly gathered; choose small or medium sized one—when large and black they are not suitable for this soup. Wash well and drain.

2. Slice and put them in a stew pan with the butter and a sprinkling of salt and pepper and cook slowly for five minutes.
3. Then add the stock and simmer until the mushrooms are quite soft—about one hour. Rub through a sieve, and then return to the stew pan.
4. Mix the flour smoothly with the milk and add to the soup.
5. Stir until boiling. Simmer for then minutes.
6. Draw the pan to the side of the stove stir in the parsley, drop in the lemon juice and serve very hot. The addition of a gill of cream is a great improvement.

   Note: Be very careful that the soup is not boiling when the cream is added, or it will curdle when the lemon juice is dropped in.

Onion Soup (Brown)

Ingredients	*Quantity*
Brown vegetable stock	1 liter
Onions	500 gram
Butter	30 gram
Bread slice	2 No.
Slice of bacon	2 No.
Salt and pepper	15 gram

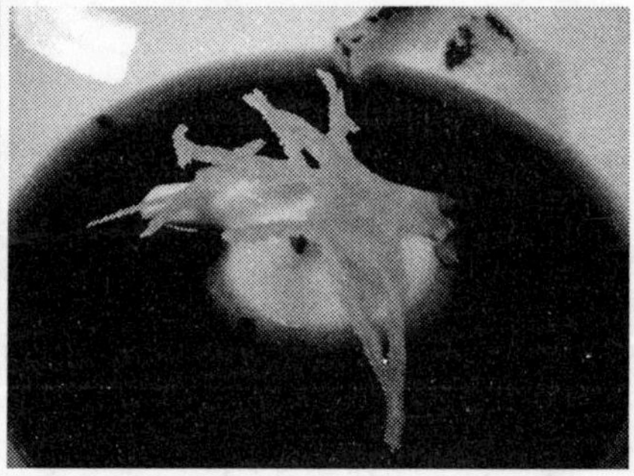

Fig 7.14 Onion brown soup

Method

1. Peel and chop the onions finely. Melt the butter in a stew pan, add the onions and fry until well browned, cover and cook very gently for half an hour.
2. Now add the stock, ham, the bread in small pieces and a good sprinkling of pepper, unless the stock is sufficiently seasoned.
3. Cover and simmer for an hour, then rub through a sieve and serve with cheese croutons.

   To make cheese croutons.
4. Cut about eight small slices from the end of a French roll, or cut a slice of bread into rounds with a biscuit cutter. Fry until crisp in apply butter, serve separately, plentifully sprinkled with grated Parmesan cheese.

Onion Soup (White)

Ingredients	*Quantity*
vegetable stock	1 liter
Onions	500 gram

Butter	30 gram
Egg	2no
Milk	200ml
Salt and pepper	15 gram
Flour	30 gram

Method

1. Melt the butter in a stew pan, and then add the onions, cut in thin slices.
2. Let these simmer slowly for half an hour. Stir in the flour, and by degrees 1½ pints of hot milk. Season with pepper and salt and cook slowly till the onion is quite soft.
3. Pass through a sieve and return to the saucepan. Beat the yolk of egg with ½ pint of milk.
4. Take the soup from the fire, add the eggs and milk, and reheat, Stir it add parsley, make very hot and serve.
5. The addition of two tablespoons of cream provides a richer soup. Do not allow the soup to boil after the eggs or cream is added.

Oyster Soup

Ingredients	*Quantity*
Oyster (fresh or rinned)	200 gram
Fish stock	1litre
Lemon juice	20 ml
Cayenne Pepper	20 gram
Butter	30 gram
Flour	20 ml
Egg yolks	2 No.
Salt and pepper	15 gram

Method

1. Put the oysters with their liquor in a small saucepan over very gentle heat.
2. As soon as they begin to simmer and before they are actually boiling, take them off the fire, strain off the liquor and reserve.
3. Bread the oysters: that is, cut off the little dark firings round the edges. Put the stock into a stew pan, add the beards and the oyster liquor and simmer for 20 minutes.

4. Then strain through a fine hair sieve, and put the liquor back in the stew pan. Melt the butter in a small stew pan, sprinkle in the flour and stir while it cooks gently for two or three minutes.
5. Add gradually a teacup of the stock, and, when quite smooth, stir this into the remainder of the stock.
6. Add the anchovy essence and cayenne bring to the boil and stir whilst boiling for five minutes. Drop in the lemon juice.
7. Cut the oysters in quarters, put them in the soup tureen pour in the soup and serve. If a richer soup is desired:
8. Add yolks of two eggs and ¼ pint of cream. Beat the yolks lightly and mix them with the cream.
9. Take the saucepan off the flame and add the mixture slowly, stirring gently all the time.
10. Reheat but do not allow the soup to boil after the eggs and cream are added. Serve very hot.

Pea Shell Soup

Ingredients	*Quantity*
Pea shells	300 gram
Vegetable stocks	1litre
Salt and pepper	15 gram
Sugar	10 gram
Onion	30 gram
Mint	20 gram
Milk	100 ml

Method

1. Well wash the pea shells, put them in a saucepan with enough boiling water to cover them, the salt and sugar, and boil until soft—about an hour according to the age of the pea shells. Then rub as much as possible through a rather coarse sieve.
2. Put the puree into a stew pan with the onion peeled and chopped and the stock. Simmer until the onion is quite soft— about twenty minutes. Stir in the hot milk and add a little finely chopped mint just before serving.

NOTE: The shells must be from fairly young peas. The shells from old peas take too long to cook.

Potato Soup (Rich)

Fig 7.15 The potato soup

Ingredients	*Quantity*
Potatoes	500 gram
Butter	20 gram
Onions	30 gram
Fresh herbs	10 gram
Vegetable stocks	1litre
Milk	100 ml
Eggs yolk	2 No.
parsley	10 gram

Method

1. Peel and slice the onions thinly, peel and cut the potatoes into quarters. Melt the butter in a stew pan, add the potatoes, onions, bay leaf and herbs and cook them uncovered until they are nicely browned; add the stock bring to the boil, and skim well.
2. Cover and simmer gently for one hour. Rub through a rather fine sieve, and then reheat in a double saucepan.
3. Beat the egg yolk, add to it the cream, stir this into the coup, and continue stirring over boiling water for five minutes. Sprinkle in the chopped parsley and serve.

Rice Cream Soup

Fig 7.16 The rice cream soup

Ingredients	*Quantity*
Vegetable stocks	1 liter
Bay leaf	2 No.
Parsley	10 gram
Thyme	5 gram
Lemon rind	20 gram
Ground rice	200 gram
Milk	100 ml
Butter	20 gram
Egg	2 No.
Salt and pepper	15 gram

Method

1. Put the stock in a stew pan, add the bay leaf, parsley, thyme and lemon rind tied in a piece of muslin, season with salt and pepper, if necessary, and simmer for half an hour. Then remove the herbs.
2. Mix the rice smoothly with the milk and pour into the stock.
3. Boil gently for ten minutes. Lightly beat the yolk or an egg, melt the butter, mix it with the egg yolk, and stir two or three tablespoons of the soup into this.
4. Then pour it into the stew pan. Add the chopped parsley and stir over low heat for five minutes, but do not let it boil. Serve very hot.

   Note: It is safest to use a double saucepan when the egg yolk has been added—unless you have a slow, simmering burner.

Scotch Broth

Ingredients	*Quantity*
Mutton broth	500 gram
Cabbage	80 gram
Carrot	80 gram
Onion	80 gram
Turnip	75 gram
Leek	50 gram
Barley	100 gram
Sweet herbs	20 gram
Parsley	10 gram
Butter	20 gram

Fig 7.17 The Scotch broth

Method

1. Peel the onion and turnip,
2. Cut the carrot and turnip into fancy shapes with a vegetable cutter, chop the onion and shred the cabbage and leek.
3. Put the butter into the stew pan and fry the vegetables in it for a few minutes.
4. Add the stock, and simmer gently with the well-washed pearl barley until the vegetables are soft—about half an hour.
5. Take out the herbs and serve the soup very hot.

Spinach Cream Soup:

Fig. 7.18 The spinach cream soup

Ingredients	*Quantity*
Spinach	500 gram
Onion	100 gram
Vegetable stock	1 litre
Flour	30 gram
Nutmeg	20 gram
Cream	50 ml
Milk	100 ml
Salt and pepper	15 gram
Garlic	30 gram

Method

1. Stalk the spinach and wash it well in several waters to remove any grit. Drain. Put it in a stew pan with the onion peeled and sliced, chopped garlic, nutmeg, pepper and half a small teaspoon of salt.
2. Cover closely and cook gently for a quarter of an hour. (The water held by the leaves is sufficient to prevent the saucepan burning).
3. Then rub through a sieve. Melt the butter in a stew pan, sprinkle in the flour, and stir well with a wooden spoon, while it cooks gently for five minutes; do not let it brown.
4. Add to it the spinach puree; stir to mix.
5. Then pour in the stock and bring to the boil. Remove the soup from the stove, stir in the cream and serve.

Sweet Corn Soup

Fig. 7.19 The sweet corn soup

Ingredients	*Quantity*
Sweet corn(tin)	1 No.
Onion	100 gram
Milks	200ml
Salt and pepper	15 gram
Butter	30 gram
Corn Flour	20 gram

Method

1. Peel and grate the onion finely, put it in a double saucepan with the corn, salt, pepper and milk, and let the water boil under it for twenty minutes.
2. Dissolve corn flour in cold water and put in boiling water, adjust seasoning and thickening of soup and serve hot.

Tomato Bisque

Ingredients	*Quantity*
Tomatoes	500 gram
Milk	150 ml
Water	150 ml
Salt and pepper	15 gram
Butter	20 gram
Flour	20 gram

Fig. 7.20 Tomato bisque soup

Method

1. Slice the tomatoes; put them in a stew pan with the salt, pepper, and ½ pint of cold water. Cover and cook over gentle heat until they are a soft pulp; rub them through a sieve, return the puree to the stew pan, and keep hot.
2. Heat the milk. Melt the butter in a stew pan, sprinkle in the flour and stir over gentle heat until it is a smooth paste; then very gradually stir in the hot milk, being careful to keep the mixture smooth.
3. Stir the tomato puree and then pour the puree in the milk. Mix well and serve very hot with cheese.

Tomato Soup

Ingredients	*Quantity*
Tomatoes	350 gram
Onion	100 gram
Butter	30 gram
Parsley	10 gram
Thyme	5 gram
Lean bacon	30 gram

Fig. 7.21 The Tomato soup

Crushed tapioca	20 gram
Cloves	2 no
Peppercorns	5 gram
Vegetable stocks	1 litre
Tomato paste	50 gram
Sugar	10 gram
Salt and pepper	15 gram
Garlic	30 gram
Milk	50 ml

Method

1. Peel and slice the onion and garlic. Fry it for five minutes in the butter, add the tomatoes cut in quarters, the parsley and thyme finely chopped, the bacon, tapioca, cloves, peppercorns and a good sprinkling and salt and pepper.
2. Pour in the stock and simmer for three quarters of an hour. Rub through a sieve. Return the soup to the stew pan.
3. Mix the flour to a very thin paste with milk, add it and stir while it simmers for five minutes. Heat the remainder of the milk, and pour it into the soup. Add the sugar, simmer ten minutes, and then serve.

LEARNING OUTCOME

- Soups of the old classical kitchen were complete dishes in themselves containing apart from the liquid and garnish, a wide variety of meat, poultry, game and fish. It is only the liquid part of the classical dishes which retains the name "Soup" today.
- Soup is immensely popular. It is warm and nourishing. The word 'soup' comes from the Latin 'suppare', which means 'soaking', and once described a dish of meat or vegetables that was soaked in the liquid in which it was cooked.
- Stock is the foundation of all good soups. Soups are made from meat stock. Meat stock is a broth made by cooking meat with water and it requires long, slow cooking. Beef, veal, lamb or chicken
- Can be cooked separately or in combinations.
- Clear soups run the gamut—from the rustic and homey chicken soup to the most sophisticated consommé. What separates clear from thick soups is that clear soups are comprised of a clear brothy liquid with things floating in it, like pieces of vegetables, meat, fish, rice, pasta, etc. while thick soups have items ground into a stock. Consommés are one of the sub

categories. Always classified sometimes thicken with tapioca. They normally inclined a light garnish matching the character of consommé. Broth is another sub category; they are not clarified like consommé. Their cleanness comes from very careful cooking. The amount of garnish (the professional term for the "things" floating) in a clear soup varies considerably. Essences are a derivation of the mentioned consommé with special flavoures. Cream soups are based on Béchamel where as veloute soups are based on veloute sauce. Some are virtually garnishing less while others are loaded with solid.

LESSON END ACTIVITY

- Try to make some basic soups.
- Try to collect more recipes of international and national soups.

QUESTIONS FOR DISCUSSION

1. Explain the term soups and with their types.
2. Describe the classification of soups.
3. Describe clear soups.
4. What are consommé and its standard preparation?
5. Explain the steps of basic clarification of consommé.
6. What are the special factors for making consommé?
7. Explain the term essence and jellied soups.
8. Explain the termed thick soups and veloute soups.
9. Explain the term vegetable soups and cream soups.
10. Explain any ten international soups.
11. What is cold soups and name any 5 cold soups?

STATE TRUE AND FALSE

- All soups can be served cold also.
- Consommé can be categorized in clear soups.
- Gazpacho is a Specialty Soup of Hungary.
- Minestrone soup is from India
- Mulligatawny is an American soup
- Chowders are from America
- Cream soups are based on Béchamel where as veloute soups are based on veloute sauce

- Bisque is a creamy puree that concentrated the essence of single ingredients into a rich performed soup.
- Jellied soups are only appropriate for serving cold season
- Essences are a derivation of the mentioned consommé with special flavoures
- The term broth and bouillon means the same
- The word 'soup' comes from the Latin 'suppare'

KEY TERMS

* Broth
* Chowder
* Croutons
* Essence
* Garnishes
* Jellied
* Nourishing
* Soups
* Thickening

Chapter 8

Sauces

After studying this chapter, the student must know

- Introduction, definition and meaning
- Essential and characteristics of good sauces
- Components of sauces
- Finalization or liaison finale
- Making of mother sauces and its physical property
- Classification of sauces
- The compound sauces
- Mother sauces with their method of preparation
- Emulsified sauces with their method of preparations
- Compound butter sauces and its some types
- Miscellaneous sauces
- Derivates of mother sauces
- Cold sauces and its types.

SAUCES

"*Sauce is to culinary art, what grammar is to language.*"

—Grimande De La Royere

The word "sauce" is a French word that means a relish to make our food more appetizing. Sauces are liquid or semi-liquid foods devised to make other foods look, smell, and taste better, and hence be more easily digested and more beneficial. Because of the lack of refrigeration in the early days of cooking, meat, poultry, fish, and seafood didn't last long. Sauces and gravies were used to mask the flavour of tainted foods. Sauces are one of the fundamentals of cooking.

Sauces may be prepared. Sauces, such as soy sauce, which are usually bought, not made, by the cook; or cooked sauces, such as Béchamel sauce, which are generally made just before serving. Sauces for salads are called salad dressing. Another variation is the pan sauce; this is made by adding an aromatic (such as chopped shallot) to a pan that has previously cooked meat, which has left hardened juices (called the fond), in the pan. A person who specializes in making sauces is often referred to as a "saucier", a French term borrowed for its situational usefulness. Sauces are an essential element in cuisines all over the world. Some famous saucier include Julia Child, Benjamin Christie, Bobby Flay, Yutake Ishinabe, and François Pierre La Varenne.

SAUCES DEFINATION

Sauce is a thickened liquid that is flavoured or seasoned to enhance the flavour of the food that it is to accompany. The sauce can be sweet, sour, spicy, or savory and may be added to the food to become part of a main dish or used as an accompaniment to the food being prepared. Sauces add a variety of features to foods, such as complimenting or enhancing flavors, succulence, attractive appearance, and additional texture.

Meanining

According to new Larouse gastronomy, sauces are hot or cold seasoned liquid either served with or uses in the cooking of a dish. Hot or cold the function of a sauce is to add flavour that is in harmony (Computable) with the ingredients of the dish.

Sauces have evolved has civilization, medieval sauces which realized on ancient condiments where very spice, sweet or sour.This was a result of necessitate they were design to mask the flavour of poorly prepared food or slightly spoil food.It was not until 17th and 18th century that more refined and aromatic preparation, béchamel, soubise and mayonnaise were appeared and mireporx been to be used. It was a CARÉME who began to classify the sauces the hot sauces which are far more at where subdivided into white or brown sauces. Cold sauces are based on mayonnaise and vinaigrette and there derivations.

The evolution of sauces continue under Escoffier and continue currently.There are many classified sauces till used however there is move towards lighter sauces.This shift to lighter sauces has been taken place for a number of year but has become intense with the increase interests of the guests in healthier meal.

Sauces are thickened liquid additions to a recipe, used to enhance the flavour or appearance, or to add moisture. In the 1800s, the French chefs Antonin Carême and Auguste Escoffier developed a systematic categorization of sauces, based on five "mother sauces". All sauces were considered to be a variation of one of these sauces. As other cuisines and ingredients have become more common to world cuisine, the number of mother sauces and sauce families has expanded slightly, but most sauces can be seen as a variation or adaptation of a few basics.

The sauces below are grouped by their family. The first five groups are the traditional sauce families, with the modern additions following. Except for the Dessert family, the top sauce in each family is that family's "mother sauce". Many of the mother sauces use a roux as the thickening agent. Roux itself is not really a sauce, as it would not be used alone.

The most crucial point in this introduction to sauces is that they are can be rushed stock, sauces takes many hours to bring to perfection are demiglaces don't rush into anything take the time.Time and care will result in the making of great sauces.

Plan ahead : Review the whole operation in your head move by move, give your ingredients and elements a chance to do their work.Set by set is how you're going to make your sauce right.

Essential of a Good Sauce

A sauce may be thick or thin, strained or contained visible ingredients. Thick or thin, light or dark, hot or cold, whatever it is must have the following characteristics:

1. It must have a distinctive flavour.
2. Glossy for a demi glace or frothy for a Sabayon (Cook in double boiler of egg and when it becomes before custard stage).
3. It must have a body with flavours. Concentrated to complement the rest of the dish.
4. The colour of the sauce must accent the dish it is being served with such as paring high white butter sauce with the Salmon Mousseline.
5. It must have the right consistency veloute sauces and white butter sauce a some transparent colour or cover the food while brown sauces should be translucent. Giving a light glaze to the meats beneath.

Note: Only white sauces, hollandaise and béarnaise (emulsion sauces) some pasta sauces and some sweet sauces are thick enough to coat the ingredients of the dish even than the shape and colour of the food beneath should understandable a sauce should never be glutens even when design to bind soufflés or to enrich gratinated vegetable.Ordinary the sauce that should be served cold need to be thicker than those to be served hot.

CHARACTERISTIC OF A GOOD SAUCE

If the sauce you have made has the characteristic of a good sauce, there are certain qualities it will add to the flavour. It is part or accompaniment. A sauce contributes to the food it is served with in five ways:

1. Moistness
2. Flavour
3. Richness
4. Appearance- Colour and Shine
5. Interest and Appetite appeal.

Components of a Sauce

Sauces are basically made-up three components:

1. Liquid this is the body of the sauce.
2. A thickening agent.
3. The flavouring and seasoning ingredients.

To understand the sauces making process you must learn to prepare the components you need an understanding of how combined and assembled them into a finished sauces. The following components are as follows;

1. **Liquid:-** A liquid provides the base of the most sauces.There are four liquids which are the base for a group of sauce termed as mother sauces, foundation sauces, base sauce or grand sauce.
   - White stock:- Chicken, veal, fish, vegetables is used for veloute sauce.
   - Brown Stock is used for espagnol (Demi glace)
   - Milk is used for Béchamel
   - Tomato sauce or stock is used for tomato sauce.
2. **Thickening Agent**: - A sauce must be thick enough to cling lightly to the food. If it is not, it will simply run off the food and form a puddle in the plate. However, this does not mean that the sauce has to be heavy or paste. Although starches are the most commonly used thickening agent there are others in order to prepare high quality sauces. You must be able to handle thickening agents of many types properly.

Roux: represent the primary thickening compound of a mother sauce. Preparation appears to be extremely simply but in reality it's crucial to making of a good sauce.

(i) **Composition of a Roux**: - Composition is a cooked mixture of 50% sifted bread flour or all purpose flour and 50% clarified fat usually butter. Fat in the roux act as a bridge between the liquid of the sauce and thickening agent. In the case of flour. To add the flour directly to the liquid would result in lumping. The fat makes the thickening agent easily soluble in the liquid clarify butter is preferred for roux because

a. The power of absorption is better in clarified in butter.

b. The water and casein in butter make it difficult to get a smooth even blend of butter and flour.

Bread flour or all purpose flour is recommended because of the high gluten content. High gluten content makes it and gives it great binding ability.

- **White roux**: is used for making cream sauces
- **Blond roux** : is used for veloute sauces
- **Brown roux**: is used for brown sauces.

White and blond roux requires less cooking time and can be made as requires. Brown roux requires a longer cooking time and it's normally cook in advance in large batch.

(ii) **Cooking of a Roux:** Time allowed for cooking of the roux that depend on the degree of heat. The more intense the heat the quicker the roux is cooked but longer and slower roux is cooked, the better it is. The roux should be cooked for a longer time until the taste, humidity and acidity of the roux flour has to be disappeared. Among the various element that makes-up flour starch has the ability to bind. The starch granules when toasted slowly begin to unbind a bit. When heat and water are both present, the granules even there and form a gel (thickener). If you try unwind them more quickly with the addition of too much water, too fast the lumps will result the toasting of starch granules in fat allows complete separation of the granules. There by effecting maximum exposure for maximum absorption, what is created it is a mass which is capable of absorbing six times its own weight of liquid if cooked.

When cooking of a roux is started with very high heat its starch get burn which destroyed the chemical group responsible for thickening of the sauces, as well as resulting in flavours changes swelling limited to only those part of the starch which are least burn the binding power of the roux is reduces greatly double or triple the amount of burnt roux is needed to gain the same consistency of the sauces.which we needed by correct roux.

The problem of burnt roux is particularly important when making brown roux.This roux is to be brown and hot burn.Brown roux is considered cooked when it has fine light brown colour and gives aroma of hazelnuts aroma characteristics of baked flour.

Roux and Aluminum pot

Attention should be paid to the metal of the utensil used for making roux. Stainless Steel pots and pans are ideal. When used aluminum utensil you have to stirred the roux. If use aluminum utensils use spatula (Wooden spoon) so that the other outer layer of aluminum will not crush. Otherwise which produces and turn the roux and their by the sauce turn it into grayish green in colour

Using the Roux

10-12 oz of roux per gallon for soup and 12-15 oz per gallon for sauce. Heavier viscosity, greater thickness is reach by reduction and but not adding more roux. Excessive roux will choked the sauces and mar the flavour. Never combine roux and stock in the same temperature. Follow the following points:-

1. Slowly adds hot stock to cold roux measure the qualities. Roux is a formula.
2. Make a solid paste with stocks and roux and then a liquid paste by whisking.
3. Continue to add reminder of the measure stock. Stirring continuously.
4. Bring sauce to a boil. Stirring often.
5. All sauce has to be brought to a boil after the roux is added. This is because:

   (a) To allow the thickness to develop to its full potential.

(b) To sterilize the sauce. This destroys bacteria present in the sauce reducing the risk of turning sour in the holding during service.

Other Starches

Basically refined wheat flour is the most commonly used starch. Other types of starches are corn starch, arrowroot, tapioca starch.

1. **Corn Starch**: Excellence all purpose starch; it is easy to work quickly and is inexpensive.But has a poor holding quality which gives to a sauces.
2. **Arrow root**: This is best starch for shine and transparency sauce but it is very difficult to work quickly. Its gives too much elasticity to sauces. It has good holding qualities.
3. **Tapioca**: Similar to arrow root but much cheaper.Easier to work with but doesn't gave much elasticity to the sauces.

Finalization or Liaison Finale

It is a French term for any mixture used for thickening or binding sauces, soups or other culinary to bind and enrich a light stock or liquid to make a thickened sauce.It refers to specifically a mixture of egg or cream used to finish the sauces and soups.

Objective of a saucier

Is to bind and enrich a light stock or liquid to make a kitchen sauces the last part of this process the last part of this process is liaison finale which is the last touch before serving. It is classified as an uncooked liaison since it is critical that the sauce should not boil ones the liaison is added.

1. **Liaison Finale with starch**: - It is potato starch or other starch dissolved in cold water and white wine and the mixture gradually poured into boiling sauce whisking rapidly.
2. **Liaison Finale with BeÊrremanie**: - For a sauce which seems to thin / butter and flour mixture is used. One part of flour to two part of butter which is whisked into the simmering. Sauce should not be re-boil. because the boil sauces develop an unpleasant taste of raw.
3. **Liaison with Egg Yolk**: - Eggs are first whipped with wire whip and cream is added if desire. A cup full of hot liquid is gradually whisk into the yolk to temper them.The mixture is then stirred into a sauces continues while its heated but not boiled. If the temperature is goes above 160° C. The yolk shell will begin harden and the sauce will curdle.
4. **Liaison with Blood**: - This is done with the blood of poultry or game or the correl of the lobster. The principle is same as with egg yolk liaison. This liaison mixed with heavy cream taking place of egg yolk. The sauce is not allowed to boil when liaisons is added.Traditional use of this finale is coqauvin (Chicken in wine) and lobster a la' American.
5. **Liaison Finale with Vegetable Pureé**: This is valuable process used in modern cuisine.Liaison is made with prescribe amount of finally puree cooked vegetables.The puree is easily made in food processor or blender.

6. **Liaison Finale with Fat**: - Based on butter, cream or foigra.

   a. **Butter**: This is to lift the sauce with butter the purpose of this liaison is not only to thicken but specially to enrich the sauces. The process is done on a very low heat.Small pieces of butter (also compound butter) are added to the hot sauces while gentling roasting the bottom of the pan on the heat. This one way of improving the sauces without changing it basic base.

   b. **Cream**: To thicken a sauces with cream usually a sauces started with pan juices of the deglazes of the sauté food item. Simply add heavy cream to sauces and bring to a boil, lower too simmer.Add reduces sauces to desire consistency.

   c. **Foigra**: This is simply to liaison with butter in a blender.Pure together a mixture of two parts of foigra and one part off heavy cream, off the heat whisk the foigra mixture into hot sauces with whire whip.

Using a Basic Liaison

1. Whisk together an egg yolk and cream in a bowl normal portion are six eggs yolk per cup of heavy.
2. Very slowly add a little of a hot sauces to the liaisons whisking constantly.
3. Remove sauce pot from heat and gradually stir in tempered liaisons.Stirring well
4. Returns the sauces to low heat to warm it gently are carefully not to go above 180degree for it will be curdle. It should never come for boil.

Wines in Sauce

The wine in the sauces for a specific purpose to add subtle flavour and richness we add wines in sauces to provide subtle flavour and richness. The guidelines for using wines are:-

1. Reduce wine by boiling. This reduces volume concentrate flavour and evaporates some of their alcohol content.
2. Reduction lessens the acidity of white wine. Acidity often causes ingredients like cream to curdle.
3. Red wine reduction makes it perfume stronger. This is also true for brandies also.
4. Fortified wine such as Port or Madeira has delicate perfumes which have easily destroyed. They work best unheated bad added at the last minute.

Milk and Cream in Sauce

Milk and sauce are not simple liquids but emulsion of fat globules in water, the emulsified agent is Casein like all emulsion, they are not stable but subject to curdling. If they are not fresh they may look and taste good but when heated the bacteria will grow and they will curdle. This wastes the product so to prevent this boil milk and cream before use.

Reduction of Sauce

Key too many sauces are reduction. Cooking over high heat to evaporate the liquid, concentrate the flavour and achieve right consistency. Reduction is essential to sauce based on stock and roux. The longer the sauce is simmered, the more subtle and mellow the taste. Uncovered pan speeds evaporation and concentration of the liquid. The normal reduction of a sauce requires gentle simmering. A hard boil may cause the sauce to become cloudy.

The making of Mother Sauces

The making can be break down into steps:

1. Produces the type of stock needed. De-grease, filter and reduce until proper concentration and taste is achieved.
2. Produce the type of roux needed.
3. Create Liaison between and stock. This involves binding the sauces with the correct percent of roux. Clean the sauce by Depouillage.
4. Develop the five physical properties:

(A) **Viscosity**: - This is the resistance of the sauce to movement.Consistency is given by thickening agent and reduction. It's best to thicken a sauce partial with roux than to bring it to proper viscosity by simmering along period.

(B) **Texture**: - Proper distribution in the sauce is given by the perfect combining and homogenizing of the roux and the stock. This perfection is achieved through simmering and de pouillement of all impurities from roux and stock. It is finally finished by straining through chinos (Strainer).

(C) **Colour**: - Proper colour is the result of its components. The stock, roux, various seasoning and flavouring all at colour to the sauce. The colour of each sauce is part of this over all character.

(D) **Luster:** - This is a degree to which sauce reflects light. This shine comes from starches used process de-poulliment which makes demiglazes shine like a mirror.

(E) **Opacity**: - This is the degree of transparency of the sauce. It is the result of gluten in roux, egg yolks, blood and milk products such as cream and butter. There are three degrees of transparency of sauces:

- Opaque (light doesn't pass through)
- Translucence (light is diffused)
- Transparent(light pass through it).

De-pouillage or Cleaning of a Sauce

Most important process in building a sauce without it you has only a gross raw product full of impurities and fat. Any sauce using a roux should be de pouilled. This brings about liaison of roux and stock. Depouillage is the removal of all the fat and the impurities of flour and the stock in the impurities. It is done in the following manner.

1. After the roux and the stock is blended. Bring the sauce to a boil.
2. Reduces the heat and let the sauce simmer this will allow the impurities and the fat to accumulate on the sides of the sauce pan/russe/ rondue.
3. Carefully skim off the accumulation.

Straining of sauce

Straining the sauce improves the smoothness and increasing the luster. The finer the masher size, the smoother and the glossy the sauce will be. The preferred utensil is the conical mash sieves.

Classification of Sauces

The four mother sauce. The name mother sauce is especially appropriate because the group spawns compound sauces. The four mother sauces are **Béchamel, Veloute, Tomato, and Espagnole.** They are always serve hot.

CHARACTERISTICS OF A MOTHER SAUCE

1. Spawns multiple compound sauces.
2. Foundation of many other culinary preparation including soups, casserole and are liquid for braising etc.
3. It is a stable structure which means it can be re-heated without breaking.
4. It is a thickened liquid base.

The brown mother sauces are Espagnole and Tomato and the whites are Béchamel and Veloute.

THE COMPOUND SAUCES

1. **Tomato**: - Provéncal and Portuguese.
2. **Demi Glaze:** - Derivatives are Mushroom, Bordelaise, Madeira, Chasseur, Robert, and Brigarde.
3. **Béchamel**: Cream, Mornay, Soubise.
4. **Veal Veloute**: - Allemande, Smitana, Poulette.
5. **Poultry Veloute**: - Albufera, Supreme, Ivoire.
6. **Fish Veloute**: - Berry Blanche, Normandy.
7. **Shell Fish**: - Shell fish sauces are Americain, Newburg.

Other Sauces

These categories are sauces which are not directly based on mother sauces.

The Hot Emulsion Sauces

Beurre Blanc (White butter sauce)

- **Hollandaise**: - Maltaise, Mousseline, Moutarde (Mustard), Noisette.
- **Béarnaise**: - Choron, Foyot, Tyrolienne, paloise
- **Butter sauces**: - Clarifies meuniere, Beurenoir, Beurrenoisette.
- **Compound Butter**:- Shallot, Maître d' hotel, Bercy, Colbert, Pimentos-Red and green butter, shrimp, Lobster, Crayfish, Chateaubriand.

Miscellaneous Sauces

Gravies, A la minute reduction, Barbeque, Nut sauces and Sweet & sour sauces.

Espangole

In the eighteen century when sauces first started being made the finest ham and essential ingredients of Espangole, was said to come from Spain two or three days were required to make this sauces.First the roux has brown slowly to develop flavour then a rich brown stock was added with pieces of veal, ham, stewing fowl or a game bird. Espagnole (pronounced like the word for Spanish: "español") is a basic brown sauce that is one of the five "leading sauces" of classical cuisine. It's also the starting point for the demiglaze, a rich and deeply flavorful sauce that is traditionally served with red meats.

Espangole sauces:

Ingredients	*Quantity*
Brown stock	6 qt.
Brown roux	13 oz.
Slab bacon, diced and blanch	8 oz.
Mireporx	2 lb
Bouquet garni —	
Thyme	2 pinches
Bay leaf	2 medium
Parsley stem	1 bunch
Tomato puree	1 qt.
Seasoning	As needed
Butter	As needed

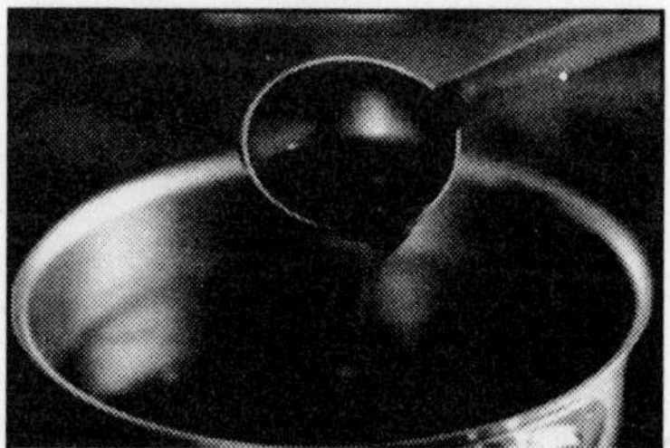

Fig. 8.1 The Espangole sauces

Method

1. In a bowl dissolve cold roux in a hot sauce making a solid paste, than liquidify the paste by adding more liquid.
2. Stir tempered roux into a boiling brown stock with spatula and whisk and bring it to a bowl.
3. Add tomato puree and bouquet garni to a boiling sauces
4. Render the bacon in a sautuir, add mireporx and sauté until golden add to boiling sauces.
5. Move pot off the centre and adjust fire to slow boil, allow scum to allocate one side than skim impurities from surface.

Note: A minimum of at least 2hours.should be considered for appropriate depouilage and reduction.

6. When reduce to one gallon add seasoning.
7. Strain through a chinois.
8. Butter top to avoid formation of skin, label, cool and refrigerator.

Preparation for Demiglazes

Espangole is the half way point in the production of traditional demiglaces by combining equal amount of Espangole and brown stock with appropriate mireporx and than continue reduction and depoulage the perfection of traditional demiglaces is achieved.

Demi Glaze

Ingredients	Quantity
Brown veal stock	1 gallon
Espangole	1 gallon
Bouquet garni with tarragon	1E.A (individual portion)
Madeira	8oz
seasoning	As needed

Fig. 8.2 The demiglazes

Method

1. Add brown veal stocks to espangole brings it's to a rolling boil.
2. Add bouquet garni, place pot off centre.
3. Simmer and reduce volume by half.
4. Depoulage frequently up to 8 hours. Until the sauce is very shiny and translucence, having remove all of the impurities.
5. Adjust seasoning strain through a chinova with muslin, add Madeira wine into it.

6. It not used immediately cool stirring frequently this will prevent formation of thick skin.
7. When completely cooled, butter top, label and cooled in refrigerate.

Jus De Veau Lie / Quick Demi glaze

Today because of concern of lighter sauces and labour factor.Chef prepares demiglazes from strong veal stock which is reduce by half with Mireporx and aromatic and then thicken lightly with modified starch. Demiglazes is well flavoured veal stock reduce to half this is the meaning of "DEMI-HALF"

White sauces : These don't required much labour as brown sauces, short cuts, lead to pasty sauces which no body like to eat to avoid this white sauces must be cook long enough to produce a silky dream white finish. It is necessary to strain sauces through muslin cloth or a fine chine cap.

Veloutes

Are finer grade of white sauces, they are made from strong flavour full liquid such as chicken broth or fish broth but not milk. *Velouté* or blond sauce is basically a *bechamel* sauce made with stock instead of milk. In preparing a *velouté* sauce, a light stock (one in which the bones used have not been roasted), such as chicken, veal or fish stock, is thickened with a blond roux.

Thus the ingredients of a velouté are butter and flour to form the roux, a light chicken, veal, or fish stock, salt and pepper for seasoning. Commonly the sauce produced will be referred to by the type of stock used e.g. chicken *velouté*

Ordinary (rich/lean)

Ordinary veloutes rich

Fig. 8.3 The oridinary veloute rich

Yield 1 gallon

Ingredients	*Quantity*
White veal stock	1 gallon
Blond roux	15 ounces
Optional (white mushroom trimmings)	5 oz.
Salt and pepper	To taste

All poultry veloutes (rich) yield 1 gallon

Ingredients	*Quantity*
White chicken stocks	1 gallon
Blond roux	15 ounces
Salt and pepper	To taste

Fish or vegetable veloutes (lean)

Yield: 1 gallon

Ingredients	*Quantity*
White fish stock or vegetable stock	1 gallon
Blond roux	15 ounces
Salt and pepper	To taste

Method and preparation of all veloutes

1. In a bowl slowly add little hot stock to a cold roux, making a solid paste, than add more liquid to make a liquid paste.
2. Whip the liquid paste into a boiling stock stirring continuously.
3. Bring to a boil.Adjust the heat source and move pan off centre of depoulage.
4. Reduce the proper consistency and depoulage occasionally establishing five physical property of the sauce.
5. Adjust seasoning.
6. Butter top to prevent formation of skin cool rapidly and label and refrigerator.

Béchamel (lean/rich)

Béchamel Lean

Béchamel sauce (pronounced 'bay-shah-mel') also known as white sauce is usually made today by whisking scalded milk gradually into a white flour- butter roux, though it can also be made by whisking a kneaded flour-butter beurre manié into scalded milk. The thickness of the final sauce depends on the proportions of milk and flour. Sauce *béchamel* is one of the very few French sauces that are easy to prepare but is flavorful and delicate enough to serve on its own or as the basis for some fifty more complex sauces. This sauce is widely used with vegetables, eggs, fish, poultry, hot hors d'oeuvres and dishes that are finished under the grill.

Fig. 8.4 The béchamel lean

Béchamel sauce is the base for a number of other classic sauces including: Mornay sauce (cheese); Nantua sauce (shrimp, butter and cream); *Crème* sauce (heavy cream); Mustard sauce (prepared mustard); Soubise sauce (finely diced onions that have been sweated in butter); Cheddar cheese sauce (cheddar cheese, dry mustard, worcestershire sauce)

Béchamel Lean

Fig. 8.5 The Béchamel rich

Yield 1 gallon

Ingredients	*Quantity*
Milk (optimal)	1 gallon (low fat milk)
White roux	15 oz.
Salt to	Taste
Nut meg	A pinch
Onions clout	1 E.A

Béchamel Rich

Yield 1 gallon

Ingredients	*Quantity*
Milk	1 gallon
Roux	15 oz.
Salt	To taste
White pepper	To taste
Nut meg	A pinch
Onion clout	1 E.A
Veal lean diced blanched	12 oz.
Onion diced sautéed	4 oz.

Method:

1. Boil milk.
2. In a bowl slow add little a cold roux to make a solid paste.
3. Add more liquid and make a liquid paste.
4. Whip the liquid paste into boil milk, stir constantly to prevent the roux from setting to bottom and burning.
5. Bring to rolling boil and onion cloute.

Note: For rich béchamel four steps are added from this point.

Veal béchamel

1. Blanched veal refresh and drain.
2. Sauté diced onions in little butter till translucency.
3. Add veal and stew lightly to a blond colour.

4. Add prepare onion and veal to sauces.
5. Cover and cook in a moderate oven at 300 degree F for 35 to 45 minute.Stir occasional.
6. When cooled remove from oven degrease adjust seasoning including a starch of nut meg.
7. Strain through a chinova muslin.
8. Butter top to prevent formation of the skin. Cool it and label and refrigerate.

Formula: = Béchamel lean + Veal + onion

Tomato Sauce

This sauce is used either on its own or as an addition to other sauces. This sauce is thickening with a roux but frequently it is made in today commercial kitchen without roux. A tomato sauce is any of a very large number of sauces

Fig. 8.6 The tomato sauce

Made primarily out of tomatoes, usually to be served as part of a dish (rather than as a condiment). Tomato sauces are common for meat and vegetables, but they are perhaps best known as sauces for pasta dishes.

Tomatoes have a rich flavour, a low liquid content, very soft flesh which breaks down easily, and the right composition to thicken up into a sauce when they are cooked (without the need of thickeners like roux). All of these make them ideal for simple and appealing sauces.

The simplest tomato sauces consist just of chopped tomato flesh (with the skins and seeds optionally removed), cooked in a little olive oil and simmered until it loses its raw flavour, and seasoned with salt.

Water (or another, more flavorful liquid such as stock or wine) is often added to keep it from drying out too much. Onion and garlic are almost always sweated or sautéed at the beginning before the tomato is added. Other seasonings typically include basil, oregano, parsley, and possibly some spicy red pepper or black pepper.

Ground or chopped meat is also common. Sauces derived from tomato sauce are: Bretonne; Tomated Chaudfroid; Portugaise; Italienne; Barbecue; Green tomato sauce; Salsa; Puttanesca; Tomato gravy

Tomato sauce yield :- 1 gallon.

Ingredients	*Quantity*
Salted pork diced or ham shank cut	6 oz.
Mireporx finally diced	1 pound
Garlic minced	2 cloves

Thyme	2 pinches
Bayleaf	2 medium
Parsley stem	One bunch
Roux blond	8 oz.
Sugar	10 oz.
Tomatoes fresh ripened peel and chop	8 pounds
Tomatoes puree can	2 ½ cans
White stock veal or chicken	2 Qt
Seasoning (salt, pepper, w.sauce)	as needed

Methods:

1. Melt pork in a rondeau and cook through blond colour.
2. Sweat mireporx garlic and aromatic in render pork fat (olive oil can be used instead of pork fat)
3. Add blond roux dilute with fond Blanc.
4. Add tomatoes, tomatoes purees and sugar.
5. Bring to a boil stirring often.
6. Cover and simmer in moderate oven 300 degree F for two hours.
7. Degrease and adjust seasoning.
8. Pass through fine food mill and than through chinova to achieve smooth texture.
9. Butter top to avoid crust forming place in a cooling bath, cool label and refrigerator.

Emulsified Sauces

Emulsion is a mixture of two liquids that normally can't be combined. Combining oil and water is the classic example. Emulsifying is done by slowly adding one ingredient to another while simultaneously mixing rapidly. This disperses and suspends tiny Droplets of one liquid through another. However, the two liquids would quickly separate again if an emulsifier were not added. Emulsifiers are liaisons between the two liquids and serve to stabilize the mixture. Eggs and gelatin are these are preparation with bring together elements which don't readily mix. Chief among the hot emulsified sauces are two egg based sauces among the foods that contain emulsifiers. In mayonnaise, the emulsifier is egg yolk, which contains lecithin, a fat emulsifier. Emulsion sauces are hollandaise and mayonnaise.

- Hollandaise flavoured with lemon juice
- Béarnaise flavoured with vinegar, shallots and tarragon.

- It is a basic butter sauce called white butter sauce or béurre blanc sauce which is not stabilized by the addition of egg yolk.

Emulsified sauces are difficult to make since they tend to separate. The key to maintain them is to create and then maintain the emulsion at the beginning, butter should be added very slowly until the sauce thicken showing emulsion is foaming. The sauce separate when they stand at too high temperature for too long. When making this sauce the base of the pan should not be more than hand hot. If it is hotter, the egg will curdle.

Hollandaise and Béarnaise sauce are both serve warm. It may be served by its self or blended with a small quantity of béchamel and veloutes and used as a coating for light meat and fish.

Production of emulsified Sauces : The production of these requires constant adjustment of heat.Heat is adjusted to prevent the sauces from curdling and separating.

The main points to remember while production is:

1. Yolk should be cooked slowly over moderate heat from time-to-time remove them from fire to lower the temperature.
2. Butter should be in the same temperature as the yolk mixture.
3. When butter is absorbed the sauce should be thick and firm.
4. When thick and firm, the sauce is brought to the correct consistency by adding a little water to lighten it slightly.
5. Emulsion sauces are usually completed by adding a few drops of lemon juice and then passed through a fine sieve or muslin cloth.

Re-montage of a broken Emulsion

Few ways to repair broken sauces:

1. If egg yolk become too thick it means that the heat is too high. Lower the heat add a few drops of cold water to mixture.
2. If the egg yolk foams but doesn't thicken the heat is too low, correct by increasing the heat slightly
3. If the sauce curdle at the end of process that means it has cooled too much or become too hot.

(A) If it is too cold put a little hot water in a bowl and gradually whisk the sauce into it.

(B) If it is too hot do the same thing with a little cold water.

Note : Both these method will save the sauces however it will not gave that lightness, should have had.

Hollandaise

The most reliable method of hollandaise is to produce a mousse by whisking egg yolks with water, one table spoon per yolk over heat on a double boiler.This process should take three minutes by which time the mousse should be light but closed textured.The mousse acts as a stabilizer allowing the melted butter to be added without the sauce separating.Formerly hollandaise was seasoned with the reduction of vinegar but today lemon juice is more common.It's a good accompliments for poached fish eggs and vegetables.

Hollandaise requires some skill and knowledge to prepare; care must also be taken to store it properly after preparation. Properly made, the sauce should be smooth and creamy. The flavour should be rich and buttery, with a mild tang added by the lemon juice and seasonings. It must be made and served warm, not hot. If the ingredients are emulsified improperly by over-or under-heating them they will separate, resulting in the sauce "breaking" from the emulsion and the yolks coagulating from excessive heat. The sauce may be portioned and frozen for future use. When ready to use, let it come to room temperature; some stirring may be required. The following list is a non-exhaustive listing of minor-sauces created by adding ingredients to Hollandaise Sauce (as a 'mother sauce'): Sauce Mousseline, Sauce Béarnaise, Sauce Maltaise, Sauce Divine, Sauce Noisette, Sauce Bavaroise, Sauce Colbert

Hollandaise

Ingredients	*Quantity*
Egg yolks	5 (E.A)
Cold water	3 oz.
White wine vinegar	1tbs
Unsalted butter melted	1 pt.
Fresh lemon juice	1no.
Cayenne pepper and salt	As needed

Fig. 8.7 Eggs yolks with cold water

Fig. 8.8 The mixing of eggs yolks

Methods:

1. Separate egg yolks from white and place yolk in a suitable bowl and cold water (Fig. 8.7).
2. Add a pinch of salt and whipped lightly (Fig. 8.8).
3. As soon as you noticed a changed in coloured from lighter yellow to darker yellow, vinegar and whipped to a froth at least until double volume.
4. Cooked over double boiler or source of allow heat (Fig. 8.9).
5. Whipping constantly until consistency reaches the soft peak (Fig. 8.10).
6. Remove from heat slowly add melted butter
7. Which is the same temperature as the egg mixture form time to time lightens the sauces by adding few drops of hot and cold water.

Fig. 8.9 The mixed of eggs yolks in double boiler

Fig. 8.10 The mixed of eggs yolks in double boiler till thicken

Fig. 8.11 The thicken egg yolks mixing constantly with drop of butter

8. Adjust seasoning with cayenne pepper and lemon juice.
9. Strain through a fine muslin cloth, label and keep warm.

Fig. 8.12 The thicken egg yolks mixing constantly till right consistency

Fig. 8.13 The hollandaise thicken with tarragon

Béarnaise

It's not hollandaise prepared with a reduction of a tarragon.Its a sauce on its own.Béarnaise is thicker and have more pungent flavour than hollandaise.Eggs yolks with a reduction of tarragon, vinegar, white wine, pepper corn and shallots. The result is a thick coarse texture mousse. Clarified butter is than whisked in it.

Béarnaise yield :- 1 qt.

Ingredients	*Quantity*
Wine vinegar	4oz.
White wine	4oz.
Shallot finely chopped	6 medium
Fresh tarragon finally chopped	3tbs
Fresh chervil finally chop	3tsp
Mignonette pepper	1tsp
Egg yolk	6 E.A
Unsalted butter melted	1 pint
Seasoning	To taste
Tarragon leaves in vinegar finally chop	1 tsp

Method

1. In a heavy stainless steel russe or roundue combined ingredients 1 to 6 bring to a boil.Reduced by 2/3 rd. remove from heat and let it cool.
2. Separate eggs yolks from white placing yolk in a bowl on a suitable size.
3. Add cool reduction and a pinch of salt, wiping slightly until changed in colour.
4. Add a little water and wiped to a froth.
5. Cook over double boiler or a source of low heat. Whipping constantly until consistency reaches a heavy peak.
6. Remove from heat slowly add melted butter which is as the same temperature as egg mixture.
7. Adjust seasoning and strain through a fine sieve.
8. Add garnish of tarragon leaves in vinegar finally chop.cool, label and keep worm.

Note: if you notice the sauces getting to thick and solid when your wiping the sauces, from time to time add a few drops of tepid water.This is preferably to certain adding extract liquid to lighten the sauces when finished.

White Butter sauce or Beurre Blanc

This sauce is originally from Loirve valley, it was made from excellent loacal butter and muscatel wine it has become sauce worldwide and develop the four basic ingredients are: White Wine, Vinegar, Shallots and butter. The first three ingredients are reduce to a thick glaze and then mounted (mix) the butter. The pan should be more than warm and vigorously whisking is needed.

Basic Beurre Blanc

Yield 1 cup

Ingredients	*Quantity*
Sweet butter	80grm
Strongly reduce fish fumet	2tbs
White wine	2tbs
Herb vinegar	2tbs
Finally sliced shallots	2tbs

Method

1. Cut the butter in the small pieces and leaves at room temperature to soften.
2. Place the shallots, fish stocks and white wine and vinegar in a heavy stainless steel sauce pan and boil on high heat. until liquid is reduced to 2 table spoon (watch against burning)

3. Turn down the heat to a very low and slowly whisking the butter 1 oz at a time.
4. Continue to stir over heat until 170degree F and than strain to a sieve.
5. The sauces should be served immediately.

Butter sauces

Butter sauces are made primarily with butters like fresh churned salted or clarified the first in the variety.

1. Beurre Noisette:- Butter heated to a light brown colour for a nutty aroma.
2. Beurre Meuniere:- Butter reaches to brown colour and then add juice of lemon and chop parsley.
3. *Beurrenoir (Black Butter):*- Means black butter but it is not actually black. It is cooked till noisette stage but little more. When the smoking point is reaches, stopped by the addition of caper and vinegar. Any acid has the effect of thickening the butter.

Compound butter

The term applies to the followings

A. Butter cooks to a various degree
B. Butter with one or more substance added usually chopped or puree
C. Complex butter such as Crustaceans butter.Used as a medium to extract the taste from various shell fish.Does yielding a large groups of sauces called shell fish sauces.
D. Hot compound butter used as a sauces such as beurre blanc and lemon butter.

SOME COMPOUND BUTTER

1. **Ail** : is a French term very common vegetable “Garlic”. Blanched garlic, cloves pounded in mortar and pestle with butter and pass through a fine sieve.
2. **Anchovies**: Anchovy’s fillets pounded in mortar with butter and pass through a sieve.
3. **Bercy** :the reduction of white wine in chop shallots add dice of poach marrow, chop parsley, salt, black pepper, lemon juice and butter soften to a cream.
4. **Beurre rouge**(rouge means red): Pound in fine powder some use of shell fish, add some butter.Melt the mixture in a sauce pan in a bain-marie.Strain through muslin into basin of iced water.
5. **Beurre Bert** (bert means green): Ponds some raw spinach and press in a bowl to extract the juices, put in a pan and let it coagulated in a bain-marie and pour it over a serviette over a bowl to drain the water collect the green colouring and mixed it with butter and pass through a fine sieve.
6. **Colbert**: Maitre d’ hotel butter mixed with meat glaze and chopped tarragon.

7. **Crevettes**: Shrimps pounded with butter and pass through a fine chives.
8. **Homard(lobster)**: Creamy parts, eggs and corals of lobster and pounded with butter and pass through a sieve.
9. **Manie**: Butter in cream and mixed with flour
10. **Meunirre**: Nutty brown cooked butter in lemon juices and chop parsley.
11. **Moutart** (mustard): Creamy butter mixed with French mustard
12. **Paprika** : Chop onions and paprika tossed in butter and mixed with creamy butter and pass through sieve.
13. **Pimentose**: Pound the pimento in butter and pass through a sieve.

MISCELLANEOUS SAUCES

1. **Gravy** : It is made from meat juices which congeal and caramelize in the bottom of the roasting pan or heavy frying pan.. For red meats gravy should be dark brown and for lighter meat it should be golden colour. Gravy can be of two types thin and thick gravy is thickened by roux.
2. **A la' Minute Reduction**:- Mostly these sauces are made when meat, fish or poultry is sautéed. If is the simple reduction of pan juices of the items sautéed after deglazing them in suitable liquid. Liquid such as stock, wine, fortified wines. Meat glazes are used which are reduced and may be thickened with liaison finale and seasoned.
3. **Barbeque sauce:-** These are now a days, mostly comes from bottles. They are highly spiced tomato based sauces with soya, sugar etc. added them. They are used for brushing meat, poultry, fish.
4. **Nut sauces:-** Two ways nuts can be used as thickener or infused in milk.Receipes of nuts sauces are the charctertics of particular region of the world. Almost these sauces popular in India and Mediterranean. Coconut sauces are typical to Asia and Caribbean. While walnut sauces are popular in south east Asia, Africa and Southern United State.
5. **Savory and Sweet Fruit sauces**:- It consists of fruit pulp and sweetness, its fruit themselves that length character to the sauces. The main ingredient in fruit which is usually served cold. Sweet fruit sauces are sweetened and thin, many are based on Jelly or jam and other from fruit puree and there flavoured can enhanced with Fruit liquor and lemon juice can be added.
6. **Savory sabayon**:- Made in a similar way as hollandaise by whisking egg yolk and fish or veal stock to form a mousse. This sauce is usually mounted with butter.
7. **Custard** : Standard portion for custard sauce are five egg yolks per two cups of milk, however more egg yolk can be added for richness classically no starch is added.Although added corn starch is an economic way to thicken sauces.

DERIVATES OF MOTHER SAUCES

DEMIGLACE

1. **Bordelaise:** chop shallots, mignonette pepper, thyme, bay leaf, redwine reduce and mix with demi-glaze and strain it.
2. **Medire**: Demi-glaze with medire.
3. **Piquant**: Chop shallots reduce with vinegar and white wine add demi-glazes pass though a Tami cloth garnish with gherkin, chervil, chop tarragon and pepper.
4. **Diable:** Chop shallots, mignont pepper reduce with white wine and vinegar add demi glazes and mustard to finish.
5. **Robert:** Chop onions cook in butter without colour moisten with white wine and vinegar and pepper, reduce to demi glazes and mustard to finish.
6. **Chasseur**: Minced mushroom tossed in butter add chop shallots moisten with white wine reduce it, add demi-glazes, butter and chop parsley.
7. **Charcuteire:** Robert Sauce garnish with juliennes of gherkin.
8. **Chaud froid**: Brown demi-glazes with aspic, essence of truffles and Madeira.
9. **Lyonnaise**: Onions partly fried in butter moisten with white wine and vinegar and reduce to demi-glazes and pass through a tany cloth.

Veloute:

1. **Allemande**: Ordinary veloute cohered with egg yolks.
2. **Aurore**: Supreme sauces slightly flavoured with tomatoes.
3. **Supreme sauce**: Reduced veloute cohered with butter.
4. **Aurore with fish**: Tomato fish veloute with butter.
5. **Fine herbs**: White wine sauce with chop herbs finished with shallots butter.
6. **Bercy:** Chop shallots tossed in light melted butter moisten with white wine for fish stock reduce and mix fish veloute and chop parsley finish with butter.
7. **Chivery**: Chicken veloute mix with an infusion of chervil, parsley, tarragon, chives, pimpernel (low growing plant with pietral flower), white wine strain and finish with chive butter.
8. **White wine sauces**: Fish stock reduce to a glaze and mixed with butter whisking gradually.
9. **Normandy**: Fish veloute with mushroom essence and oyster juice cohcard with yolks of eggs and cream. Reduced with finished butter and cream.
10. **Diplomat**: Normand sauce with lobster butter. Garnish with dice of butter and lobster.
11. **Ravigote:** Reduction of white wine and vinegar, add veloute and shallots, butter.Garnish with chervil chives and tarragon.
12. **Riche**: Diplomat finished with truffle essence and more truffle.
13. **Joinville**: Normand sauce with Cray fish and shrimps.garnish with juliennes' of truffles.

14. **Chaud froid**: Veloute made with aspic jelly.
15. **Ivory or Ivoire**: Supreme sauces with pale meat glazes.\
16. **Hongroise**: Chop onion, pepper partly fried in butter.Add paprika moisten with wine reduce and mix with supreme
17. **Poulette**: Allemande sauce with mushroom essence and lemon juice and chop parsley.

Béchamel Sauce

1. **Scotch Egg (Ecossaise):** The béchamel sauces garnish with white of egg cut in strips and hard yolk of egg passed through a sieve.
2. **Soubise**: Béchamel add cooked onion seasoned and strain.
3. **Mornay:** Béchamel mixed with butter grated gruyere and parmesan cheese
4. **Lobster sauces**: Béchamel sauces with anchovies essence garnish with diced lobster and cayenne pepper.

Tomato Sauces

1. **Portuguese:** Chop onion partly fried in oil, add tomato concasse, salt, pepper, thin tomato sauces.
2. **Provencal**: There are two types:
   a. **Tomato concasse:** Tossed in oil, salt pepper, pinch of sugar, garlic and chop parsley.
   b. **Slice mushroom:** Tossed in oil and mixed with above preparation.
3. **Italianize**: Tomato sauces add demy glaze with duellos add cooked ham finished with chop mixed tarragon, chervil parsley.
4. **Brettone**: Chopped onions partly fried in butter moisten with white wine reduces it add fresh tomatoes, tomato puree and garlic strain it. Ad butter and chop parsley.

Hollandaise

1. **Noisétte**: Hollandaise sauce with nut brown cooked butter.
2. **Moussline**: Hollandaise sauces mixed with stiffed whipped cream.
3. **Maltaise**: Hollandaise sauces with zest and add juices of oranges.
4. **Moutare**: Hollandaise with mustard.

Béarnaise

1. **Choron**: Béarnaise sauce with tomato puree.
2. **Fayot**: Béarnaise sauce with meat glazes.

COLD SAUCES

Cold Sauces are sometime given less attention than hot because they are taught to be more as salad dressing. It is true that many cold sauces are term what we term as salad dressing but these doesn't change the facts that they are sauces.They are most associated with salads sandwiches and horsd'oeuvres which are produce to the garde manager department of the kitchen.

Types can be categorized into four groups:

1. Based on basic French dressing.
2. Based on mayonnaise
3. Based on boiled dressing
4. Specialty sauces which don't relate to other sauces any of three.

1. Basic French dressing

Simplest of three primary cold sauces the basic of this sauces is nothing more than vinegar, oil and salt and pepper. It's a very temporary emulsion all those.The acidity of vinegar help to create an emulsion and but its is not able to hold it and keep it stable. Ones mixing it will quickly separate.

French dressing made from vinegar, oil, salt and pepper. It is three part of oil in one part of vinegar.

Basic French yield – 1 Qt

Ingredients	*Quantity*
Vinegar (Cider or wine)	8 oz
White pepper	½ tsp
Salt	1 tbs
Salad Oil	24 oz

Method

(i) Place vinegar in a stainless steel mixing bowl.

(ii) Add salt pepper and dissolve it.

(iii) Add oil and whisk it.

(iv) Re-whisk prior to service.

Lemon Lime French Dressing

Yield 3 cups

Ingredients	Quantity
Lemon Juice	4 oz
Lime Juice	4 oz
Sugar	½ tbsp
Salt	1 tbsp
Salad Oil	6 oz

Method

1. Place measured fruit juices in stainless steel mixing bowl.
2. Add salt and sugar whisking to dissolve them.
3. Add oil, whisk rapidly
4. Re whisk prior to service.

Emulsified French

Yield 1 Qt

Ingredients	*Quantity*
Egg Whole	2 Nos.
Dry Mustard	1 tbsp
Paprika	1 tbsp
White pepper	1 ½ tsp
Salt	1 tsp
Salad Oil	24 oz
Vinegar	9 oz

Method

1. Beat egg in stainless bowl.
2. Blend mustard, paprika, salt, white pepper and then add to egg and whisk.
3. Whisk rapidly adds oil in this increasing the quantity of oil when emulsion is formed.
4. As the sauce thicken add vinegar.
5. Ultimately add vinegar and oil till all are used.

Mayonnaise

Mayonnaise (often abbreviated mayo) is a thick condiment, whitish-yellow in colour. Mayonnaise is a basic cold sauce. It is used as a salad dressing and as an accompaniment. Mayonnaise is made by combining lemon juice or vinegar with egg yolks. Eggs (containing the emulsifier lecithin) bind the ingredients together and prevent separation. Then, oil is added drop by drop as the mixture is rapidly whisked. Adding oil too quickly (or insufficient, rapid whisking) will keep the two liquids from combining (emulsifying). But, as the sauce begins to thicken, oil can be added more rapidly. Seasonings are whisked in after all of the oil has been added. Worldwide, mayonnaise is most commonly served in a sandwich, or with salad such as potato salad or canned tuna ("tuna mayo" or tuna salad). Numerous other sauces can be created from it by adding additional seasonings.

Mayonnaise Recepies

Yield 1 Qt.

Ingredients	*Quantity*
Eggs Yolks	4E.A
Sugar	1 tbsp
Salt	2½ tsp
Dry mustard	2tsp
Oil	24 oz.
Vinegar	2 ½ oz.

Method:

1. Place eggs yolks in a mixing bowl.
2. Blend sugar salt and dry mustard.Than add to the yolk.

Fig. 8.14 The eggs yolks with constantly mixing

Fig. 8.15 The eggs yolks with constantly mixing with oil

Fig. 8.16 The sauces thicken add little vinegar

3. Beat till mix thoroughly.
4. Whisking rapidly began to add oil in a very thin stream, increasing the thickness of stream, lightly ones the emulsion began to form.
5. As the sauces thicken add the vinegar in small amount, to thin it out.
6. Alteration the addition of vinegar and until all are used.

Mayonnaise is an emulsion sauce but unlike basic French it is stable. It is used both as dressing for salad and as a spread for sandwich in the egg yolk is the primary emulsifier.

Derivatives of Mayonnaise:

Fig. 8.17 The ready mayonnaise sauces

1. **Cambridge:** Pound in mortar and hard yolk of egg, anchovies fillets, capers, chervils, tarragon, chives, Mustard, vinegar, cayenne peppers, add oil gradually as for mayonnaise.Pass through a sieves finish with chop parsley.
2. **Gloucester**: Mayonnaise sauce with sour cream, finish with ecosphere sauce and chopped fennel.
3. **Remoulade:** Mayonnaise sauce with mustard, garnish with capers, parsley, gherkins, chervil, tarragon, and finished with anchovies essence.
4. **Russe:** mayonnaise sauce mixed with cream, part of lobster, caviar puree mustard and ecosphere sauce.
5. **Tartar:** Mayonnaise with hard yolk egg, garnished with onions, gherkins and chives finally chop.
6. **Verte**: Mayonnaise sauce mixed with puree of blanched herbs like spinach, watercress leaves, parsley, chervil and tarragon and pass through a pass fine sieves.
7. **Vincent:** Half-tartar sauce and half verte mixed together are called Vincent.
8. **Andalouse**: Mayonnaise sauce mixed with tomato puree and garnished with bell peppers chopped

Boiled Dressing is an American innovation which has some similarly to mayonnaise but certain less fat and is not an emulsion sauce. This is a starch thickness sauce.

Boiled dressing Yield 2 ½ pints

Ingredients:	*Quantity*
Flour (All purpose)	1 ½ oz
Sugar	¼ oz
Dry Mustard	1 tbsp
Salt	1 tbsp
White pepper	1/3 tbsp
Paprika	1/2tsp

Beaten Egg Yolk	6 no
Milk	1 Qt
Vinegar	4 oz
Lemon Juice	2 oz
Butter	3 oz

Method:

1. Blend together flour, sugar, dry mustard, salt, white pepper and paprika.
2. Place beaten egg yolk in stainless steel mixing bowl and add the dry ingredients whisking till smooth.
3. Add milk and mix well till well blended
4. Slowly add vinegar and lemon juices.
5. Turn mixture to a double boiler and cook on low heat stirring constantly until thick.
6. Remove from heat and whisk in butter, transfer to a gloss or stainless steel container and cool.

LEARNING OUTCOME

Sauces are liquid or semi-liquid foods devised to make other foods look, smell, and taste better, and hence be more easily digested and more beneficial. Because of the lack of refrigeration in the early days of cooking, meat, poultry, fish, and seafood didn't last long. Sauces and gravies were used to mask. Sauces are an essential element in cuisines all over the world. Some famous saucier include Julia Child, Benjamin Christie, Bobby Flay, Yutake Ishinabe, and François Pierre La Varenne. Sauce is a thickened liquid that is flavoured or seasoned to enhance the flavour of the food that it is to accompany. The sauce can be sweet, sour, spicy, or savory and may be added to the food to become part of a main dish or used as an accompaniment to the food being prepared. Sauces add a variety of features to foods, such as complimenting or enhancing flavors, succulence, attractive appearance, and additional texture. Sauces are thickened liquid additions to a recipe, used to enhance the flavour or apperance, or to add moisture. In the 1800s, the French chefs Antonin Carême and Auguste Escoffier developed a systematic categorization of sauces, based on five "mother sauces". All sauces were considered to be a variation of one of these sauces. As other cuisines and ingredients have become more common to world cuisine, the number of mother sauces and sauce families has expanded slightly, but most sauces can be seen as a variation or adaptation of a few basics. The five mother sauces are: ***Béchamel*** sauces that are made with milk and pale roux. Common sauces in this group include *crème*, mornay and soubise. **Brown (demi-glace) or *Espagnole*** - sauces that are brown stock-based, such as brown sauces. Common sauces in this group include bordelaise, chasseur, chateaubriand, diable, diane, estragon, lyonnaise, *madère*, madeira, moscovite, mushroom, piquante, porto, robert, romaine, tarragon, and zingara. ***Velouté*** - sauces that are made with white stock and roux. Common sauces in this group include allemande, ravigote, *suprème*, and white bordelaise. **Red or Tomato Sauces** - tomatobased sauces. Common sauces in this category include spaghetti sauce, marinara and a wide variety of tomato sauces. **Emulsions** - sauces that are emulsified such as *hollandaise* or *mayonnaise.*

LESSON END ACTIVITY

- Prepare the different mother sauces one day each with there five derivatives of each.
- Collect the information of different herbs which are best used for sauces.
- Collect the information on "how to make quickly mother sauces".
- Collect the information on how many mother sauces are available in the marked in cooked form.Collect the information of their brands name also.

QUESTIONS FOR DISCUSSION

1. Explain the term sauces and its classifications.
2. What are the essential of good sauces?
3. Explain the charactertics and components of good sauces.
4. Descrbe in detail about the thickening agents.
5. Explain this term Liaison Finale with different types of liaison.
6. Describe the making of mother sauces.
7. Explain the charactertics of mother sauces.
8. Explain the term Espangole with their method of preparation.
9. Explain the term béchamel with their method of preparation both rich and lean.
10. Explain the term Veloute with their method of preparation.
11. Explain the term Demi-glazes with their method of preparation.
12. Explain the term tomato sauce with their method of preparation.
13. Explain the term emulsification.
14. What is emulsification sauce?
15. Explain the production of emulsified sauce and the major points to remember that emulsified sauces.
16. Write down the steps to remontage of broken emulsified sauces.
17. Explain the term Hollandaise sauce with their method of preparation.
18. Explain the term Béarnaise sauce with their method of preparation.
19. Explain the term Beurre blanc with their method of preparation.
20. Mention the name of some compound butter.
21. Mention the name of all mother sauces with six each derivatives of all with their ingredients.

22.. What are the other miscellaneous sauces?
23. Explain the term mayonnaise with their method of preparation.
24. Explain the term boiled dressing with their method of preparation.
25. Mention the derivates of cold dressings with their ingredients.

STATE TRUE AND FALSE

- Sauce is a thickened liquid that is flavoured or seasoned to enhance the flavour of the food that it is to accompany.
- Sauces add a variety of features to foods.
- Cold sauces are based on mayonnaise and vinaigrette and there derivations.
- A liquid provides the base of the most sauces.
- White and blond roux requires less cooking time.
- Time allowed for cooking of the roux that depend on the degree of heat.
- Attention should be paid to the metal of the utensil used for making roux.
- Milk and sauce are not simple liquids but emulsion of fat globules in water.
- Depouillage is the removal of all the fat and the impurities of flour and the stock in the impurities.
- Espagnole is a basic brown sauce.
- Espangole is the half way point in the production of traditional demiglazes
- *Béchamel* sauce is also known as white sauce.
- Emulsion is a mixture of two liquids that normally can't be combined
- If the egg yolk foams but doesn't thicken the heat is too low, correct by increasing the heat slightly
- If egg yolk becomes too thick it means that the heat is too high. Lower the heat add a few drops of cold water to mixture.
- Hollandaise is an emulsified sauces
- Ail is the French term for garlic.
- Bercy is derivative of béchamel

KEY TERMS

* Blend	* Lean
* Emulsification	* Mixture
* Fat	* Sauces
* Flavour	* Thicken
* Impurities	* Thickening

Unit 2
COMMODITIES AND FARINACEOUS

Chapter 9
Eggs

After studying this chapter, the student must know

- Composition and its test of freshness eggs
- Grading, storage and handling of eggs
- Various ways of beating of eggs
- Mixing eggs with other ingredients
- Different ways of cooking eggs
- Standard recipes of eggs

EGGS

Egg refers to the oval thin shelled ovum of a bird used as food. There are many types of egg such as goose duck and turkey chicken egg is most commonly used and any mention of egg in a recipe always denotes a chicken egg. Eggs are rich in nutrinent both for the invalid who requires a lightly cooked, easily digested meal as well as for the man who needs a sustaining breakfast before a day's work. Moreover, as eggs do not contain a particle of starch they can be eaten by those who wish, for one reason or another, to avoid this food. When starch is required serve untoasted bread, rice or potatoes with your eggs at the same meal. Of course, there are eggs and eggs. You find them in the shop under all sorts of names—new laid eggs; breakfast eggs; fresh eggs, cooking eggs; to name a few. Never purchase doubtful one, especially on the score of economy. Remember one new laid egg

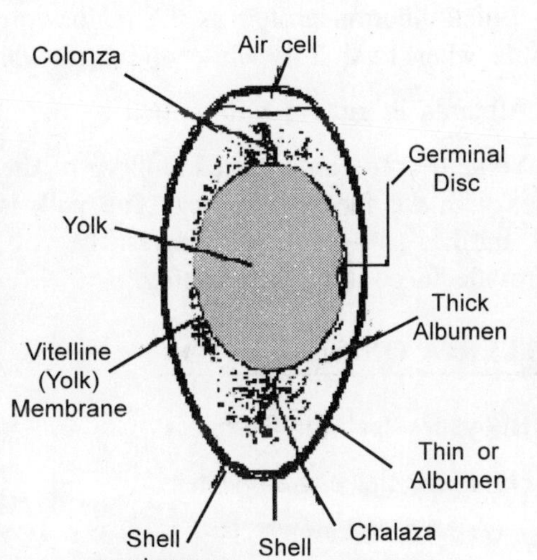

Fig. 9.1 The composition of eggs

in a cake will produce more lightness than two of a stale variety. Worse still are strong- tasting eggs; one will to taint a whole dish. It is quite impossible, too, for any cook, however good she is, to turn out a dish that depends upon stiffly beaten whites for its lightness, with eggs that are not fresh- dishes like meringues or soufflés for example.

Fortunately, with modern transport facilities they arrive in such good condition, even from far-off Australia and New Zealand, that eggs which will be quite satisfactory for all ordinary purposes can be bought for a penny or so all the year round. It is however, quite a good plan to preserve English eggs in water-glass when they are plentiful. When new laid one is unobtainable the preserved kind will be found quite suitable for all types of dishes, provided they do not demand a spongy lightness.

COMPOSITION

A whole egg made up of yolk, white and shells a membrane line of the cell at the large end of yolk. The yolk is held cemented in the egg by Chalazae. They are two white stands which are present when the egg is broken.

Shell: The shell or the outer covering of the egg may be white or brown shell it has no effect on quality. Cooking properly or nutritive value of the egg colour of the shell is determined by the breed of the chicken it is compact of calcium carbonate ($CaCO_3$) and is very fragile. It is pours white allow is to breathe.

White: - It is a food and moisture source of the embryo a fertilize egg. It accounts for 67% of the liquid weight of the egg. Egg white made-up of two parts.

- A thick white surrounds the yolk.
- A thinner mart liquid part in between the membrane and picker

Which albumin protein is the major component? It is also contain sulphur. The white is clear soluble when raw. It is white and firm when coagulated.

Albumin in egg yolk in valued by the cook and baker for its ability to hold air when beaten.

Yolk: It is the unfertilized embryo of the egg. It's yellow in colour and the depth of the colour varies with the feed of the hen. The yolk is high in fat and protein and contains iron in a large yolk and has an approx 59 calories, the yolk is valued for its richness and a texture with it which it provide in cooking and baking.

CRITERIA OF SELECTION

Buoyancy test for freshness

(1) Place the egg in water

(A) An egg newly laid is heavy. It sinks and lies flat.

(B) As the egg ages an air Pocket expands and adds bouncy. A weak old egg began to rise.

(C) A three week old egg stands upright of the air pocket expands.

TO TEST FRESHNESS OF EGGS

Dissolve a good dessertspoon of common salt in ½ pint of cold water, put an egg in gently, and if new laid it will lie flat at the bottom of the glass. It two or three days old it will lie with the large end raised a little, a few days older it will be upright with the large end uppermost. When stale it will float, the large end rising above the water in proportion to its age.

The reason is that directly an egg is laid the water in the white of it begins to evaporate very gradually, and slowly an empty space is formed in the large end. A new laid egg being quite full and has no space, but as the quantity of the white of the egg is decreased a gap is formed which as it becomes larger makes the egg light enough to float when placed in water.

GRADING OF EGGS

Egg are graded AA, A and B egg, age and handling of eggs are the primary determines or quality as the egg age the white becomes thin and the air cell between the membrane and shell enlarges. The yolk membrane and shell enlarges. The yolk membrane becomes thinner as the egg

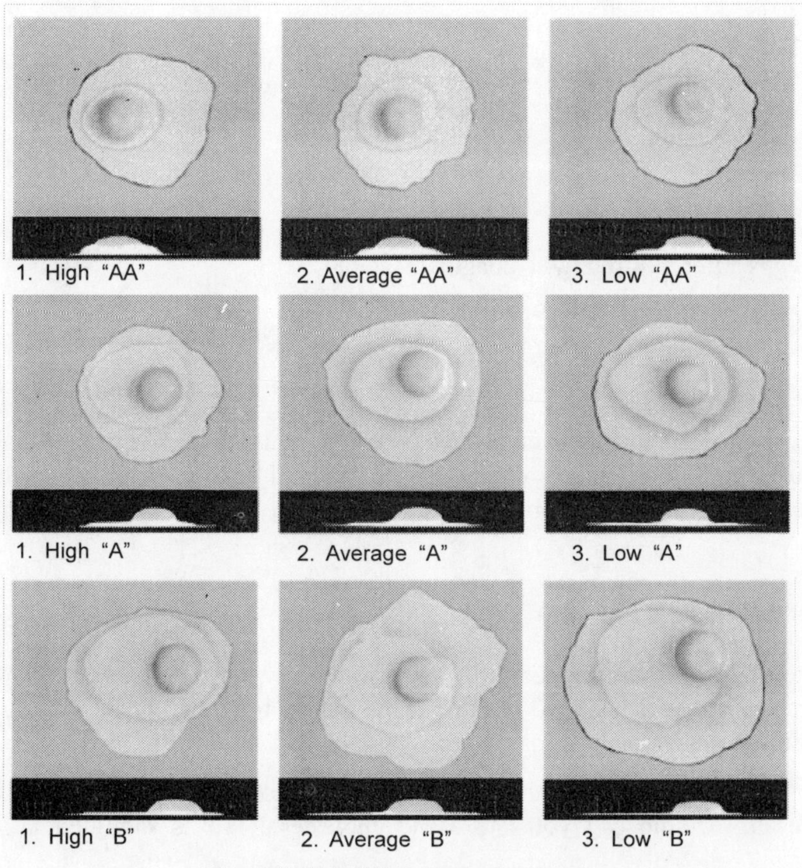

Fig. 9.2 The different grade of eggs

ages. This result in a yolk which separates makes easily and breaks easily. The yolk will be off centre in the white and flat instead of tall or rounded when the egg ages and the white thins the albumin protein has lost parts of its ability to build and maintain. It will not develop a great volume when beaten the stability with be less. The thickening emulsifying power of yolk will be less.

Grade AA: - Small spread, yolk at the centre of white. The white is thick and stand high. The chalazae are prominent round and high. There are the best eggs suitable for any type or cooking such as cooking frying.

Grade A: - Moderate spread white is reasonable thick stands moderately high most commonly used available egg.

Grade B: - Spread greatly having only small thick white, white is weak and watery chalazae are small is completely absent. Yolks are flat or broad are suitable for scrambling and baking.

Newly Liquid:

1. Yolk Compact
2. Dense White
3. Slight fluid liquid layer.

Weak Old: - Yolk moves off- centre white loosens and become fluid.

Three-week old: - Yolk flatness white thin like water.

Preparation:-

1. Whole eggs after beating will coagulate at 68° C.
2. White will coagulate between 60° C-66° C.
3. Yolks will coagulate 62-70° C.
4. Whole egg combine with liquid such as in custard coagulate and as 79-85°C

Common occurrence in egg which are cooked and held for a long period of time is the development of a green colour. This is particularly common is scrambled egg. This is the result of the iron in the egg. Yolk reacting with the sulphur in the egg white. Iron sulphide is formed causing the discoloration.

Storage and handling

Eggs loose quality at room temperature they should always be stored at 32°-42° F (0-5° C). An egg has porous shell which allows the air to be centre they should be store away from food that may pass on the undesirable odors.

Nutritional Tips: - Contain Vitamin-A, E, D, K and B complex high in Iron and Protein major concern is cholesterol. Avoid egg yolks to avoid cholesterol law is saturated fat.

BREAKING AN EGG

A little care is necessary if you want to keep the yolk whole. Tap the center of the shell sharply on the edge of a basic, and then open the shell, letting the egg fall gently into a basin. It is always advisable to break each egg into a separate cup if you have the least doubt of their freshness.

To separate the yolk and white, keep the egg upright whilst you break the shell in halves, so that the yolk will remain in the lower half, then gently pass it from one half of the shell to the other when the remainder of the white will drop into the bowl.

VARIOUS WAYS OF BEATING EGGS

The time eggs should be beaten varies according to the effect you wish to produce, and therefore it is most important to follow directions for the beating of eggs in various recipes closely, and also the different ways in which they are mixed with other ingredients.

If in a recipe you are directed to:—"Beat the eggs lightly." Beat the yolks and whites together, and only just enough to mix them well. "Beat the yolk until light and thick". Means they must be beaten by themselves until they thicken slightly becoming as thick as cream, and a little lighter in colour than when you started beating.

Beat the whites to froth. "Means beat until they are light and frothily, but still moist. "Beat the whites to a stiff froth." Beat until stiff and there is not any liquid left in the bowl.

"Beat to a stiff dry froth." Beat until they are so stiff and dry that when you tip the bowl, they remain in it. The quickest beater for egg whites is, I find, the round wire beater with a straight wooden handle. It is quite inexpensive and the process of beating is not tiring as the cook simply moves the handle quickly up and down, and a very few minutes' work will change the whites into a stiff frothy snow.

MIXING EGGS WITH OTHER INGREDIENTS

When adding eggs to other ingredients, as in batters, puddings and cakes, the directions will be, to fold, to stir or to beat. To fold is the slowest form of mixing. It is mostly employed when stiffly beaten whites are added to other ingredients and the object is to retain the air that has been beaten into them. Put the beaten egg into the centre of the ingredients, then insert the spoon, pass it down to the bottom of the basin, bring up some of the mixture, and fold it over the egg whites. Continue until well mixed, but do not employ any brisk movements. When stirring in the egg the spoon is moved round quickly in circles. When beating, a very quick movement is employed, turning the mixture constantly, so that air is beaten in.

SLOW COOKING

Dishes that contain eggs must never be subjected to fierce heat. Even when boiling eggs a better result is obtain if the water is only allowed to simmer after the eggs are put in. Fast boiling hardens the albumen and makes the eggs indigestible. When making custard, it is particularly necessary to avoid letting the mixture boil, as, if this happens, the custard will be curdled.

TO BOIL EGGS

Have ready a saucepan of boiling water, draw it to the side of the stove and lower the eggs in carefully, then place again over heat and boil gently. Allow four minutes for a new laid eggs, and three and a half minutes for eggs more than three days old. To boil hard allow ten minutes. A particularly digestible way of cooking eggs in the shell is to lower them into the saucepan as described above, then cover closely, and let them remain at the side of the stove for eight minutes. They will then be set, but soft and creamy. This method should always be employed for invalids or people with weak digestions. Eggs can be cooked firm enough to slice for salads in the same way, but they must be allowed to remain in the water for half an hour.

FRIED EGGS

When fried eggs are to be served with bacon, the bacon may be fried first, and then the eggs cooked in the bacon flat. Otherwise allow ½ oz. of butter or fat for each eggs. If too much fat is used the whites will rise in bubbles, and the yolks very often burst. Heat the fat. Break the egg into a cup. Being careful not to break the yolk. Turn gently into the hot fat, tilt the pan and cook over low heat until the whites are set. Remove carefully with a fish slice.

EGGS FRIED IN THE CANADAIN WAY

Proceed as in the previous recipe, but when the egg is almost done, turn very carefully and brown lightly on the other side.

POACHED EGGS

A nourishing dish for breakfast or for supper if served in conjunction with a vegetable puree such as spinach or green pea.

A poacher makes poaching very easy. Its great advantage is that it keeps the eggs in shape, and they do not need any trimming. Three parts fill the little pan with boiling water, add a few drops of vinegar and a pinch of salt. Being to the boil, drop the eggs into the spaces provided for them, then simmer very slowly until the whites are set. Have ready a square of hot buttered toast for each egg. Lift up the top of the poacher, take the eggs off carefully with a slice and place them on the toast.

POACHING EGGS WITHOUT A POACHER

Three parts fill a small pan with water, and add half a salt spoon of salt and a teaspoon of vinegar for a pan of medium size. Break an egg into a cup, then when the water boils, give the cup a shake so that the egg twirls round, and slip the egg gently out of the cup into the boiling water. The shake round shapes the egg. Simmer until the white is set. The water must on no account be allowed to boil after the egg is put in. Remove any scum. Take the egg out carefully on a fish slice, put the slice on a clean cloth for a minute to drain any water off, and then slide the egg on to hot buttered toast.

BAKED EGGS IN CASES

Butter little china soufflé cases, break one egg into each, put a small piece of butter or a teaspoon of cream on the top and bake in a very moderate oven until the egg is set.

EGG IN LITTLE CASSEROLES

If you have no casserole cases at hand, small white jelly-pots will do quite well. Butter each case and sprinkle a little chopped parsley on the bottom of it. Break in the egg, being careful that the yolk is kept whole. Stand the cases in a brisk oven for three to four minutes till the eggs are set quite firmly. Have ready a small square of buttered toast. Pass a knife gently round the inside of each case, tilt out the egg on to the toast and serve hot.

STEAMED EGGS

This is often appreciated by an invalid as a light supper dish. Have ready a saucepan with two inches of water boiling in it. Put a little piece of butter into a small teacup. Stand it in the saucepan and as soon as the butter melts. Break a fresh egg gently in it. Cover with a saucer and let it steam gently for eight minutes. Have ready a small square of buttered toast, turn out the egg on to it, dust with chopped parsley and serve. If liked, a little anchovy paste may be spread on the toast.

TO PRESERVE EGGS

A good store of preserved cooking eggs is very useful when fresh egg are dear. Eggs may be preserved in water-glass, but they should not be more than twenty-four hours old. Care must be taken that a cracked egg is not used. Lower the eggs very carefully into the liquid with a wooden spoon. The vessel must be kept completely covered, but as water-glass evaporates it should be looked at occasionally. Full instructions are given with each tin of water-glass.

TO PRESERVE EGGS DRY

For this purpose the eggs should be straight from the nest. Take each egg and grease it with oil or lard, being careful that every part is covered with the grease. Put a layer of bran in a box, then a layer of eggs with a little bran between each, making sure that the eggs do not touch each other. Cover with a thick layer of bran and continue the layers, finishing with a deep layer of bran.

ANCHOVY EGG

Time 10 minutes. Temperature: moderate.Enough for 4 persons.

Ingredients	*Quantity*
Eggs	8 no
Anchovies	40 gram
Butter	30 gram
Cayenne	20 gram
Lettuce	50 gram
Mustard	10 gram
Mayonnaise	40 gram
Salt and pepper	10 gram

Method:

1. Boil the eggs for ten minutes, and when cold cut them across in halves. Take out the yolks, and put them in a mortar.
2. Bone the anchovies and chop them small, add them to the egg yolks, also the butter and the cayenne and pound all to a paste.
3. Place the half white of eggs on a glass dish leveling them at the cotton so that they will stand, and f fill with the anchovy mixture.
4. Surround with salad, sprinkle with salad dressing or mayonnaise, and serve.

BUTTERED EGGS AND TOMATOES

Time: about 10 minutes. Temperature: moderate. Enough or 4 persons.

Ingredients	*Quantity*
Eggs	8no
Tomatoes	100 gram
Butter	20 gram
Salt and pepper	15 gram
Chopped parsley	20 gram
Rashers bacons	30 gram

Method:

1. Cut the tomatoes in half across the fruit and fry them lightly in 1 oz. Of butter or dripping, or bake them in the oven.

2. Place them on a hot dish, pile the buttered eggs upon them and surround with rashers of fried bacon.
3. For the Buttered Eggs.—Melt the remainder of the butter or dripping in a small saucepan, break the eggs into it, add pepper,. Salt and parsley and stir over gentle heat until set, then use as directed.

DEVILLED EGGS AND MUSHROOMS

Time: 8 minutes. Temperature: moderate. Enough for 4 persons.

Ingredients	*Quantity*
Butter toast	4no
Hard boiled eggs	8no
Butter	50 gram
Mustard	10 gram
Tomato ketchup	20 gram
Yorkshire relish	20 gram
Chopped mushroom	30 gram
Anchovy	10 gram
Salt and pepper	15 gram
Paprika	10 gram

Fig. 9.3 The devilled eggs and mushroom

Method

1. Put a quarter of the butter into a small pan with the mustard, catsups and relish. Make it quite hot, then cut the egg in quarters and put them in.
2. Have ready four rounds of toast, or cheese biscuits made hot, butter them, and sprinkle with chopped anchovy.
3. Chop the mushrooms and fry them in a little butter, place them on the toasts, put one egg quarter on each and pour a little of the sauce from the eggs over. Serve very hot.

Note : you also made a paste of ingredients and put in piping bag and remove the yolk and put that mixture on that as shown in figure

EGG AND BACON CAKES:

Time: 20 minutes. Temperature: moderate. Enough for four persons.

Ingredients	*Quantity*
Eggs	6no
Boiled bacon	100 gram

Béchamel sauce	20 gram
Bread crumbs	20 gram
Salt and pepper	15 gram
Oil	20 ml
Mashed potatoes	80 gram
Parsley	20 gram

Fig. 9.4 The eggs and bacon cake

Method:

1. The last remnant of boiled bacon or ham will do quite well for this dish.
2. Boil two of the eggs for ten minutes, then put them in cold water.
3. When cold, remove the shells and put them through a mincer with the bacon; the latter must be quite free from skin and gristle.
4. Add two tablespoons breadcrumbs, a good sprinkling of pepper and mix well. Stir in ¼ pint of freshly made white sauce. It should be quite hot.
5. Leave until cold. Then form into cakes with a little flour.
6. Dip in beaten egg, coat with breadcrumbs and fry in boiling fat. Drain well, arrange on a hot dish and garnish with parsley, or serve on a mound of mashed potatoes.

EGGS EN CASSEROLE

Time: 5 to 10 minutes. Temperature: Electricity, 375 °F. enough for four persons.

Ingredients	*Quantity*
Eggs	8 no
Sprig of parsley	20 gram
Ham	20 gram
Shallot	40 gram
Butter	30 gram
Grated cheese	50 gram
Salt and pepper	15 gram

Fig. 9.5 The egg en casserole

Method

1. Butter small casseroles or saucers. Line the bottoms with minced ham, sprinkle with very finely shredded shallot and parsley.
2. Break a fresh egg into each cover with grated cheese, and put a scrap of butter on each. Stand them in a baking tin, with a little hot water in it and cook in a moderate oven until the eggs are set. Serve at once.

3. Any other kind of meat may be used in place of the ham, or any left-over sauce could be used.

POACHED EGGS WITH HAM AND TOMATOES

Time: about minutes. Temperature: medium. Enough for 4 persons.

Ingredients	*Quantity*
Eggs	8no
Slice of cooked ham	50 gram
Rounds butter toast	4 no
Salt and pepper	15 gram
Tomatoes	30 gram
Butter	20 gram

Method:

1. Slice the tomatoes, and put them in a saucepan with the butter and a good sprinkling of salt and pepper.
2. Simmer until the tomatoes are quite soft. Then rub through a sieve and reheat the puree. Poach the eggs and just fry the slices of ham very lightly.
3. Arrange the slices of toast on a dish, place a piece of ham on each, and then a poached egg. Pour the tomato puree round and serve very hot.

SCRAMBLED EGGS

Time: about 5 minutes. Temperature: very moderate. Enough for 4 persons.

Ingredients	*Quantity*
Eggs	8no
Butter	30 gram
Milk	50 ml
Salt and pepper	15 gram
Squares of butter toast	4 no

Fig. 9.6 The scramble egg

Method:

1. Have ready four squares of hot buttered toast.

2. Beat the eggs just enough to mix the whites and yolks well. Melt the butter in a small saucepan, add the eggs, the milk and seasoning.
3. Stir the mixture constantly with a wooden spoon over gentle heat until the eggs begin to set.
4. As soon as they are sufficiently solid pile them on the buttered toast and serve immediately. Do not over-cook the mixture or it will be heavy, it should be light and moist.

PLAIN OMELET

Time: about 5 minutes. Temperature: moderate 1 omelet enough for 1 person.

Ingredients	*Quantity*
Eggs	2no
Salt and pepper	15 gram
Butter	20 gram

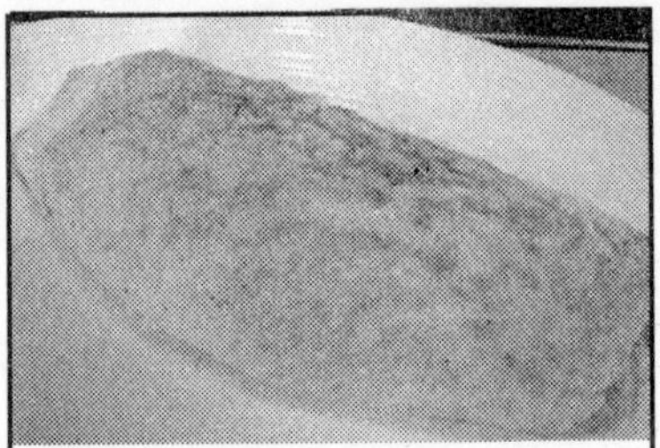

Fig. 9.7 The plain omelet

Method:

1. Beat the eggs just long enough to mix yolks and whites.
2. Add the salt and pepper. Melt the butter in the omelet pan and when it is hot, turn the eggs into it.
3. As soon as it begins to get, loosen the edges with the point of a knife, to enable the liquid part to run under.
4. Then tilt the pan and fold over to form a crescent shape. This needs a little practice, the mixture should be quite soft in the centre when the omelet is done. Then slide on to a hot plate and serve immediately.

FLUFFY OMELET

Time: about 5 minutes. Temperature: moderate. 1 omelet enough for 1 person.

Ingredients	*Quantity*
Eggs	8no
Water	5 gram
Salt and pepper	15 gram
Butter	20 gram

Fig. 9.7 The fluffy omelet

Method:

1. Separate the yolks and whites of the eggs. Be very careful not to break the yolks, as if there is any yolk mixed with the whites they will not mix to a stiff froth. Beat the yolks until they are thick and light in colour.
2. Add to them the pepper, salt, and water. Beat a minute to mix these well, them fold in the stiffly whipped whites of the eggs.
3. Melt the butter in a small frying pan, and when it is hot pour in the egg mixture, them as it begins to set, tilt the pan, loosen the edges of the omelet and form it into the shape of a half circle.
4. Serve immediately when set and lightly browned. This omelet is very good with a sweet filling, omitting the seasoning.

LEARNING OUTCOME

Egg refers to the oval thin shelled ovum of a bird used as food. Eggs are rich in nutriment both for the invalid who requires a lightly cooked, easily digested meal as well as for the man who needs a sustaining breakfast before a day's work. Moreover, as eggs do not contain a particle of starch they can be eaten by those who wish, for one reason or another, to avoid this food. When starch is required serve untoasted bread, rice or potatoes with your eggs at the same meal. Of course, there are eggs… and eggs. A whole egg made up of yolk, white and shells A membrane line of the cell at the large end of yolk. The yolk is held cemented in the egg by Chalazae. They are two white stands which are present when the egg is broken. Egg are graded AA, A and B egg age and handling of eggs are the primary determines or quality as the egg age the white becomes thin and the air cell between the membrane and shell enlarges. The yolk membrane and shell enlarges. Eggs loose quality at room temperature they should always be stored 32°F-42°F(0 -5° C). Eggs have porous shell which allows the air to be centre they should be store away from food that may pass on the undesirable odors. The time eggs should be beaten varies according to the effect you wish to produce, and therefore it is most important to follow directions for the beating of eggs in various recipes closely, and also the different ways in which they are mixed with other ingredients

LESSON END ACTIVITY

- Collect the different types of eggs and check there grade.
- Try to make some recipes on eggs as per discussed in the chapter.

QUESTIONS FOR DISCUSSION

1. Draw the composition of the eggs and explain it.
2. How to check the freshness of the eggs?

3. Discuss the grading of eggs.
4. Explain the procedure of storing and handling of eggs.
5. Explain the procedure of breaking and beating of eggs.
6. Explain the procedure of frying and boiling of eggs.
7. Explain the procedure how to preserve of eggs.
8. Why we need slow cooking for egg dishes?

STATE TRUE AND FALSE

- Egg is good binding agent.
- Eggs loose quality at room temperature.
- Eggs contain Vitamin-A, E, D, K and B complex high in Iron and Protein major concern is cholesterol.
- Whole eggs after beating will coagulate at 78°C.
- Yolks will coagulate 62-70°C.
- Egg are graded AA, A and B.
- Yolk is the unfertilized embryo of the egg.
- A whole egg made up of yolk, white and shell.
- Eggs are rich in nutrient

KEY TERMS

* Coagulation
* Composition
* Egg
* Embryo
* Nutrient
* Protein
* Unfertilized
* Yolk

Chapter 10
Rice

After studying this chapter, the student must know

- Introduction to farinaceous
- Rice composition and its types of rice
- Rice stages of processing
- Method of preparing rice
- Method of loosing nutritive value of rice

FARINACEOUS

Farinaceous cookery involves preparation or staples in the diet. "Farina" is the Italian word meaning "Flour". English term Farina word to mean "Flour" or "meal". This may be forming any of a number or product including cereals grains potatoes, nuts, beans and other. In United States Farina is applied to white granules celery made from the white inner portion or wheat cornels. Farina is other name for Camolina or wheat middling there are heard beat left in the milling machine after the finer flour has sifted out.

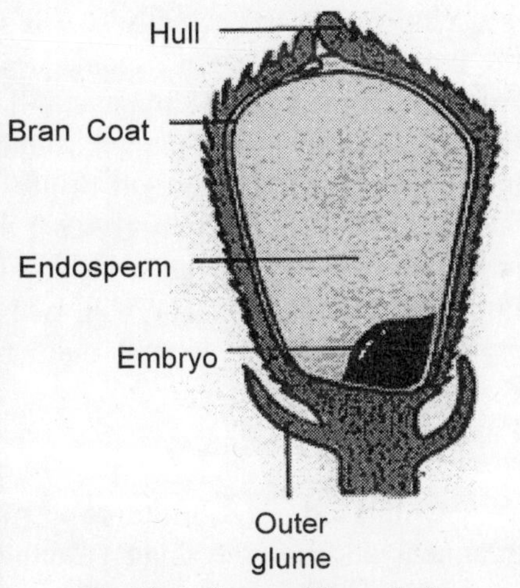

Fig 10.1 Composition of rice

Rice

Rice is important food crop it provides over one half of world population with low cost Palatable and nutritious food source. Over 90% of world rice is produce and consume in Asia and on adjacent.

The variety or Rice grown includes long grain, medium grain and short grain types. Rice is classified by the length of the grown. The term long refers to rice that is 4 to 5 times as well as its wide. Medium and short grain rice is short in relation to width of the grain.

The length of the rice affects the characters of the cook product. Long grain rice when cooked separate looks light and fluppy. There are preferred characteristics for Pilaf (Pulao) in Continental and English and side dishes eaten with curries chicken meat fishes or stew. Short grain rice when cooked is plumper and Generally tender moist and sticky. This is the preferred rice for steam rice eaten with Japanese's and Chinese Food it's valued in western cuisine for preparation of Risotto, croquettes ,pudding and molds because it's starchy consistency act as a good binder. Medium grown rice has characteristics which follow between the one or two it may be considered all purpose rice.

Grain of rice from which the germ has been removed as far superior shelf life with germ of the rice and the part most likely to become rancid or to be infested with insects.

Quick cooking: is rice cook to gelatinized starch than dried this process rice as porous structure that will permit rapid dehydration it doesn't produce long grain separate rice and has a tendency to congeal. The purpose is not nutrient but conveniences.

TYPES OF RICE

Top row, from left to right: parboiled rice, rice flour, cream of rice (Fig. 10.2).

Second row, from left to right: Carnaroli rice, Spanish rice, Bhutanese red rice (Fig. 10.2).

Third row, from left to right: long-grain rice, long-grain brown rice, wild rice (Fig. 10.2).

Bottom row, from left to right: jasmine rice, popcorn rice, Basmati rice (Fig. 10.2).

Fig 10.2 The varieties of rice

Wild Rice (Fig. 10.3)

Wild rice is not actually rice it's the grain or one of the most beautiful single steamed of an aquatic plant in America, wild grass the plant is tall round stem and has flat pointed leaves the stem is round and hallow with a hooked root which anchors it firmly to the bottom of the lakes and rivers. The Plant grows 4 to 10 feet tall the heals or the grows are Pall green with of yellow they become Purple as they mature. The wild rice kernel is ¾ inch long, cylinder, dark in colour and quite has when dried.

Fig 10.3 The wild rice

Paddy Rice

Unhusked rice in its raw stage, with no further treatment an after threshing (Contains 20-25% moisture).

Brown Rice (Fig. 10.4)

Brown rice from which the germ and out layer of the Pericarp is removed by passing grains through machine that rasp the grain, it called unpolished rice.

Fig 10.4 Brown rice (Also known as husked or whole rice)

Au-grass

Au-grass this method of cooking rice is used for Pilaf, Risotto, Paella the rice is first gently fried in fat, then its volume of stock or water is added cooking continue till the liquid absorbed.

Rice stages of processing

The Polished rice consume most widely as been through four stages of processing

1. First the rice is thrashed separating the rice grain from the stock. This result in what is called 'Paddy Rice'. The paddy rice is when mild the First time. This milling removes only the together outer husk and produces what is called whole or brown rice.
2. In the second stage the bran and embryo/Germ are removing from the rice grown by milling. This result is termed "White Rice" The Germ "Which has been removed" contains a large percentage of protein, fat minerals and vitamins.
3. The Rice is then washed clean and Polished.
4. The final step is coating the rice grain with a layer of corn syrup and take to give it Pearly texture.

METHOD FOR PREPARATION OF RICE

Since rice is clean before packing its neither necessary not desirable to wash it before cooking since it to increase the loss or soluble nutrients the use of excess water for cooking rice should be avoided nutrients are discards with the excess cooking water when the cook rice is drained. The excepted method today is to cook rice in only the amount or water or other liquid needed to achieve the correct degree of tenderness. There are a number of other factors which effect the cooking of rice to begin with each variety of rice has certain specific processing and cooking characteristics. Most long grain rice has a tendency to cook dry and fluppy. The cook grains remain intact and don't stick together. Short grains cook firmly and tend to be more sticky. The cooking method you choose must match the type of rice and type of rice most match the end product desired. Rice which yield a clear translucent grains is preferred to those which have an opaque and chalky centre.

RICE YIELD

- One cup uncooked regular white milled rice yield 3 cup cooked.
- One cup of uncooked Par boil rice yield 4 cup cooked.
- One cup of uncooked brown rice yield 4 cup cooked.
- One cup of Pre-cooked rice yield 2 to 3 cup cooked rice.

The yield and quality of rice can easily be effected by excess evaporation of water before the rice is added or mishandling of the rice during cooking. Measure cause of reduce yield and lower quality cook rice breakage of grains which compact the rice and mars (destroyed) it eye appeal.

METHOD OF LOOSING NUTRITIONAL VALUE OF RICE

Rice that undergoes various stages or milling loose many of it nutritional properties because of this several method have been devised to reduce the taste or to replace what is lost.

(1) The first method widely considered to reduce lost of nutritional value is to under milled or under polished Rice who doesn't have white shine or Polished Rice.

(2) The second method increase retaining by Par boiling the rough Rice Prior to milling commercial this type of rice is called "Converted Rice". This process allows same of the Vitamin and minerals in the germ to Permeate the Endosperm.

(3) The third method is of artificial enhancement a pre-mix is developed in this rice is wetted with a solution thiamine and niacin. The grains are then dried and covered with a protected coating a second coating of Iron Pyrophosphate is then is distributed over the Rice when dried it's again cover with Protected protein

LEARNING OUTCOME

Farinaceous cookery involves preparation or staples in the diet. "Farina" is the Italian word meaning "Flour". English term Farina word to mean "Flour" or "meal". This may be forming any of a number or product including cereals grains potatoes, nuts, beans and other. Rice is important food crop it provides over one half of world population with low cost Palatable and nutritious food source. Over 90% of world rice is produce and consume in Asia and on adjacent. The length of the rice affects the characters of the cook product. Long grain Rice when cooked separate looks light and floppy. Grain of Rice from which the germ has been removed as far superior shelf life with germ of the rice and the part most likely to become rancid or to be infested with insects. Wild rice is not actually rice it's the grain. The Polished rice consumes most widely as been through four stages of processing. Since Rice is clean before Packing its neither necessary not desirable to wash it before cooking since it to increase the loss or soluble nutrients the use of excess water for cooking rice should be avoided nutrients are discards with the excess cooking water when the cook rice is drained. Rice that undergoes various stages or milling loose many of it nutritional properties because of this several method have been devised to reduce the taste or to replace what is lost.

LESSON END ACTIVITY

- Collect the information of as much as different varieties of rice.
- Go a rice mill collect the information on their milling process
- Cook rice according to the instruction given in the chapter.

QUESTIONS FOR DISCUSSION

1. Draw the composition of rice and explain them?
2. Write a short note on rice?
3. Explain the ten varieties of rice?
4. Explain the paddy rice and wild rice?
5. Mention the steps of processing of rice?
6. Explain the method of preparing rice?
7. How we can improve the rice nutritional property with the help of which method explains?
8. Explain the term Au-grass and Brown rice?

STATE TRUE AND FALSE

- "Farina" is the Italian word meaning "Flour".
- Over 90% of world rice is produce and consume in Asia and on adjacent.
- Rice is classified by the length of the grown
- The length of the rice affects the characters of the cook product
- Grain of Rice from which the germ has been removed as far superior shelf life
- Wild rice is actually rice it's the grain or one of the most beautiful single steamed of an aquatic plant in America.
- Au-grass this method of cooking rice
- Since Rice is clean before Packing its neither necessary not desirable to wash it before cooking
- One cup of uncooked Par boil rice yield 2 cup cooked.
- One cup of uncooked brown rice yield 3 cup cooked.
- One cup of Pre cooked rice yield 2 to 3 cup cooked rice

KEY TERMS

* Aquatic plant * Farina * Flour * Grain * Opaque * Palatable

Chapter 11

Wheat and Corn

After studying this chapter, the student must know

- Introduction and composition of wheat
- Varieties of wheat
- Introduction and composition of corn
- Principles of cooking cereals

WHEAT

Is the grass of genus Tritium world wide it leads rice in the amount produce and acreage sown with it?

Wheat contents large amount of gluten is the elastic sticky tough substance formed from the insoluble protein of wheat floor during dough as it warms. This essential to leavened product wheal makes better bread than other grains because of its gluten content.

They are two variety of wheat: Hard wheat and Soft wheat.

Hard Wheat: - Contains more Protein/ Gluten they are preferred flour for bread making durum the hardest wheat is used for macaroni and Pasta Production.

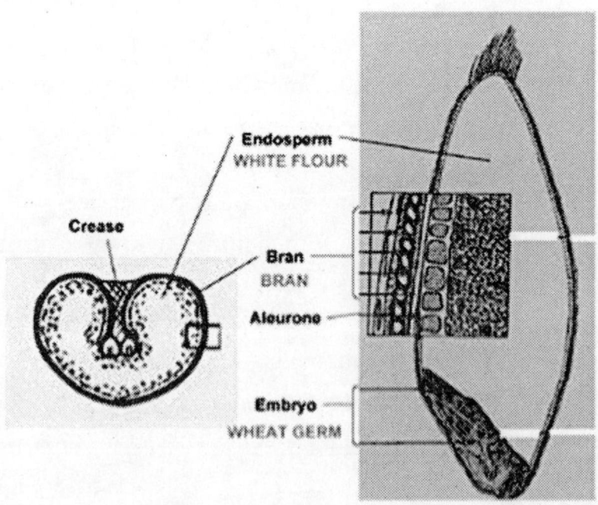

Fig 11.1 Wheat compositions

Each grain of wheat consists of a husk brand and kernel. The latter is made of starch and a mixture of Proteins called gluten. Inside the kernel is the seed or embryo (known as wheat germ) which is rich in nitrogen's and fatty substance. The external position calcium, phosphorus, and other mineral salt as well as numerous vitamins.

Soft Wheat:- Is comes from loss hardy plants contents less Protein/gluten and yield a whiter flour they are preferred from cakes, pastry, quick bread and breakfast food preparation. In these types of items the tougher chewer texture provide by the gluten is undesirable.

A grain or wheat has at its centre the endosperm or kernel. These comprise the majority of the weight or the grain it's a floury mask of starch and gluten. Incased in a layer or aleurone. This is reach in protein and minerals salt such as Phosphate of calcium magnesium and Potassium the aleuronic is part of the bran layer. This is cellulose mainly as one end of the grain and increased in the bran layer is the embryo/germ this is the leaving part of the grain. It's containing a high Protection of fat Proteins and vitamins. In the Protection of white flour the germ and bran are removed when germ and bran are left intact the product is termed whole wheat flour or graham flour depending on the processing. This are considered far more nutritious yet as with corn and rice spoil for more easily and rapidly. Whole wheat flour also produces heavier denser bread. The fine texture light and sponge bread which the American consumer comes to know the product of finely defined wheat flour.

The wheat germ, is a byproduct of milling Process is sold as separate product. It has a pleasant nutty flavored and may be added to white flour bread making. It's used as toping for soups, stews, salads, and as breakfast colours. Wheat germ may purchased lossed and vacuum package or raw. Due to its oil ones it's open it should stored under refrigeration wheat some time bleached to got a fine white colour.

CORN

Next to wheat corn is the grain most uses in the U.S. it's called Indian corn, maize and sweet corn. In the culinary sense corn means the cereal grain Zeamys which is native to America. In England this termed means wheat or in large sense any or all grains.

Corn is the grass of gramineae family. This is the Plants which grows wild in the Mexican highlands corn is cultivated all over the world today. It's one of the largest and most luxuriant of grains grasses. The corn kernel grows in rows on large areas which means upto 15 inches.

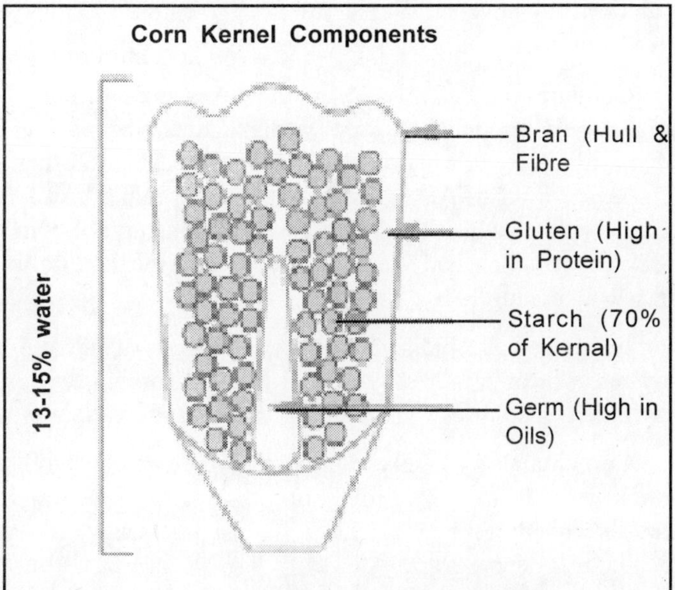

Fig 11.2 Corn composition

Dent or Field corn is the most common however this variety is used mostly for live stock feed and food processing. It's the sweet or green variety of Flint corn which is most important in culinary Preparation. There are used for caned frozen or cob corn. The ear of corn is Picked just short or rightness at this stage. The kernels are plump and well filled but still soft and milky when allowed to stay on the stock to long the kernels become tough dry.

Corn is of two types white or yellow. There is a nutrimental advantages to yellow corn. Yellow corn contains more Vitamin-A in the form of carotene both colour are rich in B Vitamin Particularly riboflavin Vitamin-C and small are of mineral including Phosphorous and Iron.

The kernel of corn consists of three parts the centre is starchy core called endosperm. Next is the embryo / germ which is composed of 50% oil the outside is hull / bran. The white and yellow corn grains are both brown into meal. Corn meals, yellow and white are made by grinding the kernels or corn to a coarse the kernel or corn to a coarse mixture. It can be Produce from the inter corn kernel or from a refined Product.

Corn meal can be prepared by grinding whole grains this type is called stone grounds it avoid heated the grain and used the whole kernel. It's excellent from simple forms of corn bread but doesn't blend that easily with wheat flour. It contain oil does difficult to store and get pest infested and rancid easily.

Fig 11.3 Corn varities

The most commonly used process called "Granulated" this process involves giving the corn on stem rollers after it has been kiln dry the rollers break and remove the husk and germ almost entirely. This gives the meal a dry and granular Feel.

Corn meal is used to make breads, cakes and pastries. In Europe Corn meal is used to make mush which has several national variations – Romania – Mama gliga, Italia's – Polenta, Frances makes a Roomette mealy Poarich, type of corn meal mush is a staple food of Africa Early attempts to make bread from meal fail. Corn meal has very little gluten without which the bread couldn't develop a structure to rise by mixing corn meal and wheat flour about which had the rich flavour and the texture of the corn yet the lighter fluppery texture of wheat bread.

In Mexico the Indian by past the process of making corn meal. Instead they boil corn kernels and mash them into a paste called Massa. This paste was used as a dough to make tortillas a thin flat unleavened bread (Something like parathas) this was also becomes Famous in U.S.

Corn Starch is highly refined and pulvarized starch made from the corn in refining the raw starch from the corn its broken up washed, Siphoned and repeatedly strained. The strained remove partials and remove fibers having been pulvarized it's dried to reduce the moisture and content to about 10 per cent.

Corn starch is chiefly used to thicken liquids. As a thickness it's first mixed with a little liquid (Cold) and mixture is than brought to boil. The mixture must be stirred constantly to prevent lumping. Corn Starch is valued for it translucent appearance that's gives to the thicken liquid. Corn starch is also used to lighter cake and pastry at a ratio at one Part of Corn starch to four part of flour.

PRINCIPLES OF COOKING CEREALS AND GRAINS

In cooking grains the essential action is gelatinization of the Cereal starch. Water driven into a Starch value by the force of heat. Unravels the Starch molecules the temperature at which this happens will varies from one type of starch to another (the norm is 160° to 180°F), but when it over is called Pasting. One's the starch molecules have unfolded the heat in the cooking process causes these molecules to from a crosslink network. That craps liquids inside the links this is called Gelatin (thickening) as the items cool the gel stiffen. Enough water and heat is uses to cereal a soft starch jell.

Cooking also bring about a change of Flour. This change due to the conversion of some complex starch into simpler sugar such as glucose, maltose and other sugar. The amount of water necessary to active the jell and flavour change of the cereal will vary with the type of grain and method by which it was process. Portion must be used in preparing all Farina. Gelatinization of starch granules takes places very quickly when the temperature is sufficiently high. This means that contains exposure to high heat can easily result in the cereal forming lumps or thicken to the pan and Scorching (burning).

Finally ground cereals tend to lump easily when they are cooked to prevent this cereals should be combined to with enough cold liquid to form a paste before it's added to the reminder to the boiling point/

Cereals must be cooked long enough to cook a starch to form a paste and to change the flavour. Because of modern methods of cereals processing long slow cooking is no longer necessary. Study have shown that the starch may be completely gelatinized when cereal is boil over a direct flamé for one to two minutes and then cooked over hot water for 10 to 15 minutes.

The amount of water used to cook the cereal should be only what is needed to achieve the correct thickness. Graining the cereal after cooking remove soluble nutrients especially thymine.

LEARNING OUTCOME

Wheat contents large amount of gluten is the elastic sticky tough substance formed from the insoluble protein of wheat floor during dough as it warms. They are two variety of wheat: Hard and Soft. Hard Wheat contains more Protein / Gluten they are Preferred flour for bread making durum the hardest wheat is used for macaroni and Pasta Production. Soft Wheat is comes from loss hardy Plants contents less Protein / gluten and yield a whiter floor they are preferred from cakes, pastry, Quick bread and breakfast food preparation. The wheat germ, a byproduct of milling. Corn is the grass of gramineae family. This is the Plants which grows wild in the Mexican highlands corn is cultivated all over the world today. It's one of the largest and most luxuriant of grains grasses. The corn kernel grows in rows on large ears which means up to 15 inches. Corn is of two types white or yellow. There is a nutrimental advantage to yellow corn. Yellow corn contains more Vitamins-A in the form of carotene both colour is rich in B Vitamin Particularly riboflavin Vitamin-C and small are of mineral including Phosphorous and Iron. Corn meal can be Prepared by grinding whole grains this type is called stone grounds it avoid heated the grain and used the whole kernel. In cooking grains the essential action is gelatinization of the Cereal starch. Water driven into a Starch value by the force of heat. Unravels the Starch molecules the Temperature at which this happens will varies from one type of starch to another (the norm is 160° to 180°F). Cereals must be cooked long enough to cook a starch to form a paste and to change the flavour

LESSON END ACTIVITY

- Collect the pictures of more varieties of corn.
- Collect the pictures of different types of wheat kernel.

QUESTIONS FOR DISCUSSION

1. Draw the composition of wheat and explain them?
2. Explain the varieties of wheat?
3. Draw the composition of corn and explain them?
4. Explain the varieties of corn?
5. Explain the principles of cooking cereals?

STATE TRUE AND FALSE

- Wheat contents large amount of gluten
- Each grain of wheat consists of a husk brand and kernel
- A grain or wheat has at its centre the endosperm or kernel
- The wheat germ, a byproduct of milling Process is sold as separate product
- Corn is the grass of gramineae family
- Dent or Field corn is the most common however this variety is used mostly for live stock feed and food processing
- Corn is of two types white or yellow.
- Yellow corn contains more Vitamin-A
- Corn Starch is highly refined and Pulverized starch

- Corn Starch is chiefly used to thicken liquids
- Cereals must be cooked long enough to Cook a starch to form a paste and to change the flavour.

KEY TERMS

* Gluten	* Kernel
* Husk	* Bran
* Granular	* Pulverized

12

Pasta, Noodles and Other

After studying this chapter, the student must know

- Introduction
- Types of pasta, its compositions and structure
- Method of preparing pasta
- Cooking pasta
- Noodles and its types
- Polenta, Gnocchi, Spatezle
- Different shapes of pasta
- Stuffed pasta.

PASTA, NOODLES AND OTHER

In its simplest pasta is combination of durum wheat, water and often egg and possible oil. It's shape in wide variety ways and can be flavoured with the addition of vegetables during Processing. Pasta is an antiquity itself. Their origins are not exploring Macro Polo introduced pasta into Italy from China In facts first known references to pasta can be traced to Sicily.

Basic pasta can be categorized into two ways ingredients and preparation methods or intended and usage the categories or ingredients and preparation methods into two major types – fresh pasta (home made pasta, pasta vatta en casa) and factory mass Produce pasta.

Factory Mass produce Pasta

It is made from dough of semolina and water seldom egg is added to the dough. The factory produce pasta is either flat or cylindrical depending on how it's Processing. Flat pasta is made by running the dough between rollers to form thin sheets. These are then into what ever shape is needed by a Punch for a stem cylindrical pasta is made by Pierced Plate (die) the size and shapes of the whole in the die determined the final shape of the pasta it may be slid like spaghetti or allow such as Penne. The drying process is important in this type of production care must be taken the pasta will mature and keep well.

Composition and structure

Factory produced pasta includes a group refers to as "Macaroni Product this group is sometimes called Alimentary Pasta it includes such products as macaroni spaghetti, vermicelli and egg noodles. The main ingredient in the macaroni group is a special durum flour which is high in gluten content. This flour is well suited to the manufacture of used product. The basic ingredients to be used in making forum flour, farina flour or any combination of two or more or there or water. The standard does allow egg whites solids, disodium phosphate, onion, celery, garlic, bay leaf and salt and other seasoning as optional ingredients.

Flour

The macaroni Products produces from durum have a characteristics yellow colour. This colour is considered a sign of good quality it's a result of the carotene pigments in the durum wheat. The type of wheat also gives the quality macaroni products it hard and translucence finish. This is highly valued by the manufacture and by the uses. It's a macaroni which is dry resistance to breakage and has a clear more uniform also takes less time to cook. Macaroni which is manufacture from blend such as durum and semolina produces a softer dough which can be feed through a Plate with less pressure. It's more resistance to over cooking thereby causes less cloudiness in the cooking water. Product made from granular type durum have properties that lies between these of the flour product and semolina product.

Egg

Any macaroni product which has the word egg added must contain egg solids. There solids can be fresh, frozen or dried they can be egg yolks or whole eggs. Egg yolks are used commonly in the production of the egg macaroni products. The uses of egg whites reduces the colour achieve with egg yolk.

Di-sodium Phosphate

This increase the alkalinity of the macaroni product. This allows the starch grains to gelatinize faster. Put simply, it allows the product to cook slightly faster. Good quality dried pasta has a dried smooth even appearance. The colour should be transparent ivory varying on yellow it should break cleanly - Good quality pasta qurduables when added.

Fresh pasta

In the fresh Pasta was only made by small business or in the home. This type of pasta is produce in large quantities and shipped and held longer due to improve packaging method. It's far more readily available for use in operation of all sizes. It can be made with flour instead of semolina and always contain eggs. Fresh Pasta must be used before it tries to gain the most benefit from the eggs.

Composition structure

The composition and structure of fresh pasta compare to factory produce pasta yields as difference in texture and taste. This fill is a result of type ingredients used and the manner in which they are handled.

Flour

Fresh Pasta is made from Flour. This flour has a softer texture and lower gluten contain. This type of flour developed into looser tough.

Egg

It is always included in fresh pasta this create a product has richer fuller flavour. It also reduce the stability of the product and shortens the shell life.

Oil

This is not a required ingredient in fresh Pasta. However when used it shortens the strengths of the gluten in the dough, allowing the leavening power of the eggs to raise the Pasta this results in a softer product than does the drum and water based pasta.

Fresh Pasta is normally rolled and cut whereas the factory produces pasta is often extruded (passing through a nozzle). The primarily Factor in handling fresh pasta are its shorter shelf life shorter cooking time and softer. The rich flavour of the Pasta is something which is valued in many dishes.

Types of Fresh and Factory mass product Pasta

The four basic categories are:

1. Pasta for soup
2. Pasta for Boiling
3. Pasta for baking
4. Filled pasta

1. **Pasta for Soup**: - is very small and made in various shapes. This group includes vermicelli linguini (small grains) Penette (small quills), stelline (little star), risoni (rice grains), conchigilettes (little shells), anellini (little rings sometimes serrated) these pasta are used in soup to provide texture flavour and slightly thickening.

2. **Pasta for Boiling:-** is largest grouping. This group includes macaroni, rigatoni, penne, pasta shell (Conchigilettes), nest (Papardelle) Butterflies (farfelle), Spirals (eliche) and spaghetti or fediline. The list is growing daily as pasta lovers on both side of the atlantic, experiments with new shape and form. These pasta are used as entire replacement or as filler in casserole fish and side dishes. They are used the main ingredients in salads.
3. **Pasta for baking:-** Must be first cooked in water or other liquid it provide flavour texture and stability to the dish. This type includes tortiglioni, Bucatini, Conchigilettes, cravatine and Lasagna (With smooth or wavers edges).
4. **Filled pasta**:- are used to incase a stuffing these pasta are stuffed with cheese vegetable meats or sweet filling for a deserts. The Pasta may come prefilled or ready to stuff depending on the type. The most common type include Cannelloni, Ravioli and Manicotti the types that are becoming more popular as the Popularity of the pasta grown are Tortellini, Tartelloni, Agnolotti (small sleepers) Capilleti (little hats) Lumancha (large shells).

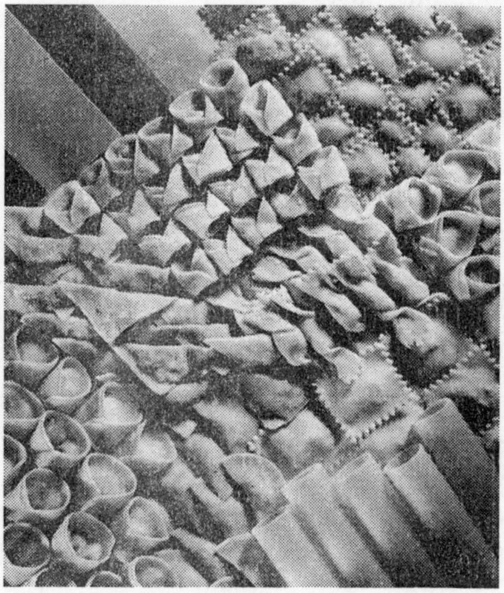

Fig 12.1 Varieties of pasta

The decision of whether to use fresh or factory Pasta will depend on the end product desire, type of operation and time requirement. There is a difference of taste due to the egg content largely in fresh Pasta and drying (edging) of the factor Pasta. Fresh pasta cook faster whereas dried Pasta takes a long time to cook.

Fig 12.2 Different varieties of pasta

Preparation method

It is not difficult to make fresh pasta. The biggest problem is that Flour differs and as to eggs. Flour varies in its ability to absorb the liquid. Egg varies in sizes thereby liquid content. Since fresh Pasta is a combination or Flour or eggs. It's difficult to be totally extract of each ingredients needed for the perfect pasta. The basic role is that for every eggs used three ounce of Flour (all Purpose or bread). Addition of water soil to fresh pasta is entirely on the discretion of the Person making it.

Cooking pasta

All pasta fresh or dried should be cooked in salted boiling water or liquid. The pasta must be added after the water is boiling to prevent the pieces sticking together the quantity of water used should be efficient to allow the pasta to swell and swim easily. It's by sealing pasta in fast boiling water that its possible to obtain the degree of the cooking knows as a' la Dante.

Small pasta should be sprinkle into briskly boiling salted water and for long pasta such as dried spaghetti gradually push it into boiling water. The allowing the longs strengths to soften and bent steering gently to prevent sticking together, it is possible to cook the spaghetti, legume or other types without breaking them into Pieces.

The handling of pasta after cooking will vary with the intended uses. If the pasta is to be used in a salad it should be drawn rinse under cold water and immediately mixed with small amount of oil to prevent starch, reducing the sticking. This also lower the temperature of the pasta. And toping the cooking process when pasta is to be refrigerator prior to services it's important to stock it with cold water. This prevents carrying over cooking after removal from heat sources.

Pasta which is served hot should be drain. It's not necessary to oil it because it can be immediately cover with sauce and serve but if it needed to cook pasta much before serving cook, rinse oil and hold in refrigerator. Before service it may be reheated by short immersion in boiling hot water.

The range of sauce for pasta is growing as rapidly as the forms and shapes. The traditional sauce like bolognaise and Melanesia based on tomato often containing ham, ground meat, seafood, cheese and anchovies and other are losing ground to newer lighter service.

Note:- All pasta served hot or cold must be well drained the water which clings to the pasta can destroyed the texture appearance and flavour of the sauce and it's to be served with.

Noodles

Are the oriental food which can be traced to both ancient Rome and China. The Italian spread throughout Asia including Japan, Southwest Asia and west-ward through Myanmar, India and Middle East.

Noodles are made from tough consisting of flour egg and water the addition of other Flavouring such as vegetable and sea food Purees is becoming more common. Also the addition of herbs is fairly common. As with pasta the egg may be deleted if desire. The word 'noodle' is derived from the German word 'noodle'. While the western noodle is produce from wheat flour the Chinese or Asia Noodle may also be produce from rice soy, mong-bean, potato or seaweed.

Types

The standard of identification from commercial produce Western Style Noodles required a minimum 5% egg solid content. Commercial noodles are sold fresh or dry. They are flat in shape with a width varying from 1/16 to ½ inches hide cuts. They are sold both fresh and dried. The wheat noodles are usually flat. Some comes one are:

1. Bean thread Noodle (Fig. 12.3)

Made from moong bean there are thin translucent noodles. Generally there are simmered in Soup or soaked in hot dishes. Japanese term for this noodles is SHIRATAKI.

Fig 12.3 Bean thread noodle

2. Shrimp Noodle

Made from the puree of shrimp (Paste) blended with wheat Flour. This South East Asian specially is an example of Flavoured Noodle which is used to compliment to particular Dishes.

3. Soba Noodles

Made from Buck Wheat Flour and have slightly Greenish in colour. This is Japanese Favorite.

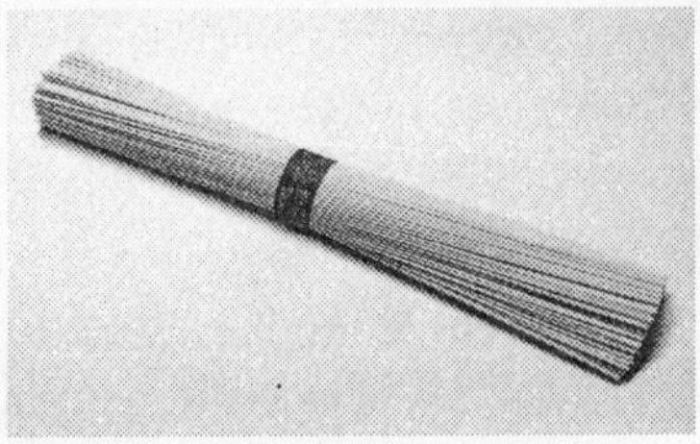

Fig 12.4 Somen noodles

4. Somen (Fig. 12.4)

This Japanese wheat Vermicelli type Noodles used in soup and Cold Dishes.

5. Udon (Fig. 12.5)

This is a thickest Japanese Wheat noodles it's used in both Hot and Cold Dishes.

Fig 12.5 Udon noodles

POLENTA (Fig. 12.6)

This is a North Italian Porridge or mush usually made from Cornmeal (Maize). However it can be made from barely meal and in certain areas from Chestnut meal (*Singhara ka Atta*). The polenta is closely related to poltos. It's prepared by boiling corn meal in salted water. Traditionally it than finished by mixing in butter or Olive oil and then pouring the mixture into a round wooden tray to cool. The cool polenta is cut into square or Lozenses. It's served pan fry baked augratin, as an accomplement served much as the same pasta or rice. Would be a polenta made with milk is often used for desert Preparation. In Italy the large grain Bergamo or Verona varies of maize are perform longer cooking time yet delivered a superior texture and flavour.

Fig 12.6 Corn meal and polenta

GNOCCHI

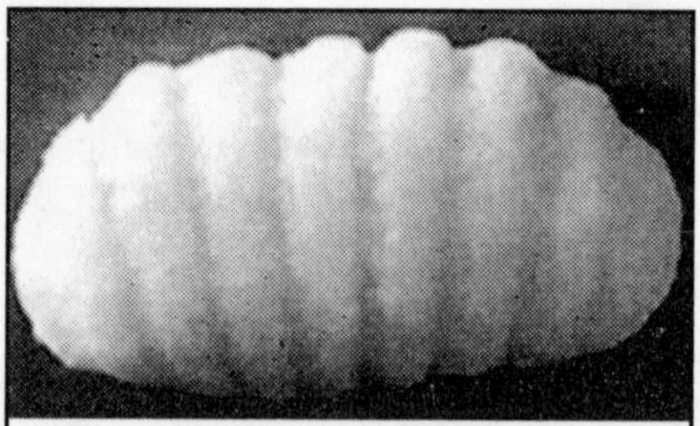

Fig 12.7 Gnocchi

Gnocchi (Fig. 12.7) are small dumplings made of Flour, Semolina, Potatoes and/or Choux pasta. The Gnocchi mixture usually includes eggs, either whole or only yolks which provide the structure of Flour. Additional liquid may be water milk or cream milk or cream is preferred choices because or richness and body they provide to the mixture. Butter or some other type of shorting is added to allow the Gluten in the mixture to stretch and rise. Achieving a tenderer product. The origin is Italian but it's also found in Astor hungering and Alsatian cookery where it's referred to as knodel, noques, knipele or quenelles. Gnocchi mean lumps. Traditions Gnocchi is first poached than cooked or gratin in the oven and served as a hot entrée. Basic ingredients are varied with the incorporation of cooked vegetable such as spinach, pumpkins, green vegetable or beet roots which gives the Gnocchi colour. Addition flavour are achieve by adding different types of Cheeses (Emmenthal, Parmesan and Ricotta) Chicken liver, Brains, Herbs and Condiments can also be includes variations.

Gnocchi Romainé: Semolina cooked in milk and butter season with salt Pepper and net meg. Raw egg yolks are blended in and then Poured in baking tins to cool. It corn than be cut in desire shape.

Gnocchi Venitienne: Two thirds mashed potatoes, 1/3 finally chop cooked chicken these are well blended in butter cream, raw eggs and grated cheese mixed is than season with salt and pepper formed into in small dumplings and poached.

Gnocchi Parisienne: Potatoes, milk, butter, raw egg and salt same basic Paste as Dutch's Potatoes mixture, add 2 to 3 ovens grated parmesan cheese to each pound of paste. Than place paste in a pastry beg in a round to be. Than mixture is pressed in the beg into boiling salted water. It's act into 1 inch Pieces as its passed. When the Gnocchi is fully cooked it rise to the top. It's than placed in a baking and lined with mornay sauces, cover with more sauce, sprinkles with Parmesan Cheese dotted with butter and browned in small oven.

SPAETZLE

Fig 12.8 Spaetzle

Means little Sparrow. It also spelled Spatzele or Spetali (Fig 12.8). It's a mixture of Flour, eggs, cream, which is formed into small dumpling which are pouched in boiling water. Especially of Alsace and Sothern Germany use to garnish Sauce meat dishes and game can be served is an entrée, augratin with cream or noisette butter or small croutons.

Basic Pasta Formula

Flour all Purpose	7 Oz
Eggs large	3

Salt	¼ T.s.p.
Olive oil	½ Ounce
Water	½ Oz

Method:

1. Breaks eggs into a bowl add salt, olive oil and water then mix well.
2. Place flour in a large bowl and form a well in a centre.
3. Pour the egg mixture into the well and gradually incorporated the flour into a egg mixture until all liquid is absorbed.
4. Scrap wall of the Bowl and incorporated well.
5. Lightly dust your hand and a flat surface with flour Place the tough or the flour surface and knead with keel of your hand for 8 to 9 minutes.
6. Cover Bowl with a lamp towel and let rest for at least 15 minutes.
7. Roll out the dough either by hand or with Pasta machine as cut as desire.

Pasta made from Flour and water dough is called pasta Secco. Pasta made Flour and egg dough called Uovo.

Different Shapes

- **Long**: - Smooth, Solid, Rod former Spaghetti and vermicelli.
- **Tubular**: - Outer surface may be smooth or corrugated example Macaroni and Mezani.
- **Flat**: - Noodles and Tagliatelle.
- **Short**: - This group contain large cut macaroni which may be straight or stand cut and large variety of Fancy shape Piece of pasta macaroni tube, Farfel.

PASTA SUITABLE FOR STUFFING FOR WITH FORCE MEAT

They are of two different types:

1. These that are stuff that pasta is on a raw stage and than cooked as Ravioli.
2. Those that are partial cook before begin stuffed and then cooking completed example Cannelloni, Pasta sheets lasagna

Small Fancy Pasta: - Used exclusive for garnishing for example Capellien, alphabetic.

LEARNING OUTCOME

Pasta is combination of durum wheat water and often egg and possible Oil. Basic pasta can be categorized into two ways ingredients and Preparation methods or intended and usage the categories or ingredients and preparation methods into two major types – fresh pasta (home made pasta, pasta vatta en casa) and factory mass Produce pasta. Factory produce pasta is made from dough of Semolina and water seldom egg is added to the dough. The factory produce pasta is either flat or cylindrical depending on how it's processing. Factory produced pasta includes a group refers to as "Macaroni Product this group is sometimes called Alimentary Pasta it includes such products as macaroni Spaghetti, vermicelli and egg noodles. In the fresh Pasta was only made by small business or in the home. This type of pasta is no produce in large quantities and shipped and held longer due to improve packaging method. It's far more readily available for use in operation of all sizes. All pasta fresh or dried should be cooked in salted boiling water or liquid. The pasta must be added after the water is boiling to prevent the Pieces sticking together the quantity of water used should be efficient to allow the Pasta to swell and swim easily. Pasta which is served hot should be drain. It's not necessary to oil it because it can be immediately cover with sauce and serve.

Noodles are made from tough consisting of Flour egg and water the addition of other Flavouring such as vegetable and sea food Purees is becoming more common. Also the addition of herbs is fairly common. Gnocchi are small dumplings made of Flour, Semolina, Potatoes and / or Choux pasta. The Gnocchi mixture usually includes eggs, either whole or only yolks which provide the structure of Flour.

LESSON END ACTIVITY

- Collect the information on varieties of pasta available in market with their brand name.
- Collect the data on pasta sauces.
- Collect the data on herbs which are used in pasta.
- Collect the data on varieties of Gnocchi.
- Bring pasta from market and boil it according to the instruction given in this chapter.

QUESTIONS FOR DISCUSSION

1. Explain what are pasta and its types.
2. Describe the classification of pasta.
3. Describe the factory produce pasta and its composition.
4. Describe the fresh produce pasta and its composition.

5. Explain in details the types of fresh and factory produce pasta.
6. Explain the procedure of cooking of pasta.
7. Explain the term noodles and its types.
8. Difference between Polenta and Gnocchi.
9. Explain the term Gnocchi and its various variations.
10. What is spatzele.
11. Explain the recipe of basic pasta dough.
12. In which different shapes pasta is available and which is the best pasta suitable for stuffing.

STATE TRUE AND FALSE

- Basic pasta can be categorized into four ways.
- Flat pasta is made by running the dough between rollers to form thin sheets.
- Factory produced pasta includes a group refers to as "Macaroni Product this group is sometimes called Alimentary Pasta
- The macaroni Products produces from durum have a characteristics yellow colour.
- Fresh Pasta is made from Flour. This flour has a softer texture and lower gluten contain.
- All pasta fresh or dried should be cooked in salted boiling water or liquid.
- Pasta which is served hot should not be drain.
- Noodles are made from tough consisting of Flour egg and water the addition of other Flavoring.
- Commercial Noodles are sold fresh or dry.
- The polenta is closely related to Polios.
- Gnocchi are small dumplings made of Flour, Semolina, Potatoes and/or Choux pasta.

KEY TERMS

* Composition
* Dough
* Dumpling
* Durum wheat
* Farina
* Gnocchi
* Noodles
* Pigment
* Polenta
* Stuffing

Chapter 13

Dairy Products

After studying this chapter, the student must know

- Introduction to dairy products
- Milk and its varieties
- Fermented milk products
- Process milk products
- Prevent curdling of curd
- Butter and its forms
- Cheese and its determined factors
- Cheese ripened process and its types with storage and service
- Standard cheese recipe.

DAIRY PRODUCTS

Milk, Cream, Butter and Cheese.

Milk: - Which the cow gives naturally. Milk as fresh whole milk the most than can be added is Vitamin. Nothing can be taken away it's certain a minimum of 3.25% of butter fat. Also termed milk fat 8.5% non-fat milk solid and 88% of water it is one of the most nutrition and whole some natural products available. It can be purchased in many form, all of which are various form of fresh whole milk after processing.

Pasteurization and Homonization:- are the process commonly used in milk Products. Pasteurized milk has been eated to kill most of the bacteria, hot and then cool, most commercial milk and cream product are pasteurized. Homonized milk is forced to a series of extremely small wholes. This separates of the fat particles in such small pieces. That they will remain suspended in the milk or cream. The result is milk or cream which doesn't readily separate. Its gives better cooking and drinking quality.

VARIETIES OF MILKS

Raw Milk is solid in some place which has not been pasteurized or homonized. This type of milk is used rarely in commercial kitchen. Pasteurized milk is also rarely used. Produced by milk of dairy cattle certified to be disease-free and kept under strict sanitary condition the milk may be sold either raw.

Fortified Milk: - Commonly there have Vitamin-A and or B possible extract no fat milk solid added to them. Other vitamin may be added to the milk but all addition must be listed on the label.

Skim or Non-Milk: - Has most or all of Fat removed it contains less than 0.5% fat (is pasteurized milk from which necessary all fat has been removed. The vitamin and mineral content is also reduced). Low fat milk contains 0.5 to 2% fat. Skim or low fat milk can't be considered as equal to whole mint. The reduction of butter fat content will change the character of the item been prepared. Butter fat gives not only richness of flavour but body and mouth feel.

Flavoured Milk: - Chocolate for e.g. have flavouring ingredients and possible sugar added. Flavoured milk drinks are skim or partly skim milk which have sugar and other ingredients added.

Cream: - Is a form of milk. The fat globules are more concentrated in it. Than in whole milk cream provides richness and body in items prepared with it. That it's readily available. It's not uncommon in institutional cooking to use whole milk in place of cream when this is done there must be the addition of a thickening agent to replace the body that the cream would have given the dish. Thickening agent with help to replace the texture but can't normally replace the rich flavour cream is less like to form a skim when heated or boiled and is for more stable than milk in cook sauces and soups.

Cream is available three market grades the name of each indicates it butter fat contents the replacement of on fat with another must be based on understanding this content. To replace heavy cream with half and half would greatly change the character of the dish been prepared.

Heavy whipping cream	36% butter fat.
Light Whipping Cream	30 to 36% butter fat
Light Cream	18 to 30%
Half and Half	A complete of milk and cream which must contain 10.5% butter fat at least.

Cream is often rich and use as a toppings for dishes or as an ingredients for dishes whipping cream a stable foam when whipped there butter fat content creates a supporting structure encapsulating air and holding it.

While it possible to whipped lighter cream and even skim milk, they will have every little stability.

Cream stability

To properly whipped a cream as much as stability as possible follow the guide as possible.

1. The equipment and cream should be as cold as possible.
2. Often sugar is added to whipped cream to increase a sweetness. This should not be done until it's whipped otherwise. It will decreased the stability of finished product powdered sugar is preferred because it has less negative effect on stability.
3. Don't over whipped the cream, stop when stiff peaks forms. It whipped to long it become granules and then form to butter.

FERMENTED MILK PRODUCTS

Cooking uses a variety of milk products produces from fermented or soured milk.When these are added to a dish produce stronger flavour to that particular dish. These also add acid to the dishes. This acid when used properly is beneficial to many preparations.

Sour Cream: - is one of the most commonly used of these product. It has been cultured (Bacteria has been intentionally added to the fermented product) or fermented or by the addition of lactic acid bacteria to cream. The bacteria grows in the cream and make acid as by product giving a cream a tangy flavour and thick texture. The Sour cream has 18% of butter fat content. It's widely use in many cooking and baking dishes.

Butter Milk: - is a fresh liquid milk (Whole low fat or one Percent) cultured by the addition of bacteria. It has a rich thick texture and a tangy acid taste. It often used as a baking powder to create leavening in bake goods. It can be used in recipe in suggesting sour milk.

YOGHURT (Fig. 13.1)

Is milk cultured with special bacteria the result is the milk product which has a custard type texture. Some time additional milk solids or flavouring fruits or sweetness are added. Yoghurt has long been associated with Middle Eastern cookery.

Fig 13.1 Yoghurt

PROCESS MILK PRODUCT

Milk is available in form other than those which must be kept refrigerated. The most commonly used in the kitchen are those from which all or part of the water has been removed.

EVAPORATED MILK (Fig. 13.2)

Can be made from whole or skim milk and contains a minimum of 7.5% butter fat. It has 60% of water removed evaporated milk is sterilize by exposure to high heat and canned and then tin. The product has somewhat cooked flavour it's used for baking and some other recipe.

Fig 13.2 Evaporated milk

CONDENSE MILK (Fig. 13.3)

It's made from whole milk with 60% of water removed the reduced milk is heavily sweetest with sugar and must contain a minimum of 8.5% butter fat. It is available can or in bulk quantities. Condense milk can't replace other milk product unless the sugar content of the recipe is adjust.

Fig 13.3 Condense milk

Fig 13.4 Dried milk

DRIED MILK (Fig. 13.4)

Have all moisture removed creating a powdered they are either available dried whole milk or dried non-fat skim milk. The Original type fried milk called "Regular" it's not easily dissolve making it difficult to used. Instant dry milk dissolves more easily and is commonly used in kitchen.

COOKING MILK AND CREAM PRODUCT (Fig. 13.5)

Curdling is problems which occur while Milk and Cream. Milk curdled when milk protein solid fried and separates from the whey. Whey is the mixture of water, salt and other solid presence in the milk. The enemies of milk in norm of cooking are Acid, Salt and heat protecting of calcium.

PREVENT CURDLING OF CREAM

1. Avoid combing milk or cream with strong acid unless starch is added when milk is stabilize with starch such as roux with flour or wax maize, it help to stabilize and protect the milk protein from separated.
2. Heat is natural enemies, reducing heat and cooking times when possible can prevent curdling.
3. Temperature of milk and cream before adding to a hot liquid temperature means to equalize the temperature of an item. This is done by adding small amount of hot liquid to a cold one staring vigorously. When the cold liquid becomes warm it is than added back to remaining hot liquid.
4. Milk scorches easily it is best heated in double boiler or a stem kettles not on direct heat. The scorching problems are caused by the proteins, natural sugar and thickness of the milk.
5. Reconstituted dry milk as will curdle quicker than fresh milk. Extreme caution is needed when using it.
6. Heated milk sauce will form a scum on top less exposes to longer this can prevented by covering then melted butter.

BUTTER

Butter is both a dairy product and a fat, by definition it's composed of 80% butter fat the reminder is milk solid and water valued as a flavouring agent and lubricant for culinary preparations, butter gives a richness and flavour to food which is difficult to duplicate.

Most butter in the markets are lightly solvent sweet and unsalted butter is also available it's more perishable then salted butter yet has a fresh sweeter taste. Butter is purchased commercially in one of the three forms.

1. Patties: Individual serving
2. Prints: Butter package in One Pound blocks
3. Tubs or bulb usually 40 to 60 pound in weight.

Some food service operation also used hiped butter. This is butter which has been expended in volume by incorporation of air some times gelatin. It has suffered consistency and improved spread of ability.

Clarified Butter

Butter from which milk solid have been removed is widely used in cooking. All butter should be stored highly wrapped or covered and refrigerated. The flavour of butter is delicate and readily absorbed other flavours. Butter will turn rancid when their at room temperature. The best temperature for storage is 35° F or below.

CHEESE

Is a food produced by separating milk solid by curdling causing the Proteins to coagulated this is done by the introduction of selected bacteria or rennet and enzymes into milk. The curdles are then drain processed and cured or aged in a variety of ways. The large variety of best cheese results from various processing techniques and types of milk used. They are 300 varieties of cheese know to the world.

The types of cheese are determined by five factors listed below:-

1. Types of milk used (Cow, Goat or sheep milk).
2. Method of curdling and temperature during the curdling process.
3. How the cruds cut and drained.
4. The ways the cruds are heat proceed or handed.
5. Condition of ripening.

Cheese is composed of three major components

Water, Fat and Protein. The Protein in cheese is derived from the milk, solids. All cheese is high in Protein. Water content of cheese will vary with the type of fresh soft cheese such as cottage cheese has 80% water. This at the top range of water content. A very hard edge cheese like parmesan is at the low end with 30% water

Fat content of cheese will vary with the type of milk used. Double cream cheese will have at least 60% fat and triple cream cheese will have at least 75% these are the richest cheese.

A flavour and texture of cheese is not only depend on its composition and but also. Good cheese is so rich in protein that it can readily take the place of meat, especially in summer. Indeed there are countless savoury cheese dishes which the family will appreciate as a pleasant change. Cheese dishes are valuable to the careful housewife from another point of view. Dry stale pieces that can no longer be enjoyed with bread or biscuits can be grated down close to the rind and served in a dozen ways Indeed for most recipes dry cheese is better than fresh

How it's ripened

Ripening a process of converting freshly made curds into distinctive flavour full varieties. Flavours are developed by introduction of certain moulds or bacteria during processing.

Cheese are classified according to ripening agent used whether it's ripens from inside or outside

1. Cheddar:- Swiss, Gouda and Parmesan are bacteria ripened from the inside.
2. Limburger and leiderkranz are bacteria ripened from outside.
3. Blue cheese including Roque fort and Stilton are more ripened from the inside.
4. Grey camembert, St.andry are most ripened from outside.
5. Cottage and bakery cheese are un ripened.

Types of cheese

Cheese are divided into large groupings:

1. **Unripened Cheese**:- are salt white, crushly made. These includes Cottage, bakery Ricotta cream, Neufchatel and Mozzarella..
2. **Semi-soft cheese**:- are more developed than un ripened but still have generally buttery texture therefore these include Fontina, Belpaese, Munster and Briok.
3. **Soft ripened**:- Cheese ripened from the outside towards the centre. When young they are formed and compact with little flavour. As they mature they soften and when full ripe may be runny these includes brie, camembert, liberkranzard, both double and triple cream cheese.
4. **Hard repined cheese**: - are curred cheeses which have firm texture. They have varies degree of mildness or sharpness of flavour depending on there age. These includes cheddar, gruyere and jarlsberg cheese.
5. **Blue veined Cheese**:- Owe there flavoured and appearance to blue and green mold which is variegated through out the cheese. These cheese includes roque ford, stilton, gorgonzola and blue cheese, blue cheesier (Cut after curdling, sometimes stirred then cultured with bacterial the time of shaping to give green or blue.)
6. **Hard grating Cheese**:- There flavour to long ageing period has two year. These cheese including Parmesan and Romano which are often sold already grated.

Goat Cheese are made from goats milks and produce in variety of forms in France called CHEVRE. Fresh un edge is most popular, having a mild flavour and very white colour with a dry texture this cheese has distinctive peppery flavour which is slightly acidic the most widely French cheese is montrachet.

Processed Cheese:- are manufactured by grading one or more natural cheese the ground cheese is than heated and blended with emulsifier and other ingredients.The mixture is passed into mould through solidify. Process is a uniform product that doesn't edge or ripened as natural cheese. It has a mild flavour and gummy texture the benefit of process cheese is its good holding or melting quality and it slope rise it's often use in cooking.A processed cheese contain at 50% dry matter and at least 40% Fat.

There are three basic type of processed cheese.

American cheese Usually refers to processed cheese made from cheddar. This is very popular for sandwich making

Processed cheese spread : Contain a lower per cent of cheese, the bulk is replaced by moisture such as milk or water. This product contains a higher level of moisture which is always in a product leveled process cheese.

Cold Packed or club cheese:- Is not heat and pasteurized like processed cheese. It's simply ground and mix with flavouring and seasoning to a separated consistency.

COOKING WITH CHEESE

The Flavour derived from the uses of various Cheese in cooking can be great. However it necessary to handle then carefully as with milk, cheese can be ruinent by heat

1. Use low heat Cheese is high in Protein which becomes stuff and stringy when exposed to excessive heat.
2. Sauces containing Cheese should not be boiled.
3. Grated Cheese melting more faster
4. Aged Cheese Melted and blend into food more easily than young Cheese.
5. Aged add more flavour to foods than yang mild Cheese so less is needed.

Cheddar,Swiss and Parmesan are three variety of Cheese used more widely in cooking. Cheddar is more widely in U.S. It's use specially in sauces and melted into food or for gratin. Swiss is used more frequently in European type dishes. These includes mornay sauces, soufflés and quiche, parmesan is used as grated topping for prepared food and as a seasoning or flavouring in dishes.

CHEESE IN SOUP

A little grated cheese makes an excellent addition to most white soups. Allow about a tablespoonful to a pint of soup. Put the grated cheese into a tureen, then pour the hot soup gently into it, stirring all the time; there is no fear of curdling, if it is added in this way

Australian Cheese Varieties

Cheese	TYPES	CHARACTERISTICS	SELECTION	WINES TO CHOOSE
Fresh Unripened Cheese 	Cottage Cheese Cream Cheese Neufchatel Ricotta Mascarpone Feta (matured in brine) Fresh Curd Quark Fromage Blanc	• Delicate milky flavour • Soft, moist, spongy body • Short shelf life • Also known as 'Fresh Curd' cheese	• Moist and fresh without excess free moisture	Lighter, refreshing wine styles that don't overpower delicate flavours: • Sparkling • Aromatic White • Medium Bodied Red • Dessert wines
White Mould Cheese 	Brie Camembert Double Brie Triple Cream Cheese (also known as White Rind cheese)	• Surface ripened • Velvety white rind • Creamy golden interior • Develops buttery, 'flowing' centre and mushroomy aroma with age • Rind is edible but if very ripe may overpower the cheese	• Rind free of hard edges or cracks • Good covering of white mould but does not have to be 'even' • Centre will soften and bulge when ready to eat	Suits a variety of wine: • Chardonnay develops a buttery texture and is ideally suited • Sparkling • Full Bodied Dry Red • Fortified wines
Blue Veil Cheese 	Made in classic styles (eg: Roquefort, Stilton, Gorgonzola) but sold by brand name	• Soft cheese with veins of green, grey or blue mould • Strong, tangy flavour with salty finish	• Veins evenly distributed • Not dull or grey in appearance • Outer edges firm but not crusted or split	Sweet wines are the best match for the tangy, saltiness of Blue: • Dessert wines • Fortified wines • Aromatic/Fruity Whites with sweet finish
Washed Rind Cheese 	Semi-soft Washed Rind Wine Washed Rind Raclette Tilsit Reblochon	• Surface ripened • Soft cheese that has been 'washed' during ageing to develop flavour • Brown, sticky rind • Golden yellow interior softens with age • Pungent aroma • Sweet tasting	• Even orange-coloured crust, free from cracks or splitting • May be slightly sticky and moist • In some styles centre will soften and bulge similar to White Mould cheese	Can be hard to match. The best styles are usually sweet and full bodied: • Dessert wine • Fortified wines • Medium Bodied Red • Sparkling red • Also good with beer

Fig 13.5 Types, characteristics, selection and wine with cheese (contd.)

Stretched Curd Cheese

TYPES	CHARACTERISTICS	SELECTION	WINES TO CHOOSE
Fresh Bocconcini Treccia Fior di Latte Matured (cooking) Mozzarella Pizza Cheese Provolone/ Provole	• Close textured semi-soft cheese • Textured appearance when 'torn' • Fresh types are moist and delicate in flavour • Matured types are prized for their 'stretch' when cooked • 'Stretched Curd' refers to method of manufacture	• Uniform white, pale yellow to yellow colour • Slightly soft and resilient • Smooth, even surface	For matching with fresh types, choose light, refreshing wines: • Sparkling • Aromatic White • Medium Bodied Red

Eye Cheese

TYPES	CHARACTERISTICS	SELECTION	WINES TO CHOOSE
Edam Emmenthal Fontina Gouda Gruyere Havarti Swiss-style	• 'Eyes' or 'holes' produced by carbon dioxide during maturation • Slightly sweet, subtly piquant flavour • Firm but moist body with open texture • Buttery, golden yellow colour	• Smooth close-textured and even in colour • 'Eyes' may be unevenly distributed, but should be round and glossy • No cracks between eyes	Quite versatile to match with wine: • Full Bodied Dry White • Medium Bodied Red • Dessert wines • Fortified

Cheddar and Cheddar-styles

TYPES	CHARACTERISTICS	SELECTION	WINES TO CHOOSE
Mild Cheddar Aged 3mths Matured (Tasty) Aged 3-12 mths Vintage Aged over 12 mths Flavoured Processed Colby Red Leceister Cheshire Lancashire	• Semi-Hard cheese • Flavour varies from bland and buttery (Mild) to the sharp bite of Vintage • Texture becomes drier and more crumbly with age	• Free from dryness or cracks • Texture will vary, depending on age - from smooth and pliable to crumbly and dry	Suits a variety of wines: • Full Bodied Dry White • Full Bodied Dry Red • Dessert wines • Fortified wines

Hard Grating Cheese

TYPES	CHARACTERISTICS	SELECTION	WINES TO CHOOSE
Parmesan Pecorino Romano Pepato	• Mostly used for grating but also excellent table cheese • Almost translucent golden yellow • Sharp, robust flavour • Grainy texture • Piquant finish	• Appear hard and granular • No evidence of large cracks or slits	Choose intense wines to match • Full Bodied Dry White • Full Bodied Dry Red • Fortified wines • Sparkling wines also match as acidity contrasts with texture of cheese

Fig 13.5 Types,characteristics, selection and wine with cheese (contd.)

STORAGE AND SERVICES

The holding quality varied widely and the term the more edged the cheese. The longer the time it will kept for example cottage cheese must be used in a week. Parmesan may keep for a week or long, soft ripened cheese such as camembert and brie detoured rapidly once they have full repined. In general store cheese under refrigerate oxygen is an enemies of cheese it will change drastically ones it's cut. Cheese will also dried up rapidly when expose to the air wrap cheese lightly with heavy plastic wrap for storage.

Serve Cheese expect unripened cheese at room temperature only at room temperature both flavour fully developed. Cheese should be cut just prior to services to prevent drying and flavour loss.

SOME STANDARD CHEESE RECEPIES

Bread And Cheese Pudding

Time: about 45 minutes. Temperature: Gas,. Electricity, 325° F. Enough for 4 to 6 persons.

Ingredients	*Quantity*
Bread slices	10 no
Butter	75 gram
Cheese	75 gram
Salt and pepper	15 gram
Mustard	20 gram
Egg	6no
Milk	200ml

Method:

1. Line a pie dish with small pieces of bread and butter, sprinkle them with coarsely grated cheese, salt, pepper and a little made mustard.
2. Then put over it more bread and butter, repeat the seasoned cheese layer and top with bread and butter.
3. Beat the egg, mix the milk with it. Pour this in and bake in a very slow oven.

Cheese Custard

Time: about 30 minutes. Temperature: Electricity, 325° F. Enough for four persons.

Ingredients	*Quantity*
Milk	300ml
Eggs	4 no
Grated cheese (processed)	100 gram
Bread crumbs	50 gram
Salt	15 gram
Cayenne pepper	10 gram

Method

1. Beat the yolks of the eggs with a good pinch of salt and a few grains of cayenne. Add the milk, breadcrumbs, and grated cheese.
2. Mix well. Then stir in the whipped whites of the eggs. Turn into a buttered dish and bake in a very slow oven until set.

Cheese Fingers

Time: about 10 minutes. Temperature: moderate. Enough for 8 fingers.

Ingredients	*Quantity*
Bread slices	10 no
Cheese	5 gram
Salt and pepper	15 gram
Mustard	20 gram
Oil	200 ml

Method

1. Remove the crust from the bread, then cut each slice into four narrow strips. Then fry them a golden brown in boiling fat.
2. Drain well, then spread a little mustard on each, cover each one with a thin layer of cheese and put under a hot grill until the cheese is hot and soft. Serve very hot.

Cheese Pudding (I)

Time: about 25 minutes. Temperature: Gas, electricity, 450° F. Enough for four persons.

Ingredients	*Quantity*
Dry cheese	100 gram
Butter	60 gram
Flour	60 gram
Milk	100ml
Egg	4no
Pepper and salt	15 gram

Method

1. Melt the butter in a small saucepan, mix the flour with it and stir for four minutes over gentle heat.
2. Mix in the milk gradually and stir until it has boiled for five minutes. Remove from heat. Then add the cheese, finely grated, and the whipped yolk of the egg. Season well with pepper and salt.
3. Then stir in the stiffly whipped white of the egg. Pour into a fireproof dish, sprinkle a little grated cheese over, and bake in a quick oven for about a quarter of an hour. Serve hot.

Cheese Pudding (2)

Time: about 25 minutes. Temperature: Gas, electricity, 450° F. Enough for four persons

Ingredients	*Quantity*
Dry cheese	100 gram
Butter	60 gram
Potatoes	100 gram
Egg	4 no
Pepper and salt	15 gram

Method

1. Steam the potatoes and then mash them very smoothly, add the cheese finely grated, the pepper and salt, then the egg well boated, and mixed with the milk.
2. Put the mixture in a well buttered pie dish and bake in a moderate oven for half an hour. Skinned tomatoes baked with a little butter are good served with this dish.

Cheese Puffs

Time: 10 minutes. Temperature: Gas. Electricity, 450° F.

Ingredients	*Quantity*
Flour	100 gram
Butter	50 gram
Cheddar cheese	30 gram
Parmesan cheese	30 gram
Egg	2 no
Salt and pepper	10 gram

Method

1. Grate the cheeses and keep them separate.
2. Season the flour with salt and pepper and stir into it very gradually a breakfast cup of cold water.
3. Melt the butter in a stew pan and add the flour, stir while it boils five minutes,.
4. Then stir in the Cheddar cheese. Remove from the fire and beat in two well whisked eggs.
5. Drop dessertspoons of the mixture on a buttered baking tin.
6. Put a little of the Parmesan cheese in the centre of each. Bake brown in a hot oven and serve hot at once.

LEARNING OUTCOME

Milk is what the Cow gives naturally. Is this term fresh whole milk to be termed as fresh whole milk the most than can be added is Vitamin O. Nothing can be taken away it's certain a minimum of 3.25% of butter fat. Also termed milk fat 8.5% non fat milk solid and 88% of water it is one of the most nutrition and whole some natural Products available. There are many varieties of milk available in the market such as raw milk, fortified, skim milk,flavoured milk. Cream is a form of milk. The fat globules are more concentrated in it. Than in whole milk cream provides richness and body in items prepared with it. That it's not readily available in other wise. Cream is available three market grades the name of each indicates it butter fat contents the replacement of on fat with another must be based on understanding this content. Cooking uses a variety of milk products produces from fermented or soured milk.When these are added to a dish produce more stronger flavour to that particular dish. Fermented milk product are yoghurt, curd, butter milk and sour cream. Curdling is a problem which occurs while Milk and Cream. Milk curdled when milk protein solid fried and separates from the whey. Whey is the mixture of water salt and other solid presence in the milk. The enemies of milk in norm of cooking are Acid, Salt and heat protecting of calcium.

Butter is both a dairy product and a fat by definition it's composed of 80% butter fat the reminder is milk solid and water valued as a flavouring agent and lubricant for culinary preparations butter gives a richness and flavour to food. Is a food produced by separating milk solid by curdling causing the Proteins to coagulated this is done by the introduction of selected bacteria or Rennet and enzymes into milk.Cheese is composed of three major ingredients such as water,fat and protein. Ripening a process of converting freshly made curds into distinctive flavour full varieties. Flavours are developed by introduction of certain moulds or bacteria during processing. The Flavour derived from the uses of various Cheese in cooking can be great. The holding quality varied widely and the term the more edged the cheese. The longer the time it will keep for example cottage Cheese must be used in a week. Parmesan may keep for a week or long, soft ripened cheese such as camembert and brie detoured rapidly once they have full repined

LESSON END ACTIVITY

- Collect the information of different types of milk available in the market.
- Collect the information on tetra pack milk available in the market with their brand name.
- Collect the information on different varieties of cheese available in the market.
- Which brand name cheese is more consumed in the industry.Go to the different hotels to get the information?

QUESTIONS FOR DISCUSSION

1. Explain the term milk and there composition.
2. Difference between Pasteurization and Homonization.
3. Explain the different varieties of milks.
4. Difference between skim and fortified milk.
5. Write a short note on cream.
6. Write a short fermented milk and its types.
7. Explain the term processed milk product.
8. Difference between evaporated and condense.
9. How to prevent the curdling of cream?
10. Define butter and its composition.
11. What is cheese and its types?
12. Explain the components of cheese.
13. How cheese is ripened?

14. Write a short note processed cheese.
15. What are the steps to keep in mind while cooking with cheese?
16. Explain the procedure of storing the cheese.

STATE TRUE AND FALSE

- Milk contains 88% of water.
- Homanized milk is forced to a series of extremely small holes.
- In skim milk all fat is removed.
- Cream is a form of milk.
- Heavy whipping cream contain 30% butter fat
- Light whipping cream contains 30% butter fat.
- Cream is often rich and use as a toppings for dishes
- Skim milk and contains a minimum of 7.5% butter fat.
- Curdling is problems which occur while Milk and Cream.
- Milk scorches easily it is best heated in double boiler or a stem kettles not on direct heat.
- Butter is both a dairy product and a fat by definition it's composed of 80% butter fat.
- Butter will turn rancid when there at room temperature.
- Cheese is composed three major components water, Fat and Protein.
- A very hard edge cheese like parmesan is at the low end with 30% water
- Ripening a process of converting freshly made curds into distinctive flavour full varieties.
- A processed cheese contain at 50% dry matter and at least 40% Fat.
- Cheddar,Swiss and Parmesan are three variety of Cheese used more widely in cooking.
- Serve Cheese expect un ripened cheese at room temperature only at room temperature both flavour fully developed.

KEY TERMS

* Butter fat
* Curdling
* Fortified
* Globules
* Homonized
* Pasteurized
* Processed cheese.
* Rancid
* Scorches
* Skim
* Whipping

Unit 3
MEAT AND SEAFOOD COOKERY

Chapter 14

Meat

After studying this chapter, the student must know

- Introduction and choosing your meat
- Boiling and storing of meat
- Freezing meat
- Cooking frozen meat
- Thawing frozen meat
- Storing cured meat
- Storing of minced meat, sausages and variety of meat
- Standard cuts of meats and there uses
- The art of carving meat and seafood.

MEAT

Meat is classified into three categories

The French word for meat is Viande, comes from the Latin *'vivenda'* meaning "that which maintain life". The tenderness of meat depends on the age and their feeding. Meat should be hung before sale. Because hung process is necessary to tenderlized their tissues. The sketal muscles are made-up of fibre which are composed of proteins, salt and nitro-genous extractives. There are two types of connective tissues:-

1. Collagenous or white connective tissue.
2. Elastin or Yellow connective

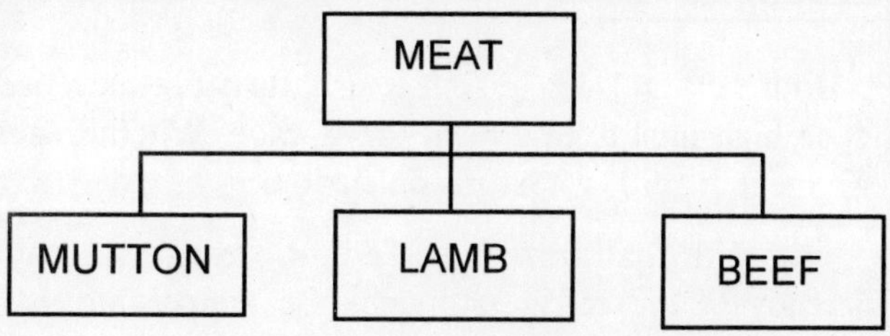

Fig 14.1 Classification of meat

The taste and flavour of meat is determined by various factors such as age, eating style and maturity, older the flesh toughness the tissue and younger the meat more tender and sweet in taste.

Immediately slaughter meat should be hung till tender.

HOW TO CHOOSE YOUR MEAT

Meat from young stock such as lamb, veal and yearling beef, tends to be tendered than mutton or beef from animals of a more mature age.

The amount of work done by a muscle while the animal was active and its affects on its tenderness for instance, the muscles in the rump and loin regions of a steer do less work than those of the leg and, as rule, rump is superior tenderness.

However, meats which are less tender, from more mature animals or parts of the animal which do more work, can be made tasty and tender by adopting the proper cooking method.

Several other factors influence the choice of meats cuts.

Large families usually buys large joints of meat for roasting are pot roasting these cuts lipe the tender cuts suitable for grilling are available only from a sum all proportion of the carcass, they are therefore in demand and so tend to be more expense.

Various cuts of the meat are more suited for meals of breakfast, lunch or way family meals are organized.

There are several into suitable for barbecuing, cold buffets and for approval occasions.

It is always worth considering the time available for the preparation of meat when buying meat. As a rule the cheaper cuts require longer working time, but larger cuts such as joints for roasting also require long time. Steaks chops and some variety of meat are tender and can be quickly prepared. The cheaper cuts however can be first tender and nutritious when cooked correctly.

STORING MEAT

Meat like other natural foods, is subjected to spoilage and loss if it not handles properly throughout all stages of preparation, distribution and storage. Because of the need to ensure that high standards of animal health and hygiene are maintained:

FREEZING MEAT

Both raw and cooked meat usually store extremely well in the freezer. But it is important to choose high quality raw meat for storage. Whether fresh or frozen, since freezing does not improve poor meat in either texture or flavour.

The time that frozen, chilled or fresh meal can be stored in a refrigerator varies with the efficiency of the refrigerator and the temperature at which it is set. The three main storages of a refrigerator are:

1(a) Deep freezer compartment temperature 18°C (0°F) or lower.

1(b) Freezer compartment temperature well below 0°C (32°F) below freezing point.

2. Cold storage meat compartment. Temperature about -2°C (28°F) close to freezing point.

3. Cold storage compartment. Temperature 72°C (36°F) just above freezing.

Once good compromise is to use to freezer for keeping special high quality cuts or those which are not often obtainable such as pork fillet, veal and fillet steak, together with a variety of prepared dishes made from the cheaper cuts which are useful when time is to likely to be short for food preparation.

COOKING FROZEN MEAT

Frozen meat can be cooked when thawed or unthawed but partial or complete thawing helps it to retain its juiciness. Thin cuts of meat and minced meat may toughen if cooked while still frozen. All meat should be thawed in its wrapping and preferably in a refrigerator since slow thawing is required. Allow 5 hours per lb in a refrigerator and 2 hours per lb at room temperature. If it is really necessary to hurry thawing can be done in cold water but meat flavour will not be so good. If meat must be cooked from the frozen state, unthawed large cuts will take 1½ times as long as fresh ones, smaller thin cuts will take 1¼ times as long. When thawing sausages and mince, allow 1½ hours at room temperature or three hours in a refrigerator for 1 lb of meat.

THAWING FROZEN MEAT

Meat may be safely thawed before cooking most people prefer to cook fresh or thawed meat, believing it to have better flavour, tenderness and juiciness. However, it may be cooked from the frozen state provided adequate cooking time is allowed.

To thaw meat, place the frozen package in the cool storage compartment of the refrigerator and slit open top of the wrapping.

Thawing in a refrigerator may take up to 8 hours per pound, depending on the thickness of the meat. In cool climates, the meat may be thawed at room temperature but it should be cooked as soon as thawing is complete.

It is normal for some moisture to escape from meat during showing. This moisture can be disposed of by removing the moisture proof wrapping during the final stages of thawing. The surface of the meat will quickly dry off to fresh appearance when exposed to the atmosphere.

Neither partially thawed or fully thawed meat should be re-frozen.

STORING CURED MEATS

Uncooked sliced smoked or cured meats should be wrapped in grease. Proof paper or open clear plastic and stored in the cool storage compartment of the refrigerator until required for cooking.

Storing Minced meat, Sausage and variety meats:-

Meat in this group, when purchased in a fresh chilled state, should be prepared for cooking without undue delay. Between purchase and cooking, minced meat, sausage, liver, brains, kidney etc. may be wrapped and stored in the Freezer compartment of the refrigerator, but they are better purchased close to the time when they are to be cooked. Never stored partially cooked meat.

CUTS AND THEIR USES

Beef

The better cuts	*Suggested Uses*
Sirloin	Roasting, Preferably on the bone. Grilling as sirloin steak entrecote steak porterhouse steak to bone steak.
Fillet	Roasting in Pastry case grilling as chateaubriand fillet steak.
Tournedos Rump Steak	Roasting in the Piece grilling
Fore ribs, Wing ribs, Back ribs	Roasting preferably on the bone.
Tops Ribs	Grilling as minute steaks (thin)
Top Side	Roasting, if larded
The Economy Cuts	*Suggested Uses*
Top Rump of thick Flank	Pot roasting
Flank	Pot roasting (if boned and rolled)
Brisket	Slow Roasting (if de-fatted and rolled) pot roasting
Silver Side	Pot Roasting
Shin	Stewing / Stock
Leg	Stewing / Stock
Neck and Clod	Stewing / Stock
Chuck Blade	Stewing / Pies and Pudding
Skirt	Stewing / Pies and Pudding

Lamb and Mutton

The Better Cuts	*Suggested Use*
Saddle (Double loin)	Roasting
Loin	Roasting

The Better Cuts	*Suggested Use*
Leg	Roasting
Shoulder	Roasting

The Economy Cuts	*Suggested Use*
Best end neck	Roasting, Stewing
Middle neck	Stewing
Scrag End of neck	Stewing
Breast of lamb	Roasting,
Pork	Stewing
Leg	Roasting
Loin	Roasting
Blade	Roasting
Sparerib	Roasting
Hand and Spring	Roasting
Belly	Roasting and Grilling

ROASTING TIMES FOR MEAT

	Oven Temperature	*Total Cooking Time*
Beef	325-350° F	Rare 20 minutes per Lb
		Well done 30 minutes per Lb
Lamb	325-350° F	25minutes per Lb
Pork	325-350° F	30 minutes per Lb thick cuts 40minutes per Lb

CUTTING TIMES FOR MEAT

Cuts meat at room temperature	*Grilling time in minutes*	
Sirloin Steak	Rare	: 6-7
1 inch thick	Medium Rare	: 8-10
	Well done	: 14-16
T-bone Steak	Rare	: 7-9

Cuts meat at room temperature	*Grilling time in minutes*	
1½ -2 inches thick	Medium	10-12
Fillet Steak	Rare	6
1-1½ inches thick	Medium rare	7
	Well done	10
Chateau-Briand	Rare to medium rate	16-20
3-4 inches thick		
Pork Chops	20-25	
Lamp Chops	10-Aug	
Sausages	Thick 10-15	
	Thin 8-10	
Bacon	Slice 3-4	
	Rolls 5-6	

THE ART OF CARVING

A knowledge of carving is invaluable to the chef. Food will go so much further if it is carefully served and not only will every portion look appetizing but the joint will be still presentable on its second appearance. Of course, carving is, to a great extent, a matter of experience only learnt by practice. But good tools and some knowledge of anatomy are also necessary. Nowadays most people prefer to carve from a dinner wagon or a side table instead of on the dining table itself. If they are inexperienced their efforts are not watched, and if any mishap occurs it does not spoil the appearance of the cloth.

FISH

Carve fish with a slice or fish servers if you have them. Otherwise use a fish knife and fork, or a fork and a knife of stainless steel. A large, thick fish, such as cod or salmon, should be placed on the table with the thin part towards the server. When the fish is hot it is a matter of opinion whether the skin should first be removed or not. It is the more modern way of carving when several portions are required. On the other hand, the skin keeps the fish moist and some people prefer to cut the fish with the skin still on it so that any part that is left is not unprotected. First make an incision right along the back the whole length of the fish. Then cut narrow portions right across, either removing the skin first or keeping each piece intact. Next slip the fish slice between a portion and the backbone and lift it neatly off. This method of carving is used for the thick parts of all round—as distinct from flat—fish. As you get nearer the tail you will, of course, serve wider pieces. When the top piece has been served, take out the centre bone and cut the underside in the same way.

Cod and large fresh haddock are often scored whilst raw, the marks dividing the fish into portions. Serve smaller fish—such as mullet, whiting and mackerel—one to each person, if they are on the small side. Alternatively they may be cut into two portions by dividing them down the back. Slide the server under and remove one half of the fish. Then take out the centre bone and serve the remainder. To fillet flat fish, such as plaice and soles, when they have been cooked whole, first remove the head and tail and the bones along the sides. Then cut down along the centre of the fish and slide the server under the fillets, one on either side of the bone. Take out the backbone and serve the under portion.

These directions apply mainly to steamed or grilled fish. It is difficult to carve fried fish neatly, much better fillet it before it is cooked so that it is ready to serve. With turbot and halibut, first cut down the centre of the fish from head to tail. Then cut across in sections, the width, of course, depending upon the size of the portion required and the thickness of the fish. Slip the server underneath the piece against the bone to remove it. The white skin-side of these fish is considered the best and generally served first. Often the underside is left to make a fish pie or fish *au gratin.* If, however, more of the fish is needed the bone must be removed and the underside cut into portions as before If fish is served as a course, it is best to put it in portions on the plates from which it is to be eaten, garnished and covered with sauce

MEAT

It is always best to carve from a dish that is too large rather than from one that is too small. Gravy should not be poured round the joint unless the dish has a well; it will only encourage splashes on the cloth. See that your knife is really sharp *before* it leaves the kitchen. The rasp of a sharpener is not a good start to a meal; never on any account should the knife be used for any other purpose. A two-pronged fork with an efficient guard is equally necessary. Make sure always that the guard is in position before you begin. Meat is always cut across the grain except in the case of a saddle of mutton. Here are simple directions for carving.

BEEF

Sirloin. The undercut, considered the choicest part of this joint, is generally served hot. Carve it is thick slices, cutting through the fat towards the bone of the joint. With the upper part, first cut away the little bone at the bottom of the joint. Then cut in thin slices right along, detaching the cut pieces from the middle bone by cutting between the bone and the meat at the side of the joint.

Ribs of Beef. Although this joint is similar in form to a sirloin, it does not possess an undercut. It is therefore carved in the same way as for the upper part of the previous joint.

Rolled Ribs, Aitchbone and Round of beef. These cuts are simply sliced across as thinly and evenly as possible, so that the joint, when cold, does not look ragged.

Ox Tongue. Start by cutting the tongue nearly through a few inches from the root.

Then serve rather thick slices—cutting them from both ends, remembering that the centre is thought to be the choicest part. If fat is wished it will be found at the root of the tongue.

MUTTON AND LAMB

Leg of Mutton or Lamb— Place the joint with the knuckle on the left side, and the thickest part of the leg away from you. Then raise the joint slightly towards you by putting the fork into the thickest part. Cut through the centre of the joint right to the bone, and then cut slices from either side. They should be fairly thick—mutton is not cut as thinly as beef.

The knuckle—a favourite portion with many—is cut in slices slanting towards the joint.

Shoulder of Mutton or Lamb. —The under part of the shoulder—some-times called the "oyster"- is best served hot. If you do not require many portions, cut them from this part and you will leave a very presentable cold joint. Serve fairly thick slices as with the leg. To carve the upper part, have the knuckle on your left, raise the joint with the fork, and cut slices through the centre to the bone. The meat on either side of the blade bone is cut in long, narrow slices

Loin of Mutton or Lamb. —This is a simple joint to carve if your butcher has jointed it well. Place the thickest part towards the carver so that chops can be cut right through between the bones. With a whole loin slices are also cut from the chump end.

Neck of Mutton or Lamb. — This joint (the best end of the neck) makes an excellent roast for two. Carve it in exactly the same way as loin.

Saddle of mutton or Lamb. —This cut, which consists of the two loins is the one joint that is carved against the grain of the meat. Slice it *across* the ribs, serving a little fat, taken from the under part of the joint, with each portion together with a slice of the kidney. The tail-end is usually placed to the left.

Forequarter of Lamb. —This is one of the most difficult joints to carve. First detach the shoulder from the breast by cutting right round the shoulder, raising it and taking it away.

Be careful to leave plenty of meat on the breast bones—the part of the joint which is best served hot. Often the shoulder is put aside on another dish and the breast divided into cutlets. If both parts of the joint are served hot a cutlet and a slice from the shoulder are usually combined for each portion.

PORK

Carve the leg and the loin in exactly the same way as mutton. The hand and the belly—both usually salted—are simply cut in slices.

Sucking Pig.—Half a sucking-pig is the joint that is usually served. Remove the shoulder as described for a forequarter of lamb, and cut off the leg. The various portions are then carved like lamb.

Ham.—Cut ham as you would a leg of mutton, but in very thin slices. The centre of the joint is the choicest part. The knuckle is apt to be salt.

VEAL

Breast.—This joint consists of the ribs and brisket. First cut through the centre, then serve slices of both brisket and ribs.

Fillet of Veal. —Carve exactly in the same way as a round of beef in thin, even slices. Knuckle of veal. –Cut slices through to the bone as described for a leg of mutton.

Loin of Veal. —This joint corresponds to a loin of mutton. Sometimes the chops are too large for one portion. They should then be sliced as for ribs of beef.

Calf's Head. —The bones are usually removed before this dish is served, so that the only carving that is necessary is to cut the meat in thin slices.

Serve a little of the tongue and brains with each portion. If the bones have not been taken out slices should be cut from the ear to the nose and served with a slice of the throat sweetbread. The meat round the eyes and the palate are considered tit-bits.

POULTRY AND GAME

A poultry knife is a great help when it comes to the carving of poultry or game. It is shorter and more curved and pointed than the knife used for a joint. A cook's kitchen knife is a good substitute. Birds that fly have the plumpest breasts, but the legs of birds that swim are considered the choicest part.

Fowls.—You carve a fowl in the same way whether it is roast or boiled. Place the bird with its breast bone towards you and take a firm grip with your fork, one prong on either side towards the back of the breast bone. Start by pressing back the leg so that you can get at the breast more easily, getting the knife between the body and the thigh and forcing the joint. Some carvers take the leg off altogether, others prefer only to force it to one side.

With a medium sized chicken it is usual to make three breast portions, one at each side cut down so that it consists of a wing and a good slice of the breast and the third the centre part round the breast bone, with the wish bone—a favourite tit-bit—in front. With a very small chicken, sufficient only for two, the whole of the breast at one side is served with the wing portion. On a large bird, which a careful carver is eking out to go round, the breast iss cut in long, thin slices and served with a slice of leg meat from the thigh. Or, the thigh can be served as a portion; some people prefer it even to the breast. The drumstick is not considered a choice cut and is reserved for a made up dish if any chicken is left.

The oyster—A small piece that lies on either side of the back—is really more like a mussel in shape; is generally though a very choice morsel. Turn the carcass over and remove it with the point of the knife.

The parson's nose—The Australians call it "the last bit that flew over the fence"—is also prized by some.

If the bird is stuffed a slice of stuffing is cut with each wing portion and a small piece served with every other helping.

Duck.—The joints of this bird are more in the body and therefore harder to find. Use the point of the knife and it will be easier to gauge the right spot. The breast is sliced thinly and the legs and wings served much in the same way as for a fowl.

Turkey and Goose.—With birds of this size, unless the family is large, the breast only will be needed at the first carving. It is more economical however, to serve slices of leg and slices of wing in every portion. If the birds are stuffed a small piece is served with each portion.

Pheasant.—The breast and wings are the choice parts of this bird and a leg is never served along. Carve in the same way as for a fowl.

Pigeon, Partridge and Grouse.—These birds are cut straight through the body if they are a good size, half being served to each person. Small same are served whole, one to each portion and small pigeons and grouse are used in the same way.

Hare.—Place the dish with the head at your left. Start carving by putting in the knife and cutting along the backbone from the centre to the end. Cut through the middle and you have two of the choicest portions of meat. Two more will be found on the other side of the bone. Next cut off the hind leg and the foreleg, removing the meat from the bone in slices. Whole legs are seldom served.

LEARNING OUTCOME

The French word for meat is '*Viande*', comes from the Latin word '*vivenda*' meaning "that which maintain life". The tenderness of meat depends on the age and there feeding. Meat should be hung before sale. The taste and flavour of meat is determined by various factors such as age, eating style and maturity, older the flesh toughness the tissue and younger the meat more tender and sweet in taste. Meat from young stock such as lamb, veal and yearling beef, tends to be tendered than mutton or beef from animals of a more mature age. Meat like other natural foods is subjected to spoilage and loss if it not handles properly throughout all stages of preparation, distribution and storage. Both Raw and Cooked meat usually store extremely well in the freezer. But it is important to choose high quality raw meat for storage. Frozen meat can be cooked when thawed or unthawed but partial or complete thawing helps it to retain its juiciness. Thawing in a refrigerator may take up to 8 hours per pound, depending on the thickness of the meat. In cool climates, the meat may be thawed at room temperature but it should be cooked as soon as thawing is complete. A knowledge of carving is invaluable to the chef. Food will go so much further if it is carefully served and not only will every portion look appetizing but the joint will be still presentable on its second appearance.

LESSON END ACTIVITY

- Collect the information of different varieties of meat available in your areas
- Collect the information how they cut their meat.
- Collect the information of meat processing companies.

QUESTIONS FOR DISCUSSION

1. Explain the classification of meat.
2. Explain the procedure how to choose meat.
3. Explain the procedure how to store and freezing the meat.
4. Explain the procedure how to cooked frozen meat.
5. Explain the procedure of thawing meat.
6. Explain the procedure of storage cured meat, sausages and minced meats.
7. Name the standard cut off beef with suggestive use.
8. Write the temperature for roasting of beef, lamb and pork.
9. Mention the cutting temperature of meats and its grilling time in minutes.
10. Describe the art of carving in details of each meats including fish.

STATE TRUE AND FALSE

- The tenderness of meat depends on the age and there feeding.
- Meat should be hung before sale
- hung process is necessary to tenderealized there tissue
- As a rule the cheaper cuts require longer working time.
- Meat like other natural foods is subjected to spoilage and loss if it not handles properly.
- Both Raw and Cooked meat usually store extremely well in the freezer.
- Deep freezer compartment temperature 18° C (0° F) or lower.
- Cold storage compartment. Temperature 72° C (36° F) just above freezing.
- A knowledge of carving is invaluable to the chef

KEY TERMS

* Carving
* Fowls
* Freezing
* Hung
* Knuckle
* Tenderealized
* Tenderness
* Thawing

Chapter 15

Lamb and Mutton

After studying this chapter, the student must know

- Introduction of meat
- Cooking of meat
- Frozen meat
- Preparing and marination for meat
- Gravy for roast meat
- Time table for cooking meat
- Standards cuts of lamb and mutton
- Grading quality
- Standard recipes of lamb and mutton

LAMB

Meat is such an important item of both catering and cookery that the chef will take the trouble to find out how and where to buy the best joint at the cheapest prior, and then how to cook it to perfection. Correct cooking makes all the difference to the flavour, the appearance and the amount of nourishment left in the meat. Deal, first of all, at a reliable shop where only meat of the best quality is sold. Make friends with your butcher and show him that you both know what you want, and appreciate the best when you have obtained it. So called inferior joints can often be obtained at a first-class shop at a lower price, because there is not the demand for them there, and if the butcher knows just how much you can afford to spend, he will probably let you have a piece of greater value for the money because he happens to have a surplus of that kind of joint. With meat, more perhaps than with any other food, the personal shopper scores all the time, as naturally those who order without seeing must often have goods the personal shopper has refused. Now for some hints on cooking the various kinds of meat. The novice and the experienced cook alike will benefit from a careful study of the points mentioned.

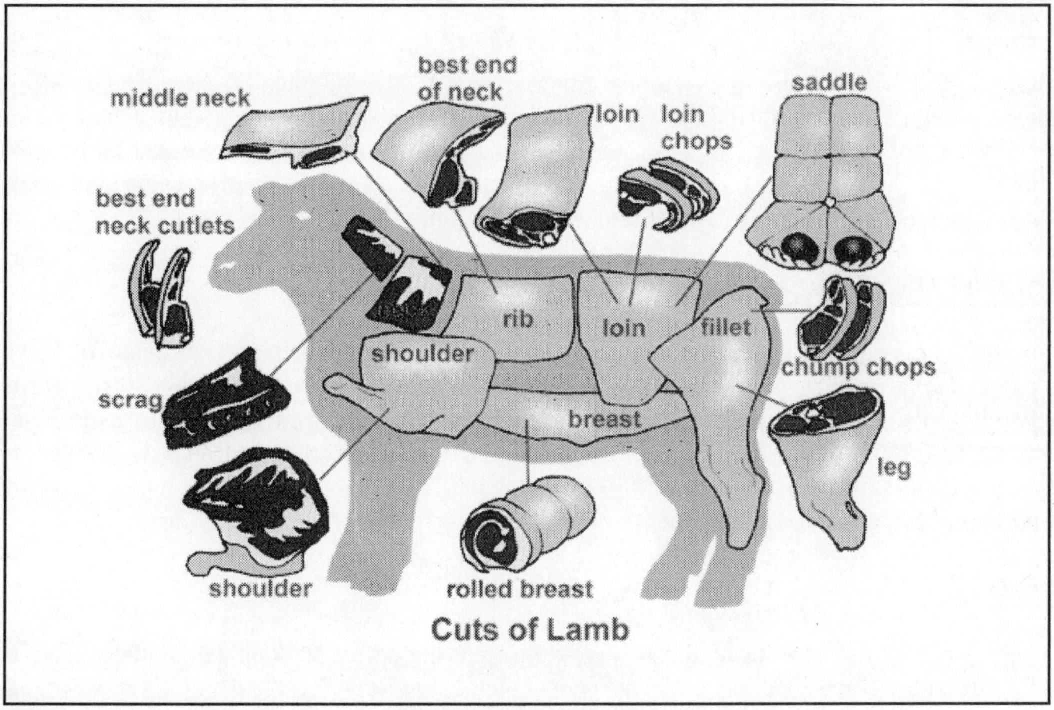

Fig 15.1 The cuts of lamb

BOILING

Put fresh meat into fast boiling water, let it boil for five minutes, then reduce the heat and simmer very gently until it is quite tender; meat that is boiled all the time is tough. When simmering, the water should be just moving gently all over the surface. Salted meat is put in cold water, the water is then brought gently to boiling point, then simmered until done. Serve boiled meats with a suitable garnish of diced vegetables, and skimmed broth handed in a well heated tureen.

ROASTING

The correct method is on a spit in front of a fire, but few commercial kitchen have a suitable grate for this now, and oven roasting has become the present day method. The great point is to keep the even, sides as well as shelves, scrupulously clean. To keep the goodness in roasting meat, the joint must be put into a hot oven and the beat maintained for the first ten minutes. This hardens the albumen and keeps the juices in the meat. Afterwards slacken the heat to moderate. Basting is important. If a joint is not basted, it will be dry and flavourless. Baste about every fifteen minutes.

Increase the heat when the point is nearly done if it is not sufficiently brown; if, on the contrary, it is becoming too brown, cover with greased paper until done. A roast joint must be served very hot; have the dish, plates and gravy tureen well heated.

STEWING

Stewing is the best method to employ for the tough parts of meat. A casserole is nicest, but a stew pan with a closely fitting lid may be used. Any kind of fresh vegetables may be stewed with the meat, but if dried peas or beans are used, they must be soaked for twenty four hours first. The time needed will depend on the toughness of the meat. Cover with cold water and cook very slowly. Long stewing will make the toughest meat tender.

GRILLING OR BROILING

See that the grid-iron is scrupulously clean, grease it well, then heat it and rub off the grease with paper. Have ready a clear, hot smokeless fire, or if you are using a gas or electric griller, light it fully five minutes before it is required. Regrease the grid-iron, put the meat on it, and let it be close to the heat for a minute, and then slacken the heat. When sufficiently cooked on one side, turn with a slice or grilling tongs. A fork must not be put in meat that is being grilled, or the goodness will escape. Grilled meat should be served immediately it is done.

FRYING

There are two methods used for frying, drying frying and the deep fat method. The first is used for sausages, chops, steaks, etc. The frying pan is greased, the meat put in and cooked over a fierce heat for the first two or three minutes, then moderate heat is employed, but grilling is a far better way of cooking chops and steaks. When frying sausages, prick them well first, and then cook very slowly to prevent the skins bursting. Deep frying is employed for outlets, rissoles and any meat that is enclosed in batter or egg/and breadcrumbs. Use plenty of fat, and when a thin blue smoke is rising, put in the prepared meat and fry a golden brown. Drain well before serving (for "frying", *see also fish section.*)

BRAISING

This is a delicious way of cooking meat, as it remains rich in flavour, all the goodness being retained. A shallow saucepan is needed with a closely fitting lid. Dust the meat very sparingly with flour, put about 1 oz. Of dripping or butter in the saucepan, put in the meat and brown in on both sides. Add some vegetables, cut in small pieces, a bay leaf, a sprig of parsley, thyme and marjoram, ½ pint of stock or water and a good sprinkling of salt and pepper. Cover closely and cook gently until the meat is quite tender, allowing twenty-five minutes to the pound and twenty-five minutes over.

Serve on a hot dish with the vegetables round. Skim the gravy; boil it rapidly until reduced to about a gill, and pour round the meat just before serving.

FROZEN MEAT

To defrost frozen meat, hang it in a draught for at least twenty-four hours. On no account should artificial heat be employed in thawing the meat. When sufficiently hung it requires no different treatment from our killed meat.

PREPARING MEAT

To Bone

Though the butcher will always bone meat for you, it is as well to be able to do it yourself. A very sharp knife is needed and they are consists of keeping the knife as close to the bone as possible, so that very little meat is left on it. The best way to learn is to watch your butcher at work, for it is a process that is not easily learned from a book.

To Lard

Larding is used on lean or dry meat to keep it moist. To lard correctly a larding needle is necessary. It is a needle without an eye, but they are slits at the thick end and the strips of fat bacon are put in these slits. The fat bacon is cut into strips, usually about two inches long and not more than quarter of an inch in width, but for very small joints or birds they will necessarily be a little smaller.

To lard, put a strip in the larding needle then on the point of the needle take up about half an inch of flesh and draw the bacon fat partly through. When the needle is taken out, there should be an equal length of the fat at each end of the "stitch". This process is repeated in even rows. A simple way to lard is to place a thin rashers of fat bacon over the joint or bird, and tie it in place with tape or thread, removing it about then minutes before the joint or bird is done so that it may brown.

To Pickle

The following is sufficient for a joint of beef or pork or a tongue: 4 quarts of cold water, 4 oz. Of Demerara sugar, 1½ lbs. Of bay salt, 1 oz. Of saltpeter. Put all the ingredients into a stewpan and bring to the boil and remove any scum. Then boil gently for twenty minutes. Turn the pickle into a deep earthenware bowl and leave until quite cold before putting in the meat. If the pickle does not quite cover the meat, it must be turned each day. It should remain in the pickle for at least a week—but it can be kept in for a fortnight if not wanted before.

MARINADE FOR MEAT

A process that helps to make tough meat tender, and also to improve the flavour. Mix together three tablespoons of olive oil with three dessertspoons of vinegar. Add a good sprinkling of salt and pepper, a slice of onion or shallot, a sprig of lemon, thyme or any herbs preferred. Put the mixture in a dish and place the meat in it. Let it remain in the marinade for one or two hours. If the mixture does not cover the meat, turn and baste it several times during the process. Drain before cooking, but do not dry it. A marinade greatly improves a steak if allowed to remain in it for an hour before grilling.

GRAVY FOR ROAST MEAT

Gravy served with roast meat should be the gravy that belongs to it without any addition from the stockpot. If there is a knuckle bone belonging to the joint, simmer it well and use the liquor to make the gravy, otherwise use water. Pour the fat from the pan very slowly, leaving all the brown sediment, for this is the essence of the meat, then add about half a small teaspoon of salt and ½ pint of the bone broth or boiling water. Place the pan over gentle heat and stir until all the brown sediment is well mixed with the liquid. Strain and serve in a hot tureen. Sometimes with lamb it is necessary to add a drop or two of browning, but be very sparing with it.

To Curry

Curries are excellent fare if well made, but they do not consist of just an ordinary mince with the addition of only a curry powder thickening as many cooks seem to imagine; there is a great deal more than that to be thought of. The most delicious curries are undoubtedly made with fresh meat, but it is also one of the best ways of reheating cold meat and poultry. Curries made of fresh meat need very slow cooking; the meat must be very tender and thoroughly impregnated with the curry flavour. Cooked meat should be put in the sauce and allowed to remain in it for not less than one hour.

The best utensil in which to make a curry is a glazed earthenware pot or casserole. Buy the best curry powder and paste for your curries; they are cheapest in the end, and good curry can not be made with poor or stale powder and paste. Shallots are used in curries in preference to onions. They are first fried in a little butter or fat, but be sparing with the fat, as a greasy curry is a point one. Some enjoy a little garlic in curry, but it should be a very small quantity. It is so powerful that a scrap too much may spoil a whole dish. The safest way to use it is just to rub the casserole inside with a piece of cut garlic. All curries should contain a sweet and a sour element. This is accomplished by the blending of such things as lemon juice or vinegar with sweet chutney or red currant jelly and is the making of the curry. Coconut milk is a great improvement in curry, but when you see this ingredient mentioned in a recipe, do not confound it with the milk drawn from a coconut. It is an infusion made as follows:—

COCONUT MILK

Scrape some of the white part of a coconut into a cup or basin, according to the quantity required. Just cover it with boiling water and leave to soak for an hour, and then squeeze the juice through muslin. Stir the liquid into the curry just before serving.

ALMOND MILK

This is sometimes used in place of coconut. Put 4 oz. Of ground almonds or pounded sweet almonds in a mortar with two shredded or pounded bitter almonds. Mix well together. Cover with a teacup of boiling milk and water mixed. Leave for ten minutes, then strain off and use.

TIME TABLE FOR COOKING MEATS

The following time-table will be a help to the beginner, but it is impossible to give exact time for cooking; so much depends on the thickness of the joint. For instance, a thick leg of mutton will need longer than a long thin loin of equal weight. Then, again, some people like underdone meat, others like it very well done. But experience soon teachers us how to cook it to suit the tastes of our own family. If a joint is stuffed, five minutes more time should be allowed for every pound of meat.

TO BOIL

Bacon.—Put it in cold water, bring to the boil, then simmer, allowing half an hour to the pound.

Ham —-Put it in cold water, bring to the boil, then simmer, allowing half an hour to the pound for hams not more than 10 lb. In weight; allow a quarter of an hour's simmering for every pound after 10 lb.

Salt Beef.—Put it in cold water, bring to the boil then simmer, allowing twenty-five minutes to the pound.

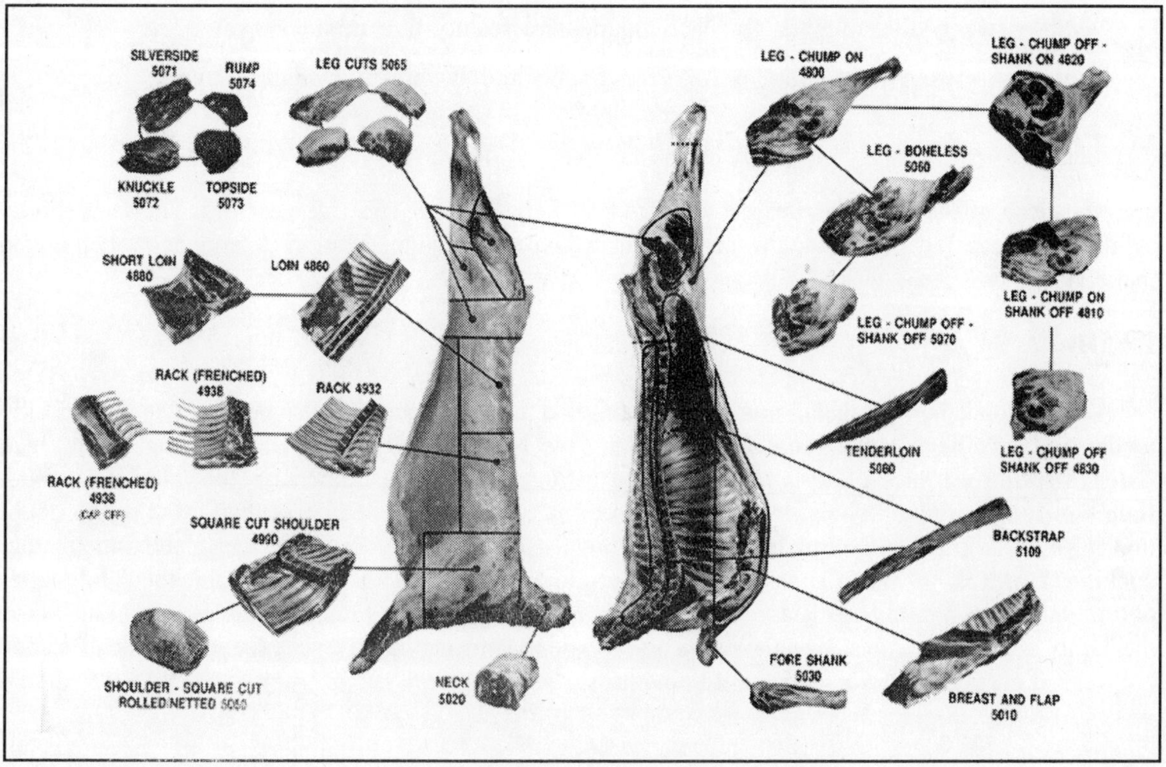

Fig 15.2 Primal cuts of lamb

Salt Pork.—Put it in cold water, bring to the boil, then simmer gently, allowing twenty-five minutes to the pound.

Calf's head.—-Put in cold water, bring to the boil, then simmer for three hours.

Sheep's Head.—Put in cold water, bring to the boil, and simmer for two hours.

Ox Tongue.—-Put in cold water, bring to the boil, and simmer for two and a half hours.

Mutton. —-Put in boiling water, then simmer, fifteen minutes for each pound and fifteen minutes over.

Veal. ——Put in boiling water, then simmer, allowing twenty minutes for every pound and twenty minutes over.

TO ROAST

Beef.—-Quarter of an hour for each pound, and quarter of an hour over.

Lamb.—Twenty-five minutes for each pound and twenty minutes over.

Mutton.—-Twenty minutes for each pound and twenty minutes over.

Pork.—-Twenty-five minutes for each pound and twenty minutes over.

Veal.—-Twenty-five minutes for each pound and twenty-five minutes over.

Venison.—-Twenty-five minutes for each pound and twenty-five minutes over.

MUTTON

The flesh of the sheep is considered at its best between four and five year old. The lean should be rather a deep red in colour, the fat very firm and quite white. Mutton should be well hung to make it tender

LAMB

When lamb is born in shelter and reared mainly on milk, it is called house lamb and is wonderfully tender and succulent, but, naturally, expensive. This is obtainable in the first months of the year. Later in spring we have grass lamb, reared out of doors and not as expensive, but almost as good. Lamb must be very well cooked to be digestible. Many cooks do not realize this, thinking no doubt that a young animal will need less cooking, but as a matter of fact the young need much more cooking. Lamb is cut into the same joints as mutton, except that the leg and join, the hindquarter or the shoulder, breast and neck—the forequarter—are generally each cooked as one joint when the lamb is small. Lamb's sweetbreads are very good and not nearly so expensive as calf's they are very digestible and so valuable for invalids.

STANDARDS CUTS OF LAMB AND MUTTON

Breast

This cut is one of the cheapest cuts and whilst the price is similar to scrag end, but is much more versatile. It can be roasted on the bone, boned, stuffed and rolled, or when well trimmed, can be used for mince, burgers or skewers (kebabs). Some butchers also sell this cut in strips which are ideal for barbecues. Excellent flavour, but rather fat. It is often used in Irish stew or Haricot Mutton, but makes quite a good roast, boned and stuffed with a savoury stuffing and well browned; the fat is then delicious

Flank

Unlike other cuts from the loin area, the flank is much tougher and is usually sold as mince.

Fore shank

Also known as Lamb shanks, this cut is suitable for slow roasting, stewing and braising. It has become very popular in recent years especially when braised when a whole shank with the bone is served per person. It is a very flavourful cut of meat.

Leg

This is a prime cut with little fat which is excellent for roasting as a joint. It is often cut into lamb steaks suitable for frying or grilling or into cubes for lean kebabs.

Loin

The loin is the most tender part of the lamb. It is from this area that loin chops come from as well as medallions, noisettes as well as roasting cuts. Suitable for roasting although the joints tend to be small unless you have a whole saddle which is made up of a double loin roast, from both sides of the backbone. Frying and grilling are excellent for the smaller cuts.

Neck

This is one of the tougher cuts and is generally sold as Stewing lamb or made into mince (ground) meat. When sold in pieces it is only suitable for very long, slow, moist cooking. Although tough the flavour is very good so well worth the extra cooking. Best End of neck is traditionally used for Lancashire Hotpot.

Rack

A "rack of lamb" is the name given to the whole rib section on either side of the backbone between the shoulder and the loin. A tender and flavoursome cut, it is also expensive and it is suitable for dry heat cooking such as roasting or grilling. This cut has a layer of fat which, although it can be trimmed down, is best left on when roasting as it melts and bastes the meat during cooking. Racks are often "Frenched" which means that the upper ends of the rib bones are scraped clean of meat and fat thereby exposing the bones which sometimes have paper frills popped over the top. Once frenched, it can be used to create a "Crown" where two racks are tied together to form a circle, the middle of which is then stuffed or a "Guard of honour" where the two sides of the rack are stood vertically with the bare bones uppermost and rib ends interlocked to resemble soldiers' swords. Racks are not large pieces: one rack of lamb is usually large enough to serve three people.

Scrag

Also known as scrag end or neck end, this is one of the tougher cuts and is therefore one of the cheaper ones. The meat from this area is often more fatty than other cuts and is usually sold chopped or diced for use in stews and casseroles.

Shoulder

Shoulder is often sold as two separate joints, blade and arm (knuckle). The whole shoulder is also sometimes called "square cut" which consists of the arm, blade, and rib bones. Suitable for roasting, shoulder is a relatively expensive cut, even more so if you buy it boned and rolled although adding a stuffing before rolling makes it more economical. Many cooks prefer to buy it this way as the structure of the bones in the joint can make carving difficult. Shoulder meat is also often trimmed of fat and sold as cubes for curries, kebabs and casseroles. **Shoulder chops** are suitable for pan-frying, grilling or braising.

The Neck

The best end is considered one of the primmest parts. It is generally used for cutlets and made dishes, and is a delicious roast for a small family. A whole neck or target is a good joint to buy, as cutlets, a small roast and a stew from the scrag can be obtained from it.

The Head

A very cheap and nourishing joint. May be stewed or used to make a pie, and also makes good broth. It is a joint that should not be despised, for it contains a great deal of nourishment very cheaply.

The Liver. Sheep's liver is cooked in the same way as calf's or lamb's liver, but it is not nearly as tender and should therefore be cooked more slowly.

The Heart. Very good stuffed and roast or stewed.

Kidney. The kidney of mutton and lamb are tender and delicious. they may be cooked in various ways; the favourite perhaps is grilled.

Quality Grading

These are some standards based on meat carcass grades and yields. These standards are used by meat purchasers, local, and state agencies as well as hospitals, schools, state institutions, the Department of Defense, and consumers to help determine lamb quality, nutrition and palatability.

The inspects each lamb carcass and gives it a grade based on palatability or quality, leanness, conformation or muscular development, marbling, and flank streaking. Prime, Choice, Good, and Utility are the four grades that a carcass could receive. It does not matter what sex the lamb is.

Prime refers to the best cut of carcass being well muscled, with minimum fat streaking range requirements in the flank being small to abundant, and lean flesh.

Choice refers to a carcass that is slightly muscled, with minimum fat streaking range requirements in the flank being trace to abundant, and the carcass has a minimum amount of external fat covering.

Good refers to slightly thin muscled. Carcass is thin with tapering legs with slightly narrow thin backs. The of flank streaking is practically devoid to modest.

Utility refers to the low end of the scale. An ovine carcass given a utility grade has the characteristics that are lower than the minimum requirements of good.

Yield grades are used commercially, because they can provide additional information. Five yield grades can be assigned to a carcass based on fat percentage, with 1 being the leanest to 5 representing the fattest. The yield grade can be computed by measuring the fat thickness over the ribeye muscle, amount of kidney pelvic fat, external fat, and leg conformation grade

RECIPES OF LAMB AND MUTTON

Roast and Boiled Mutton or Lamb

Time: 20 to 25 minutes to the lb. according to the thickness of the joint. Temperature: low.

Ingredients	*Quantity*
Leg, neck, or breast of mutton, lamb	750 gram
Water	2 litre
Salt	15 gram
Onion	100 gram
Turnip	50 gram
Onion	100 gram
Parsley	10 gram
Caper	10 gram
Hollandaise	50ml

Method

1. For boiling, choose a leg, neck, or breast. If the joint is fat, trim some off before cooking leaving only as much as will be required.
2. If more vegetables are needed it is best to cook them separately, as too many vegetables spoil the flavour of the meat.
3. Wash the meat, scrape the carrot, peel the onion and turnip and cut them in quarters. Put the meat and vegetables in a stew pan containing sufficient boiling water to cover well, add a teaspoon of salt and bring to the boil again.
4. Skim well and reduce the heat, then simmer slowly until the meat is quite tender; being careful that it does not boil. Onion, or Parsley, or Caper Sauce is generally served with boiled mutton.
5. Hollandaise Sauce is extremely good and if a little is used to mask the mutton sprinkled with parsley, it turns an otherwise rather uninteresting looking dish into a very delightful one.

Roast Mutton Or Lamb

1. The leg, should and loin are all good roasting joints, while best end of the neck is a delicious little joint for a small family.
2. Mutton and lamb need careful roasting. A well cooked joint is evenly done throughout without being dry, and nicely browned without being burnt.
3. Mutton and lamb should be well-basted lamb will need some additional fat to keep it moist.
4. Baste about every quarter of an hour. If sufficiently browned before it is done, cover with a well greased papper.
5. Mutton will need twenty minutes for each 450 gram and twenty minutes over.
6. Lamb needs rather more cooking: twenty-five minutes to the pound and twenty-five minutes over. Mutton and lamb should be served very hot.
7. See that everything is ready and hot before you start dishing up.
8. Serve onion sauce with shoulder of mutton, and red currant or crab apple jelly with other joints.
9. Mint sauce or jelly is served with lamb, but gooseberry sauce is also good.

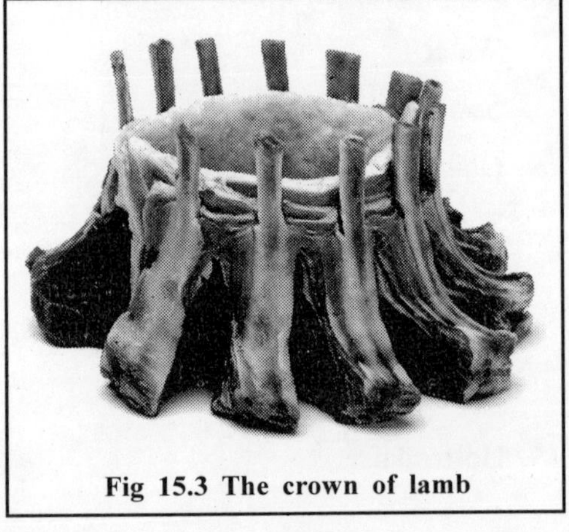

Fig 15.3 The crown of lamb

Crown Of Lamb or Mutton

Ingredients	*Quantity*
Best end neck of mutton	750 gram
Mushroom	100 gram

Flour	50 gram
Salt and pepper	15 gram
Tomato	100 gram
Butter	50 gram
Boiled potatoes	100 gram
Fat for roasting	50 gram
Rashers of bacon	30 gram
Milk	30 ml

Time 1½ to 1¾ hours according to the thickness of the cutlets. Temperature: Gas 4. Electricity, 450° F, reduces to 375° F. After 10 minutes enough for 4 to 6 persons.

Method

1. Have the mutton well chopped between the bones and trim down each chop bone as you would for cutlets, but without separating them.
2. Then roll the joint round in the form of a crown—with the bone part of the chops inside the crown.
3. Put a thin strip of fat bacon round each cutlet bone so that the bones will not be burnt, tying it on with shread.
4. Sprinkle the joint with flour, pepper and salt. Put a little hot fat in a baking tin and put in the joint.
5. Cover the joint with well buttered paper, and put it in a hot oven.
6. After ten minutes reduce the heat to moderate, and bake for about one hour more.
7. Remove the paper a quarter of an hour before the joint is done, so that it may be nicely browned.
8. It is most important that the heat should be reduced after ten minutes cooking, or the meat will be dry.
9. When cooked, take off the bacon, and put a cutlet frill round each bone.

To Make the Gravy

10. Drain off the fat from the tin, stir in ½ pint of the stock, add a tomato and a dessertspoon of mushroom catsup, and boil for two or three minutes.
11. Rub through a sieve, and use. Serve potatoes mashed with butter and milk and piled in the centre of the brown.

Leg of Lamb

Ingredients	*Quantity*
Leg of lamb	750 gram
Thin rashers fat bacon	30 gram
Dripping	20 ml
Lemon	2 no.
Stock	1litre
Castor sugar	20 gram
Salt and pepper	15 gram
Red currant jelly	10 gram

Method

1. Make the stock with the knuckle bone. Cover the joint with the rashers of bacon, tying them on with thread.
2. Melt the dripping in a baking tin, and when it is quite hot put in the lamb and roast in the usual way.
3. Remove the bacon about a quarter of an hour before the lamb is done, so that it may be nicely browned.
4. Strain the juice of half a lemon over it a few minutes before dishing up, and serve with red currant gravy.

To make the Gravy

5. Put the joint on a hot dish and keep it hot (hall cold lamb is most unappetizing).
6. Pour off all the fat from the pan, being careful to keep back the meat essence at the bottom.
7. Pour in the stock and boil for four minutes, stirring well at the bottom of the baking dish.
8. Next add the sugar, a good sprinkling of salt and pepper, and the red currant jelly. Stir well, and bring to the boil. Strain and serve.

LEARNING OUTCOME

Meat is such an important item of both catering and cookery that the chef will take the trouble to find out how and where to buy the best joint at the cheapest prior, and then how to cook it to perfection. Correct cooking makes all the difference to the flavour, the appearance and the amount of nourishment left in the meat.

Put fresh meat into fast boiling water, let it boil for five minutes, then reduce the heat and simmer very gently until it is quite tender; meat that is boiled all the time is tough. Stewing is the best method to employ for the tough parts of meat. A casserole is nicest, but a stew pan with a closely fitting lid may be used. To defrost frozen meat, hang it in a draught for at least twenty-four hours. On no account should artificial heat be employed in thawing the meat. When sufficiently hung it requires no different treatment from our home killed meat. Larding is used on lean or dry meat to keep it moist. To lard correctly a larding needle is necessary. It is a needle without an eye, but they are slits at the thick end and the strips of fat bacon are put in these slits. Gravy served with roast meat should be the gravy that belongs to it without any addition from the stockpot. If there is a knuckle bone belonging to the joint, simmer it well and use the liquor to make the gravy, otherwise use water. When lamb is born in shelter and reared mainly on milk, it is called house lamb and is wonderfully tender and succulent, but, naturally, expensive. This is obtainable in the first months of the year. The standard cuts of meats are very important to learn such as ribs, chunk etc.

LESSON END ACTIVITY

- Go to the butcher shops and learn the method of cutting of lamb.
- Try to make some lamb and mutton dishes according to the recipe given above.

QUESTIONS FOR DISCUSSION

1. Draw a picture of lamb which shows the standard cuts of lamb.
2. Explain the process of boiling of lamb.
3. Explain the process of stewing of lamb.
4. Explain the process of braising and stewing of lamb.
5. Explain the process of preparing meat.
6. Mention the timetable for cooking meats.
7. Write the down the standards cut of lamb.
8. How to check the quality grading of meats.
9. Write down the process of roasting lambs.
10. Mention the recipes of boiled lamb.

STATE TRUE AND FALSE

- Salted meat is put in cold water.
- Stewing is the best method to employ for the tough parts of meat.

- Grilled meat should be served immediately it is done.
- Use plenty of fat, and when a thin blue smoke is rising.
- To defrost frozen meat, hang it in a draught for at least 24 hours.
- Larding is used on lean or dry meat to keep it moist.
- A process that helps to make tough meat tender, and also to improve the flavour.
- Gravy served with roast meat should be the gravy that belongs to it without any addition from the stockpot.
- To roast beef 25 minutes for each pound and 20 minutes over.
- To roast veal 25 minutes for each pound and 20 over.
- Mutton should be well hung to make it tender.
- The loin is the tenderest part of the lamb.
- Shoulder is often sold as two separate joints, blade and arm (knuckle).

KEY TERMS

* Grading	* Mutton
* Joints	* Scrag
* Knuckle	* Strip
* Lamb	* Tender

16

Poultry and Game

After studying this chapter, the student must know

- Introduction
- Popular breed of poultry
- Choose quality of poultry
- Draw and truss of poultry
- Classification and selection of chicken
- Steps to cut chicken
- Cooking of chicken with nutritional facts
- Safe storage of chicken
- Recipes of chicken
- Introduction to games with its cooking techniques
- Varieties of games

POULTRY

Poultry is universally loved and as widely available at its flavorful best when freshly killed, it does not require lengthy preparation and may appear as easily in a pleasant dish redolent of garlic as in an elegantly sauce creation suited to champagne taste.

Because it's delicate flesh is easily digested. Poultry caries a layer of fat under the skin and several larger fat deposits near the tail. The latter are easily removed. A whole chicken destined for the roasting oven needs its skin as a protective layer to prevent the meat from drying out during cooking but the skin is easily removed once the chicken is cooked. Individual pieces of chicken may be skinned before or after cooking. Chicken will not brown quite as well as when skinned. The use of paprika will help the process without changing the flavour. Whether broiled, fried, roasted or simmered in a pot, the chicken and it relatives deserve the high position they hold in world cookery.

Similar to other meats, poultry must undergo a mandatory inspection for whole sameness. Depending on the various factors such as carcass shape and the ration of meat to bone. Once inspect, birds are plucked cleaned, chilled and packaged. They may be purchased whole or in parts. Poultry is classified by age. The younger the bird, the more tender the flesh. Poultry is the catch-all term for domesticated birds that are meaty enough to eat. Poultry tends to be lower in saturated fat than other meats, so it's a good choice for health or weight. The fat can be still more lowered by removing the skin and by using light meat from the breast instead of the darker meat from the thighs and legs. Younger birds are tenderer than older ones, so they're best for grilling, roasting, and frying. Older, tougher birds do better if they're cooked in stews or soups.

Those who are fortunate enough to have their own chickens, know the old from the young; but it is a different matter when we have to purchase them, and a certain amount of knowledge is necessary if we are to obtain good value for our money.

Poultry includes the different varieties and sizes of chicken, turkey ducks; geese and guinea fowls.

Chicken is the meat derived from the chicken. It is the most common type of poultry in the world, and is frequently prepared as food in a large number of ways.

Duck this fatty bird makes a divine roast, but it's hard to cook without setting off the smoke alarm. It helps to pour off the fat while it's roasting. Wild ducks are less fatty than store-bought ducks. A young duck, called a duckling, broiler duckling, roaster duckling, is tenderer than an old duck or mature duck. High fat meats like duck generally should be cooked at a higher temperature and for a longer time than low-fat meats.

Goose the meat is dark and fatty, and more like beef than chicken. Young goslings are the priciest, and the tenderest. Wild goose is tougher and has a much stronger flavour than a domesticated goose. High-fat meats like goose should be cooked at a higher temperature and for a longer time than low-fat meats. Frozen goose is a good substitute for fresh.

Guinea fowl this small bird is very lean and tastes like a pheasant. It's very lean, so bard it before roasting, or marinate it before putting it on the grill.

Poussin is a very young chicken, and it has a very delicate flavour and very little fat. They're available in some gourmet markets

The Breed of poultry are listed below:

American Class

Breeds	*Varieties*
Chantecler	Partridge, white
Holland	Barred, white
Java	Black, Mottled

Breeds	*Varieties*
Plymouth Rock	Barred, Blur, Buff, Columbian, Partridge, Silver penciled, White
Rhode Island Red	Rosecomb, Single comb
Wyan Dotte	Black, Buff, Silver, laced, Silver Penciled
Asiatic Class	
Brahmas	Buff, Dark, Light
Langshan	Black, White
Cochin	Black, Brown, Buff, Partridge, Golden laced, Silver laced, White
English Class	
Dorking	Colored Silver Gray, White
Sussex	Light Red, Speckled
Orpington	Black, Blue, Buff, White
Mediterranean Class	
Anconas	Rose Comb, Single Comb
Minorca's	Single Combs (Black, Buff, White) Rose combs (Black, White) White faced black.
Continental Class	
North European:-	Black, Golden Penciled, Golden and Pangled, Silver Penciled, Silver Spangled White.
Hamburgs	
Campiness	Golden silver

Note : The King of chicken Breeds is "BRAHMA".

Choosing quality of poultry

The breast of a young fowl is gristle at the end, and this can be easily felt. If it is all hard bone, it is not suitable for roasting. The comb of a young cockered is bright red and quite smooth, and the legs are smooth also, and spurs quite small. A young hen's comb is bright, soft and small, and the legs smooth. Choose poultry that is plump without being over-fat. The presence of too much fat can be felt under the skin. Birds with dark skin and legs are best in flavour, and should be chosen for roasting, but white birds are more delicate for boiling.

Fowls for roasting and grilling must be young, but for braising, boiling or stewing old birds are quite good. Ducks for roasting should be about three months old. To tell if they are young, see if their feet are pliable and yellow. The breast should feel firm; if it feels flabby, it is too fat, and will be oily in flavour. Goose are useless for cooking when more than a year old. When young they have pliable yellow feet, a smooth yellow bill, and white skin. The best turkeys have white skins, with smooth black legs. Choose a bird not under 10 lb. in weight, and one that is plump and feels heavy for its size. When buying pigeons, see that the feet are smooth and supple and the bird plump. All poultry, unlike game, should be eaten while quite fresh. Twenty-four hours after killing is long enough in hot weather, but in very cold weather they may hang a day or two.

TO DRAW AND TRUSS

Place the bird on a board, breast downwards, and cut a long slit in the skin of the neck, then a small one across the top, thus forming the letter T. Turn the skin back on either side, pull up the neck and cut it off at the root, not leaving any stump. Lay the bird on its back and take out the crop through the opening. You will find it between the neck bones, like a bag of skin. Turn the bird round and draw it between the tail and the vent an opening large enough to take your thumb and first two fingers. Now hold the bird firmly by the back with the left hand and loosen the entrails with the right hand, being very careful not to press them, for if the gall bladder is broken it will give a bitter taste. Take hold of the gizzard (it is easily found, as it is the one hard entrails) and pull and you will find, as a rule, that the whole of the entrails will come out with it. Put your fingers in again to make sure that nothing has been left. Examine the gall bladder (a little long-shaped green bag) and if intact, the bird need only be wiped inside with a damp cloth, but if the bladder is broken the bird must be thoroughly washed. Now cut off the pinions and truss the bird. The bird can be trussed either with skewers or a trussing-needle threaded with fine string, but the former is the simpler method. Put the bird breast upwards on the board and put the wings in position, turning in the ends. Then press a skewer through the first joint of the wing, then through the bird and through the other wing. See that you have both sides alike.

Draw up the legs into position and put a skewer right through the first joints. Stuff the bird and secure the flap of skin at the neck with a small skewer. If you are not satisfied with the shape of the bird, shape it up in position with your hands and tie a string round to keep it in position. If there has been any down left on the bird after it has been plucked a lighted tapers should be passed quickly over it before it is trussed. Be careful not to burn the skin.

The bird is now ready for the baking tin. Lard it with plenty of dripping and fat bacon before putting it in the oven to roast. A turkey is drawn and trussed in a similar way to a fowl, but the sinews of the legs must first be removed, otherwise the legs would be uneatable. This is not difficult if done in the following way. Break the leg about the foot, and fasten the foot down on a board or table with a strong skewer or bradawl. Pull, and you will find the sinews will come out without much trouble.

For boiling a fowl is drawn in the same way, but the legs are then cut off half-way up. Cut the skin round the leg at this joint. Crack the joint and pull the shank part and you will find the sinews will come with it. Then loosen the skin of the leg from inside the body, working round the leg. Make a small cut across the leg in the drumstick. Press the legs inside with the loosened skin drawn over them. Press the rump in and draw the skin over so that the opening is closed. The truss as for roasting.

Classification of Chicken

Chickens are first classified by age and weight. Young chickens are tender and cook quickly; older chickens need slow cooking to make them tender. For best results, it's important to know which type of chicken to buy for cooking.

Broiler-fryers are young chickens weighing from 1½ to 3½ pounds. Only 7 to 10 weeks old, they yield tender, mildly flavored meat and are best when broiled, fried, or roasted.

Roasters are 4- to 6-pound chickens that are 16 weeks old. As the name implies, they are perfect for roasting and rotisserie cooking.

Capons are young, castrated roosters that weight from 5 to 7 pounds. These richly flavored birds have a higher fat content and yield more meat than roasters.

Stewing Hens are adult chickens from 1 to 1½ years old. They weight from 4½ to 7 pounds and have tough, stringy meat and require prolonged cooking for more than an hour or two to make the meat edible. Stewing hens are excellent for stocks, soups, or stews, since moist-heat preparation tenderizes them and enhances their flavour.

Whole chicken of every type are available with the neck and giblets wrapped separately and stuffed inside. Look for livers and giblets packaged separately in the shops for use in stuffing's, soups, and specialty dishes.

Selection of Chicken

1) Soft fluffy feathers should be all over the body, especially concentrated under the wings.
2) The feathers should be easy to pull out.
3) The skin should be clear and smooth with no bluish tinge spots.
4) The feet should be supple with smooth overlapping scales, and if fresh, moist.
5) Combs and wattle (the skin hanging near the beak) small and well-developed. The comb should be bright red.
6) Conformation or the shape of the bird is important, and the bird should be free from deformity.
7) The eyes should be prominent and clear.
8) It should not have a marked unpleasant smell.

STEPS TO CUT CHICKEN

1. PLUCKING

Place the bird upon the knees with the feathers lying away from you. Beginning with the legs, take a few feathers between the thumb and forefingers, bend them back with a slight jerk in the opposite way to which they grow (this is to break the main quill) and then pull them sharply forward and away.

2. REMOVING THE NECK

Cut a long slip in the skin of the neck, then a small one across the top, thus forming the letter T. Turn the skin back on either side, pull up the neck and cut it off closely at the root. Leave plenty of loose skin, which will be needed to cover the stuffing.

3. DRAWING

First cut an opening between the tail and the vent large enough to insert the thumb and first two fingers. Hold the bird firmly with the left hand and loosen the entrails with the right take hold of the gizzard which is the only hard entrail, and pull; the entrails will all come away easily.

4. SINEWS

Cut the skin round the leg at the first join and pull the shank part very firmly. The sinews will come with it. It is usually only necessary to remove the sinews when the bird is to be boiled, but the sinews of a turkey must always be removed otherwise the legs will be uneatable.

5. SINGEING

At this stage it is sometimes necessary to singe the bird, as some of the close under-feathers or down may have been left behind after plucking. Hold the bird up by the leg and quickly pass a lighted taper all over the body. Care must be taken not to turn the skin or to discolor it.

6. STUFFING

Chickens may be roasted without stuffing, but forcemeat is a great improvement. It is put in at the neck end, inserting as much as will be covered by the loose skin flap left from cutting off the neck. Fasten with a small skewer. An onion may be put in the body of the bird if liked.

7. WINGS

Put the bird, breast upwards, on the board and fold the wings in position by turning in the end under the body. Then press a skewer through the first joint of the wing, then through the bird and through the other wing. See that you have both sides alike. A skewer is sometimes not necessary.

8. LEGS

Fold the legs into position and put a skewer right through the first points. If you are not satisfied with the shape of the bird, press it into position with the hands and tie a string round to keep it in position. The bird is now ready for the baking tin.

CHICKEN CUTS

Picture of the main different cuts of chicken are as follows:

Whole Chicken

Halves

Breast Quarters

Split Breast

Split Breast without Back

Boneless, Skinless Breast

8-Piece Cut

Whole Chicken Wing

Wing Drummettes

Wing Mid Section with Tip

Wing Mid Section

Whole Chicken Leg

Boneless, Skinless Leg

Thigh

Boneless, Skinless Thigh

Drumsticks

Giblets

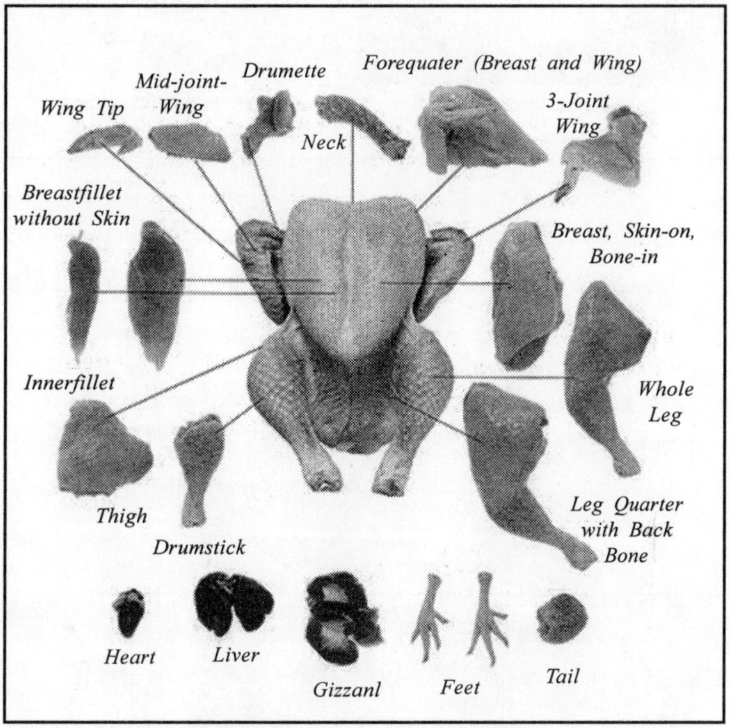

Fig 16.1 Cuts of Chicken

Whole Chickens

Whole Chickens are marketed either fresh or frozen (Fig 16.2).

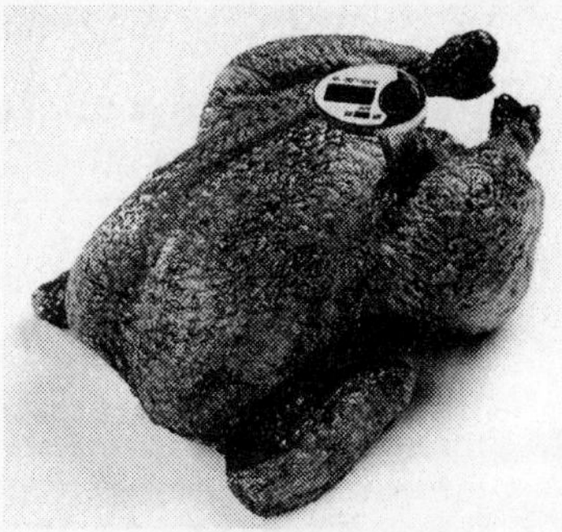

Fig 16.2 Whole Chicken

Halves: The bird is split from front to back through the backbone and keel to produce 2 halves of approximately equal weight (Fig 16.3).

Breast Quarters: Halves may be further cut into which include the wing. A breast quarter, including portions of the back, is all white meat (Fig 16.4).

Split Breast: A breast quarter with the wing removed (Fig 16.5).

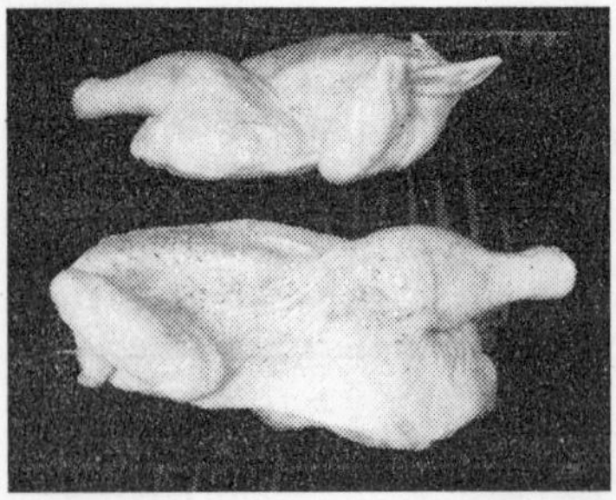

Fig 16.3 Halves of Chicken

Fig 16.4 Breast quarters of Chicken

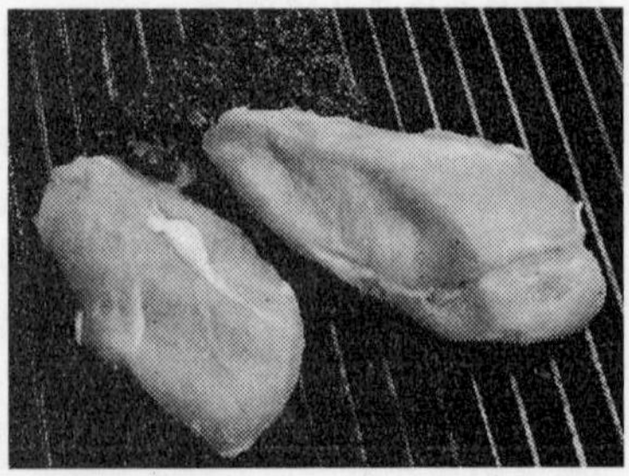

Fig 16.5 Split breast of Chicken

Split Breast without Back: A breast quarter with wing and back portion removed (Fig 16.6).

Boneless, Skinless Breast: Split breast that has been skinned and deboned (Fig. 16.7).

8-Piece Cut: The whole bird is cut into 2 breast halves with ribs and back portion, 2 wings, 2 thighs with back portion and 2 drumsticks. The parts may be packaged together and labelled as whole cut-up chicken. These are usually sold without giblets.

Whole Chicken Wing The Whole Chicken Wing is an all white meat portion composed of three sections; the drumette, mid-section and tip (Fig 16.9).

Wing Drummettes The first section between the shoulder and the elbow (Fig 16.10).

Fig 16.6 Split breast of Chicken without back

Fig 16.7 Boneless breast of Chicken

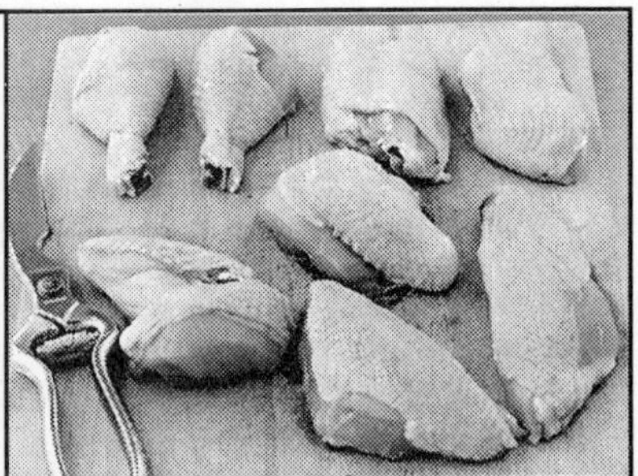

Fig 16.8 Eight pieces of chicken

Wing Mid Section with Tip The flat centre section and the flipper (wing tip) (Fig 16.11).

Wing Mid Section The section between the elbow and the tip, sometimes called the wing flat or mid-joint (Fig 16.12).

Whole Chicken Leg The Whole Chicken Leg is the drumstick-thigh combination. The whole leg differs from the leg quarter in that id does not contain a portion of the back (Fig. 16.13).

Fig. 16.9 Whole Chicken Wing

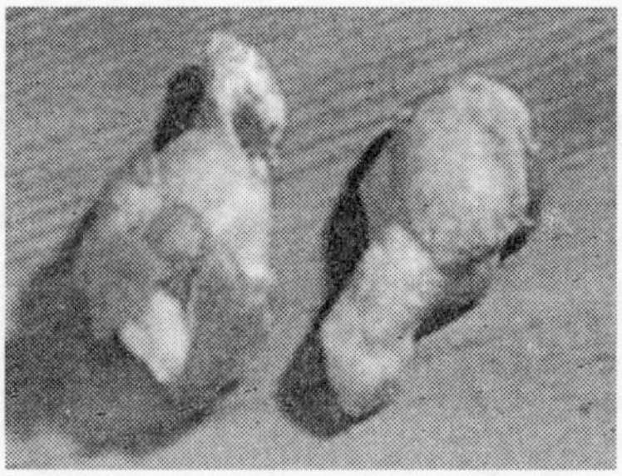

Fig 16.10 Wing drummettes

Fig 16.11 Wing mid section with tip

Fig 16.12 Wing mid section

Fig 16.13 Whole chicken leg

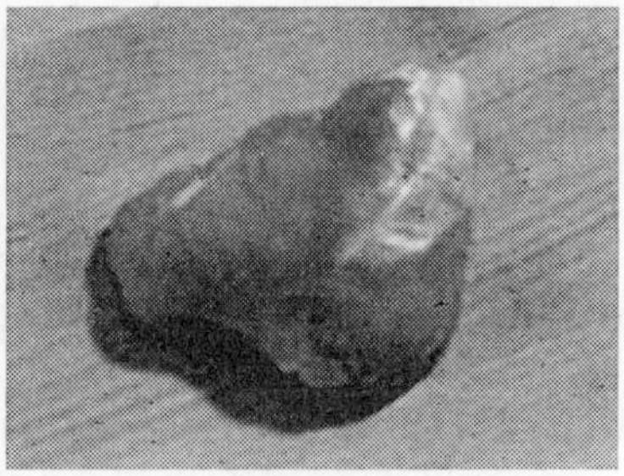

Fig 16.14 Bonesless leg

Boneless, Skinless Leg Whole chicken leg with skin and bone removed (Fig. 16.14).

Thigh The thigh is the portion of the leg above the knee joint (Fig. 16.15).

Boneless, Skinless Thigh Thigh with skin and bone removed (Fig. 16.16).

Drumsticks Drumsticks include the lower portion of the leg quarter (the portion between the knee joint and the hock) (Fig. 16.17).

Giblets Includes heart, liver and neck (Fig. 16.18).

Fig 16.15 Chicken thigh

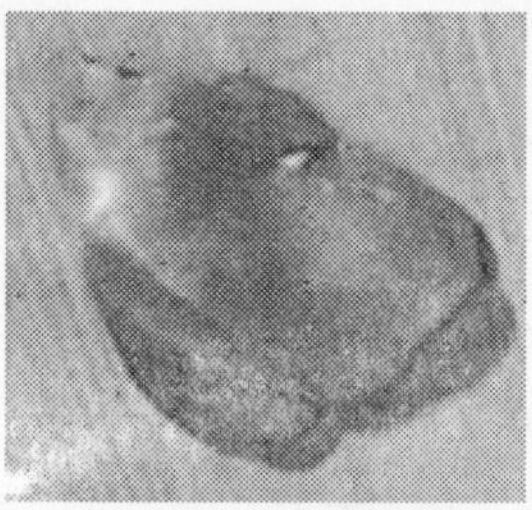

Fig 16.16 Boneless chicken thigh

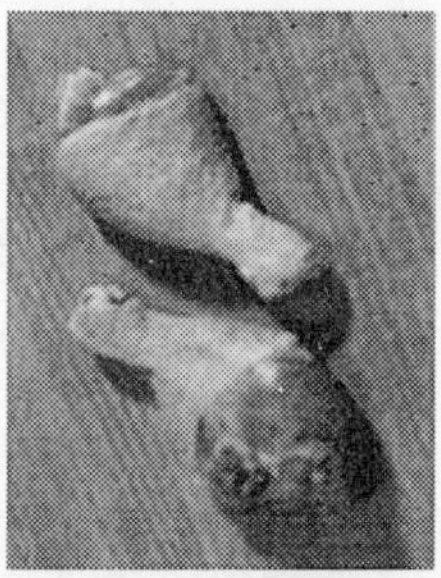

Fig 16.17 Chicken drumsticks

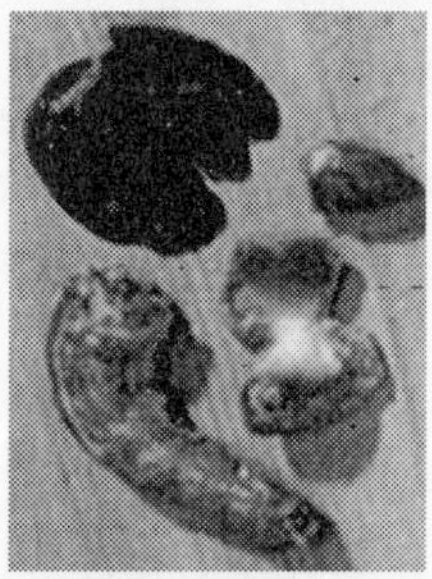

Fig 16.18 Chicken giblets

HOW TO CUT A CHICKEN

This is a basic method for cutting up and disjointing a whole chicken with the least amount of waste.

1. Remove the legs

Place the chicken breast side up on a solid Cutting board. Pull one leg away from the body and cut through the skin between the body and both sides of the thigh.

Bend the whole leg firmly away from the body until the ball of the thighbone pops from the hip socket. Cut between the ball and the socket to separate the leg. Repeat with the other leg.

Fig 16.19 Removal of chicken legs

2. Divide The Legs

Place the chicken leg skin side down on the cutting board. Cut down firmly through the joint between the drumstick and the thigh.

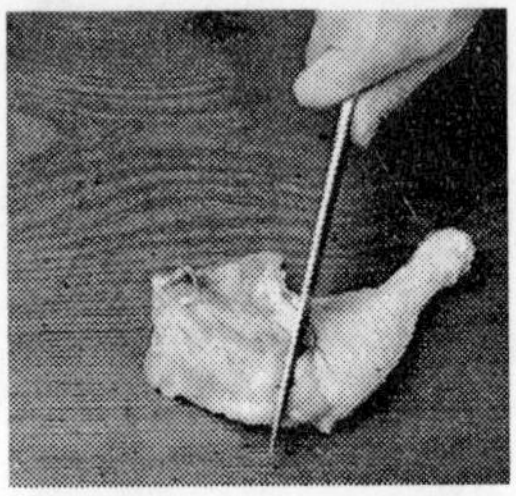

Fig 16.20 The division of chicken leg

3. Remove the Wings

With chicken on it's back, remove wing by cutting inside of wing just over joint. Pull wing away from body and cut from down through the skin and the joint. Repeat with the other wing.

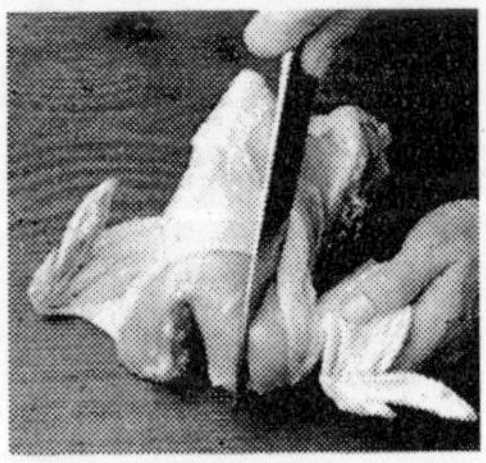

Fig 16.21 Removal of the wings

4.Cut Carcass in Half

Cut through the cavity of the bird from the tail end and slice through the thin area around the shoulder joint. Cut parallel to the backbone and slice the bones of the rib cage. Repeat on the opposite side of the backbone

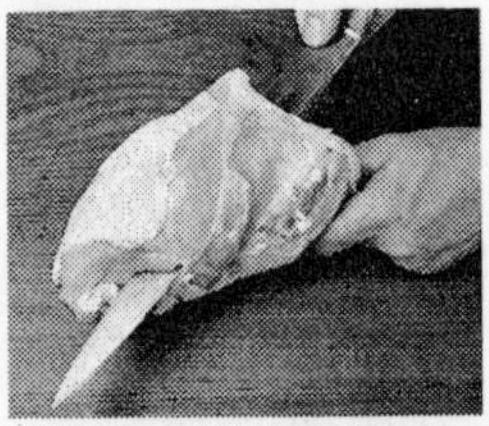

Fig 16.22 Cutting of carcass into half

5.Remove The Breast

Pull apart the breast and the back. Cut down trough the shoulder bones to detach the breast from the back. Cut the back into two pieces by cutting across the backbone where the ribs end.

6. Cut Breast In Half

You may leave the breast whole if your recipe requires. To cut in in half, use a strong, steady pressure and cut downward along the length of the breastbone to separate the breast into two pieces (Fig. 16.24).

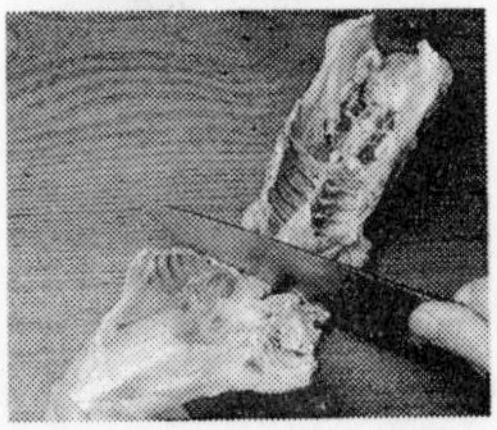

Fig 16.23 Removal of the breast

Fig 16.24 Cutting of breast

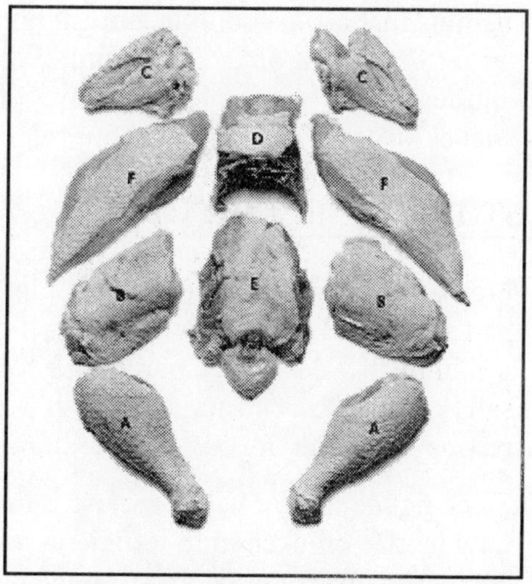

Fig 16.25 Standard cut of chicken
The picture on the left shows a whole chicken cut in 10 pieces.
a. Legs, b. thighs, c. wings, d. part of back portion. e. tail end of back portion. f. breasts, and c. wings.

COOKING OF CHICKEN

Chicken is incredibly versatile and can be cooked in many different ways. Each method of cooking helps bring out the individuality of the pieces and flavors of chicken.

Baking—Baking is an oven-based technique that is considered to be among the healthiest methods for cooking chicken.

Poaching—Poaching is a technique that cooks chicken slowly and gently in a simmering, but not boiling, liquid that covers the food. The poaching liquid may be flavored or seasoned.

Browning—Browning chicken is the first step in many recipes for cooking chicken.

Braising—Braising is a moist-heat cooking method used to tenderize tough cuts of meat. Chicken is normally browned first and then braised.

Stir-Fry—Stir-frying quickly cooks bite-size pieces of chicken over very high heat in a small amount of oil.

Roasting—Roasting is a technique often performed in the broiler.

CHICKEN NUTRITIONAL FACTS

Chicken is high in protein, low in fat and low in cholesterol, making it a good selection for a healthy diet. Our bodies require a certain amount of protein daily and the body does not store protein so we need to replenish it each day. A 3-ounce portion of chicken provides a large amount of our daily requirement for protein. Our bodies also require fat in our diet, which allows us to absorb vitamins that are fat-soluble and energy producing. But, too much fat is not healthy. Chicken is lower in fat than most other meats and over half of the fat is unsaturated fat, the type that helps lower cholesterol. The white meat is lower in fat than the dark meat of the chicken but the dark meat is higher in iron, an important nutrient for a healthy body.

SAFE STORAGE OF CHICKEN

- Fresh, raw chicken can be stored in its original wrap for up to two days in the coldest part of the refrigerator. However, freeze chicken immediately if you do not plan to use it within two days after purchasing. You can freeze most chicken in its original packaging safely for up to two months; if you plan to freeze it longer, consider doublewrapping or rewrapping with freezer paper, aluminum foil, or plastic wrap.
- Stocking the freezer with boneless, skinless chicken breasts and thighs can be a real timesaver. Divide the chicken into efficient, meal-size portions and package for freezing. These convenient packages defrost and cook quickly and eliminate leftovers.
- Airtight packaging is the key to freezing chicken successfully. When freezing whole chickens, remove and rinse giblets (if any) and pat dry with paper towels. Trim away any excess fat from the chicken. Tightly wrap, label, date, and freeze both chicken and giblets in separate freezer-strength plastic, paper, or foil wraps.
- Thaw frozen chicken, wrapped, in the refrigerator for best results. Thawing times for frozen chicken can vary depending on how thoroughly frozen the chicken is and whether the chicken is whole or cut up

RECEIPES OF CHICKEN

To Roast Poultry

Roast Fowl Or Chicken

Time: 45 minutes to 1½ hours according to the age of the fowl. Temperature: Gas, electricity, 450° F.

Ingredients	*Quantity*
Chicken	1 no.
Slices of fat bacon	50 gram
Dripping for hasting	50ml
Forcemeat (optional)	50 gram
Onion (optional)	50 gram

Fig 16.26 Roasted chicken

Method:

1. Fowls and chickens may be roasted without being stuffed, but forcemeat is a great improvement.
2. Herb, sausage, mushroom and chestnut are all suitable; it is just a matter of taste.
3. Having prepared the bird for roasting, put in the forcemeat at the neck end, putting in as much as the loose skin will cover, fasten it with a small skewer—put a little dripping and an onion in the body of the bird if the flavour is liked.
4. Cover the breast with fat bacon, heat some dripping in a baking tin, put in the bird, place it in a hot oven, and baste well during the cooking to keep it moist. Time will depend entirely on the age of the bird—quite a young chicken will only need forty-five minutes, a fully grown fowl!
5. One and a half hours. Remove the bacon five minutes before the bird is done, to brown the breast.
6. Turkeys and guinea fowl are roasted in the same way, also geese and duck, but the two latter are stuffed with sage and onion, and the bacon is omitted.

Gravy For Roast Poultry

- This is far more important than most cooks realize. Remember it more or less flavors the whole meal. So it is necessary that it should agree with the roast and enhance and not detract from its natural flavour.
- For poultry, the foundation of the stock should be the giblets of the bird.
- The Giblets—bunch of savory Herbs such as thyme, Marjoram and Parsley— Onion—salt spoon Salt—sprinkling of pepper—teaspoon Brown roux—dessertspoon,Mushroom.
- Wash the giblets, and cut them up and put them in a stewpan with the herbs and seasoning.
- Pour over 1 pint of cold water, bring to the boil, remove any scum, and simmer for two hours. Pour off all the fat from the baking tin in which the bird was cooked, strain into it ½ pint of the giblet gravy, a teaspoon of brown roux or a teaspoon of flour mixed with a teaspoon of liquid butter, add a dessertspoon of mushroom catsup and a few drops of browning, if necessary. Boil three minutes in baking tin, stir well and strain into hot tureen.

Blanquette of Chicken

Time: 1 ½ hours. Temperature: moderate Enough for 4 persons.

Ingredients	*Quantity*
Chicken	1 no
Carrot	100 gram
Onion	100 gram

Celery	50 gram
Clove	5 gram
Peppercorns	2 gram
Mace	2 gram
Parsley	10 gram
Thyme	2 gram
White stock	1 litre
Butter	20 gram
Flour	100 gram
Yolks	2 no
Eggs	2 no
Cream	100 ml

Method

1. Cut the chicken into neat joints. Into a stewpan put the carrot, onion and celery, all thinly sliced, the clove, peppercorns, mace and herbs.
2. Place the joints of chicken upon this. Bring the stock to the boil and pour it in. Add salt if it is unseasoned, then cover closely and simmer for half an hour.
3. Melt the butter in another stewpan, and stir in the flour. Stir for four minutes over very gentle heat. Remove it from the fire and gradually strain in the stock from the chicken. Mix well until it is perfectly smooth.
4. Then stir over gentle heat until it boils. Draw to the side of the stove or place over a very low gas where it will simmer very gently, and leave for half an hour.
5. Stir in the lightly beaten yolks of the eggs and the cream.Strain it into the pan containing the joints of chicken. Make very hot and serve.

Fricassee of Chicken

Time: about 20 minutes. Temperature: moderate.

Ingredients	*Quantity*
Boiled chicken	500 gram
Butter	20 gram
Flour	30 gram
Yolks of eggs	2 no

Lemon juice	10 ml
Cream	50 ml
Mashed potatoes	100 gram
Potatoes	50 gram
Mushrooms	50 gram

Fig 16.27 Fricassee of chicken

Method

1. Melt the butter in a small pan, add the flour, and stir over gentle heat until smooth. Do not let the mixture burn.
2. Then add gradually ½ pint of liquor in which the chicken was boiled and stir until it has boiled for five minutes.
3. Beat the yolk of an egg, stir in the lemon juice and cream and add this to the sauce.
4. Cut the chicken in neat joints and heat them in the sauce. If you are using a fresh chicken this is not necessary, as it will be hot in the broth.
5. Turn on to a hot dish. Garnish with mashed potato pressed through a forcing bag, and some mushrooms which have been fried in a little butter; or the fricassee may be served plain.

Game

Though game is an expensive luxury at the beginning of the season, it is the reverse once it becomes plentiful. One just needs to watch the market and know how to buy. Only young birds should be roasted, and these may be recognized by the quill feather in the wings: in young birds these are soft and not fully grown. The legs should be smooth and the toes soft and supple. If your game is a present, you will have to pluck, draw and truss it. Grouse, partridges, pheasants, black cock, and capercailzie are drawn and trussed in the same way as a fowl, the only difference being that with such a small bird as grouse you cannot put your hand inside to draw it. For these, after cutting off the head, loosen the inside at the neck and squeeze out the entrails. With the larger birds—partridge and pheasant—you can put in your hand.

Be careful when removing the head to leave enough skin to skewer back. Then bring the legs up close to the breast, and pass a trussing needle and thin string through the pinions and thick part of the thigh; tie round securely. To truss snipe, plovers, quails and woodcock, after clucking the birds, wipe them outside with a clean damp cloth, but do not draw them. Twist the legs up close to the body, skin the neck and head and bring its beak round under a wing. Wild duck, teal and widgeon are trussed like chickens, but the pinions are cut off at the first joint like geese.

Cooking of game

To braise game: Put the giblets into a saucepan with two onions, a little bunch of sweet herbs, a small blade of mace, two bay leaves, and ½ pint of stock or water. Cover the bird with fat bacon and put it in on the giblets. Cover closely and simmer until the bird is quite tender, one to two hours, according to age. Remove the fat bacon from the breast about ten minutes before it is done. Then strain off the liquor and skim off any fat. Put it in a saucepan and boil rapidly until it is reduced to a gill. Pour this over the bird and serve.

Grilled Game: Cut the birds in half and wipe the inside with qa damp cloth. Brush them over with liquid butter, sprinkle with salt and a little cayenne or white pepper as preferred. Place them on a hot, well greased grid-iron over a clear, bright fire or under a grill and cook about eight minutes each side for a bird the size of a partridge, twelve minutes each side for pheasant. Serve with maitre d'hotel butter or see special sauce for game.

GAME VARIETIES

Game varieties could be broadly grouped into two: birds and animals:

Quail Quails have dark meat that's quite tasty. They're very lean, so they are generally bard before roasting or marinated grilling. Quail are commonly eaten complete with the bones, since these are easily chewed and the small size of the bird makes it inconvenient to remove them.

Wild Duck The meat of a duck is mostly on the breast and the legs. The meat of the legs is darker and somewhat fattier than the meat of the breasts, although the breast meat is darker than the breast meat of a chicken or a turkey. Being waterfowl, ducks have a layer of heat-insulating subcutaneous fat between the skin and the meat. Boneless duck breast is also called "magret" and can be grilled like steak, usually leaving the skin and fat on. Internal organs such as heart and kidneys may also be eaten; the liver in particular is often used as a substitute for goose liver in foie gras.

Partridge These small, plump birds are related to pheasants, and very tasty. Varieties include the chukar, redlegged partridge or French partridge, and grey partridge or English partridge.

Pigeon Pigeon meat is dark and very tender. Varieties include the squab, which is a young pigeon that's never flown, the wood pigeon, rock dove, and ring dove.

Venison The term venison applies to deer meat, elk meat, moose meat, caribou meat, and reindeer meat, all of which can be used interchangeably. Venison is very lean, so it's important not to overcook it. The best cuts are from the back strap, or loin area.

Alligator Alligator meat is lean and mild and people say it tastes like a combination of pork, chicken, and rabbit. The best meat comes from the tail.

Antelope Antelope are related to goats, but the meat resembles strongly-flavored venison.

Bear Compared with beef, bear is high in protein and low in fat and calories. Make sure you cook it thoroughly— it's possible to contract trichinosis from undercooked bear meat.

Bison Buffalo (Bison) meat tastes like beef, but it's a lot leaner. Tougher cuts are cooked very slowly over low heat. Meat is pale coloured and slightly sweetish.

Rabbit Rabbit is low in fat and similar in taste and texture to chicken.

Boar Boar (also known as wild boar) meat is similar to pork, only leaner, redder, and stronger-tasting. It should be cooked thoroughly, it's possible to contract trichinosis from undercooked boar meat.

Grouse This is possibly the most choice of all game birds, with flavorful, dark meat. Varieties include the ptarmigan, capercaillie, and blackcock.

Kangaroo Kangaroo meat is becoming increasingly popular in Australia. It has a very strong, gamy flavour that's a bit like venison. It's very lean, so overcooking should be

avoided.

Turtle (also called cooter) Turtle meat is very flavorful though it's somewhat chewy. It often goes into soups

LEARNING OUTCOME

Poultry is universally loved and as widely available at its flavorful best when freshly killed, it does not require lengthy preparation and may appear as easily in a pleasant dish redolent of garlic as in an elegantly sauce creation suited to champagne taste. Similar to other meats, poultry must undergo a mandatory inspection for whole sameness. Depending on the various factors such as carcass shape and the ration of meat to bone. Once inspect, birds are plucked cleaned, chilled and packaged. Poultry includes the different varieties and sizes of chicken, turkey ducks; geese and guinea fowls. The breast of a young fowl is gristle at the end, and this can be easily felt. If it is all hard bone, it is not suitable for roasting. The comb of a young cockered is bright red and quite smooth, and the legs are smooth also, and spurs quite small. A young hen's comb is bright, soft and small, and the legs smooth. Choose poultry that is plump without being over-fat. Chickens are first classified by age and weight. Young chickens are tender and cook quickly; older chickens need slow cooking to make them tender. For best results, it's

important to know which type of chicken to buy for cooking. Chicken is incredibly versatile and can be cooked in many different ways. Each method of cooking helps bring out the individuality of the pieces and flavors of chicken. Chicken is high in protein, low in fat and low in cholesterol, making it a good selection for a healthy diet. Our bodies require a certain amount of protein daily and the body does not store protein so we need to replenish it each day. A 3-ounce portion of chicken

LESSON END ACTIVITY

- Bring a whole chicken from the market and cut according to the instruction given in this chapter.
- Collect the information on how varieties of chicken available in the market.

QUESTIONS FOR DISCUSSION

1. Explain the term poultry and its types.
2. Mention the name of the popular breed of poultry.
3. Explain the procedure to choosing the quality of poultry.
4. How to draw and truss of the poultry.
5. Explain the classification of chicken.
6. Explain the procedure of selection of chicken.
7. Explain the steps to cut the chicken.
8. Mention the name of the different chicken cuts.
9. Explain the procedure to how to cut chicken.
10. Explain the different methods of cooking chicken.
11. Explain the procedure of storage of chicken.
12. What are the nutritional facts in chicken.
13. Explain the term game.
14. Explain the different cooking method used for games.
15. Explain different game varieties.

STATE TRUE AND FALSE

- Poultry caries a layer of fat under the skin.
- Chicken will not brown quite as well when skinned.
- A poussin is a very young chicken, and it has a very delicate flavour and very little fat.
- The breast of a young fowl is gristle.
- Roasters chicken are 4- to 6-pound chickens that are 16 weeks old
- Capons chicken are young, castrated roosters that weigh from 9 to 10 pounds
- Chickens are first classified by age and weight.
- Chicken is high in protein, low in fat and low in cholesterol
- Fresh, raw chicken can be stored in its original wrap for up to two days
- Quails have dark meat that's quite tasty.

KEY TERMS

* Fowls
* Giblets
* Lean
* Partridge
* Pheasant
* Plucking

Chapter 17

Pork

After studying this chapter, the student must know

- Introductions
- Standards cut off pork and with their use
- Ham, Bacon and Gammon
- Standard pork of recipes.

PORK

Pork, to be digestible, needs to be very well cooked. Underdone pork is dangerous. It should be so well done that there is not a tinge of pink in the gravy that runs from it. It is in season from September to April, and it is not advisable to eat it during the summer months. Always buy dairy fed pork. The skin should be thin, pale and cool to the touch, the lean finely grained, and the fat quite white and firm. Choose it with a moderate amount of fat. Very lean pork is poor in flavour; very fat port is wasteful.

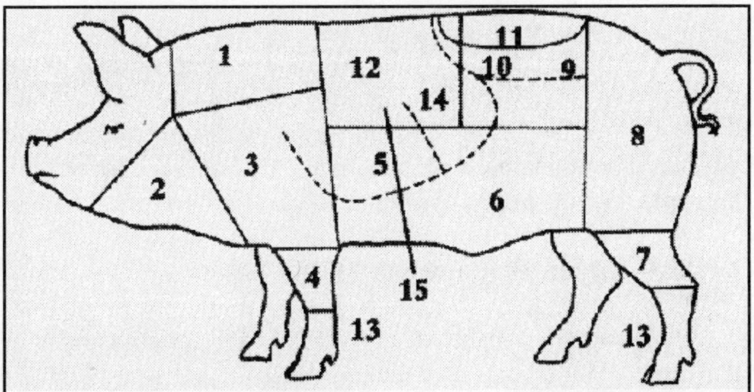

1. Chine, Neck
2. Pork, Cheek
3. Shoulder
4. Foreleg
5. Forelib
6. Belly, Lean
7. Hindleg
8. Ham, Hind quarter
9. Loin
9. Pork cutlet with fillet
11. Fillet
12. Cutlet
13. Foot
14. Middle pork rib
15. Lard, pork fat

Fig 17.1 The pork's cuts

Beware of pork with very thick skin; it will be old and tough.

STANDARD CUTS OFF PORK

Pork Shoulder Arm Picnic (Fig 17.2)

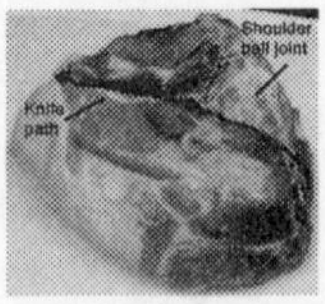

Fig 17.2 Pork shoulder arm picnic

Pork shoulder arm picnic contains arm bone, shank bone, and a portion of blade bone. It also contains shoulder muscles interspersed with fat. The shank and part of the lower area are covered with skin. It is usually prepared by roasting.

Pork Shoulder Arm Roast (Fig 17.3)

Fig 17.3 Pork shoulder arm roast

Pork shoulder arm roast is cut from pork shoulder arm picnic. The shank is removed, leaving the round arm bone and the meaty part of the arm picnic. The outside is covered with a thin layer of fat. Pork shoulder arm roast is usually prepared by roasting.

Pork Shoulder Arm Steak (Fig 17.4)

Fig 17.4 Pork shoulder arm steak

Pork shoulder arm steak has the same muscle and bone structure as pork shoulder arm roast, only cut thinner. It contains round arm bone and the meaty part of the arm picnic. The outside is covered with a thin layer of fat. It is usually prepared by braising or pan-frying.

Pork Shoulder Blade (Boston) Roast (Fig 17.5)

Fig 17.5 Pork shoulder blade

Pork shoulder blade (Boston) roast contains the top portion of whole shoulder, the blade bone exposed on two sides, and some intramuscular fat. It is usually prepared by roasting.

Pork Shoulder Blade Steak (Fig 17.6)

Fig 17.6 Pork shoulder blade steak

Pork shoulder blade steak is cut from pork shoulder blade Boston roast. It contains blade bone and several muscles and is usually prepared by braising, broiling, grilling, panbroiling, or panfrying.

Pork Cubed Steaks (Fig 17.7)

Pork cubed steaks are square or rectangular. The cubed effect is made by a machine that tenderizes the meat mechanically. The steaks may be made from muscles of several primal cuts and are usually prepared by braising, broiling, grilling, or panbroiling.

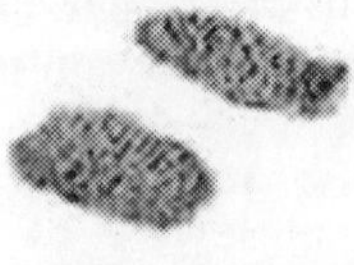

Fig 17.7 Pork cube steaks

Pork Cubes for Kebabs (Fig 17.8)

Pork cubes for kabab are boneless, lean, and cut into cubes. They are usually prepared by broiling, grilling, braising, panfrying, or roasting.

Fig 17.8 Pork cube kebabs

Pork Hocks (Fig 17.9)

Pork hocks are cut from picnic shoulder and are similar to pork shank cross cuts. They contain two round shank bones exposed at both ends and are usually prepared by braising or by cooking in liquid.

Fig 17.9 Pork hock

Pork Loin Blade Roast (Fig 17.10)

Pork loin blade roast contains part of the blade bone, rib bones, and backbone. It also contains large loin eye muscle surrounded by several smaller muscles. It is usually prepared by roasting.

Fig 17.10 Pork loin blade roast

Pork Loin Blade Chops (Fig 17.11)

Pork loin blade chops are cut from the blade end of loin and contain the same muscle and bone structure as pork loin blade roast, including part of the blade bone, rib bones, backbone, large loin eye muscle and several smaller muscles. Pork loin blade chops are usually prepared by braising, broiling, grilling, panbroiling, or panfrying.

Fig 17.11 Pork loin blade chops

Pork Loin (Fig 17.12)

Pork loin country-style ribs are made by splitting the blade end of loin into halves lengthwise. The ribs contain part of the loin eye muscle and either rib bones or backbones. They are usually prepared by roasting, baking, braising, broiling, grilling, or by cooking in liquid.

Fig 17.12 Pork loin rib

Pork Loin Back Ribs (Fig 17.13)

Pork loin back ribs are cut from the blade and center sections of loin. They contain rib bones, meat between the ribs called finger meat, with a layer of meat covering the ribs that come from the loin eye muscle. Pork loin back ribs are usually prepared by roasting, baking, braising, broiling, grilling, or by cooking in liquid.

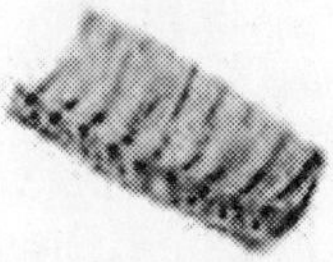

Fig 17.13 Pork loin back ribs

Pork Loin Center Rib Roast (Fig 17.14)

Pork loin center rib roast is a cut from the center rib area of loin. It contains loin eye muscle and rib bones, and is usually prepared by roasting.

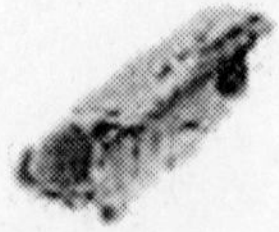

Fig 17.14 Pork loin centre rib roast

Pork Loin Rib Chops (Center Cut Chops) (Fig 17.15)

Pork loin rib chops, also called center cut chops, contain eye muscle and backbone. Rib bone may also be present, depending on the thickness of the cut. Fat covers the outside edge. These chops are usually prepared by braising, broiling, grilling, panbroiling, or panfrying.

Fig 17.15 Pork loin rib chop

Pork Loin Center Loin Roast (Fig 17.16)

Pork loin center loin roast is a cut from the center of loin. It contains rib eye, tenderloin muscles, rib bones, T-shaped bones, and a thin fat covering. It is usually prepared by roasting.

Fig 17.16 Pork loin centre

Pork Loin Top Loin Chops (Fig 17.17)

Pork loin top loin chops contain top loin muscles and backbone running the length of the cut. The tenderloin is removed, and there is an outside covering of fat. These chops are usually prepared by braising, broiling, grilling, panbroiling, or panfrying.

Fig 17.17 Pork loin top loin

Pork Loin Butterfly Chops (Fig 17.18)

Pork loin butterfly chops are a double chop, about two inches thick, which comes from the boneless loin eye muscle. It is sliced in half to form two sides resembling a butterfly. Butterfly chops are usually prepared by braising, broiling, grilling, panbroiling, or panfrying.

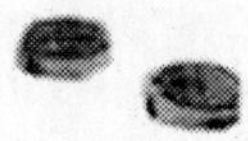

Fig 17.18 Pork loin butterfly chops

Pork Loin Top Loin Roast Boneless (Double) (Fig 17.19)

Pork loin top loin roast boneless (double) is two boneless loins reversed and tied together with the fat side facing out. It is used to make boneless roast and is usually prepared by roasting.

Fig 17.19 Pork loin top loin

Pork Loin Chops (Fig 17.20)

Pork loin chops are cut from the sirloin end of loin. The eye muscle and tenderloin is divided by a T-shaped bone. The chops also contain backbone and are usually prepared by braising, broiling, grilling, panbroiling, or panfrying.

Fig 17.20 Pork loin chops

Pork Loin Sirloin Roast (Fig 17.21)

Pork loin sirloin roast contains hip bone and backbone. The largest muscle is the eye of loin, separated from the smaller tenderloin muscles by finger bones. It is usually prepared by roasting.

Fig 17.21 Pork loin sirloin

Pork Loin Sirloin Chops (Fig 17.22)

Pork loin sirloin chops are cut from the sirloin end of loin. They have the same muscle and bone structure as pork loin sirloin roast, containing hip bone and backbone. The largest muscle is the eye of loin, separated from the smaller tenderloin muscles by finger bones. Pork loin sirloin chops are usually prepared by braising, broiling, grilling, panbroiling, or panfrying.

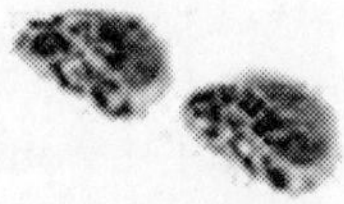

Fig 17.22 Pork loin sirloin chops

Pork Loin Sirloin Cutlets (Fig 17.23)

Pork loin sirloin cutlets are boneless slices cut from the sirloin end of loin after the tenderloin, hip bone, and backbone are removed. They are usually prepared by braising, broiling, grilling, panbroiling, or panfrying.

Fig 17.23 Pork loin sirloin cutlets

Pork Loin Tenderloin Whole (Fig 17.24)

Pork loin tenderloin whole is a boneless cut taken from the inside of loin. The largest end is round and gradually tapers to the thin flat end. Very tender, it is usually prepared by roasting, baking, braising, broiling, or grilling.

Fig 17.24 Pork loin tenderloin

Pork Spareribs (Fig 17.25)

Pork spareribs are cut from the side. They contain long rib bones with a thin covering of meat on the outside and between the ribs. They may also contain rib cartilage. Pork spareribs are usually prepared by roasting, baking, broiling, grilling, or by cooking in liquid.

Fig 17.25 Pork spareribs

Fresh Side Pork (Fig 17.26)

Fresh side pork is the same cut as slab bacon but it is fresh. It is taken from the section of side that remains after the loin and spareribs are removed. The layered lean from fat is generally used as a seasoning. Fresh side pork is usually prepared by cooking in liquid.

Fig 17.26 Fresh side pork

Pork Leg (Fresh Ham) Whole (Fig 17.27)

Fig 17.27 Pork leg

Pork leg (fresh ham) whole is a bone-in hind leg, usually covered with skin and fat about halfway up the leg. It is usually prepared by roasting.

Pork Leg (Fresh Ham) Shank Portion (Fig 17.28)

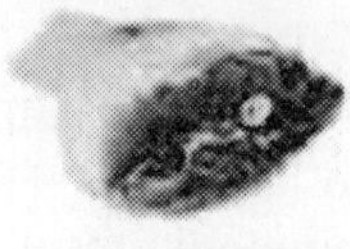

Fi 17.28 Pork leg shank

Pork leg (fresh ham) shank portion is the lower portion of the leg. It contains shank bone and part of the femur bone. Skin covers the shank and a small portion of the outside muscle. It is usually prepared by roasting or by cooking in liquid.

Ground Pork (Fig 17.29)

Fig 17.29 Ground pork

Ground pork is unseasoned and ground from wholesale cuts that are generally in limited demand. It is also made from lean trimmings and sold in bulk form. Ground pork is usually prepared by broiling, grilling, panbroiling, panfrying, roasting, or baking.

Smoked Pork Shoulder Picnic Whole (Fig 17.30)

Fig 17.30 Smoked pork

Smoked pork shoulder picnic whole has the same muscle and bone structure as fresh pork shoulder arm picnic. In addition, it is cured and smoked. It contains arm bone, shank bone, and a portion of blade bone with shoulder muscles interspersed with fat. The shank and a part of the lower area are covered with skin. It is usually prepared by roasting, baking, or by cooking in liquid.

Smoked Pork Shoulder Roll (Fig 17.31)

Fig 17.31 Smoked pork shoulder

Smoked pork shoulder roll is the cured and smoked meaty boneless eye of pork shoulder blade Boston roast. It is usually prepared by roasting, baking, or by cooking in liquid.

Smoked Pork Hocks (Fig 17.32)

Fig 17.32 Smoked pork hocks

Smoked pork hocks contain two round shank bones exposed at both ends. They are oval-shaped, two to three inches thick, cured, and smoked. They are usually prepared by braising or by cooking in liquid.

Smoked Pork Loin Canadian-Style Bacon (Fig 17.33)

Smoked pork loin Canadian-style bacon is made from boneless loin, a single elongated muscle with little fat. Cured and smoked, it is usually prepared by roasting, baking (if sliced), broiling, grilling, panbroiling, or panfrying.

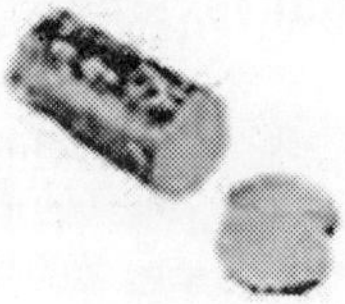

Fig 17.33 Smoked pork loin

Smoked Pork Loin Rib Chops (Fig 17.34)

Smoked pork loin rib chops have the same muscle and bone structure as fresh pork loin rib chops, but they are also cured and smoked. They contain loin eye muscle and backbone. The rib bone may also be present. They are usually prepared by roasting, baking, broiling, grilling, panbroiling, or panfrying.

Fig 17.34 Smoked pork loin rib

Smoked Pork Loin Chops (Fig 17.35)

Smoked pork loin chops have the same muscle and bone structure as fresh pork loin chops, but they are also cured and smoked. They are cut from the sirloin end of loin and contain eye muscle and tenderloin divided by a T-shaped backbone. They are usually prepared by roasting, baking, broiling, grilling, panbroiling, or panfrying.

Fig 17.35 Smoked pork loin chops

Smoked Ham Whole (Fig 17.36)

Smoked ham whole has the same muscle and bone structure as pork leg (fresh ham) whole, but it is also cured and smoked. It contains the bone-in hind leg. It is usually prepared by roasting or baking.

Fig 17.36 Smoked ham whole

Smoked Ham Shank Portion (Fig 17.37)

Smoked ham shank portion has the same muscle and bone structure as pork leg (fresh ham) shank portion, but it is also cured and smoked. The lower potion of the leg, it contains shank bone and part of the femur bone. It is usually prepared by roasting or baking.

Fig 17.37 Smoked ham shank

Smoked Ham Rump Portion (Fig 17.38)

Smoked ham rump portion is a portion of cured and smoked ham that contains the aitchbone and part of the leg bone. A thin layer of fat covers the outer surface. It is usually prepared by roasting or baking.

Fig 17.38 Smoked ham rump

Smoked Ham Center Slice (Fig 17.39)

Smoked ham center slice is cut from the center portion of cured, smoked ham. It contains top, bottom, tip muscles, and round bone. It is usually prepared by broiling, grilling, panbroiling, panfrying, roasting, or baking.

Fig 17.39 Smoked ham slice

Slab Bacon (Fig 17.40)

Slab bacon is cured and smoked side. It contains steaks of lean and fat on one side. The other side may be covered with skin. Slab bacon is usually prepared by broiling (if sliced), panbroiling, panfrying, roasting, or baking.

Fig 17.40 Slab bacon

Sliced Bacon (Fig 17.41)

Sliced bacon is sliced from slab bacon. It may be shingled with the outer skin removed. It is usually prepared by broiling, panbroiling, panfrying, roasting, or baking.

Fig 17.41 Sliced bacon

Sausage Links (Fig 17.42)

Sausage links are made from ground, fresh meat and with seasonings such as salt, pepper, and sage. These are stuffed into casings and shaped into links. Sausage links are usually prepared by braising, panfrying, roasting, or baking.

Fig 17.42 Sausages links

DIFFERENCE BETWEEN HAM BACON, AND GAMMON

Ham is a pig's hind leg, first cut off the carcass and then smoked, salted or dried (or a combination of these) for preservation. Gammon also comes from the hind leg but it is cured as part of a side of bacon and cut off after wards. Gammon may be smoked separately or left unsmoked but it is not matured long enough to have a strong ham flavour and does not keep for as long as ham, which is generally cured more slowly. While some hams are meant for further cooking, some such as Parma and Bayonne hams are simply eaten in the 'raw' cured state, having been salted and then dried over several months to preserve the flesh.

Hams may also be smoked over a slow fire, and the different types of wood used, such as beech, juniper or oak, will each produce a distinctive flavour. Unsmoked hams are also known as green hams and have a milder flavour.

You can buy an uncooked whole ham to bake as a special dish, but in most stores, the ham is sold cooked and sliced, and is used for salads and sandwiches, or included in recipes where it just needs to be heated through. Gammon can be hard to find, but is available from specialist butchers especially if they sell traditional British cuts. It is sold in joints, rashers or steaks for cooking at home

BACON

Bacon is any of certain cuts of meat taken from the sides, belly or back of a pig that may be cured and/or smoked. Meat from other animals may also be cured or otherwise repared to resemble bacon, such as beef, lamb, chicken, goat or turkey bacon. In continental Europe, it is used primarily in cubes (lardons) as a cooking ingredient valued both as a source of fat and for its flavour

ROASTED PORK

The leg or loin is generally chosen for roasting, and the skin must be well scored. A leg is scored round and round in narrow rows from the knuckle; a loin the way of the chop bones. The crackling is one of the tit-bits of roast pork, but often we find when it comes to table it is hard, tough and uneatable. This is easily prevented by brushing it well over with salad oil before putting it into the oven. It will then be crisp, but not tough. The joint must be put into a hot oven, which should be kept at a fairly fierce beat for ten minutes, then slackened to moderate until the meat is thoroughly done through, basting it occasionally to keep it moist. Allow twenty-five minutes for each pound, and twenty minutes over. When cooking pork in the oven it is a good plan to wrap it in greaseproof paper.

Pork must be served very hot. Do not start dishing up until the dish, plates and gravy tureen are all hot. Put the joint on the dish, and keep it hot while you make the gravy. Slowly pour off all the fat from the dripping pan, leaving just the brown sediment at the bottom. Add to this half a saltspoon of salt, and ½ pint of boiling water or broth made from the knuckle bone, stand the pan over gentle heat, and stir whilst it boils for a minute, scraping every particle of meat essence from the bottom of the tin. Strain into a hot tureen. Serve sage and onion and apple sauce with roast pork.

Boiled Pork

Time: about 25 minutes to the lb. and 25 minutes oven. Temperature: low.

Ingredients	*Quantity*
Leg of pork	1kg
Parsnip	100 gram
Carrot	100 gram
Onion	100 gram
Strip of celery	50 gram
Pease pudding	100 gram

Method

1. Wash the joint well. Prepare the vegetables and cut them in strips.

2. Any kinds may be used. Put them with the pork into a stewpan and cover with cold water if the pork is well salted, if only slightly salted use warm water, but not hot.
3. Bring slowly to the boil, then simmer very gently until the meat is quite tender. Serve with pease pudding.
4. Place the vegetables round the meat, and serve some of the broth in a tureen. If to be eaten cold, leave the meat in the water until it is cold.

Note: Salt meat, especially pork, needs very careful cooking. The secret of success is slow simmering. If allowed to boil it will be hard and tough, if cooked at a slow simmer it should be soft as marrow. The time must vary according to the thickness of the joint. A thick leg will need thirty minutes to the pound. A whole leg is too large a joint for a small family; a good plan is to ask your butcher to put the knuckle in pickle for a week and roast the remainder.

Faggots

Time: 45 minutes. Temperature: Gas, Electricity 450° F.

Ingredients	*Quantity*
Pigs liver	400 gram
Pork fat or bacon	50 gram
Onions	100 gram
Sage leaves	10 gram
Fresh herbs	10 gram
Dried herbs	5 gram
Bread slice	2 no
Salt and pepper	15 gram
Pig caul	30 gram

Method

1. Remove any hard crusts from the bread and cut it in small pieces. Cover it with warm water, and when quite soft drain off the water, press the bread as dry as possible and beat it smooth with a fork. Wash and dry the liver.
2. Remove any rind from the bacon (either bacon or pork must be all fat), then cut liver and bacon into small pieces, and mix them with the onions, peeled and sliced. Put these through a mincer.
3. To the bread add the herbs finely chopped and a good seasoning of salt and pepper. Now add the minced meats, and when thoroughly mixed, form the mixture into balls. Wash the caul and cut it is squares with scissors.
4. Wrap each ball in a piece of caul, and pack them closely together in a baking tin. Bake in a hot oven for about three quarters of an hour.

5. They should be nicely browned when done. Serve hot or cold.

Ham (To Cure)

Ingredients	*Quantity*
Ham	500 gram
Salt	20 gram
Vinegar	20ml
Brown sugar	30 gram
Black pepper	20 gram
Salt peter	10 gram

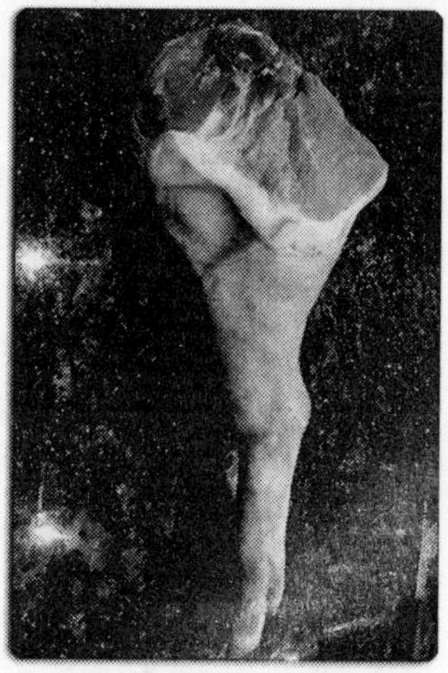

Fig 17.43 Pork leg

Method

1. Put the ham in an earthenware pan (a large bread pan answers very well), and sprinkle the saltpeter over it, especially round the bone and knuckle (Fig. 17.43)
2. Leave it for twelve hours. Sprinkle the pepper, sugar, and salt on the ham, pour over the vinegar, and let it remain again for twenty-four hours.
3. Then well rub the ham all over with the mixture once a day, until you have liquid enough to baste the ham with a spoon.
4. Continue basting it each day with the liquid for a month.
5. Now hang it up in a warm place for a week to drain and dry, and after wards put it in a bag, being careful to close it so that it is impossible for files to get to the ham.
6. Hang it in a dry place and do not use for at least three months.

Ham or Bacon (Boiled)

A ham or half a Ham, or Gammon of Bacon—Bay leaf—little bunch of fresh Herbs—cold Water—Bread rasping or Glaze.

Time: after coming to the boil, 30 minutes to the lb. for a ham not more than 10 lb. in weight, and 15 minutes for every lb. after the 10 lb. Temperature: low.

Ingredients	*Quantity*
Ham or bacon	750 gram
Bayleaf	2no
Bunch of fresh herbs	5 gram
Cold water	1litre
Bread rasping	50 gram

Method

1. Soak the ham overnight in lukewarm water. Then scrub it well and scrape off all discoloured parts.
2. Put it in a stewpan with sufficient cold water to cover it well. Herbs and bay leaf improve the flavour of the ham if you have them, but they can be dispensed with.
3. Bring it slowly to the boil, then skim well and simmer gently until done.
4. To test, see if the rind will come off quite easily; if so, it is ready.
5. If the ham is to be served hot, lift it out on to a dish, remove the skin and trim it round, sift bread rasping over it and put a paper frill round the knuckle, then place it on a clean hot dish.
6. If it is not wanted until it is cold, leave it in the water it was cooked in until almost cold, then take it out, remove the rind and trim it, coat with rasping or brush over with glaze.

Pork Chops With Tomatoes

Time: about 10 minutes. Temperature: moderate. Enough for 4 persons.

Ingredients	*Quantity*
Thins chops	750 gram
Tomatoes	250 gram
Butter	20 gram
Pickled gherkin and onion	50 gram
Salt and pepper	15 gram

Fig 17.44 Pork chops with tomatoes

Method

1. Cut eight thin chops from a lean loin of pork, and trim them.
2. Sprinkle well with pepper. Grease a grid-iron, put on the chops and grill over a clear hot fire or under a gas grill.
3. Turn several times while they are grilling, so that they may be done through without being dry. They will need about fifteen minutes. Place them on a hot dish and surround with a piquant tomato sauce.

   To Make the Sauce:

4. Slice—ripe tomatoes into a saucepan, add butter. Simmer until the tomatoes are quite soft, then rub through a sieve.
5. Return the puree to the saucepan, add a pickled gherkin and onion finely chopped, and a seasoning of salt and pepper and serve.

LEARNING OUTCOME

Pork, to be digestible, needs to be very well cooked. Underdone pork is dangerous. It should be so well done that there is not a tinge of pink in the gravy that runs from it. Beware of pork with very thick skin; it will be old and tough. Ham is a pig's hind leg, first cut off the carcass and then smoked, salted or dried (or a combination of these) for preservation. Gammon also comes from the hind leg but it is cured as part of a side of bacon and cut off after wards. Gammon may be smoked separately or left unsmoked but it is not matured long enough to have a strong ham flavour and does not keep for as long as ham, which is generally cured more slowly. Bacon is any of certain cuts of meat taken from the sides, belly or back of a pig that may be cured and/or smoked. The leg or loin is generally chosen for roasting, and the skin must be well scored. A leg is scored round and round in narrow rows from the knuckle; a loin the way of the chop bones. The crackling is one of the tit-bits of roast pork, but often we find when it comes to table it is hard, tough and uneatable.

LESSON END ACTIVITY

- Go to the butcher shops and learn the cutting process of pork.
- Collect the information on different varities of pork.

QUESTIONS FOR DISCUSSION

1. Draw a pork cuts with suitable diagram ?
2. Explain in details the cut of pork?
3. Explain the difference between ham, bacon and gammon
4. Explain the procedure of roasted pork?
5. Difference between slab bacon and sliced bacon ?

STATE TRUE AND FALSE

- Ham and bacon are same thing.
- Ham can be a substitute of bacon
- Gammon can be subsited of bacon
- Underdone pork is good for health
- Ham is a part of hing leg of pork.

- Slab bacon is cured and smoked side.
- Sliced bacon is sliced from slab bacon.
- Smoked ham rump portion is a portion of cured and smoked ham that contains the aitchbone and part of the leg bone.
- Smoked pork loin chops have the same muscle and bone structure as fresh pork loin chops, but they are also cured and smoked

KEY TERMS

* Bacon	* Ham
* Crackling	* Hock
* Digestible	* Rib
* Gammon	* Unsmoked

18

Beef and Veal

After studying this chapter, the student must know

- Introduction
- Standards cut off beef with their use
- Standard recipes of beef.
- Veal introduction and its standard cut
- Standard recipes of veal.

BEEF CUTS

The lean of good beef if young will be a light, bright red ingrained with tiny streaks of fat. The fat will deep cream, and the suet firm and hard. Moist flabby meat is inferior in qualify.

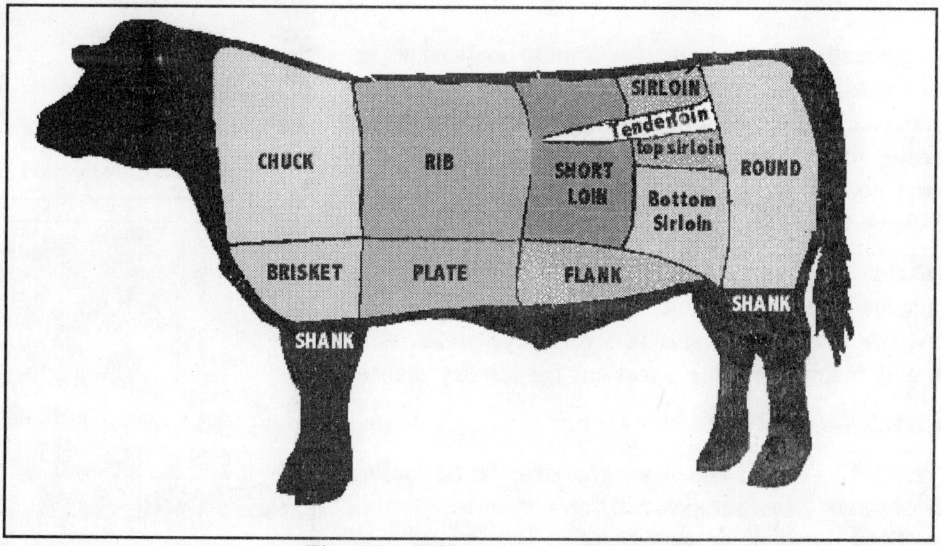

Fig. 18.1 Different cut of beef

The best beef is from an animal of about two years old. When it is not from a young animal there will be quite a wide streak of gristle between the fat and the lean; this is especially noticeable in the sirloin. Be careful therefore when choosing this joint.

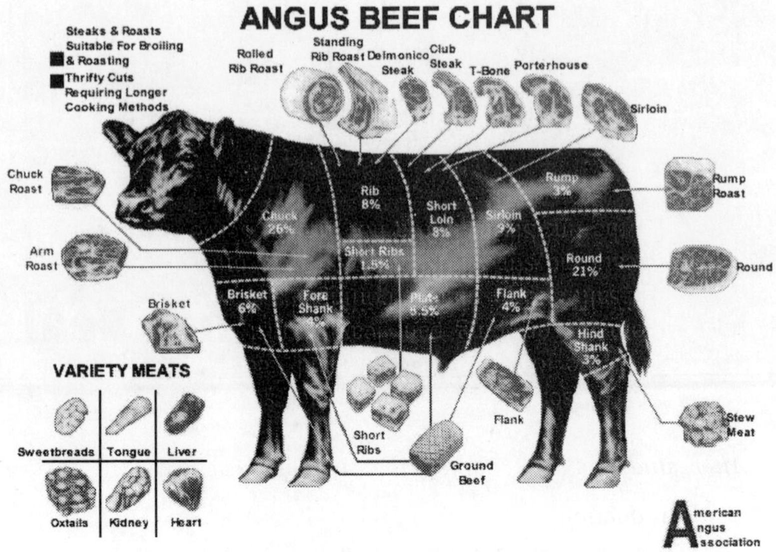

Fig. 18.2 Different varieties of beef

The Sirloin. "loin of beef"—evidently his cook knew how to roast it to perfection, and probably he had come in hungry from the chase. The sirloin is undoubtedly the best of all joints, and though the price is high, there is no waste, and it can be divided to very good advantage so as to make several fresh hot meals. The sirloin is a roasting joint; when buying it, choose the centre cut for that is where the undercut—the tit-bit is thickest. The followings cuts are as follows:

STANDARD CUT OFF BEEF

Chuck (Fig. 18.3)

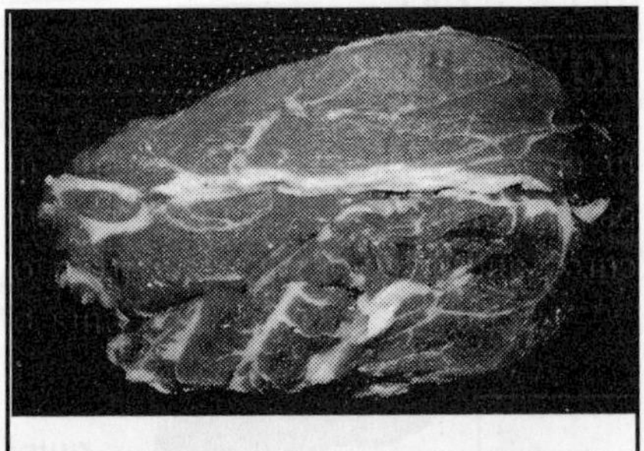

Fig. 18.3 Chuck part of beef

Meat is basically muscle, and the chuck happens to be a heavily exercised area. Luckily, this area contains a great deal of connective tissue, including collagen. Collagen melts during cooking, making the meat intensely flavourful. Cuts from this area benefit from slow, wet cooking methods like stewing, braising or pot-roasting (Fig. 18.3).

Blade Roast—an inexpensive cut which lies next to the ribs; more tender than most chuck; makes an excellent roast. Alternatively, the roast can be cut into a rib-eye steak, with meat above and below the bone excellent for stir-fry dishes.

Chuck Steak—a good choice for kabobs if well marinated

Fig. 18.4 Ribs of beef

Rib (Fig. 18.4)—Tender and flavourful ribs can be cooked any number of ways. Most recipes call for ribs to be roasted, sauteed, pan-fried, broiled, or grilled.

Rib Roast—known as a standing rib roast (bone left in), or without the bone for convenient slicing. Excellent when dry roasted. A seven-bone prime rib roast can be quite a hefty addition to the dinner table. It is great for a crowd, but for a small family a bone roast will do. Many butchers will cut a roast to order for you.

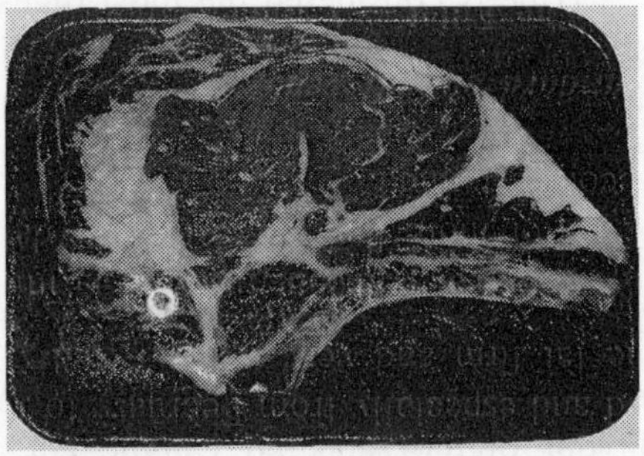

Fig. 18.5 Rib steak of beef

Rib Steak (Fig. 18.5)

Also cut from the rib section, these tender steaks can be purchased bone-in or as boneless rib-eye.

Short Loin (Fig. 18.6)

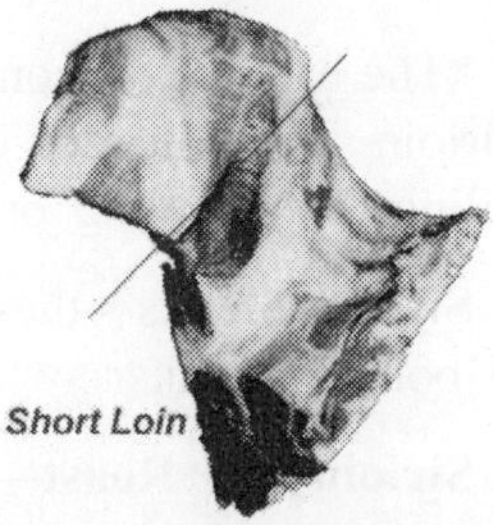

Fig. 18.6 Flank and short loin of beef

This area boasts extremely tender cuts and can be prepared without the aid of moist heat or long cooking times. Cuts from the short loin may be sautéed, pan fried, broiled, pan broiled or grilled.

Porterhouse Steak (Fig. 18.7)

a very popular steak cut from the rear end of the short loin; the name originated from the days when it was served in public alehouses that also served a dark beer called porter. The porterhouse consists of both tenderloin and strip steak. The tenderloin is often served separately as filet mignon

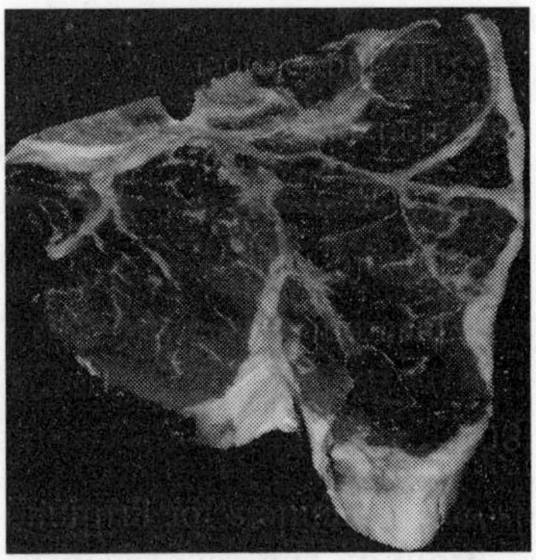

Fig. 18.7 Porterhouse Steak

T-bone Steak (Fig. 18.8)

cut from the middle section of the short loin; similar to the porterhouse steak; has a smaller piece of the tenderloin; usually grilled or pan-fried

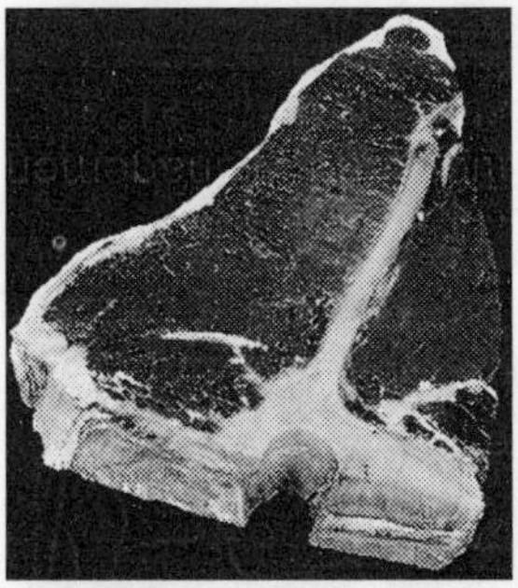

Fig. 18.8 T-bone Steak

Tripe

The inner lining of the stomach of animals that chew the cud. There are different kinds, the so-called honeycomb and blanket are the most popular. Good tripe is thick and white; it should be used while very fresh. Tripe is usually prepared and boiled before being offered for sale. When purchased in its raw state it must be washed and blanched several times and then boiled until tender before bring cooked in the usual ways.

Tripe is considered the most digestible part of the animal and is therefore often prescribed for invalids. It is generally boiled or stewed in milk and served with onion sauce. It may also be cut in strips and fried in batter.

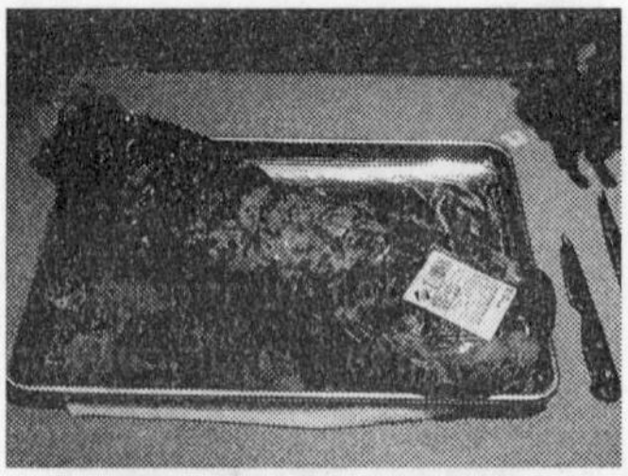

Fig. 18.9 Tenderloin

Tenderloin (Fig. 18.9)

Tenderloin often considered the most tender cut of beef; responds well to sauces, meaning the meat does not overpower the flavour of the sauce. It can be cut as the whole strip, or into individual steaks for filet mignon

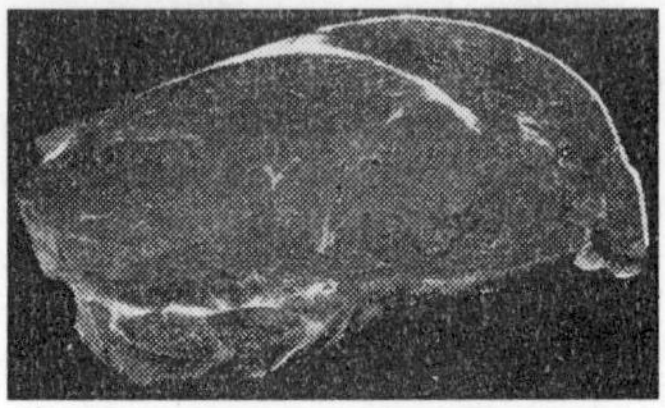

Fig. 18.10 Sirloin

Sirloin (Fig. 18.10)

"The backbone's connected to the … hipbone"—not a song, but a sirloin. These tender cuts respond well to sautéing, pan-frying, broiling, pan-broiling or grilling.

Sirloin Steaks—these steaks are available in a variety of boneless and bone-in steaks

Sirloin Tip Roast—excellent when dry roasted or marinated.

Fig. 18.11 Flank of beef

Flank (Fig. 18.11)

This meat is lean, muscular and very flavorful. Flank is primarily used for flank steaks and rolled flank steaks. It can also be used for kabobs.

Flank Steak—This steak has a great flavour, and should be sliced thin against the grain for maximum chewability. Use to make the classic London broil

Fig. 18.12 Short plate of beef

Short Plate (Fig. 18.12)

This section is best used for stew meat, where its rich, beefy flavour can be appreciated.

Round: The round consists of lean meat well-suited to long, moist cooking methods.

Top Round: This is the most tender part of the round; it can be prepared as pot roast or cut into thick steaks for braised dishes

Fig. 18.13 Rump roast of beef

Rump Roast (Fig. 18.13)

A very popular cut for pot roast, but can also be roasted at low temperatures.

Shank/Brisket (Fig. 18.14)

Traditionally used for corned beef, brisket is best prepared with moist heat. Suitable preparation methods include stewing, braising and pot-roasting.

Fig. 18.14 Shank of beef

Foreshank (Fig. 18.15)

Brisket First Cut: a leaner cut of the brisket, for those who want the flavour but not the fat of a brisket pot roast

The Cheek: Suitable for stews, also used to make brawn

The Heel: Very good for making stock, as it is very gelatinous. It is only used with meat when a jelled substance is required.

The Tail: A very nourishing, joint, delicious stewed or braised with vegetables. The small joints may be used separately to make soup.

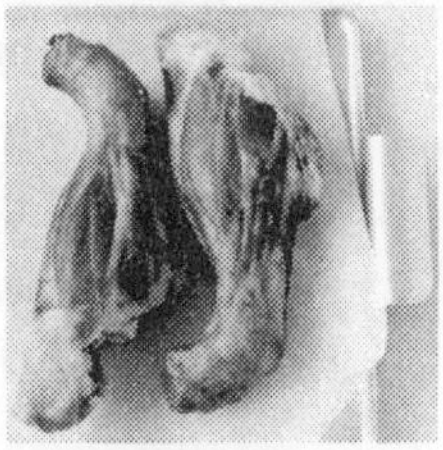
Fig. 18.15 Fore shank of beef

The Heart: May be stuffed and braised or roasted, but being rather coarse and tough, needs long slow cooking.

The Tongue: Should be salted and boiled. A very good dish.

The Liver and Sweetbreads: May be stewed or fried, but need to be well and slowly cooked.

STANDARD RECEIPES OF BEEF

Boiled And Roast Brisket Beef (Boiled)

Ingredients	*Quantity*
Brisket	1kg
Onions	100 gram
Carrot	50 gram
Cloves	10 gram
Bunch of herbs	10 gram
Mace	5 gram
Celery	20 gram
Salt and pepper	20 gram

Fig 18.16 Boiled and roast brisket of beef

Time: 2 to 3 hours. Temperature: low. Enough for 6 to 8 persons.

Method

1. Wipe the meat with a damp cloth or wash it if it seems necessary.
2. Trim it and tie it in shape with tape or twine.
3. Scrape and quarter the carrots, peel the onion and stick the cloves in it.
4. Put the meat into a stewpan with the vegetables, herbs, mace, and the celery cleaned and cut in strips.
5. Add enough boiling water to cover it well, the salt and a sprinkling of pepper. Bring to the boil. Skim thoroughly.
6. Then cover closely, reduce the heat and simmer gently until the meat is quite tender.
7. Take the meat out and remove the tape, put it on a hot dish with the vegetables round, and serve some of the broth separately.

Salt Beef (to serve hot)

Ingredients	*Quantity*
Round or silver side of beef	750 gram
Carrots	75 gram
Turnips	75 gram
Small onions	100 gram
Potatoes dumplings	80 gram
Cold water	3litre

Time: 2 ½ to 3 hours. Temperature: low. Enough for 6 to 8 persons.

Method

1. Wash the meat well and tie it into shape. If there is a marrow bone it may be taken out and reserved for a savoury.
2. Put the meat in a stewpan with enough cold water to cover it well, and bring to the boil.
3. Then skim thoroughly, reduce the heat and simmer gently until the meat is quite tender.
4. The carrots scraped and cut in quarters may be put in with the meat.
5. Peel the onions and turnips and add them when the beef is half done.
6. Add the dumplings twenty minutes before the beef is ready.
7. Remove the tape before serving and garnish with the vegetables and dumplings. Serve some of the broth separately.

Salt Beef (To Serve Cold)

Ingredients	*Quantity*
Brisket of beef	750 gram
Rashers fat of bacon	50 gram
Carrot	100 gram
Spanish onions	100 gram
Cloves	10 gram
Whole spice	10 gram
Cold water	2 litre

Method

1. Wash the meat and tie it into shape. Put two rashers of bacon in a stewpan, then put in the beef, and put the other rashers on the top.
2. Scrape and slice the carrot, peel and slice the onion, and put these vegetables round the meat, add the spices and cloves tied in a piece of muslin and just cover all with cold water.
3. Bring to the boil, remove any scum, cover closely and simmer slowly until tender. Then lift out the meat, remove the bones and press it between two dishes with a weight on the top.
4. Leave until quite cold. Then trim off any rough edges and brush over with melted glaze.

Roast Beef

Temperature: Gas regular, reduce to 4 after about 10 minutes. Electricity, 475° F. Reduce to 375° F.

1. For roasting we have a choice of sirloin, ribs, round of beef or aitchbone. If the round or aitchbone.
2. If the round or airchbone is chosen, it should be well hung or it will not be tender.
3. Wipe the joint with a damp cloth, and trim off any discoloured pieces.
4. Tie it in shape if this has not already been done, and weigh it. Then put it in the baking tin in a hot oven, maintain the heat until the meat begins to brown—ten to fifteen minutes.
5. Then reduce the heat. Baste about every quarter of an hour; if the meat is very lean, you will need some dripping to baste well. This is a very important process.

Fig 18.17 Roast beef

6. Remember beef should be served underdone, so allow a quarter of an hour for each pound, but add an additional quarter of an hour for the joint if it is not liked very much underdone.
7. Remove any skewers or string before serving. Serve very hot as soon as it is ready. A clear unthickened gravy is best for beef. Pour off all the fat from the pan— reserving all the sediment.
8. Add ¼ to ½ pint of boiling water, or plain beef bone stock—to the pan, regulating the quantity according to the size of the joint.
9. Then stir the bottom of the pan well with a wooden spoon to mix all the sediment, which is essence of meat.
10. Add salt to taste, bring to the boil, strain and use.
11. Have plates and dishes hot before you start dishing up. With roast beef serve batter pudding, grated horseradish or horseradish sauce.

Roast Beef With Gherkins And Suet Pudding

Ingredients	*Quantity*
Roast beef	750 gram
Egg yolk	2 no
Mustard	5 gram
Salt and pepper	15 gram
Vinegar	10 gram
Gherkins	20 gram
Suet roll(plain)	2no
oil	10 gram

Method

1. Roast the beef and serve with the gherkin sauce.
2. Make a plain suet roll, let it cool, then cut it in slices.
3. Pour a little of the fat from the beef into a frying pan and when it is very hot, put in the slices of pudding and brown them on both sides.
4. Serve them round the meat.

   To make the Sauce.—

5. Put the yolk of an egg into a basin with a quarter of a teaspoon of made mustard, and a sprinkling of salt and pepper.
6. Stir with a wooden spoon until well mixed, then add drop by drop, stirring all the time, enough salad oil to form a thick paste.

7. Next stir in a dessertspoon of vinegar from clear pickle and a tablespoon of finely chopped gherkins. Serve in a sauce tureen.
8. If more convenient to use mustard pickle, omit the mustard from the seasoning.
9. In Norfolk tiny dumplings are served in this way.
10. Make them by mixing together ½ lb. of flour with a small teaspoon of baking powder and half that quantity of salt, then adding about a quarter of a pint of milk to form a soft dough.
11. Drop teaspoons of the dough into boiling stock or broth and boil very gently for fifteen minutes. Cool; then fry in some hot beef dripping.

Steak

Rump or fillet for grilling or frying—chuck or buttock for stewing.

To Grill

Time: 5 to 10 minutes according to thickness.

1. Choose rump or fillet and beat it well.
2. A rolling pin is the best utensil for this process. The reason for beating is to break the fibres, and so to make the meat more tender.
3. See that the grid-iron is scrupulously clean, grease it well, heat it and rub off the grease with paper.
4. Have ready a perfectly clear smokeless fire or a hot gas or electric grill; regrease the grid-iron and put the meat on it, let it be chose to the heat for a minute, then slacken the heat.
5. When sufficiently cooked on one side turn with a slice or grilling tongs. A fork must not be put in meat that is being grilled or the goodness will escape.
6. Grilled meat should be served immediately it is cooked if it is to be as its best.

To Fry

Time: 5 to 10 minutes according to thickness of the meat.

- Grease a frying pan and make it hot; put in the meat and cook over fierce heat for the first two or three minutes, then reduce to moderate until the meat is sufficiently cooked.

Fig 18.18 Fillet steak milanese

Fillet of Steak Milanese

Ingredients	*Quantity*
Fillet of steak	750 gram
Tomatoes	100 gram

Macaroni	20 gram
Pimento sauce	30 gram
Butter	20 gram
Salad oil	10 gram
Salt and pepper	15 gram

Time: 20 minutes to boil the macaroni—10 to 15 minutes to grill the steak. Temperature: moderate. Enough for 4 persons.

Method

1. Brush the steak over with the oil, sprinkle with salt and pepper, and leave for an hour.
2. Boil the macaroni until tender. Reserve one tomato.
3. Slice the others and stew them with the butter and some salt and pepper.
4. When quite soft, rub through a sieve, mix with the pimento sauce and make very hot. Slice and fry the remaining tomato.
5. Grill the steak, surround it with the macaroni. Pour the sauce over. Garnish with fried tomato.

Veal

Veal is considered at its best when the calf is from two to three months old and especially from February to July. The flesh should be pinky white, and the fat firm and very white. Red veal with and very white.

Red veal with but little fat is inferior and unwholesome. It should not be hung for more than three or four days, as the flesh of a young animal soon becomes tainted.

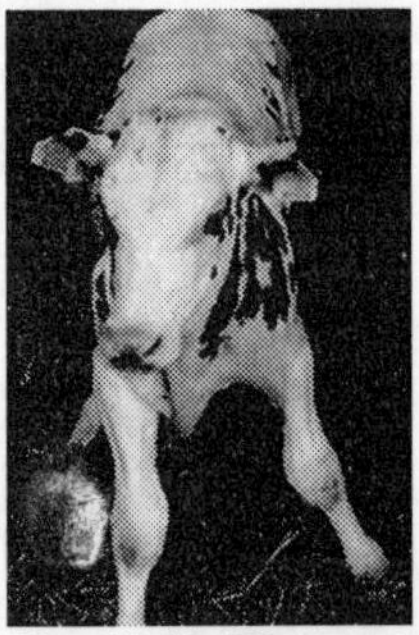

Fig 18.19 The veal

Standard cut off veal

The Fillet.—A joint without any waste. May be roasted, but is generally used for cutlets and fancy dishes such as Veal Olives.

The Loin.—A tender joint, may be roasted or cut into chops.

The breast. —A tender joint to roast, or may be braised or stewed. Boned, stuffed, and roasted. it is good hot or may be served cold for supper or picnics.

The Neck.—May be roast, stewed or braised; also makes cutlets for grilling or frying in egg and breadcrumbs.

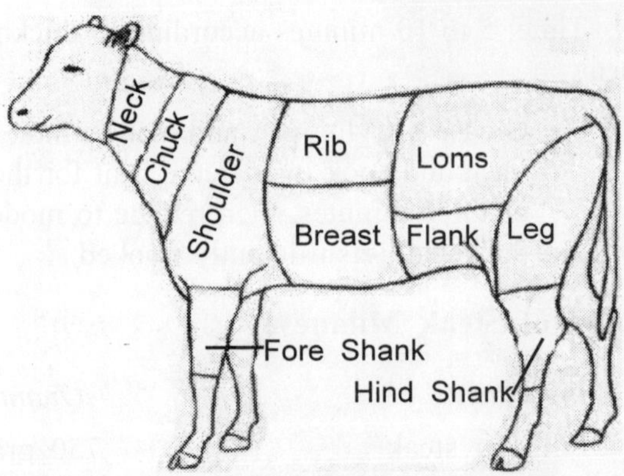

Fig 18.20 Cuts of veal

The Knuckle:—Stewed or boiled, the knuckle makes very nourishing soup, and the meat can be served with parsley sauce.

The Head.—Nourishing and digestible. Boiled and served with brain sauce. Also used to make the very popular. Mock Turtle Soup.

The Feet.— makes good stock for soup. Should be stewed with vegetables, as, though nourishing, they are somewhat flavourless. Also useful for making jellies.

The Sweetbread.—very nourishing and delicious and easy to digest. The heart is the best and most expensive but the cheaper throat sweetbreads are also very good.. They may be cooked in many ways.'

The Liver. —No longer a very cheap dish, as the demand is great now it is recognized as a cure for anemia. May be plainly fried, or in egg and breadcrumbs and served with bacon.

Kidney.—The kidney is a great delicacy, sometimes sold with the loin, but can also be bought separately. Makes a delicious roast for two, or a delicate braise or stew. Kidney from a calf of good quality will have a rather thick boating of very white suet round it. A very lean kidney is inferior.

Brains.—These are generally served with the head, but are also used for other dishes, such as Mock Sweetbreads.

Heart.—This may be stuffed and roasted, or braised.

RECEIPES OF VEAL

Ragout of Veal

Time: 1½ to 2 hours. Temperature: low. Enough for 4 to 6 persons.

Ingredients	*Quantity*
Breast of veal	1kg
Veal stock	1litre
Clove	5 gram
Onion	100 gram
Turnip	50 gram
Mace	10 gram
Parsley	10 gram
Lemon whole	1no
Allspices powder	5 gram
Mushroom	50 gram

Tomato paste	20 gram
Rasher of bacon	30 gram
Butter	20 gram
Salt and pepper	15 gram

Method

1. Cut the meat into small joints and fry them brown in the fat.
2. Drain and put into a saucepan. Just cover them with water or stock, and put in also the onion with the clove stuck in it, the mace, yellow part of the lemon rind, allspice, parsley and a good seasoning of salt and pepper.
3. Cover closely and simmer very gently until the meat is so tender that it will come easily from the bone.
4. Strain from it a pint of the liquor, skimming off as much fat as possible. Mix smoothly together the flour, tomato paste, browning, a good teaspoon of the juice of the lemon and stir this into the stock until it has boiled five minutes.
5. Put the joints of meat on a hot dish pour on the gravy, surround with the rashers of bacon lightly fried, and serve.

Veal Stew

Time: 30min to 1 hour. Temperature: low. Enough for 4 persons.

Ingredients	*Quantity*
Lean veal	750 gram
Lemon	1 no
Sprig of parsley	10 gram
Thyme	5 gram
Marjoram	5 gram
Bay leaf	2 no
Onion	100 gram
Flour	20 gram
Milk	50 ml
Butter	10 gram
Mace	5 gram
Salt and pepper	10 gram

Fig 18.21 Veal stew

Fried bacon	20 gram

Method

1. Cut the veal into small pieces, and dust it lightly with flour mixed with a sprinkling of salt and pepper.
2. Put it in a stewpan with the herbs, bay leaf, a strip of lemon rind (yellow part only), the onion peeled and sliced, a good sprinkling of pepper and just enough cold water to cover.
3. Bring slowly to boiling point and then simmer very slowly until the meat is tender, adding a teaspoon of salt when the meat is beginning to soften.
4. Do not add it too soon as salt put in at first has a tendency to harden veal.
5. Draw off a teacup of the stock and skim off any fat. Mix a tablespoon of flour with a little cold milk, put the remainder of the milk in a saucepan with the mace, and bring slowly to the boil, take out the mace, mix the boiling milk with the flour and the skimmed stock.
6. Melt the butter in a saucepan, put in the stock, etc., and stir till it has boiled for five minutes.
7. Add a squeeze of lemon juice. Strain the remainder of the stock from the veal.
8. Arrange the meat in a mound on a dish. Pour the sauce over. Garnish with fried bacon

Fricassee of Veal

Time: 45 minutes. Temperature: low. Enough for 4 persons.

Ingredients	Quantity
Veal cutlet	500 gram
Onion	100 gram
Butter	20 gram
Thyme	5 gram
Parsley	10 gram
Marjoram	3 gram
Flour	30 gram
Bay leaf	2no
Salt and pepper	15 gram
Mashed potatoes	50 gram
Tomato sauce	20 gram

Method

1. Beat the meat with a rolling pin and cut it in cubes, put them in a stewpan with the onion stuck with the clove herbs and bay leaf in a muslin bag, and the salt and pepper.

2. Bring to the boil, skim well, then simmer until the meat is quite tender; about forty-five minutes.
3. Melt the butter in a small frying pan, stir in the flour, and cook gently for five minutes, but do not allow to colour.
4. Remove the onion and herbs from the veal. Stir in a little of the liquor into the flour and butter, then add them to the veal.
5. Simmer for ten minutes. Force a wall of mashed potato with tomato sauce round a dish, turn the veal into the centre and serve at once.

LEARNING OUTCOME

The lean of good beef if young will be a light, bright red ingrained with tiny streaks of fat. The fat will deep cream, and the suet firm and hard. Moist flabby meat is inferior in qualify. The best beef is from an animal of about two years old. When it is not from a young animal there will be quite a wide streak of gristle between the fat and the lean; this is especially noticeable in the sirloin. Be careful therefore when choosing this joint.it better tto proper knowledge of all cuts. Meat is basically muscle, and the chuck happens to be a heavily exercised area. Luckily, this area contains a great deal of connective tissue, including collagen. Tender and flavorful ribs can be cooked any number of ways. Most recipes call for ribs to be roasted, sauteed, pan-fried, broiled, or grilled. Veal is considered at its best when the calf is from two to three months old and especially from February to July. The flesh should be pinky white, and the fat firm and very white.

LESSON END ACTIVITY

- Go to a butcher shops and learn the process of cutting beef.
- Learn to cook the different varieties of steak.
- Learn to cut the different varieties of steak.

QUESTIONS FOR DISCUSSION

1. Draw a cut of beef with their diagram?
2. Explain in brief the standard cut of beef?
3. Explain the followings :
   i) T-bone steak
   ii) porter steak
   iii) tenderloin
   iv) sirloin

4. Mention the cut of beef which are excellent for stew.
5. Write the standard recipe of boiled beef.
6. Write the standard recipe of cold salted beef.
7. Write the standard recipe of hot salted beef.
8. Write the standard recipe of roasted beef.
9. Explain the term veal and draw their standard cuts.
10. Explain the standard cut of veal.

STATE TRUE AND FALSE

- The lean of good beef if young will be a light, bright red ingrained with tiny streaks of fat.
- The best beef is from an animal of about two years old.
- The sirloin is undoubtedly the best of all joints, and though the price is high, there is no waste.
- Tender and flavorful ribs can be cooked any number of ways.
- The tenderloin is often served separately as filet mignon.
- Tripe is considered the most digestible part of the animal.
- The round consists of lean meat well-suited to long, dry cooking methods.
- Veal is considered at its best when the calf is from two to three months old

KEY TERMS

* Fillet
* Flabby
* Ribs
* Shank
* Streaks
* Suet
* Tenderloin

Chapter 19

Fish and Sea Food

After studying this chapter, the student must know

- Introduction
- Fish structure
- How to check the freshness of fish and its storage
- Universal freezing method
- Classification and choosing of fish
- Preparing of fish
- Filleting and method of fillet a fish
- Method of cooking fish
- Varieties of sea food with their used
- Standard recipes of seafood
- Point to remember to cook fish

FISH

A Fish is any aquatic vertebrate animal that is typically ectodermic (or Cold blooded) covered with scales and equipped with two types of paired fins and several unpaired fins.

Fish Structure

The structure of Fish varies depending on the Fish habit. The skeletal structure of fish is a useful means of separating finfish into smaller grouping. The three types of fin fish.

Round Fish have middle back bone with one fillet on either side and one eye on each side of the head.

Flat Fish have a back bone that runs through the centre of the Fish, two upper and two lower fillets and both eyes on the same side of the head.

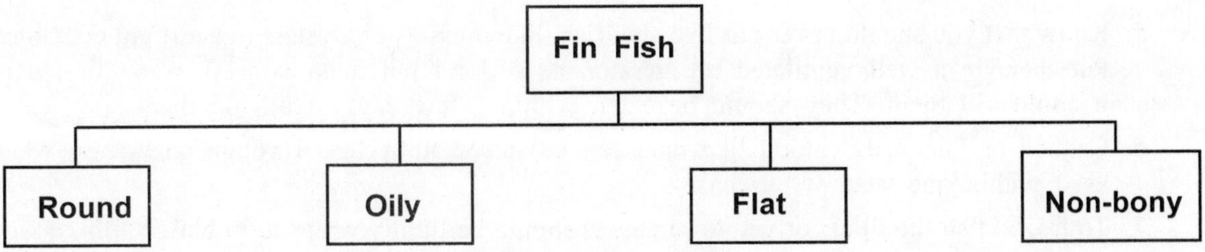

Fig. 19.1 Fish structure

Non-bony Fish have cartilage rather than bones.

Freshness Check

1. Look for firm, shiny flesh. It should be bounced back when touched.
2. **Sniff the Fish**. A "Fresh" Fish should not smell "Fishy" but should have the odor of the Ocean.
3. **Check the eyes**: If the head is on fresh fish should have clear eyes, no cloudiness should be present. They should bulge a little.
4. **Check the gills:** - If whole they should be bright Pink / Red and Wet not slimy or dry.
5. **Check cuts of Fish**: - Fish fillet and steaks should be moist and without discoloration.
6. On Fillet and Steaks, look for flesh separation and gaps. If the meat separates from itself it's not fresh.
7. Look for discoloration, brown or yellow edges and a spongy consistency; these are all signs of aging fish.
8. Fish should be received at a temperature of 40°F/4°C or less.

How to store Sea Food

Sea Food is different from other types of Food, because freshness is key for safety and flavour, it must be stored differently under correct storage conditions fish and shellfish can be held for several days without losing any appreciable quality follow points are remember for storing seafood:

1. Do not let frozen seafood thaw until you are ready to use keep it frozen.
2. Wrap cooked seafood in moisture proof paper or put in an airtight container. If you are refrigerating seafood, don't let the juices from one seafood drop to other seafood.
3. Always keep fish at a proper storage temperature and handle it as little as possible. Fin Fish: 28° to 32°F / -2° to 0°C live mussels : 35°F to 40°F / 2° to 4°C, live crustacean 39° to 45°F / 4°C to 7°C; Caviar 28° to 32°F / 2° to 0°C smoked fish 32°F/0°C.
4. Hard shell seafood like Oysters and calms cannot be frozen, but they should last for several day. If you keep them on ice in a refrigerator.

5. Know that you should never put live shellfish, like mussels or Oysters in a airtight container. Put them in a well ventilated refrigerator. Also don't put them in fresh water or Ice or it could kill them. They should be eaten within a few days of buying them.
6. Canned or Punched seafood like tuna can be stored for years. Through taters best when used within one year of purchase.
7. To frozen fish the fillets or whole carcasses should be tightly wrapped in plastic film, taking care to exclude as much as air from the package as possible.
8. Put seafood on ice in the refrigerator in the freezer, immediately after buying it.

Note:- Do not accept any frozen fish with white frast on its edges. This indicates freezer burn the result of improper packaging or thawing and refreezing of the product.

Universal Freezing Methods

There are four ways of preparation fish for freezing, the first two being the most common.

(a) **Dry pack**:- Separate pieces of fish with double thickness of cellophane, wrap in moisture-vapour-proof paper, bag, seal and freezer. Be sure the paper is in close contact with the fish to exclude air which will dry the fish and make it tasteless freeze quickly on the floor of the freezer.

(b) **Brine Pack**:- This is not suitable for fatty fish as tends to xidise and lead to rancidity. Dip Fish into cold salted water (1 tablespoon salt to quarter water), drain, wrap and seal. Do not keep brine dipped fish longer than three months.

(c) **Acid pack:** - Citric Acid preserves the color and flavour of fish ascorbic acid is an antioxidant which stops the development of rancidity in fish which can cause off flavour and smells. A chemist can provide an ascorbic acid power to be diluted in a proportion of 1 part powder to 100 parts of water. Dip fish into this solution drain, wrap and seal.

(d) **Solid Ice pack:** - Small Fish, Steaks or Fillets can be covered with water in refrigerator trays or loaf tins and frozen into solid block. The fish should be separated by double paper as usual remove ice blocks from pan wrap in freezer. Paper and store. The Fish can also be frozen in a solid ice pack in large waxed tubs. Cover the fish completely to within ½ inch of container top and crumple a pieces of cellophane over the top of the fish before closing a lid. The advantage in this solid ice method is a saving of container and wrapping material.

CLASSIFICATION OF FISH

Fish is high protein food supply on an average a little more than 5 gram of protein per addible ounce. Fish could be got from lakes, rivers and sea fresh water fish are cinder be superior in flavour than salt water Fish and active fish is more superior in flavour than lean fish.

Fish has fewer calories than meat. All fish is low in fat and extremely nutritious. An average serving supplies one third to one half of the daily protein requirements as well as vitamin-B thiamin,

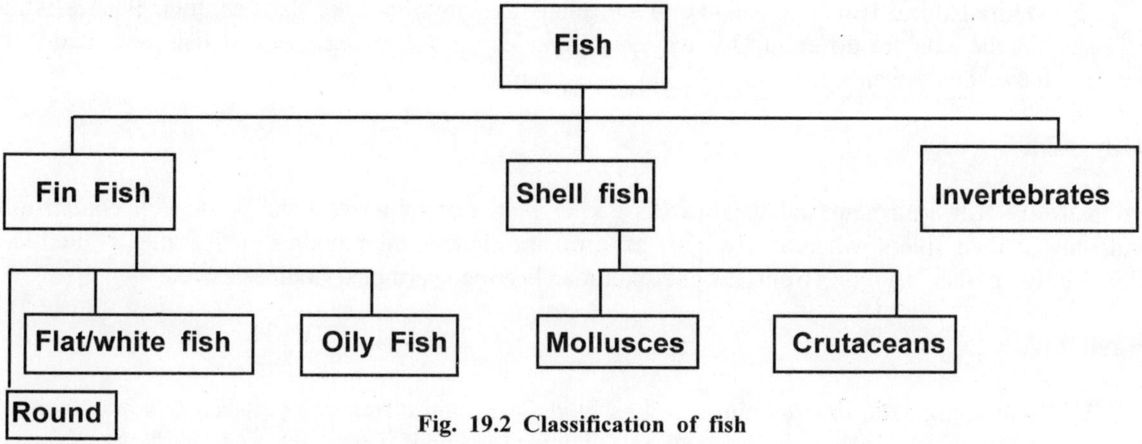

Fig. 19.2 Classification of fish

riboflavin and niacin. Most fish also provide iodine, copper and iron and if cooked with the bones, calcium and Phosphorus.

Fish requires more attention from the cook than meat whether it is cooked whole, filleted or cut into steaks. Leaving Fish whole with head and tail intact prevents loss of natural juices. Particularly when broiling is the cooking method. The skin of broiled fish is delicious Crisp.

A quick and easy method of cooking fillets or steaks is to dip them in flour or cracker meat and sauté them in Oil, burning once and basting after burning. When fish is done, remove to a heated Platter, squeeze raw garlic through a press into the cooking oil, add lemon juice and pour over the fish.

Fish is also excellent baked, steamed, Poached or in stews when Poaching or stewing do not allow the cooking liquid to boil only to simmer a little on the surface.

FIN FISH

Fin fish are cold-blooded vertebrates with gills. Fin fish have skin and scales which cover the body. They move with the help of fins. True fish have an internal skeleton and a backbone. Most fish have a bony skeleton but some fish like sharks have a skeleton made up of pieces of cartilage (hard connective tissue). Fish can be divided into various sub-categories according to habitat, shape and flesh type.

WHITE FISH

Fresh white fish has the following characteristics: firm flesh, clear and shiny eyes, red gills and a clean smell. There are two types of white fish: Round fish and Flat fish.

1) **White Flat fish** - have white flesh and are flat. Turbot, brill and halibut are very large flat fish, but are readily available from suppliers and popular in many fine restaurants. The cuts of flat fish are different to those of round fish. This category includes the following types of fish: plaice, Dover sole, lemon sole, turbot, brill, halibut, etc.

2) **White Round fish** - are round and are relatively common. Like flat fish, their flesh is white but the cuts are different.This category includes the following types of fish: cod, haddock, hake, huss, whiting, monkfish, etc.

Oily Fish

All oily fish are round and the flesh is darker than that of white fish. White fish contain oil, but only in their livers, whereas oily fish have oil throughout their bodies. This category includes the following fish: salmon, trout, mackerel, tuna, herring, sardines, anchovies, etc.

Shell Fish

Shellfish are aquatic invertebrates used as food. The main difference between fish and shellfish is their skeleton. Shellfish have an external skeleton or shell. There are two main categories of shellfish, crustaceans and molluscs.

Crustaceans

Crustaceans have multi- jointed shells. The shells of crustaceans do not grow with the fish; they shed each year with a new one forming to suit their new size. Examples of Crustaceans are: Lobsters, Crawfish, Prawns and Crab.

Molluscs

Molluscs shellfish have shells but they are not multi-jointed. Some molluscs are eaten raw, such as oysters, but the remainder need very little in the way of cooking through. Too much cooking will affect their texture and taste. Examples of molluscs are: Mussels, scallops, Oysters.

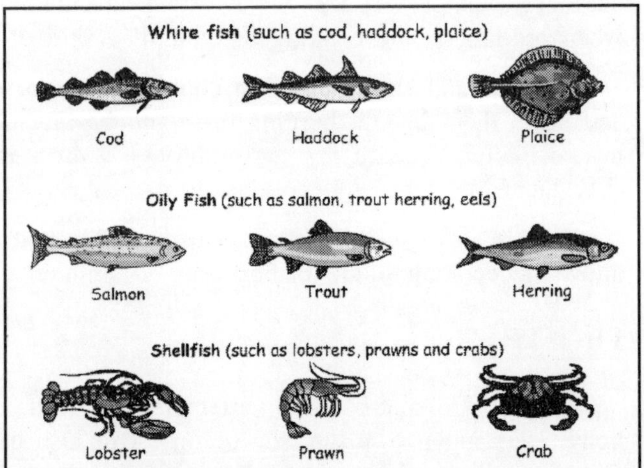

Fig. 19.3 Different varieties of seafood

Invertebrates

Invertebrates are spineless marine animals with no outer shell. They include the squid and octopus family

FISH

Fish is nutritious and easily digested, invaluable to the invalid, and almost essential to the brain worker. Use more fish in your household. It need not be an expensive item; indeed, some of the cheapest kinds are the best. If mackerel were as expensive as salmon we should esteem it far more than we do. Watch the markets and buy what is plentiful. Fish is at its best when in season and even the most expensive varieties have their cheap times. When there is a glut of soles they can be purchased almost as cheaply as hake or haddock. Certain fish is dear because it is always in great demand. It is a mistake always to buy those popular kinds. The reason why most people tire of fish is because so few varieties are purchased. Even the kinds bought are generally prepared in the same way.

With fish so much depends upon the cooking. Believe it; a well cooked dab is far nicer than a badly cooked sole. Then there is the sauce that is where most British cooks fail. The French chef will serve fillets of inferior fish under the name of sole, and we know no difference, because he has disguised them so cleverly in a delicious creamy sauce. There is no reason why you should not learn the same secrets. Let us begin right at the beginning with a hint or two about:

CHOOSING FISH

Freshness is the first essential. Always deal at a reliable shop, but at the same time, learn to judge for yourself. When fish is fresh the gills are red and moist, the eyes bright and full and the flesh firm but elastic. If pressed the mark of the finger fades at once. Spots on plaice should be bright red; they turn greenish-brown when the fish is stale. Never choose then, ill-nourished-looking fish. Thick plump ones are always superior in flavour. This is especially noticeable with such fish as turbot, halibut, sole and codfish. As a rule fish of medium size are the best purchase. In small fish the bones are too much in evidence. On the other hand, very large fish are often coarse-flavoured.

The tails of such fish as lobsters, crayfish, prawns and shrimps are well curled round when fresh.. If they are pulled out they will immediately fly back. When buying a lobster or crab, choose one that is heavy for its size. The flesh of a cock lobster is considered the best, but the hen is more sought after as the spawn (coral it is called) is so useful for enriching sauces and for garnishing. Mackerel should be bright with a silvery sheen that seems to reflect a rainbow. The cheapest cuts of fish are not always the most economical. Though the prime cuts cost more, every flake can be utilized, whereas, with the cheapest parts often half is wasted. Oily fish such as salmon, mackerel and herring, also all freshwater fish, should be cooked as soon as possible after being caught. Soak fresh water fish in slightly salted water to remove the muddy taste they often posses. Frozen fish such as Canadian salmon should be thawed before it is cooked. This can be done by soaking it in cold water for a quarter of an hour.

QUANTITIES

With boiled fish, half a pound is the usual allowance for each person if the dish is to form the principal part of a meal. When serving several courses half that quantity will be enough. Err, if you must, on the generous side. A glance at the recipes given in the Left Over's section will show that cold fish never need be wasted. There are many delicious ways in which it can be served again. When fish is to be fried, one goodsized fillet is allowed for each person as a course, doubling the quantity for a meal. Slips are served one to each person—also small mullet and fish of that kind.

Allow three or six smelts, according to size, for each person and a quarter of a pint of whitebait. One small mackered or half a large one is enough for each person. Scallops are served in threes and oysters in threes or sixes. The French serve them in the deep half of their shells, but in this country they are generally placed in the shallower portion.

PREPARING

It is well to know how to prepare the fish from start to finish, in case ardent fisher-friends present you with part of the catch when the fishmonger is too far away to lend a hand.

To Clean—-With flat fish such as sole or plaice, first scrape off the scales with a small knife, working towards the head—a knife that has been broken and rounded is, I find, an ideal tool to keep for this purpose. Then make a slit in the throat or underpart of the head and remove the inside washing the fish out well with salted water afterwards. To clean the other kinds such as fresh haddock and whiting, make a slit in the under-part of the fish about three parts down the fish from the head to the tail, then empty them and wash in salted water.

Red mullet and smelts are exceptions; these are not emptied but just drawn through the gills. If there is any black skin lining the fish, rub it off carefully as it is invariably bitter in taste. Roe, unless very small, should be removed from the fish as it takes longer to cook and therefore is best cooked separately. When the fish is to be served whole, the fins must be cut off; this is best done with scissors. Eyes also should be removed.

To Skin Flat fish.— Cut the skin across at the tail end with a wet knife. Then lift the skin and loosen the edges all round the sides with the first finger. Now, holding the fish firmly down on the board with one hand, take the skin between the first finger and thumb of the other hand and draw it off from the head towards the tail. You will not find any difficulty in this process, provided you have loosened it well all round first.

Round fish are also skinned from the head downwards. First cut the skin through on both sides quite close to the fins, then make a cut just below the head. Loosen the skin and then pull gently down towards the tail. Then turn the fish, and remove the skin on the other side the same way. Watch your fishmonger when he is skinning a fish and you will see the exact process far better than it can be described.

SALT FISH: Remember that salt fish must first of all be well washed and then put in cold water to soak for several hours before it is cooked.

FILLETING

To fillet flat fish such as a sole, cut off the fins, then with a sharp knife cut down the fish right along the side of the centre bone from head to tail. Now slide the knife along between the bone and the flesh and cut off the fillets neatly. Draw away the fillet with the left hand as you cut. Try to keep the knife as close to the bone as possible, then you will not leave any pieces of flesh behind. Remember, in cutting off a left-hand fillet that you cut towards the tail. For a right-hand one, turn the fish round and work towards the head. Illustrations of these processes will be found farther on in this section. To fillet round fish such as herrings, cut off the fins. Then cut right down the middle of the back—cutting to the bone. Then with the tail towards you cut away the fillet on the left hand side, keeping the knife as close to the bone as possible, then with the head towards you, remove the other fillet in exactly the same manner.

How to Fillet a Fish

Here are a series of 15 pictures describing the simple techniques of filleting reasonable sized fish like coral trout, barramundi, mangrove jack, salmon etc. This method can be adapted to suit most fish species with scaled skin, and the end result will give you beautiful clean fillets, little bones and virtually no wastage.

1. What is required is a simple cutting board or flat surface, a thin flexible blade for cutting along the backbone, and a broad flat blade for removing the hard skin.
2. Holding the fish flat on the cutting board, and while using the thin knife, pierce the skin behind the front dorsal fin.
3. Slice the knife diagonally across the fish, cutting to, but not through, the backbone.
4. Hold the fish by the head and run the blade down the backbone towards the tail with a sawing motion. Do not try to cut too much of the fillet off the backbone at this stage, this will come later.

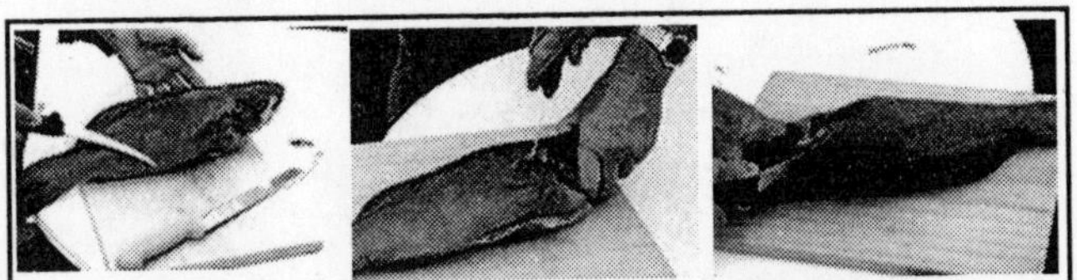

Fig. 19.4 Slicing of fish with different steps

5. When near the tail region, hold the knife flat against the backbone and push the point right through the side of the fillet. With the knife protruding out the other side, cut right through the remaining fillet towards the tail.
6. Peel the fillet back with one hand while cutting the fillet away from the backbone using small slicing motions. Don't try to cut too much away in one stroke. It is better to use many small cuts, guiding the knife along any bony structures and removing all that beautiful flesh.

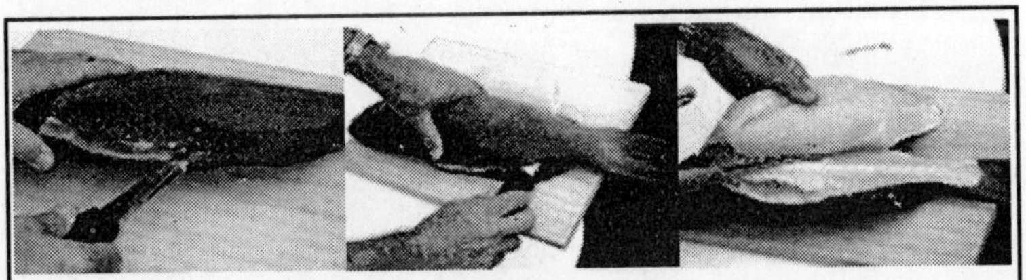

Fig. 19.5 Cut of fillet from bones

7. The most difficult task is to remove the fillet from the rib cage area. A very sharp knife is essential here. Using small strokes again, just feel your way around the bones, eventually completely removing one side of the flesh.
8. Turn the fish over making sure to hold the fish fairly flat on the cutting surface, and repeat the procedure to remove the other fillet. Some fisherman will keep the first fillet loosely

attached to the backbone to improve the "shape" of the fish and making it easier to work for removing the second fillet.

Fig. 19.6 Cutting of fillet from the bones

9. The fish "wings" are regarded by some culinary experts as the second best eating part of any fish, second only to the meat found at the back of the head. Break or cut them off whole and save them for the BBQ.
10. And there you have it, two superb fillets, the wings and the carcass.
11. Next comes the removal of the skin, note that the fish has not been scaled and this is not necessary.Hold the tough skin in one hand and using the flat bladed knife, slice a small portion of the flesh away from the skin.

Fig. 19.7 Cleaning of fillet

12. Cut a "finger hole" into the skin.
13. Hold the skin by the finger hole, and using the broad bladed knife, gently remove the skin from the remaining fillet. It is important to hold the knife at the correct angle and to pull on the skin, not push or cut with the knife. Holding the blade too flat will result in a jagged cutting action and probably leave some skin on, hold it too upright and you will slice through the skin and make it difficult to re-start the procedure. There is no substitute for practice, so go catch a few and give it some trial and error until you work the right angle to suite your blade.
14. The completed job.

Fig. 19.8 Removing of skin from the fillet

METHODS OF COOKING

TO BOIL : Large fish may be boiled, but steaming is really a better method for small or cut fish. The success of boiled fish depends a great deal upon its appearance; be careful, therefore, not to let it break and also see that it is a good colour. To keep fish white, rub it over gently with a slice of cut lemon before cooking and be very careful to skim well when the water comes to boiling point. If your fish kettle is not fitted with a strainer the fish should be enclosed in a bag of thin muslin, otherwise it will be very difficult to remove it from the fish kettle without breaking the fish. Having prepared and washed the fish, and, if necessary, tied it in shape, put it on the strainer. Have enough warm—not boiling—water in the kettle to cover it well, and lower the fish into it. The exceptions are salmon and salmon trout; these fish are put into gently boiling water to preserve their colour. Add a dessertspoon of salt and a large teaspoon of vinegar to every quart.

When the water comes to the boil, skim thoroughly, then reduce the heat and simmer until the fish is sufficiently cooked. The time to cook is about ten minutes to the pound and ten minutes over. Only experience can teach the cook the exact time, for it depends so much more upon the thickness of the fish than upon the actual weight. A short thick fish will therefore take much longer than a larger flat one. The only way you can test, is to lift the fish out on the strainer and try with the tip of a fish knife or a skewer to see if it separates easily from the bone. Drain carefully. The simplest plan is to lift the fish out on the strainer and place it across the fish kettle for a minute or two, then slide the fish on to a hot dish—a really hot one, please—there is nothing more unappetizing than just warm fish ! Garnish daintily and serve with a good sauce.

TO STEAM: Prepare and wash the fish, sprinkle it with lemon juice and salt. Put it in a steamer over boiling water. A fish kettle will answer the purpose, if you put the fish on a strainer that has legs. In fact anything that will raise it above the water will do. You will only need a few inches of water in the kettle. Cover closely and keep the water boiling until the fish is done. If more water is needed during the cooking only water that is actually boiling must be used. Remember when steaming, that the water must be kept boiling all the time and the lid tightly closed. The time required will vary according to the thickness of the fish, but steaming takes longer than boiling. For fish of medium thickness, allow fifteen minutes to the pound and fifteen minutes over. A delicious method for fillets or small pieces of fish is to steam them between two plates, they then retain all their delicious flavour.

Grease a deep plate or soup plate with butter, put the fish on it, season with salt, pepper and lemon juice, cover with butter paper. Place the plate on a saucepan of boiling water and cover with another plate or a saucepan lid if it is not too shallow. See that the water boils fairly briskly until the fish is done. A fillet or slice of fish will take twenty to twenty to twenty-five minutes.

TO FRY IN EGG AND BREADCRUMBS: When you are able to fry fish to perfection you have mastered one of the most important parts of cookery. So many cooks fail and go on failing, because they will not trouble to follow the few simple rules that spell success. First wash it in cold water, then drain, dry thoroughly and flour lightly. Fish must be perfectly dry before it is put into the beaten egg, otherwise the egg will not stick to the fish because the water still clings to it, and your finished effect will have a patched appearance. The fat must be at the right temperature when you put the fish in. If it is not hot enough—that is, when it is only sizzling but no smoke rising, the heat will not be sufficient to set the albumen in the egg.

The fat will penetrate to the fish and the fish will absorb the grease. This then is the cause of greasy fish. To avoid it, make sure that you wait until a thin blue smoke arises from the fat and the fat itself is perfectly still. Then the egg and crumbs will coat your fish, so that, when served, it will be dry, slightly crisp and golden hued. The pan used should be deep and strong. If possible have enough fat to cover the fish. Oil is excellent for fish but clarified dripping is very good, or one of the cooking fats now on the market. It is not extravagant to use plenty of fat, as if it is carefully strained after use it can be used again.

PREPARING FISH FOR FRYING

Fish may be fried whole or in fillets; the latter is the easier method unless the fish are small. Wash the fillets in cold water, and dry them thoroughly with a soft cloth (I always keep a special cloth for this purpose). Flour them, and if they have been properly dried first, the flour should remain quite dry upon them. Take a fresh egg and beat it well on a deep plate. Dip in the fillets one by one, brushing them well over with the egg to make sure that every particle is covered. Have ready plenty of the breadcrumbs seasoned with salt and pepper, and put these on a sheet of kitchen papper. Drain a fillet from the egg and place it on the breadcrumbs, tossing them over on to the fillet from either side. When the fish is well coated with crumbs, par it to make them stick. Then just hold up the fillet and very gently shake off any superfluous bread. Be careful not to be too vigorous or you may find a patch uncoated. Treat each piece in this fashion, and then put into your frying basket as many as it will conveniently hold. The many as it will conveniently hold. The fillets must not be close enough to touch each other. Lower your basket into a deep pan of boiling fat (don't forget the blue smoke now) and fry until the fish is a golden brown. One more warning. Don't think that bubbling fat is boiling fat ready to be used. The sizzling will stop when the smoke appears.

If you do not possess a frying basket or a deep pan, follow the rules I have given, but in place of the frying basket, you must put each fillet straight into the boiling, fat, and gently turn it when one side is brown. If the fillets are thick, or you are frying whole fish, such as whiting, lessen the heat a little as soon as the fish begins to brown, otherwise the outside will be overcooked before the fish is done. When your fish is cooked drain it well on a hot sieve, and arrange it on a very hot dish. Serve at once garnished with parsley (only a little), and if liked, cut lemon. Fried fish should never be covered, as it so soon becomes sodden if the steam cannot escape.

VARIETIES OF FISH WITH THERE USED

Bass Fish (Fig. 19.9)

A fish of quite good flavour, should be cooked in the same way as codfish.

Fig. 19.9 Bass fish

Bream Fish (Fig. 19.10)

Freshwater bream is flavourless and not worth the trouble of cooking, but sea bream is quite good eating, a cheap and satisfying fish. It may be grilled, baked or fried. To Grill. After washing, wipe perfectly dry and dredge with a little flour. Grill under moderate heat or over a clear fire. Turn the fish several times while cooking; it should be well browned on both side. Serve with anchovy or any well-flavoured sauce or a tomato puree.

- Time: 20 to 30 minutes according to the thickness of the fish. Temperature: moderate. Allow 1½ lb. For 4 persons.
- To Bake. Stuff the fish with herb or chestnut forcemeat and bake on a well buttered tin. Either cover it or baste while it is cooking with the liquor that comes from it.

Fig. 19.10 Bream fish

- Time: 30minutes in a moderate oven, as it is a rather solid fish. Temperature: Gas. Electricity, 375° F.
- To Fry. Bream should be filleted, cut in pieces of a convenient size, and fried either in egg and breadcrumbs or butter. Serve very hot with a good sauce.

Brill Fish (Fig. 19.11)

- This is an excellent fish, somewhat similar to turbot, but the flesh is not so white; in fact, it is almost yellow.
- Bream may be cooked in the same way as turbot, it is particularly good steamed and served with lobster sauce.
- Rub it over with a little salt and a slice of lemon before cooking, to improve the colour.

Fig. 19.11 Brill fish

Carp (Fig. 19.12)

Carp is a pond fish without much flavour, but as it is plentiful in some parts of the country where sea fish is not always obtainable, it is as well to know how to cook it.

Fig. 19.12 Carp fish

- Carp, like all freshwater fish, should be soaked in salted water for at least an hour before cooking. Remove the gills before soaking, as they are inclined to give a muddy flavour to the fish.
- It is best stuffed with a savoury forcemeat; celery stuffing is very good.
- Wrap it in buttered paper and bake for about half an hour in a moderate oven. Or, instead of buttering the paper, soak the fish in a tablespoon of lemon juice and a tablespoon of oil and a seasoning of salt and pepper for an hour before cooking. Then put it in a paper bag with the oil and lemon.

Char and Chub (Fig. 19.13)

Should be cooked in the same way as carp.

Fig. 19.13 Char and chub fish

Cockles (Fig. 19.14)

Fig. 19.14 Cockles shell fish

This shell fish is peculiar to certain coasts.

To Boil. Wash the cockles in several waters and scrub the shells, then leave them in slightly salted water for an hour, allowing about one pint of cockles for each person. Drain and put them in a stew pan with about two tablespoons of water at the bottom, cover with a clean cloth, and cook over gentle heat. As soon as the shells open (which will be in about five minutes) they are done. Shake the saucepan two or three times to prevent burning. Serve very hot on a napkin. Any of the recipes for mussels may be used for cockles.

Cod (Fig. 19.15)

Fig. 19.15 Cod fish

- Another cheap fish somewhat lacking in flavour. Either choose a savoury method of cooking, or if plainly boiled or steamed serve with well flavoured sauce.
- For boiling or steaming choose a middle cut or head and shoulders.
- Codfish is never cooked whole, as the different parts vary so much in thickness, that it would be impossible to have the shoulders sufficiently cooked, without overcooking the tail.
- The salt cod generally sold during Lent is not a profitable purchase—it needs long soaking in lukewarm water, changing the water several times, and should then be gently simmered in milk and water and served with egg sauce. Do not choose an anchovy or shrimp sauce as the fish, however well soaked, remains salt.

FRIED COD: - Cod cutlets about 1 inches in thickness, 2 tablespoons Flour, Salt and Pepper, good pinch of powdered Mace or Nutmeg, Lard or Dripping for frying, Maitre d'Hotel Butter.

Time: about 15 minutes. Temperature: moderate;. Enough for 4 persons.

- Wash and very thoroughly dry the fish. Mix a sprinkling of salt, pepper, and, if liked, the mace or nutmeg, with the flour, and dust the fish with this. Put the cutlets into boiling fat that covers them and fry until nicely browned - you can then lessen the beat a little.
- When done, the flesh should come easily from the bone with a skewer or the tip of a knife. Drain the fish well on a sieve or soft paper and serve very hot with a pat of maitre d'hotel butter on each cutlet.

CREAMED COD: - Cod cutlets, 1 inches in thickness. 2 Butter, scrap of Mace, Lemon, tablespoon Flour, 2 teaspoon finely chopped Parsley, Salt, pint milk.

Time: 15 minutes to steam the fish. Temperature: moderate. Enough for 4 persons.

- Rub the fish with a little salt, sprinkle with lemon juice and steam it. Put the milk into a saucepan with a quarter teaspoon of salt, the rind of half a lemon, yellow part only, and the mace.
- Stand this over very gentle heat, where it will get quite hot, but will not boil. Leave in a warm place until it is well flavoured, then strain.
- Melt the butter or margarine in a small stewpan, add the flour very gradually and stir over slow heat until it forms a paste.
- Add the flavoured milk a little at a time stirring all the while and being careful to keep it quite smooth.
- Boil gently for four minutes. Remove the skin from the fish. Place the cutlets on a hot dish, pour the sauce over, sprinkle with very finely chopped parsley and serve at once.

Fig. 19.16 Conger eel fish

Conger Eel (Fig. 19.16)

These sea eels are larger than fresh-water eels and the flesh is not as delicate. Choose the smallest; the very large ones are coarse. For methods of cooking.

Crab (Fig. 19.17)

- Choose a crab by its weight; the heavier it is for its size the better. Crabs of medium size with large claws are best.
- To Boil. First tie the claws, then put the crabs into very fast boiling water which must be sufficient to cover them well, add a large dessertspoon of salt to every quart of water. Continue boiling quickly until the crabs are done. They will need from twenty to thirty minutes according to size.

Fig. 19.17 Crab

Dressed Crab

Pick out all the meat from the crab, take away what is called the apron (it lies just under the head) and the gills. (This must always be done whatever recipe is used.)

- Mix the contents of a moderate sized crab with a tablespoon of oil, a tablespoon of vinegar, a good sprinkling of salt and pepper and half a teaspoon of made mustard.
- The fishmonger will sometimes dress a crab if asked, and in some shops it is sold ready prepared.

- Wash and dry the shell and rub it over with a little oil to brighten it. Put the mixture in the centre, arranging the meat from the legs of the crab at the sides. Garnish with watercress.

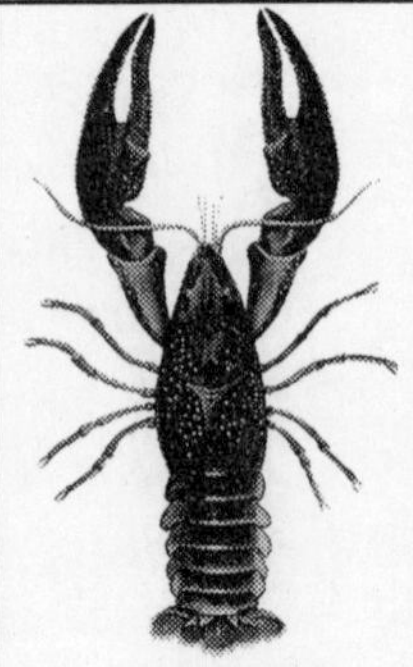

Fig. 19.18 Variety of cray fish

Crayfish (Fig. 19.18)

A very similar fish to the lobster, but it has no large claws and the flesh is not so delicate in quality. It is cooked in the same way as lobster.

- A miniature lobster, very delicate in flavour, delicious either hot, or cold with salad; extremely useful for decorating other dishes.
- To Boil.—Wash the crayfish well, put them in boiling water with a teaspoon of salt to every quart of water.
- They should be a brilliant red when cooked sufficiently. Drain and pile them on a napkin. Time to cook about ten minutes.

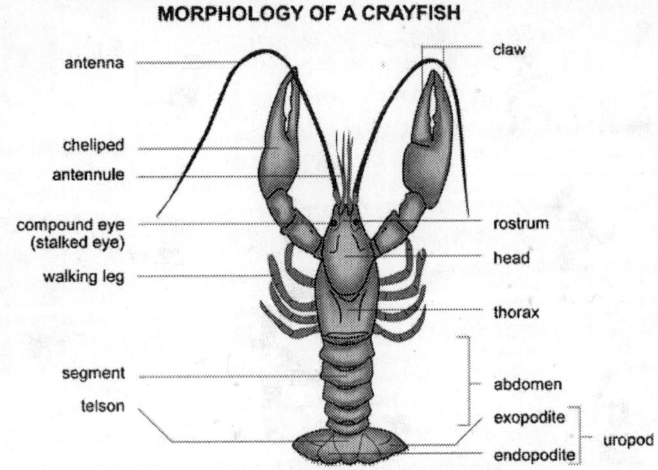

Fig. 19.19 Structure of cray fish

Dabs (Fig. 19.20)

- Dabs are similar in shape to plaice but a much better flavour.
- The small ones may be fried or grilled whole. If the black skin is removed when filleting large dabs, you can cook them as you would soles.
- They are very good fried in egg and breadcrumbs and served with tartar sauce.
- They are very moderate in price and any of the recipes for cooking the cheapest kinds of fish can be used for them.

Fig. 19.20 Dab fish

Dory (Fig. 19.21)

- An inexpensive and satisfying fish with flesh as firm as a turbot and of a delicious flavour.
- It may be boiled and served with a good sauce, filleted and fried, or stuffed and baked.
- The dory possesses a very ugly head and that part is seldom sent to table.
- **To Boil**. - Empty and thoroughly cleanse the fish. Remove the head, cut off the fins and rub the inside of the fish with salt.

- Put it in a fish kettle with sufficient cold water to cover and a dessertspoon of salt to a quart of water.
- Bring slowly to the boil, and simmer until sufficiently cooked.
- Being a thick solid fish it will need from twenty to twenty five minutes to cook according to thickness.
- Serve with a good sauce such as lobster, anchovy or shrimp also for curried fish.

Fig. 19.21 Dory fish

Eels (Fig. 19.21)

- Eels are most nutritious, but they must be eaten while very fresh, that is why they are usually sold alive.
- To kill an eel, cut through the spine just below the head. Split the fish down the belly and clean it out.
- To skin it, cut the skin in a ring at the back of the gills, and, holding the fish firmly with a cloth, pull off the skin. Some cooks use a pair of tweezers to do this.
- Eels make a pleasant change for the invalid. Being so very nutritious, they are excellent body builders, and if attractively garnished, will be readily taken by the convalescent.

Fig. 19.22 Eels

STEWED EELS: - Eels of moderate size, 500 gram Veal Stock, pinch of powdered Mace, Salt and Pepper, sprig of parsley and Lemon Thyme, 1 oz. Butter or Margarine.

Time: 1½ hours. Temperature: Gas, Regular. Electricity, 375 F. Enough for 4 persons.

- Cleanse and skin the eels. Cut them into two-inch lengths and sprinkle the pieces with salt, pepper and mace.
- Grease a fireproof dish, put in the eels, and the parsley and thyme finely chopped, pour in the stock, put the remainder of the butter in small pieces on the eels.
- Cover and cook in a moderate oven for one and a half hours. They can be served hot or cold.

FLOUNDER (FIG. 19.23)

A flat fish similar in shape to plaice but darker in colour. It may be cooked in the same ways as plaice.

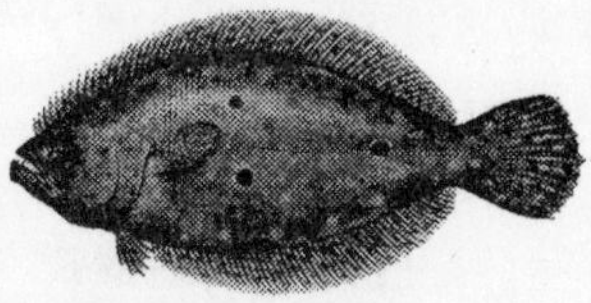

Fig. 19.23 Flounder fish

Grayling (Fig. 19.24)

Fig. 19.24 Grayling fish

A pretty silver grey fish, peculiar to rivers in the north of England. It should be baked, fried or grilled.

Gurnet (Fig. 19.25)

A round fish with a large and ugly head, but the flesh is form and of good flavour. It may be boiled, stuffed and baked, or filleted and fried in batter or egg and breadcrumbs.

Fig. 19.25 Gurnet fish

Haddock

- **Dried**—The best smoked haddocks come from Aberdeen; in fact, they get their name Finnan from the village of Findon, a few miles from Aberdeen, where they were originally prepared.
- **Fresh**—This is one of the cheapest of fish and may be cooked in many ways. Choose fish of average size, as the small ones are very bony. As well as the following recipes, all those for cooking the cheapest kinds of fish are suitable.

Fig. 19.26 Haddock fish

CREAMED HADDOCK: 750 gram Fresh Haddock, 2 oz. Butter, 2oz. Flour, pint milk, Egg 2 no.,100 gram Breadcrumbs, Salt and Pepper, 2 dessertspoon grated cheese.

Time: 40 minutes. Temperature: moderate to steam. To bake: Gas,. Electricity, 450° F. Enough for 4 persons.

- Steam the fish for twenty minutes, then remove all skin and bone and divide it into flakes.
- Melt the butter in a stewpan, stir in the flour and continue stirring whilst it cooks gently for two or three minutes, then add the milk gradually and stir whilst it boils for five minutes.
- Add the flaked fish and a seasoning of salt and pepper.
- Let it cool a little, then stir in the well beaten yolk of egg, and lastly, the stiffly whipped white.
- Turn the mixture into a fireproof dish, sprinkle with the breadcrumbs and grated cheese, and bake in a hot oven until lightly browned.

Hake (Fig. 19.26)

- Hake is a cheap, good and easily digested fish. It may be steamed and served with a sauce, sliced and fried, baked, or curried.

Fig. 19.27 Red hake fish

- Hake can also be cooked in the same manner as cod or haddock, but baking is usually the most palatable form of serving this useful fish.
- Plenty of flavouring should be allowed as otherwise the flesh is inclined to taste rather insipid.

Halibut (Fig. 19.28)

Fig. 19.28 Halibut fish

- Halibut is similar to turbot in appearance. Although not quite as full flavoured, the flesh is very delicate and digestible.
- A middle cut or head and shoulders is considered best, the tail being somewhat flavourless.
- Halibut may be boiled, steamed, baked, fried or cooked in any of the ways advised for turbot.

Herring (Fig. 19.29)

Fig. 19.29 Herring fish

- The herring is the cheapest of fish and one of the best.
- Being rich in flavour and very nourishing, it is a veritable poor man's friend, for when plentiful, and that is when at its best, a good-sized fish may be purchased very cheaply.
- The fish fried, grilled or soused will make a nourishing meal, while the roe can be cooked separately and served as a savoury.
- Choose plump herrings with a bright silvery hue and refuse those which are red round the eyes, for they are sure to be stale.

Herrings Grilled

- Make two or three incisions across the fish each side with the point of a knife, flour slightly, and brush over with salad oil or liquid butter.
- Place on a well greased grid-iron, and cook over a clear bright fire for about ten minutes, turning once or twice during the process.
- Serve on a hot dish garnished with parsley.
- When using a gas or electric grill, place the prepared herrings or bloaters on the bars of a toaster with a tin underneath, and put a little water in the tin.
- In this way the fish will keep moist, otherwise a gas grill is inclined to dry them too much.

Ling (Fig. 19.30)

Fig. 19.30 Ling fish

- This fish is very like the cod both in appearance and flavour, but more slender in form. The liver yields a similar oil.
- Any of the recipes given for cod, also for cooking the cheapest kinds of fish, may be used for ling.

Lobster (Fig. 19.31)

Fig. 19.31 Lobster

- This very popular shell fish is in season from the beginning of April until the end of October, it is therefore, at its best when oysters are out of season.
- It is a favourite dish in summer served with mayonnaise. Choose lobsters that are heavy for their size and have broad tails.
- This fish should only be eaten when very fresh. When choosing, see that the tail springs back into curled position when fish is extended.
- If it hangs limply the lobster is not fresh. When alive they are blue-black colour, but become a brilliant red when boiled.

To Boil.—Tie the claws with fine string or hemp and wash the fish well. Have ready a pan of fast-boiling water slightly salted. Plunge the lobster in head first, then boil gently, allowing twenty-five minutes for a lobster weighing about two pounds.

To Serve.—leave the fish until quite cold. Then remove the claws, place the lobster on a board, spread out the tail, press it down firmly and with a very sharp-pointed knife, make an incision just where the head and body shells join. A strong pocket knife is quite good for this purpose. Then with a large sharp knife cut straight through the tail. Next turn the lobster round and still holding it firmly cut right through the centre of the head. Crack the claws gently with a hammer, being careful not to splinter the shell or it will injure the flesh. Place the head upright on a dish lines with lettuce, with the claws and tail pieces round. Serve with oil and vinegar or a plain dressing.

Mackerel (Fig. 19.32)

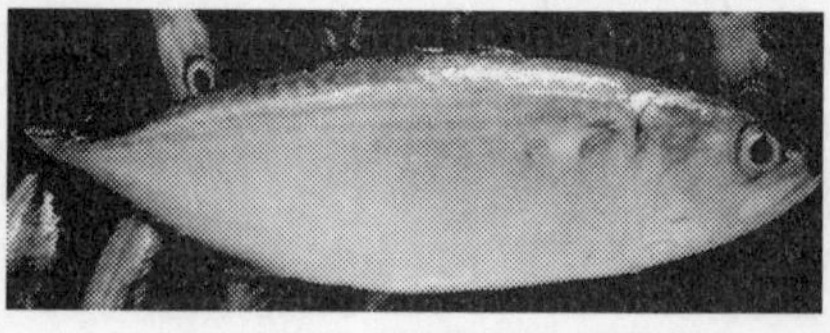

Fig. 19.32 Mackerel fish

- A rich and nourishing fish, so plentiful at times that they can be bought almost as cheaply as herrings.
- To obtain the true full flavour they should be absolutely fresh; in fact they are never quite as good as when out of on the fishing smack.

- When buying this fish, see that the skin is bright and silvery, and the eyes full and not sunken.
- When mackerel are boiled or soused, they should be just cleaned and washed out with salted water, but if they are to be grilled or fried they should be split also.
- This is not a difficult matter. Start at the head and cut the fish right along the back. Keep the knife just to the right of the centre bone, but be careful not to cut through the underskin at all, the object being to split the fish, not to divide it into two parts.
- The large centre bone can then be removed. Draw it off with the left hand and cut away the fish with a knife.

Megrim (Fig. 19.33)

- The megrim is sometimes called the smooth sole and the scald fish. It is also known as the grey sole, although this is usually a West of England definition.
- It is one of the cheapest of fish and may be cooked in any of the ways directed for them. The megrim should be eaten as fresh as possible, for it soon loses flavour.

Fig. 19.33 Megrim fish

Grey Mullet (Fig. 19.34)

Grey mullet does not bear any resemblance to red mullet, and has but little flavour.

Fig. 19.34 Grey mullet fish

Red Mullet (Fig. 19.35)

- The red mullet is a fish that is good to look at and very good to cat, for its colour is a rosy red and the flavour delicious.
- Red mullet are never drawn; pull out the gills but leave the trail.
- The liver is a great delicacy.
- Wash this fish carefully and handle as little as possible, as the skin is very easily broken.
- Red mullet is best when cooked in simple ways such as grilling or baking. It is spoilt when boiled and is too easily broken to be successfully fried.

Fig. 19.35 Red mullet fish

Mussels (Fig. 19.36)

- Mussels are found in large quantities on the rocks of our coasts.

Fig. 19.36 Mussels

- They are a very favourite shell fish, but like the lobster do not agree with everybody. When quite fresh the shells are very rightly closed.
- Another test for freshness is by weight; if they are so light that they float on the water they will not be wholesome.
- The shells should be well washed and thoroughly scrubbed, then soaked in salted water to rid them of sand, and finally rinsed well in a colander under running water before cooking.

To Boil.—Cleanse as directed above and put the mussels while quite wet into a strong stewpan. Cover and place over moderate heat. Shake the pan, and as soon as the mussels open they are done. Strain off the liquor and reserve it (as it is an excellent foundation for fish sauces, or to flavour fish soup). Turn the mussels into a bowl, beard them and serve on a napkin. The beard is the little black weed-like part. It can be easily removed with scissors. Allow about one dozen mussels for each person.

For Garnish or Sauce.—Boiled mussels are excellent as a garnish for boiled or baked fish; they also make a good sauce.

Fig. 19.37 Oyster

Oysters (Fig. 19.37)

Oysters should only be eaten when in season, that is from September until the end of April; when there is an "r" in the name of the month. They should also be eaten as soon as they are opened. If long exposed to the air, their delicate flavour deteriorates. Oysters eaten raw are a popular form of hors d'ceuvre.. To open an oyster, hold it very firkmly in a cloth to protect the hand, then take a sharp-pointed knife and force the point just under theedge of the upper shell. Press the knife in, so that you feel it along the surface of the under shell, then force it towards the fringe of the shell. Raise the knife sharply towards the right and the shell will come off. Serve on the half shells with cut lemon and brown bread and butter.

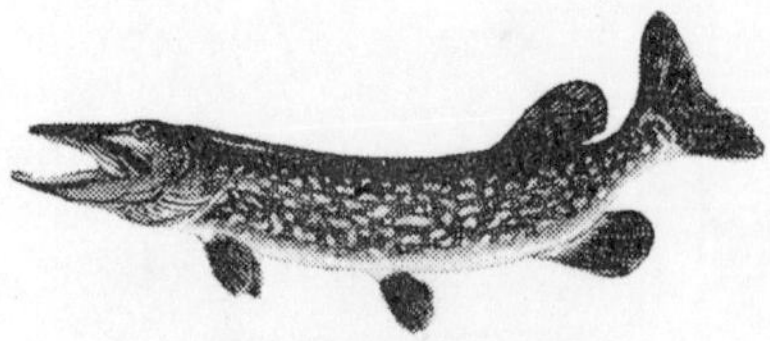

Fig. 19.38 Pike fish

Pike (Fig. 19.38)

Pike is at its best when baked, though it is often served boiled. Remove the roe when cleaning the fish, as it is not good eating.

Fig. 19.39 Plaice fish

Plaice (Fig. 19.39)

One of the most popular of the cheap fish, of good flavour and tender flesh. Excellent when filleted and fried in egg and breadcrumbs or butter. Plain boiling is not to be recommended, but this fish is very good cooked in milk. If the dark skin is removed, both appearance and flavour are improved.

Prawns (Fig. 19.40)

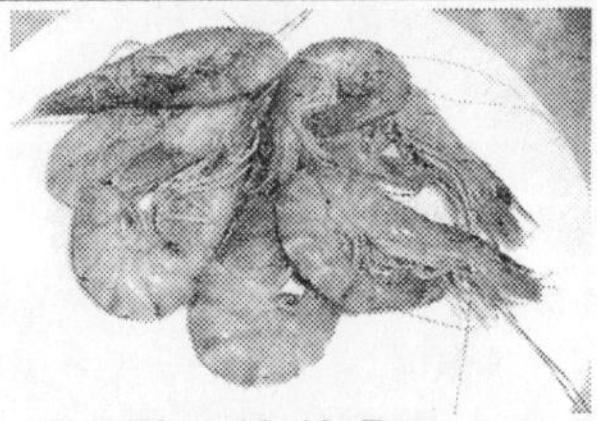

Fig. 19.40 Prawn

A delicious little shell fish in form like the shrimp but larger. When alive they are grayish in hue and very transparent, when cooked they become almost as bright a red as lobster. They are sold ready boiled but when fresh caught they should be boiled in the same way as shrimps. Unless you live near where they are caught, English prawns are a somewhat expensive luxury; imported ones are quite cheap, but have not the same delicious flavour or firm flesh. Prawns are generally used to garnish other fish dishes or as an hors d'ceuvre, but they are very good fried or curried; these two modes of cooking are especially to be recommended for the imported fish as it improves their flavour. The following recipes give instructions for their preparation.

Rock Salmon (Fig. 19.41)

Fig. 19.41 Rock salmon

A cheap and rather flavourless fish. No special recipes are needed, but it can be cooked in the same way as cod and the cheapest kinds of fish.

Salmon (Fig. 19.42)

Fig. 19.42 Salmon

This king of all fish is rich and delicious in flavour; in fact, no other fish can compare with it. It is most plentiful and cheapest in July and August, makes a perfect summer time meal, and being so satisfying can take the place of meat and need not therefore be considered extravagant. Salmon is most delicious when freshly caught; when it has been kept for a few days it loses the creamy curd from between the flakes. Salmon required rather longer cooking than other fish and is very unwholesome when underdone. It is seasonable from February until August. Salmon on sale at other times of the year comes either from Canada or Holland. The flavour of chilled salmon is not so fine as that of the fresh variety, but never-theless it is very good eating. The addition of a little olive oil to the water in which it is cooked improves the flavour and adds moister to the fresh. It can also be cooked in the ways given for the cheapest kinds of fish.

To Boil. - The head and shoulders or a middle cut are best for boiling. Scrape the scale of carefully, cut off the gills and the fins. Wash the fish thoroughly and see that it is quite free from blood or the colour when cooked will be spoilt. The fish should be put in boiling water with a dessertspoon of salt for each quart of water. Bring the water to the boil again and skim well. Then simmer, allowing ten minutes to the pound and ten minutes over for a thick piece of fish, eight minutes if only moderately thick. When done it should come easily from the bone. Serve with cucumber and any sauce. Preferred, such as tartar or hollandaise. Green peas and new potatoes are very good accompaniments.

Scallops (Fig. 19.43)

Fig. 19.43 Scallops

The scallop is a delicious shell fish with an orange-red roe and firm white fresh. Like all shell fish they must be cooked while very fresh. They need careful cooking at a moderate temperature. If boiled quickly they at once become hard and indigestible. They are very good parboiled and then fried in egg and breadcrumbs.

To Prepare. - Well wash the fish and remove the beard and black portion.

Shad (Fig. 19.44)

A fish of but little flavour which is best baked.

Fig. 19.44 American shad fish

Shrimps (Fig. 19.45)

There are two mainly varieties of shrimps, brown and pink. The brown shrimp is caught near the shore; the pink shrimp out at sea. The brown has more flavour, but the pink more delicate fresh. They should only be eaten when freshly boiled. State shrimps are very unwholesome. To boil, put them into boiling water and boil quickly for five minutes. Shrimps are used principally for sauces and garnish. They are also used in salads, or as hors d'ceuvre, and make excellent paste for sandwisches etc.

Fig. 19.45 Shrimp

Skate (Fig. 19.46)

Skate is a cheap fish of good flavour. It is generally sold cut in pieces or crimped. It may be streamed, boiled, fried, curried or baked, but whichever way it is cooked, it must first be skinned. It improves in flavour if kept a day before being cooked. As a rule the pieces vary very much in thickness and this must be taken into consideration when it is boiled or steamed. Put the thick pieces in the fish kettle first, and the thin pieces about five minutes after. It is very good cooked in Court Bouillon served with black butter or tartar sauce. Before boiling or steaming, roll the pieces and tie them with thread to keep them in shape. Skate is in season from August until April and is not wholesome when out of season.

Fig. 19.46 Skate fish

Smelts (Fig. 19.47)

Fig. 19.47 Smelts fish

Smelts to be good must be very fresh; if fresh they have a silver hue and a smell similar to that of cucumber. They are generally fried in egg and breadcrumbs, but they may also be grilled or baked.

To Fry. - Dry them carefully, and sprinkle with salt and pepper. Roll Them first in flour, then in beaten egg, and finally in very fine breadcrumbs. Use a frying basket if you have one as smelts are easily broken if not very carefully turned; their appearance is then spoined.

To Grill. - Flour the fish and cook under gentle heat, turning them once very carefully,

To bake. - Clean and carefully dry eight smelts and cut off the fins with a pair of scissors. Well butter a fireproof dish, lay the fish in it in a single row, sprinkle them with salt, pepper and lemon juice. Chop very finely a small shallot, mix with it a teaspoon of finely chopped parsley, quarter teaspoon anchovy essence and two tablespoons of breadcrumbs. Put these on the fish, then put 1 oz. Of butter or margarine in small pieces on the top, cover with greaseproof paper and bake fifteen minutes in a moderate oven.

Sole (Fig. 19.48)

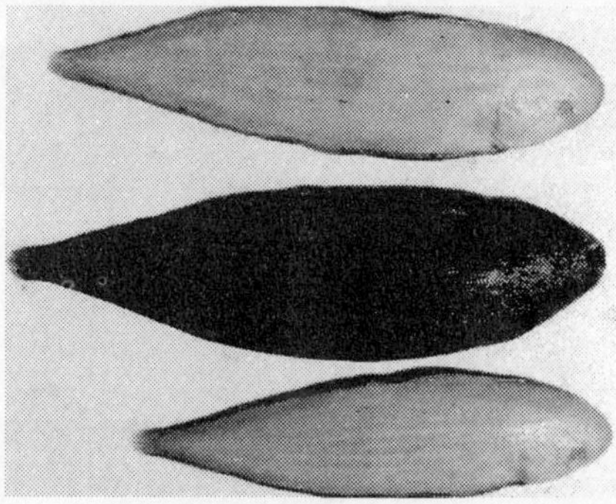

Fig. 19.48 Sole fish

The sole is the king of flat fish, highly esteemed for its firm flesh and delicious flavour. It is seasonable throughout the year, and may be prepared in so many different ways. In choosing sole, be sure that it is perfectly fresh. The gills should be red and moist, and the eyes bright and full.

- The real sole is the so-called Dovers sole, but the lemon sole is very good eating though inferior in both texture and flavour; it is rounder and wider than the Dover sole.
- Then the Witch is often called Torbay sole—probably to make it more saleable. Soles are good cooked in almost any way, but their delicious flavour is best retained perhaps by frying or grilling. Although we are inclined to think of the sole as an expensive fish, large ones may be bought very cheaply when plentiful.
- They should either be filleted or cut in pieces across the flesh and fried in egg and breadcrumbs.
- The latter is really the better method as filleting somewhat detracts from the flavour.
- Slips are small soles; these should be fried whole. Any kind of sauce can be served with soles, but their own flavour is so good that the simple accompaniment of cut lemon is by many considered sufficient

Sprats (Fig. 19.49)

Fig. 19.49 Sprats fish

Sprats are both nourishing and appetizing if well cooked, and should be far more popular than they are being such good value for money. Dry and flour them, fry in boiling fat and drain thoroughly. Mustard butter is a very good accompaniment. To make this, beat 2 oz. Of fresh butter to a cream, then season it with a sprinkling of pepper, a saltspoon of French mustard, or oridinary mustard made with vinegar, and then add drop by drop a teaspoon of tarragon vinegar. Mix well and use.

Sturgeon (Fig. 19.50)

Fig. 19.50 Sturgeon fish

The sturgeon is called a royal fish because at one time it had, when caught, to be sent to the reigning sovereign. In ancient days it was thought so much of that a band marched before it when it was sent to table. It has solid flesh somewhat resembling veal. Its roe is used to make caviar.

TO BOIL. - Clean, skin and bind it with a piece of tape. About 1 lb. is sufficient for four persons. Put it in a stewpan with a small bunch of fresh herbs, an onion stuck with a clove, a teaspoon of salt, and a dessertspoon of vinegar. Cover with warm water. Bring to the boil, skim well, and simmer for about three quarters of an hour. Serve with lobster or any other sauce preferred. It may also be stewed, baked or fried, but whatever mode is employed, remember it needs more cooking than other fish because the flesh is so firm.

Trout (Fig. 19.51)

Fig. 19.51 Trout fish

This fish has a beautiful appearance with silver and gold colouring and is very highly esteemed for its delicious flavour. The larger trout, caught in lakes and in the sea, are cooked in the same way as salmon. River trout, caught in rivers and streams, are a smaller fish but just as delicious, and should be baked, grilled or fried, but not boiled. Trout should be cooked as soon as possible after purchase. When quite fresh the eyes are bright and the gills red. Trout may be fried, grilled or stuffed and baked, the last named being the most popular method.

River Trout (Fig. 19.52)

Fig. 19.52 River trout

River trout are very good baked without any flavouring other than lemon juice. Butter a fireproof dish, put in the trout, sprinkle with lemon juice, cover and bake in a moderate oven fifteen to twenty minutes.

Turbot (Fig. 19.53)

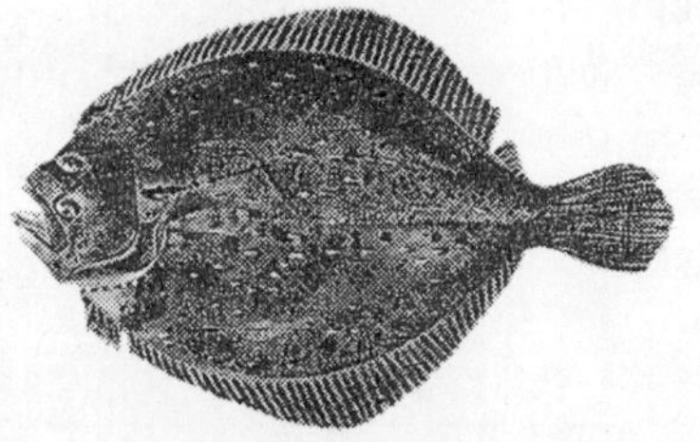

Fig. 19.53 Turbot fish

A very nourishing fish of excellent flavour with firm creamy white flesh, which, when stale, turns a bluish tint. Choose thick turbot; the middle cut is a good purchase as there is no waste, but the head and shoulders when bought cheaply make an economical dish. The fins of turbot are never cut off; they are very gelatinous and considered a great delicacy. Turbot is generally boiled and served with lobster, hollandaise or shrimp sauce; it is also very good baked or flaked and fried.

Whiting (Fig. 19.54)

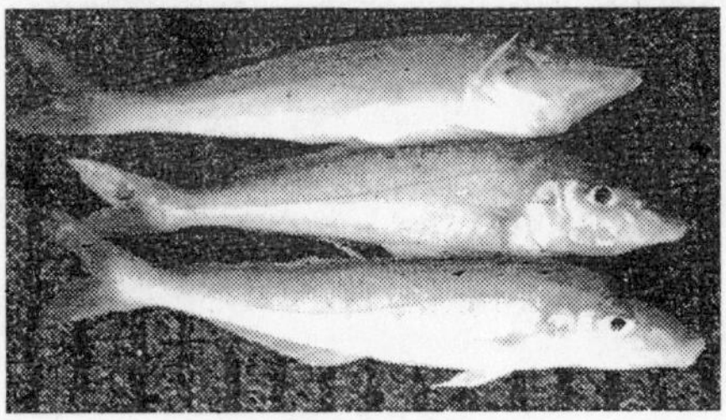

Fig. 19.54 Whiting fish

The whiting is a fish of delicate flavour and so easy to digest that it is a valuable food for invalids. It may be steamed or fried, or cooked in any of the ways given for the cheapest kinds of fish. When whiting is to be fried, the skin is removed and the tail fastened through the eye-holes. It is best fried in deep fat.

Whitebait (Fig. 19.55)

Fig. 19.55 Whitebait fish

Cooks with little experience frequently find difficulty in cooking this little fish crisp and dry, the reason being either that they do not dry the fish sufficiently, or that the fat is not smoking when the fish is put in. Wash the fish in very cold water, drain well in a colander, and finish drying with a soft cloth. Take another dry cloth and sprinkle over it 2 oz. of flour for 1 pint of whitebait. Well toss the fish in this, then put on a sieve and shake to remove any superfluous flour. Have ready a pan of hot smoking fat. Warm the frying basket, put in the whitebait, plunge the basket into the fat and fry till crisp. It only takes two or three minutes. Take out the basket, shake it, drain well and serve at once, with cut lemon and brown bread and butter,.

RECIPES FOR COOKING THE CHEAPER KINDS OF FISH

These recipes have been created to make the cheapest fish as appetizing and attractive as the more expensive varieties. The cheapest fish are by no means the least nourishing, but many of them need just some ingredient to improve their flavour. This, however, does not apply either to herrings or mackerel, for though cheap, these fish are by no means wanting in flavour. Fillets of fish can be bought very cheaply by the pound, and being free from bone, they are a very good purchase.

They vary in kind, being fillets of whatever fish is most plentiful at the time. The heads of large fish such as cod, turbot or salmon can often be bought for a few pence with sometimes quite a nice piece of shoulder with them. These can be steamed and served with sauce; or small fillets can be cut from them and used in any of the following recipes and the head itself boiled to make fish stock, the foundation of many good soups.

FISH BOILED IN COURT BOUILLON

Real Court Bouillon consists of a mixture of white wine, sherry, herbs, spices and vegetables, but it find the following a very good substitute; it gives a delicious flavour to an otherwise ordinary fish and so very much enhances the value of the cheapest kinds, such as haddock or megrims, or freshwater fish, which is often lacking in flavour. Prepare and cut in small pieces a medium sized carrot, onion and a stick or two of celery. Put them into a stewpan with a small bunch of fresh herbs, three peppercorns, a teaspoon of salt, a tablespoon of vinegar, and 1 ½ pints of water or veal broth. The latter makes a very good bouillon. Bring to the boil, skim well and then simmer for an hour. Strain off and use in place of water to boil any kind of fish. The liquor may afterwards be used as stock for soup or some of it to make sauce for the fish. A wineglass of sherry or white wine is a great improvement..

STANDARD RECEPIES

To Fry Fish in Batter

Ingredients	*Quantity*
Flour	100 gram
Oil	20 ml
Butter	20 gram
Egg	2 no
Salt and pepper	10 gram

Method

1. Mix the salt and pepper with the flour and sift well.
2. Stir in gradually the oil or melted butter and mix until quite smooth, then stir in a gill of just warm water.
3. Mix to a smooth cream and stir in the well whipped white of an egg. Dry the fish well, dip it in the batter, then immediately immerse it in the boiling fat and fry a golden brown.
4. There must be a sufficient quantity of fat to cover the fish, as it will not then be necessary to turn during frying.
5. Drain well and serve as soon as possible.

6. Fillets will take five to ten minutes to fry, according to thickness; cod steaks and thick fish about fifteen minutes.

To Fry Fish Without Breadcrumbs or Batter

1. Fish steaks may be fried without either batter or breadcrumbs. Cut codfish, haddock or any similar fish in slices across.
2. Dry them well and dust over with seasoned flour.
3. Heat enough fat in a frying pan to prevent the fish sticking (about 2 oz.), and, when it is quite hot, put in the fish slices and fry over moderate heat until brown on both sides, turning over with a fish slice.

To Bake

1. There are several ways of baking fish, the main point is to see that it does not become dry in the process.
2. Fat of some kind or a liquid is used to keep it moist. The following is a simple way for fillets of fish or flat fish such as soles or dabs.
3. Clean and remove any dark skin from the fish. Well grease a fireproof dish with butter or margarine.
4. Wash the fish, but do not dry it. Put it into the greased dish and sprinkle with salt and pepper; a little lemon juice also improves the flavour.
5. Place a few scraps of butter or margarine on the top; cover and bake in a moderate oven from ten to fifteen minutes, according to the thickness of the fish.

To Bake Fish In Milk

1. This is a very nourishing way to serve fish. It is often recommended for invalids, and also particularly suitable for fish that is inclined to be dry or flavourless.
2. Grease a fireproof dish with butter or margarine, and put in the fish; a little thinly sliced onion can be added if liked.
3. Just cover with milk and cook in a moderate oven ten to twenty minutes according to the thickness of the fish.
4. It can be served as it is, or the milk can be drained off and used to make any suitable sauce such as shrimp, lobster or anchovy. This can be poured over the fish before serving.

To Bake Stuffed Fish

Time : Whole fish from 15 to 30 minutes according to size.

Fillets from 15 to 20 minutes. Temperature: Gas, Regular.

Electricity, 375F.

Fig. 19.56 Stuffing in the fish

1. Round fish, such as fresh haddock, whiting or herrings are excellent stuffed and baked.
2. Wash and clean the fish, cut off the fins and the end of the tail with scissors. Dry them.
3. Then fill the opening through which the fish has been cleaned with any good forcemeat—herb for example. Sew up the opening with a needle and coarse thread.
4. Be sure to leave an inch or two of thread at one end so that you can draw it out easily before serving. Allow 1 oz. Of butter or dripping for the smaller fish such as whiting—2oz.
5. For a haddock. Put the fat in a baking tin or fireproof dish and heat in the oven. Lay the fish in the tin and with a spoon, pour a little of the fat over it. Sprinkle with breadcrumbs.
6. For preference, and bake in a moderate oven, basting it with the fat several times during the cooking. If using a casserole or a fireproof dish serve it in the dish.
7. If preferred you can lift the fish on to a hot dish and pour the liquor round. Either way the thread must be removed before serving.

Fillets of fish can also be stuffed and baked.

1. Season the fillets with salt and pepper, spread a little forcemeat on each one, and roll them up neatly, tying each one with thread or thin string.
2. Pack them upright in a well greased tin, put a scrap of butter or dripping on each, cover with greased paper and bake in a moderate oven.
3. Tomato, anchovy, or shrimp sauce may be served with baked fish, but it is quite good served with its own liquor, if it has not been overcooked.

Baked Fish To Serve Cold

Temperature: Gas. Electricity, 325° F.

1. Clean and wash the fish, any kind may be used.
2. Mackerel are very good cooked this way.
3. Mix together a teaspoon of salt, quarter teaspoon of pepper and powdered cloves mixed. Rub the fish with this seasoning.
4. Lay in a fireproof dish, add a bay leaf, cover with vinegar, then with greaseproof paper and bake one hour in a moderate over. Serve cold.

Stewed Fish

Time: 15 to 20 minutes according to the thickness of the fish.

Temperature: Gas, Regular, Electricity: 325° F.

Fig. 19.57 Stewed fish

1. This is a very tasty and nourishing way to cook either small fish or fillets.
2. It is most important to prevent the liquid from boiling. Just a gentle simmering is required, either in quite a moderate oven or over very gentle heat.
3. Put the fish in a glass or earthenware casserole or an enameled saucepan, cover either with fish stock made from fish bones or equal parts of milk and cold water.
4. Season with salt and pepper if the stock is not already seasoned, cover, and cook very gently until done.

5. The liquor can then be drained off and used to make any suitable fish sauce, which should be poured over the fish and served very hot. Hollandaise sauce is particularly good.

To Grill

Temperature for grilling: Hot to start—reducing to medium as necessary.

1. Grilling is one of the most delicious ways of serving fish.
2. But care must be taken than it is not overcooked outside before is sufficiently cooked through.
3. This is by no means an easy method when only a coal fire is available, for it must be perfectly clear and smokeless. Cinders should always be kept to make up a fire before grilling.
4. A little salt thrown on to the fire will help to clear it. But nowadays the majority of hotels used a gas or electric grill, and with either of these grilling is simplicity itself.

Fig. 19.58 Grilling of fish

5. When using an electric grill, it should be switched on high for two minutes before using. With a gas grill, turn the flame on full for four minutes before using.
6. Then the heat in each case must be reduced as found necessary, according to the thickness of the fish.

Point to remember to cook fish

1. A grid-iron or grid-pan should be kept exclusively for fish and absolute cleanliness is most essential. Before using the grid, first warm it and then rub well with kitchen paper.
2. When fish, such as bloaters or herrings, are grilled whole, remove the heads and tails, clean the fish thoroughly and dry them. Then make two or three cuts just through the skin to prevent it bursting while cooking. Dust lightly with flour.
3. Brush over with liquid butter or oil, season with salt and pepper and place on the grid-iron. Then put it under the hot grill, turning once or more if it is a thick fish but being careful not to break it. Do not stick a fork into the flesh, but turn with grilling tongs or a fish slice.
4. Roes are best taken out and cooked separately, otherwise it is difficult to cook them sufficiently without over-cooking the fish.
5. Delicate fish such as trout or red mullet are often grilled wrapped in buttered or oil paper, but care must be taken that the paper does not burn, and they should not be put too close to the heated grill.

6. Fish may also be split before grilling. Remove the large bone, flour and brush over with liquid butter or oil. Slices of fish may also be cooked in this way, such as a cod or salmon steak.
7. Maitre d'hotel butter, tartar or mustard sauce is a good accompaniment to grilled fish.
8. Remember grilled fish must never be kept waiting, the quicker it is served the better it will be.
9. See, therefore, that the dish and plates you are using for serving are heated before you start to grill.
10. Fish without much flavour are greatly improved if marinated before being grilled. The method consists of mixing oil and vinegar together in the proportion of one tablespoon of vinegar to two tablespoon of oil.
11. Put them in a rather deep dish with a sprig or two of savoury herbs, a little chopped shallot or onion, a sprinkling of salt and pepper and a pinch of grated lemon rind.
12. Put in the fish and let it remain for at least one hour, turning it occasionally

LEARNING OUTCOME

A Fish is any aquatic vertebrate animal that is typically ectodermic (or Cold blooded) covered with scales and equipped with two types of paired fins and several unpaired fins. The structure of Fish vary depending on the Fish habit. The skeletal structure of Fish is a useful means of separating finfish into smaller grouping. Sea Food is different from other types of Food, because freshness is key for safety and flavour, it must be stored differently under correct storage conditions fish and shellfish can be held for several days. There are four ways of preparation fish for freezing, the first two being the most common are dry, brine, acid pack and solid ice pack. Freshness is the first essential. Always deal at a reliable shop, but at the same time, learn to judge for yourself. When fish is fresh the gills are red and moist, the eyes bright and full and the flesh firm but elastic. If pressed the mark of the finger fades at once. Spots on plaice should be bright red, they turn greenish-brown when the fish is stale. Never choose then, ill-nourished-looking fish. The tails of such fish as lobsters, crayfish, prawns and shrimps are well curled round when fresh.. If they are pulled out they will immediately fly back. When buying a lobster or crab, choose one that is heavy for its size. The flesh of a cock lobster is considered the best, but the hen is more sought after as the spawn (coral it is called) is so useful for enriching sauces and for garnishing. To fillet flat fish such as a sole, cut off the fins, then with a sharp knife cut down the fish right along the side of the centre bone from head to tail. Now slide the knife along between the bone and the flesh and cut off the fillets neatly. Draw away the fillet with the left hand as you cut. Try to keep the knife as close to the bone as possible, then you will not leave any pieces of flesh behind. When you are able to fry fish to perfection you have mastered one of the most important parts of cookery. So many cooks fail and go on failing, because they will not trouble to follow the few simple rules that spell success. First wash it in cold water, then drain, dry thoroughly and flour lightly. Fish must be perfectly dry before it is put into the beaten egg, otherwise the egg will not stick to the fish because the water still clings to it, and your finished effect will have a patched appearance.

LESSON END ACTIVITY

- Collect the information of different varieties of fish available in your local market.
- Bring fish from market and debone that fish.
- From bones made a fish stocks.

QUESTIONS FOR DISCUSSION

1. Explain the term fish and its structure.
2. Explain the procedure to check the freshness of the fish.
3. Explain the procedure to store the fish.
4. Explain the procedure of the universal freezing of the fish.
5. Explain the classification of the fish.
6. Write a short note on white fish and oily fish.
7. Difference between crustaceans and shell fish.
8. Explain the procedure of choosing fish.
9. Explain the procedure of preparing fish.
10. How to skin the flat fish?
11. Explain the procedure of filleting the fish.
12. Explain the different methods of cooking fish.
13. Mention the varieties of any 10 fish with their used.
14. Mention the standard recipes of cream cod.
15. Draw the structure of Cray fish.
16. What are the point to remember when your are cooking the fish?

STATE TRUE AND FALSE

- The structure of Fish varies depending on the Fish habit.
- Round Fish have middle back bone with one fillet on either side.
- Sea Food is different from other types of Food, because freshness is key for safety and flavour.

- Do not let frozen seafood thaw until you are ready to use keep it frozen.
- Hard shell seafood like Oysters and calms cannot be frozen.
- Canned or Punched seafood like tuna can be stored for years.
- Fish is high protein food supply on an average a little more than 5 gram of protein per addible ounce.
- Fish has fewer calories than meat.
- Fish requires more attention from the cook than meat whether it is cooked whole, filleted or cut into steaks.
- Fish is also excellent baked, steamed, Poached or in stews.
- Crustaceans have multi- jointed shells.
- Mollusces shellfish have shells but they are not multi-jointed
- Large fish may be boiled, but steaming is really a better method for small or cut fish.
- Bass fish is variety of shell fish
- Brill is resemble to turbot.
- Courtbouillon is poaching liquid

KEY TERMS

* Aquatic
* Brine
* Calms
* Courtbouillon
* Ectodermic
* Fillet
* Freshness
* Invertebrate
* Oyster
* Safety
* Skeletal